SLAUGHTER ON A SNOWY MORN

SLAUGHTER ON A SNOWY MORN

A TALE OF MURDER, CORRUPTION AND THE DEATH PENALTY CASE THAT SHOCKED AMERICA

COLIN EVANS

ICON BOOKS

First published in the UK in 2010 by Icon Books Ltd

This edition published in the UK in 2011 by
Icon Books Ltd, Omnibus Business Centre,
39–41 North Road, London N7 9DP
email: info@iconbooks.co.uk
www.iconbooks.co.uk

Sold in the UK, Europe, South Africa and Asia
by Faber & Faber Ltd, Bloomsbury House,
74–77 Great Russell Street,
London WC1B 3DA or their agents

Distributed in the UK, Europe, South Africa and Asia
by TBS Ltd, TBS Distribution Centre, Colchester Road,
Frating Green, Colchester CO7 7DW

Published in Australia in 2011
by Allen & Unwin Pty Ltd,
PO Box 8500, 83 Alexander Street,
Crows Nest, NSW 2065

ISBN: 978-184831-216-6

Printed and bound in the UK by
CPI Mackays, Chatham ME5 8TD

Contents

Colin Evans is the author of several books specialising in forensics. These include *The Casebook of Forensic Detection: How Science Solved 100 of the World's Most Baffling Crimes*, and *The Father of Forensics* (Icon, 2008).

List of Characters

Victims
Charles Phelps

Margaret Wolcott

Defendants
Nelson Green

Charles Stielow

Stielow Family Members
Mary Jane Green: mother of Laura Stielow, Nelson Green, Raymond Green and Olive Smith

Raymond Green: brother of Nelson Green and Laura Stielow

Olive Smith: sister of Laura Stielow

Roy Smith: son of Olive

Ethel Stielow: eldest daughter of Stielow

Irene Stielow: second daughter of Stielow

Laura Stielow: wife of Charles Stielow

Roy Stielow: eldest son of Stielow

Neighbours
Adelbert Benson: son of Jesse Benson

Jesse Benson

Erma Fisher: Benson family housekeeper, later Adelbert's wife

Melvin Jenkins: nephew of Charles Phelps

Howard Kohler

Winifred Kohler

Wallace Moone

William Pogle

Police Officers

Chester M. Bartlett: sheriff of Orleans County

Andrew Van Dell: Orleans police chief

Charles B. Nichols: sheriff of Cattaraugus County

J. Scott Porter: under-sheriff of Orleans County

John Rice: deputy sheriff of Orleans County

John Stork: Medina police chief

Prosecutors

Harold S. Blake: assistant prosecutor

Nona Gleason: court stenographer

Thomas A. Kirby: associate of Knickerbocker

John C. Knickerbocker: district attorney for Orleans County

Private Detectives

George W. Newton: lead detective in the Stielow investigation

Thomas O'Grady: private investigator hired by *The World*

Henry Schultz: chauffeur for Newton

Charles Sparacino: Newton agent

Robert A. Wilson: Newton agent

Prosecution Expert Witnesses

Albert H. Hamilton

Charles Newton

Stielow Support Team

Mischa Appelbaum: founder of the Humanitarian Cult

Inez Milholland Boissevain: New York lawyer

John Clute: Nelson Green's trial lawyer

Grace Humiston: New York lawyer

Stuart M. Kohn: New York lawyer

James W. Osborne: appeal lawyer

Arthur E. Sutherland: appeal lawyer

David A. White: Charles Stielow's trial lawyer

Sing Sing Personnel

Dr Calvin Derrick: acting warden

Frederick Dorner: principal keeper

John W. Hulbert: state executioner

George W. Kirchway: acting warden

John Lowry: pastor

Spencer Miller: assistant warden

Thomas Mott Osborne: warden

Reverend Anthony N. Petersen: chaplain

John B. Riley: superintendent of prisons

Medical Personnel

Dr Fred Eckerson: Medina physician

Dr Edward Munson: coroner

Dr George F. Rogan: Medina physician

Forensic Experts

Sergeant Harry F. Butts: NYPD ballistics expert

Lieutenant James A. Faurot: chief inspector of the New York Detective Bureau

John H. Fisher: physicist

Major Calvin H. Goddard: firearms expert

Philip O. Gravelle: microphotographer

Albert Llewellyn Hall: early American ballistics expert

Captain William A. Jones: NYPD ballistics expert

Max Poser: opticals expert

Dr Otto Schultze: pathologist

Government Officials

George H. Bond: lawyer detailed to investigate the Shelby shootings

William E. Orr: secretary to Charles Whitman

Charles E. Waite: lawyer detailed to investigate the Shelby shootings

Charles S. Whitman: governor of New York State

Judges

George W. Cole: circuit judge

Charles L. Guy: circuit judge

George H. Larkin: surrogate (later county) judge

Cuthbert W. Pound: trial judge

Adolph J. Rodenback: circuit judge

Other Suspects

Erwin King: itinerant horse trader

Clarence O'Connell: itinerant burglar

Sundry Players

Frank W. Buell: Orleans County deputy treasurer

Irving L'Hommedieu: senator for Orleans County and head of
local Republican party

Harry R. Kidney: warden of Auburn Prison

Mrs Elmer Klutz: friend of the Smith family

The Laskey family: alibi witnesses

William Munson: district attorney of Orleans County

Charles F. Rattigan: warden of Auburn Prison

Charles Scobell: bloodhound handler

Louis Seibold: reporter for *The World*

Isaac Swart: sheriff of Orleans County

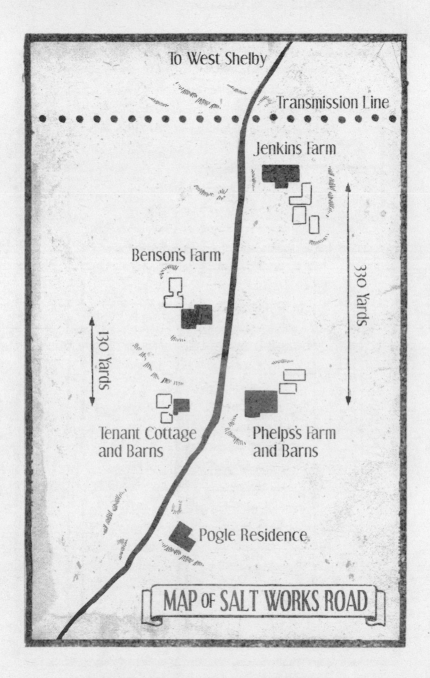

Map showing the layout of houses along Salt Works Road

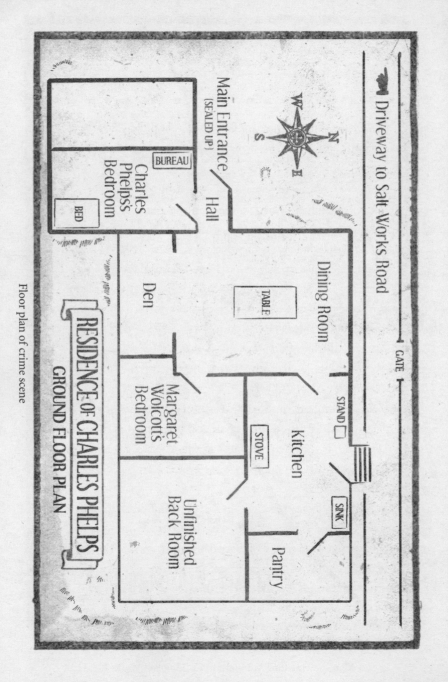

Floor plan of crime scene

RESIDENCE OF CHARLES PHELPS
GROUND FLOOR PLAN

Driveway to Salt-Works Road

GATE

Main Entrance
(SEALED UP)

Hall

BUREAU

Charles
Phelps's
Bedroom

BED

Den

Dining Room

TABLE

Margaret
Wolcott's
Bedroom

STOVE

Kitchen

STAND

Unfinished
Back Room

SINK

Pantry

Preface

History gets made in the unlikeliest places. In early 1915, with the world's horrified gaze fixed on the gas-filled trenches of Flanders, the homicidal events that rocked a sleepy little backwater tucked away in the far western corner of New York State received, understandably, little media coverage beyond the county line. The crime was appalling, no doubt about it, but no worse than scores of others across America that year. Certainly, there was nothing to suggest that it would make history and spark a forensic revolution.

At first – or even second – glance, Orleans County might seem an improbable delivery room for the birth of modern ballistics analysis. Residents of this overwhelmingly rural district tend to care more about the soil than the laboratory, always keeping one anxious eye on the changeable skies, the way that farmers do. Lying an hour's steady drive east of Niagara Falls, Orleans County is a profoundly peaceful place, and yet almost a century ago, among the skein of apple orchards, mist-covered lakes and potato fields that winds for miles through this rich and alluring landscape, a grotesque tragedy unfolded that would change for ever the face of crime-fighting around the globe.

Charlie Stielow wasn't anyone's idea of the great American hero, and no pretence can or should be made that he was anything other than a very ordinary man trapped in most extraordinary circumstances. His only crime was to get caught up in a whirlwind that dumped him in places that, mercifully, few of us will ever visit. This is his story.

PART I

1

Pity The Poor Immigrant

28 June 1914 was not a good day for Archduke Franz Ferdinand. His morning drive through the broiling streets of Sarajevo had been marred when a Serb terrorist hurled a grenade at his car. Quick action by the archduke – he knocked the grenade away with his hand so that it exploded harmlessly in the car's wake – prevented a disaster, but the heir to the Austro-Hungarian throne was still quivering with rage when he reached the town hall. As the mayor began his welcoming address, Franz Ferdinand interrupted him testily. 'What is the good of your speeches? I come to Sarajevo on a visit, and I get bombs thrown at me. It is outrageous!'[1] The archduke's ill-humour was short-lived and so was he. That afternoon the Serb nationalists tried again. And this time they succeeded. A motorcade bearing the archduke and his wife, Sophie, on a tour of the blistering city was so poorly guarded that a nineteen-year-old fanatic named Gavrilo Princip had no problems in opening fire with a pistol. Both royals were mortally wounded. There was nothing to suggest that the assassination of an unpopular royal in a little-known Balkan country would trigger the start of history's bloodiest conflict. Yet barely five weeks later Europe was in flames.

It all happened with bewildering haste. On 28 July, Austria-Hungary declared war on Serbia. Russia, tied by treaty to Serbia, then mobilised its forces. Four days later, Germany, straining at the leash for a chance to flex its military muscle and allied by treaty to Austria-Hungary, declared war on Russia and France. On 4 August, when German troops overran neutral Belgium, treaty obligations forced the final European heavyweight, Britain, into the fray.

From one end of the continent to the other, recruiting offices on both sides were stormed by millions of bright-eyed, eager young men, all bursting with patriotic fervour. 'Don't worry,' they reassured anxious relatives, 'it will be over by Christmas!' By the spring of 1915, what would become the 20th century's cruellest cliché had been well and truly buried beneath a welter of blood and bullets. March of that year saw the great armies of Europe digging in along a line that stretched from the North Sea to the Franco-Swiss border. All along this Western Front, the Great War slowly degenerated into the Great Stalemate, as mechanised slaughter on a scale hitherto unimaginable made any kind of advance prohibitively expensive in human terms. A few yards of blood-drenched soil gained one day: those same few yards lost the next. It all seemed so pointless.

Across the Atlantic, most Americans were convinced that Europe had gone crazy. But not everyone felt this way. Many of that nation's more recent immigrants agonised over the reports that filled their daily newspapers each morning. For them the battlefields – Marne, Tannenburg and Ypres – were not just marks on some vague map but the stuff of childhood memories. And as the fighting intensified, no immigrant group was more affected than the 8 million American citizens of German birth or extraction. They were trapped in a kind of citizenship no man's land, walking on eggshells every step of the way. Many of the more thoughtful kept a wary eye on Washington, DC. Although the nation's overriding mood was for non-involvement in the war, they knew that the capital's elite power-brokers – overwhelmingly pro-British – were exerting relentless pressure to intervene. The press, too, had sided with Britain and her allies and slanted their coverage accordingly. It was a case of common language; common cause. They fed off an Allied propaganda machine that ran rings around its German counterpart when it came to moulding American opinion. Every act of war was skilfully morphed into yet another example of Teutonic barbarity. Well, what else could you expect from the homeland of Nietzsche, Treitschke and all those other militaristic anti-Semites?

Such unremitting bias infuriated the German-American community. In New York City, an immigrant pressure group railed against those influential papers that had 'an English correspondent tied to its stirrups', and vowed to establish a daily newspaper that 'would tell the truth about Germany'.[2] Elsewhere in America the pretence of neutrality was, at times, paper thin. When Harvard University portentously announced that, in the interests of impartiality, it was withdrawing all invitations to visiting German professors, it notably did not extend this embargo to lecturers from France. All in all, it wasn't a good time to be a German in America.

Just ask Charlie Stielow.

Although this 36-year-old Berlin-born farmhand was insulated from the worst of the Hun-baiting – he couldn't read and could barely write his name – his empty pockets provided eloquent proof of the hardening animosity. It was the same right across upstate New York, as German immigrants, especially those like Stielow, anchored to the bottom of the economic scale, suddenly found themselves on the business end of some witheringly mean stares from their neighbours.

The past winter had been the toughest that Charlie could remember. By the beginning of March 1915, his back was pressed tight to the wall. Troubles were piling up like snowdrifts at his door and there was no sign of a spring thaw. Debts, domestic worries, the threat of imminent homelessness, no job, no prospects, no money, Stielow had 'em all, in spades. What he didn't have was luck. Nothing new about that, though. Somehow Dame Fortune had always danced tantalisingly out of reach for this burly farm worker. For most of his adult life, and even before that, he'd bent his back in the windswept fields that lie south of Lake Ontario. He followed the crops and the picking seasons, managing to save just enough money each summer so that he and his family could hibernate through the vicious winters, all the while praying for spring to come early. As a way of life it was brutal, but it was an existence that Charlie shared with hundreds of other indentured farm labourers in this part of the world, and he'd always scraped by, somehow. Until now.

In Niagara County agriculture was king. If you were rich, you owned a farm; if you weren't, you worked for someone who did. Charlie epitomised the contract farm worker. The system was rigid and simple: hire on for a calendar year with one of the wealthy land-owners, do a good job, keep your nose clean, and maybe there would be the option of a renewal if the boss liked you. Usually Charlie got asked to stay, because he was broad-backed, honest, didn't complain and could work like a mule. He'd been with one landowner, Ernest Schrader, for the best part of five years, until that relationship fizzled out in the spring of 1914. There was no rift, Charlie just needed a change. He already had another job lined up with a new boss named George Terrell. The pay was nothing special, just $28 a month, but the job did come with feed for Charlie's cow and a pen for his hogs.

As always, Charlie worked round the clock during his time with Terrell and looked set for another lengthy stay when, suddenly, in an unprecedented and wholly unexpected splash of entrepreneurial verve, the lowly farmhand traded a hog for one of Terrell's horses, signing a note for $30 to cover the difference. Charlie Stielow was stepping into uncharted, possibly treacherous waters. And the expansion didn't stop there. Reasoning that two horses would gener-ate more income than one, he promptly doubled the size of his team by buying another animal, this time from a trader named Charles Speck, who lived in nearby Lockport. He financed the deal by mort-gaging the entire rig – both horses, his wagon and harness – to Speck and by signing yet another promissory note.

This was a high-risk strategy and, who knows, it might have paid off, except that calamity struck – Charlie got laid off. Terrell, caught in a financial crisis of his own, had to cut costs ruthlessly and that meant canning the hired help. Overnight, Charlie's cash flow dwindled from meagre to non-existent, and with no funds to make the payments, his world began to implode. Speck, as unsentimental as he was pragmatic, attached Charlie's harness and wagon, a manoeuvre that pushed the farmhand to the brink of financial ruin. No doubt about it, grabbing even a small slice of the American dream was proving awfully elusive for Charlie Stielow, just as it had been for his parents.

Julius and Hannah Stielow were working a farm on the outskirts of Berlin when Charlie entered this world on 15 October 1878. Whatever joy Charlie's arrival brought to the family was counterbalanced by the harshness of their bleak existence. The 'Iron Chancellor', Otto von Bismarck, might have pulled off one of history's great feats of political legerdemain in unifying the disparate Teutonic states under a single German flag, but precious few benefits had filtered down to those families that barely had one foot on the lowest rung of the socio-economic ladder. Hunger was commonplace, poverty rife. The Stielows rubbed their groaning bellies and, like millions of other Europeans before and since, cast envious eyes westwards, beyond the Atlantic. Miracles were possible across that ocean, so they'd heard, and like almost everyone else floundering at the bottom of the financial barrel they had no problem in suspending disbelief. Every spare pfennig was stashed with just one goal in mind. It was a struggle but their diligence paid off. Two long years after Charlie was born, the Stielows had enough in the family kitty to pay for the steerage-class tickets that allowed them to join the vast migratory flood to America.

They landed at the immigration centre at Castle Garden, on the southern tip of Manhattan, in early 1881. All around them New York was in the midst of its first great building boom. Apartment houses were mushrooming everywhere as the middle classes abandoned their fine single residences and took to apartment living with well-financed relish. The non-stop construction guaranteed plenty of work for those newly arrived off the boat and meant that thousands of immigrants would spend their entire lives within a few miles of the landing stage at Castle Garden. But the Stielows were country people. All they'd ever known was farm life. New York with its hectic bustle and roaring growth wasn't for them. They had their eyes fixed on the lush farmland of western New York State, already a magnet for so many of their fellow countrymen. Their 4,000-mile odyssey from Berlin terminated in Niagara County.

The county is home to one of America's curious topographical idiosyncrasies: more of its jurisdiction lies below water than above it. This is because the county's northernmost boundary stretches far out into the icy depths of Lake Ontario. The trade-off comes in fertility. The part of the county that remains dry – the Ontario plain – provides some of the best growing soil in the north-east, and it was this fecundity that attracted the first European settlers in the early 19th century. The Stielows set up home in Wolcottsville, a small hamlet subsumed by the larger township of Royalton, which lies some twenty miles south of Lake Ontario and twice that distance north-east of Buffalo. Owing to the large number of Germans hereabouts, Wolcottsville was known locally as Prussia, and most newcomers clung to their native tongue. As a result, Charlie grew up in a German-speaking household, an act of parental short-sightedness that left him permanently handicapped when it came to coping with the language of his adopted homeland. For the rest of his life he would retain a slight accent and often adopt a clumsy and irregular form of phraseology.

The Stielows were hard workers, thrifty and resourceful, and after a few years spent tending other people's crops and stock, they had scraped together the deposit for a two-acre smallholding of their own. Here they raised Charlie, his brother Gus and sister Mary, along with two much older half-sisters from Hannah's first marriage, Pauline and Augusta Krause.

In 1902 Julius Stielow died, as much from hard work as anything else, and nine years later he was followed to the grave by Hannah. Her death opened up a deep family rift. Originally, she had willed the farm – which had grown in size to ten acres – to Charlie alone, but just before her death some last-minute estate-juggling meant that it was left jointly to all five children, an unsatisfactory compromise that triggered a bitter argument.

The feuding lasted for years. When the dust finally settled, Charlie retained a fifth share of the Wolcottsville farm and got to stay in the main house, with his wife, Laura, and their two children. But for how much longer? Settling with his siblings had taken every cent he had and more. As a result the farm was mortgaged up to the chimney stack and, in March 1915, with news of Charlie's horse fiasco common knowledge in Wolcottsville, the woman from nearby Middleport who held the note on the property was threatening foreclosure. If Charlie couldn't find some money fast, not only would he be flat busted and out of work, but he and Laura and the kids wouldn't even have a roof over their heads. Adding to his headaches was the bittersweet realisation that in a month's time there'd be one more mouth to feed, seeing as Laura was pregnant with their third child.

Charlie Stielow was close to his wits' end, but not quite. He still had one ace left to play. On 2 March 1915 he set out on a five-mile trek from Wolcottsville, skirting the northern edge of the Tonawanda Swamp – at that time the largest marshland in New York State – until he reached Newton's Corners, in the village of West Alabama. Here, close to where the Newton family had opened the inn that gave the district its name, local businessmen and farmers gathered every Tuesday for the weekly auction. All kinds of farm machinery, horse tack and feed found its way to the auctioneer's gavel, but Charlie wasn't in the market for bid and buy on this March morning; he was after a job. The auction also acted as a kind of *ad hoc* labour exchange. Charlie worked his way through the milling crowd until he saw a familiar face. He and William Warner swapped problems for a while, and when Charlie explained his predicament, Warner thought for a moment, then recalled that 'Phelps wanted to get a man'.[3]

In such a close-knit agricultural community all the big farmers had big reputations, and Stielow didn't need any further clarification. Charles B. Phelps lived just across the border, in adjoining Orleans County. He owned a decent-sized spread on Salt Works Road, and, if you believed the rumours, had saved nearly every cent he'd ever made. For most of his life he'd run the farm on his own, but in recent years advancing age had caught up with him – he was now aged 70 – and getting the crops in on time needed outside help. This posed a dilemma. Because the cussedness of his personality was legendary, most local farmhands gave Phelps a wide berth. As a consequence, the old man was forced to dip into a pool of casual labour known locally as 'swamp angels', a rag-tag bunch of pedlars and itinerants who roamed the back roads of upstate New York. These swamp angels drank hard, played hard, and many of them stole pretty hard as well. Phelps didn't trust them an inch. Neighbours grew accustomed to seeing the crusty old-timer lay into the help when dissatisfied with either their work or their demands, which was most of the time. Come payday, Phelps could always be relied upon to stage a spirited defence of his wallet. Curses and threats were commonplace as disgruntled ex-employees trudged off down the road, shouting back over their shoulders with beer-stained breath at their tight-fisted tormentor.

Phelps might have been the doomsday option, but for Charlie Stielow, penniless, out of work and stretched to the limits of his endurance, he represented a flicker of hope. And in what had been a gloom-laden world, that amounted to quite a lot.

———

Eight days later saw Charlie Stielow making his way north-east along Salt Works Road, in the direction of West Shelby. The long, weaving highway had been named for the well where locals came to buy their salt, essential for preserving meat through the long, harsh winters. As he tramped steadily northwards into Orleans County the scrubby pines of the Tonawanda gave way to lush, rolling countryside, a place where almost anything grew in the rich, loamy soil. West Shelby was one of four hamlets – East Shelby, Millville and Shelby itself were the others – that together made up the township of Shelby. In 1910 the accumulated population was recorded as 3,945, though each year that number shrivelled by just a few as low-income families, beaten down by the hardships of indentured rural life, packed their bags and headed for Buffalo in search of a more certain income in the canning factories and on the docks. Those that stayed remained rooted in the 19th century. Many houses had not been hooked up to the electricity grid, automobiles were still a novelty on the dirt lanes, outnumbered by buggies and horses, and most people, like Charlie Stielow, got around on foot.

He trudged to a halt outside the Phelps place, a mile south of West Shelby. It was an imposing two-storey frame house set some way back from the main dirt road. A solitary tree with spiky, bare branches towered over the driveway, while several similar trees ran in a straight line alongside the house. On the north side of the property a telephone post signalled Phelps's one and only concession to modernity. There was no evidence of electricity cables. Around the back, a gated fence divided the various barns, sheds and an orchard from the main living quarters. And beyond all this, the sweeping, snow-flecked fields stretched clear to the wooded horizon. Even on a grey, wintry day it was an impressive landscape.

Not that Charlie noticed. He was too busy sizing up the house. The overarching impression was one of extreme isolation, bordering on desolation. Apart from a small, deserted-looking cottage that stood directly opposite on the other side of Salt Works Road, the nearest neighbour on Phelps's side of the road was more than 300 yards to the north. The seclusion was deliberate and desired. For the most part the families who lived along Salt Works Road were well-to-do farmers, the kind who expected their privacy, and respected the privacy of others.

Phelps certainly fell into this category. A lifelong bachelor, he occupied this large house with just his 50-year-old housekeeper Margaret Wolcott for company. Miss Wolcott was clearly blessed with almost supernatural reserves of patience, judging from the way she'd managed to endure her boss's tantrums for more than five years without quitting, although her lack of any close family might have eased her critical faculties in that respect somewhat.

As Charlie Stielow clumped up the long driveway, he saw that the front of the west-facing house had been boarded up for the winter, a common enough cost-cutting exercise, designed to keep out the frigid winds that came howling off Lake Ontario and preserve valuable heat (it would later be found that Phelps had caulked up the front doors for the same reason). Charlie slowly worked his way around the north side of the house until he located an unsealed door. He climbed the couple of steps and knocked, then retreated to ground level to wait.

After a few moments Phelps appeared. He was tall and spare, with a bony face that glowered over a large beard that reached to his chest. In his gruff way he demanded to know what Charlie wanted. He was looking for work, was the answer. Phelps ran a flinty eye over the caller and liked what he saw. The man standing sheepishly at the foot of the steps was built like an ox, five-ten or so tall and about seventeen stone, all of it muscle. Best of all, so far as Phelps was concerned, he was clearly cut from a different cloth than those damned swamp angels who just drifted through with their sticky fingers and cavernous pockets. There looked to be nothing shifty about him. Charlie had a cannonball-round face, under-slung with the beginnings of a double chin, thin tufts of dark reddish hair plastered flat across his head and a Zapata moustache that gave him an almost cartoonish look. But it was a pleasing overall appearance, one dominated by the eyes; deep and blue, and exuding an earnest, almost childlike honesty. His clothes – dungarees and a heavy, padded jacket – might have been shabby, but at least they were clean. Phelps grunted his approval and invited the stranger into the welcome warmth of the large kitchen, then sat down and listened while Charlie haltingly out-lined his work experience.

Since leaving school at age twelve, unable to read or write, he had spent his entire life working on farms from one end of Niagara County to the other. There wasn't anything he didn't know about picking apples or hoeing potatoes; he could plough fields, work a team, slaughter livestock, dig irrigation ditches, fix wagons; in fact, he could turn his hand to just about anything agricultural. For close on a quarter-century, Charlie Stielow had been a hard-working son of the soil, unnoticed by the world at large, and in all that time he'd never once run foul of the law.

After some hemming and hawing, Phelps agreed to hire Charlie for one year, beginning on 1 April. The terms were surprisingly gen-erous, an indication of just how much Phelps was impressed by the newcomer: Charlie could live rent-free in the tenant house directly opposite, have pasturage for his cow, feed for his horse, all the pota-toes and fuel he needed for himself and his family, and in addition he would receive $400 a year. Charlie stammered his thanks, hardly able to believe his good fortune. Shoving all the dark rumours he had heard about Phelps welshing on promises to the furthermost recesses of his mind, he stuck out his big, work-callused paw and shook on the deal.

But the crafty Phelps smelled an opportunity. Why not, he sug-gested to Charlie, move into the tenant house as soon as possible; that way he could carry out a few chores around the farm – without pay, of course – until his yearly contract commenced on 1 April? It prob-ably didn't occur to Charlie that he was being taken for a sucker, and if it did, well, he kept his disappointment to himself. Over another handshake he agreed to take up occupancy the following Saturday, 13 March.

When Laura Stielow heard the news that evening her relief was almost overwhelming. Here, at long last, she saw a chance for some much-needed domestic stability. She'd been sixteen years old and three months pregnant with Ethel when she and Charlie married in 1902. Roy had come along one year later. Since then, matrimonial life had been one long, relentless grind. In the dozen years since they were married, she and Charlie had lived in ten different homes. The constant upheaval had worn away at her frail, tiny body and left her nerves wound tighter than piano strings. This time around, with another baby due in the next few weeks, she was determined that things would be different.

Laura's delight lasted all of 48 hours. On the following Friday evening Charlie came home, all out of breath and giggling in that strange high-pitched way of his. He excitedly told how he'd been selling a few household effects to a group of pedlars, when one of them mentioned that some temporary paid work was coming up locally that week. Was he interested? Charlie laid out the proposition to Laura: maybe they ought to delay moving out to the Phelps place until his official start of 1 April? This way, maybe he could make a few extra bucks to take with them?

Laura's Lilliputian stature concealed a fiercely determined nature. Her brown eyes flashing angrily, she prodded her big, dumb husband a couple of times in the chest and insisted that he adhere to the original agreement. Old man Phelps wasn't the kind to be monkeyed around with, she said. If he thought Charlie was playing him for a fool, he might turn nasty and hire someone else. She didn't want to hear any more of this nonsense!

The dressing-down from Laura clearly had its intended effect. Overnight, Charlie came to realise the wisdom of her words, and the next morning he got his Democrat wagon – a high, horse-drawn, lightweight two-seater – out of hock, loaded it with the family's mainly second-hand furniture, and set out on the five-mile journey to West Shelby. Laura, shrugging off her eight months' pregnancy like it wasn't there, drove a second horse-drawn wagon they had rented from a local hotel keeper named Fred Pechuman.

Riding alongside Laura were her two children, her 53-year-old mother, Mary Jane Green, and her younger brother, Nelson Irow Green. The Greens had travelled over that day from the family home in Royalton Center, to help Laura settle in after the move. Mary Jane intended to remain throughout her daughter's confinement and beyond, until Laura regained her strength. Nelson jabbered non-stop all the way over. He didn't have anything to say; he just talked a lot. Just over a week shy of his nineteenth birthday, he was lean and strong, and not much else. Like Charlie, he'd also known nothing except farm labouring since leaving school, and, like Charlie, he was functionally illiterate. Where they differed was in mental acuity. Nobody ever accused Charlie Stielow of being smart, but compared to his brother-in-law he was a tower of intellectual strength. When a newspaper report later branded Nelson as 'not mentally bright',[4] it was a cruel, if accurate, assessment. He had the mind of an infant and an almost foetal suggestibility, but come harvest-time his grown-up brawn more than compensated for any cerebral shortcomings. And it was the same when it came to moving house. Nelson could work all day and not break a sweat. On days like this he was invaluable.

With flakes of snow swirling around them the two wagons crossed the county line and rolled slowly up Salt Works Road. Phelps was on hand to greet them and show them the ropes, and that Saturday the Stielow family got to spend their first night in the small two-storey tenant house. They later learned that Phelps had only bought this property the previous week from a neighbour, for $1,700. It had stood empty ever since the previous occupant, Kirk Tallman, a Canadian apple picker who'd had a falling-out with Phelps, had left in a huff. When the time came to close the deal, Phelps had drawn just $500 from the bank, paying the $1,200 balance from banknotes he pulled randomly from various pockets. His attorney shook his head in disbelief: the damned old fool might not trust banks, but did he really need to advertise his prejudices so publicly? Local gossip had always insisted that old man Phelps kept thousands stashed in his house. Stunts such as this did nothing to quash those rumours.

Once inside the tenant house, Mary Jane Green directed the sleeping arrangements. She was a forceful woman, short on patience and, having given birth to no fewer than twelve children, she was used to taking charge. She announced that she and Laura would share a small downstairs bedroom; that way she could keep an eye on her heavily pregnant daughter. Charlie and Nelson were ordered to bunk down together in another ground-floor room, while the two children made do with an upstairs room. That night after supper everyone retired early, worn out by the exertions of what had been a long day.

Next morning Charlie got up early and familiarised himself with the layout of the farm and his duties. Most of Phelps's acreage was given over to potatoes and a small herd of cows. In the back yard he also kept a few chickens for his own use. It was the middling kind of farm that Charlie had worked on all his life. He didn't foresee any difficulties.

Just after dawn on the Monday, Phelps, in a rare act of magnanimity, hitched up his own lumber wagon and drove Charlie back to Wolcottsville to pick up more personal effects. Two days later he repeated the favour, when he and Charlie went back for the final time and collected the Stielow family's last few odds and ends, including the kitchen range. No doubt about it, the boss and his new employee were already acting like the best of pals.

When Charlie and Laura Stielow settled into their new house on that March weekend they had just three dollars in the world between them. But they felt like royalty. As far as they were concerned, the crisis had passed. After years of weary struggle, a glimmer of light flickered at the end of what had been a perilously long tunnel. They had a roof over their heads, a new baby just around the corner, and Charlie had just landed the best job of his life. The family's future had never looked brighter. So it was with some surprise that, just four months later, Charles Frederick Stielow found himself on death row at Sing Sing prison, awaiting an appointment with the electric chair.

2

Bodies In The Snow

Sunday 21 March 1915

The shots were fired at some time around 10:45pm. Two in quick succession, then a third, followed by a final blast a short while later. At least, that was the way it sounded to Erma Fisher.

Ordinarily, the 45-year-old housekeeper to the Benson family – they lived on the same side of Salt Works Road as the tenant house – would have been fast asleep. But on this particular night, after retiring at 10:00pm, she had felt unwell and had gone to the kitchen for a glass of water. While there she had heard the sudden staccato bursts. Pulling back a curtain, she squinted into the murk. Instinct told her that the shots had come from the Phelps place, which stood approximately 120 yards to the south, on the opposite side of the road. Unfortunately for the inquisitive Erma, visibility was poor that night. The quarter moon was buried deep in a thick layer of cloud that left the Phelps house shrouded in darkness.

Still curious, she switched her gaze to the small tenant cottage opposite the Phelps place, where the hired help stayed. She knew that a new family – German, by all accounts – had moved in just one week beforehand, and the thought occurred that they might be embroiled in some kind of domestic flare-up. If so, it wouldn't be anything out of the ordinary. Old man Phelps was forever hiring hobos to tend his farm, and after-hours drinking and fistfights were common among those damn swamp angels. But that house, too, was wreathed in darkness, and offered no clue.

Erma, still not happy, called for Adelbert Benson, the 47-year-old son of her employer, to join her in the kitchen. At the same time she eased the kitchen window open just a crack. A few flakes of snow brushed against her cheek as she strained to hear any further noises. Nothing. Just a frigid silence. She shivered in the cold night air and chided herself for her foolishness. Probably just some farmer with a shotgun trying to scare off a raccoon or a cat, maybe, she thought, and began to close the window. Suddenly a shrill scream cut through the silence. Then another. According to her first reported account – although subsequent events demonstrated that Miss Fisher's memory shifted like quicksand – this was followed just moments later by the sound of rapping at a door, and a woman's anguished voice crying out: 'Let me in, I am dying.'[1]

In the midst of all this nocturnal activity, Erma had been joined in the kitchen by Adelbert. According to Benson's unswerving testimony, which held up under numerous retellings, he never heard any shooting, any screams, or anyone crying out for help. All he heard was what sounded like a single knock at someone's door. He lingered in the kitchen for a few minutes, until frustration got the better of him. Probably just some family argument, he shrugged to Erma, best not to interfere. With that he returned to the warmth and comfort of his bed.

But Erma wasn't so easily swayed. Convinced something dreadful had happened, she stationed herself by the window and maintained a keen-eyed vigil. Moments later she was rewarded by the sight of a flickering light in the Phelps kitchen, which was on the north side of the house, facing in her direction. Half expecting more disturbances, she continued waiting at the window, only to be disappointed. Several minutes passed. Whatever had caused the commotion now appeared to have died down. Puzzled more than anything else, Erma Fisher pulled the kitchen window shut and retired to bed.

Once again a brooding silence descended over the houses along Salt Works Road.

Next morning at five o'clock, Charlie Stielow eased himself quietly out of bed. He leant over and gave the still-slumbering Nelson a shake, then began dressing. It had been an icy night with a fresh fall of snow, so he dressed quickly, pulling on blue dungarees over the shirt that he habitually slept in, slipping stockinged feet into felt boots covered with rubber overshoes and finally donning a black cap that covered his ears. Rubbing his hands together against the cold, he went into the small kitchen to build the fire. A few moments later, Nelson stumbled into the kitchen, yawning. Today was his birthday – he was nineteen years old – but there was no time or money for celebrations. As far as Nelson was concerned, today would be a day like any other. Charlie, after telling his young brother-in-law to continue tending the fire, readied himself to go across to the Phelps house where he would start straining the milk, his first chore of the day. As quietly as he could – his bulk and natural clumsiness made silence an impossibility – he threaded his way through the quiet household and opened the front door. A blast of icy air stung his face as he stepped outside onto the wooden veranda, into what was still an inky morning. He'd gone no more than a stride when his foot brushed up against an obstacle of some kind. He peered down. His eyes struggled to adjust to the dark. When they did so, he recoiled like he'd trodden on a rattlesnake.

Margaret Wolcott had been dead for hours. Her body, shoeless and clad only in a white nightdress, lay like a frozen mummy on the snow-covered porch. When Charlie bent down and reached out a tentative hand the tiny housekeeper felt icy to the touch, utterly lifeless. An ominous dark halo stained the snow around her upper body. Charlie withdrew his hand quickly, his mind a whirligig of confusion. What on earth had caused this diminutive, middle-aged woman to abandon the warmth and security of her home on a winter's night, cross a snow-covered road in her bare feet and wearing only a nightdress, then to collapse and die on his doorstep? Only one answer made any sense. Charlie raised his fearful gaze to the big timber-framed house that stood opposite. From this angle and distance the building seemed to be in total darkness, but as he stood up and edged his way across the snow-covered road, into the driveway and around towards the side of the house, he could see a low light burning through the kitchen window.

Then he stopped. The outer kitchen door, usually secured, was lolling back on its hinges.

Another couple of strides told him why. Charles Phelps, wearing just a cotton undershirt, lay sprawled on the kitchen floor, his head about six inches from the corner of the sink, his bare feet propping open the door. A flickering oil lamp on a stand just beside the door illuminated what was a grisly scene.

The old man's head had been mashed to an ugly pulp, but he was still alive, even if his breath did come in stertorous, jerky gasps. Charlie, panic-stricken, backed out through the kitchen door, gulping in huge draughts of the cold morning air as he tried to gather his scrambled thoughts. His eyes scanned the road in both directions. Off in the distance, on the same side of Salt Works Road, a single gleam of light flickered. It triggered a memory. Old man Phelps had mentioned something about that farm belonging to his nephew, Melvin Jenkins.

Charlie cut through a small gate and began running, as fast as his boots would carry him. Within a few yards he was panting for breath. Although an enormously strong man, stamina was not his strong suit; any kind of prolonged aerobic activity took its toll. Wheezing and weaving an uncertain path through the darkness, his lumbering stride left clear footprints in the overnight snowfall as he blundered along. As he neared the light he realised that it came from a barn situated some way behind the main house.

The Jenkins place was more than a fifth of a mile distant, and Charlie's lungs felt close to bursting by the time he staggered into the barn. Inside, a well-built man in his late thirties, with brown curly hair, was already hard at work cleaning some tack by lamplight. He looked up, startled by the intrusion.

Melvin Jenkins's blue eyes hardened as Charlie panted out his news, that there had been 'some robbering [sic] going on at Phelps, and they must have been shot.'[2] Jenkins acted quickly. He told Charlie to alert any other neighbours he could find, then arranged to meet him back at his uncle's house. Like his uncle, and unusually for these parts, Jenkins was hooked up to the telephone line and he then called a local physician, Dr Fred Eckerson who lived in Shelby. Eckerson digested the details and told Jenkins to immediately notify the coroner, Dr Edward Munson. Munson, like Eckerson, informed Jenkins that he would get to the Phelps place as soon as possible.

Meanwhile, still breathing hard from his exertions, Charlie trundled back down Salt Works Road. On the way, he stopped off at the tenant house and summoned Nelson out to the porch. The teenager's eyes widened to the size of saucers when he saw Margaret Wolcott lying there. Charlie grunted for him to fetch a tarpaulin from the buggy shed out back and to cover Miss Wolcott's body; he didn't want any of the womenfolk to witness the awful spectacle draped across their doorstep. He also instructed Nelson to stand guard over the body. Moments later, Charlie resumed his heart-bursting laps of Salt Works Road, this time running half a mile south to the Kohler residence.

It had been Howard Kohler who'd handled the paperwork on behalf of the previous owner – a relative – when Phelps had recently purchased the tenant house, and he was still in bed when Charlie hammered at the front door. It took him several minutes to answer the knock. Charlie, half-apologetically, said, 'We've had a little trouble at our place and I wish you'd come down.' Asked to elaborate, he said, 'A woman is dead at my place and a man is hurt.'[3] Thinking that this sounded a hell of a lot worse than just 'a little trouble', Kohler rushed to finish dressing. More garbled exchanges followed.

When questioned later, Kohler said he was certain that during this conversation Stielow had mentioned that the victims had been shot. For now, though, he and Charlie headed north back towards the Phelps place.

In the meantime, Jenkins had already made his way down Salt Works Road from the opposite direction. On his way he passed the Benson household. Jesse, the 75-year-old head of the house, and his son Adelbert were standing on the porch, with Erma just behind them, demanding to know what all the ruckus was about. Scarcely breaking stride, Jenkins hollered out what little he knew and kept on running.

He reached the house just after 5:30am and cautiously entered the kitchen. His uncle didn't stir. Jenkins bent down and cradled the old man's head. 'What happened?' he asked. 'Who did this?'[4] For a moment the old man's eyes flickered open, but the look was uncomprehending and maddeningly brief. An instant later, they fell shut again.

Realising that any further communication was hopeless, Jenkins gently laid his uncle's head on the floor, then stood up and began, tentatively, to explore the house. He did so edgily at first, still unsure what he might find. He began with his uncle's bedroom. It looked as if a hurricane had blown through; clothes and paperwork were strewn everywhere, the obvious legacy of a thief's attentions. Jenkins continued his inspection. He crossed the dining room and entered Margaret Wolcott's bedroom. Apart from the bed, which had clearly been slept in, this room looked neat and tidy. Without thinking, Jenkins now committed a cardinal but wholly understandable sin: he grabbed a handful of blankets from the rumpled bed, and used them to make his uncle comfortable.

In the early 20th century – with American interest in scientific forensic investigation still largely confined to the pages of Sherlock Holmes books – even big cities struggled with the concept of crime scene preservation, so there was very little chance of this rural outpost providing a textbook example of investigative rectitude. And so it proved. Jenkins's blunder, however understandable, came to exemplify the entire inquiry, as indiscretion was heaped on top of error, assumption on top of suspicion, until all that was left was a confused parody of reality.

Jenkins returned to the kitchen to check on his uncle. Still unconscious. Moments later he crossed the road to the tenant cottage, his heart heavy with despair. Even though the first shafts of daylight were beginning to dissipate the gloom, nothing could lift the dark sense of tragedy that had befallen this snowy country road. Serious crimes of any description were rare enough in the Shelby area; homicidal robberies came along once, maybe twice in a generation.

Nelson Green watched as Jenkins approached slowly. He had taken Charlie at his word and stood guard-like over his charge. Jenkins introduced himself, then bent down and lifted the canvas shroud. He shuddered. The farmhand's assessment had been correct; the poor woman was far beyond medical assistance. She appeared to have been shot just once in the chest. He could barely believe that a single wound had caused so much havoc, but her nightdress was saturated with blood. With the morning light improving all the time, Jenkins noticed something else – a trail of bloody handprints reaching up across the Stielows' front door and big splotches of blood on either side. Moving closer he could see the deep grooves that had been made by Margaret Wolcott as she clawed at the door with her bloodstained fingernails in the final few moments of her life. Jenkins, aware that there was nothing more to be done here, trudged sadly back to his uncle's house. Behind him, Nelson resumed his role as guardian of the corpse.

After checking once more on his still-comatose uncle, Jenkins stepped back outside. There were several footprints around the house, in the soft earth and snow of the driveway and on the east side of Salt Works Road, heading north. Judging from their size, the prints had been made by someone quite large. Another flurry of footmarks ran from the kitchen door of the Phelps house, going back and forth to a henhouse in the back yard.

Then he spotted a quite different set of tracks. These had been made by a bare foot in the snow, and led from the kitchen door, alongside the house, past a rosebush and out to the road. The prints – small, dainty even, and showing the clear imprint of the toes – had obviously been made by the terrified Margaret Wolcott as she had attempted to flee her assailant.

While Jenkins struggled to absorb all this, Howard Kohler appeared. Charlie trailed some way behind, obviously feeling the effects of his unaccustomed exertions. As Jenkins and Kohler talked and took control, a sense soon developed that the hired hand was being sidelined, shoved to the margins. This impression was reinforced a few minutes later when Jenkins and Kohler were joined by another neighbour, William Pogle. In a well-intentioned but hopelessly misguided gesture, the three men fanned out in a search for clues, little realising that every footprint they left in the soft mud and snow would only amplify the subsequent confusion. But their efforts were not without success. After a few moments, Kohler pointed out a mop handle lying beside the house. It appeared to have been freshly broken off. When someone suggested that it might have been used in the murderous break-in, the others nodded sagely. After that, with the dawn sky lightening around them, they decided to widen their search and began scouring the road for clues, footprints mostly. They needed to be quick, because the snow was beginning to melt.

The medical men were true to their word. By 8:00am Munson and Eckerson had reached the Phelps house and both were working feverishly over the stricken owner who still lay sprawled across the kitchen floor. They began by cleaning his wounds, wincing when they saw the full extent of the injuries. Phelps had received a savage blow low down on the left side of his face that had knocked loose four teeth, cut his tongue and the inside of his mouth, and left ugly bruising from cheek to jaw. But the life-threatening damage had been caused by bullets. He had been shot three times – in the head, chest and left arm – with a small calibre weapon, possibly a .22. Although there was little visible blood loss, either on the body or the kitchen floor, the internal injuries were catastrophic. Munson and Eckerson shook their heads. Neither held out much hope for their 70-year-old patient. They summoned Stielow, who was waiting dutifully outside the kitchen, and between them the three men hefted the still-unconscious Phelps into the sitting room, where he was laid on a sofa.

Having done all they could for Phelps, the two doctors hurried across the road and examined Margaret Wolcott's rapidly stiffening body. She had been killed by a single bullet that had entered her chest under the left arm. The question now confronting Munson and Eckerson was one that perplexes pathologists and medical examiners to the present day: at what time did this murder victim die? Unless the death has been witnessed – which rarely happens – there are no absolutes in this trickiest of all forensic conundrums. At best, it is an informed guess; at worst, it may be dangerously misleading.

Three factors generally come into play: *rigor mortis*, the stiffness of the body caused by muscles contracting after death; *hypostasis* or lividity, the dark discoloration of the skin resulting from the gravitational pooling of blood in the veins; and *algor mortis* or body temperature. Of these, the core body temperature is the most useful indicator of time of death, especially if the victim has been dead for less than 24 hours, but other factors, such as musculature and ambient temperature, have to be considered. For instance, someone obese will cool much more slowly than a lean person; and someone who dies in a warm room will retain more body heat than someone who succumbs outdoors in cold weather. Clothing, too, is important, as a naked body can cool 50 per cent faster than a clothed one.

In this instance, *rigor mortis* was already well established in Margaret Wolcott's face and upper body; dark red blotches of blood were visible in the lower reaches of her body; and her core body temperature had plunged precipitously. Factoring in the overnight cold, which would have hastened rigor and accelerated heat loss from such a lightly clad victim, Munson and Erickson were jointly satisfied that the time of death was probably no later than midnight. As it turned out, this proved to be an accurate assessment.

It was 9:00am before Sheriff Chester M. Bartlett arrived from the county seat of Albion, some twenty miles away. An imposing figure of huge girth, the 49-year-old Bartlett had been a patrolman until taking up the elected post of sheriff on 1 January 1914. Since that time he'd broken up his share of drunken brawls, domestic and otherwise, jailed a few arsonists – barn burnings were a common form of revenge in rural communities – and occasionally acted as intermediary in disputes between aggrieved farmers. Significantly absent from his CV was any meaningful experience of homicide investigation. This lack soon became all too apparent. In his defence, it should be stressed that he had inherited a horribly contaminated crime scene. News of the double tragedy had spread like wildfire through this small community, and spectators were converging on the farm like locusts. Most lined the road outside, craning their necks from a semi-respectful distance; but anyone with even the most tenuous family connection wandered at will throughout the murder house and its environs, rearranging furniture, obliterating finger and foot prints, and generally making a nuisance of themselves.

A trained investigator would have immediately assumed an iron-fisted control of the crime scene, but in 1915 very few jurisdictions in small-town America could afford the luxury of a dedicated detective force. Because rural crime tended to be sporadic, petty and overwhelmingly indigenous – the automobile had yet to come into its own as the lawbreaker's best friend – most investigations were handled by the local sheriff. Bartlett, and the thousands like him, generally did a satisfactory job, solving most of the crimes that came their way. But the world was moving on. In Europe, especially, an entirely new culture of crime investigation had taken hold. There, the investigators were not gun-toting lawmen who headed up posses, but scientists in laboratories and highly skilled pathologists, keen-eyed observers determined to bring method to what had been investigative chaos.

The recent groundbreaking discovery that no two people shared the same fingerprints might have revolutionised crime-fighting globally, but fingerprint analysis represented only the tip of an ever-expanding forensic iceberg. The dawn of the 20th century had brought with it a string of landmark scientific breakthroughs. Most were chemistry-based. In 1900 a test developed in Germany made it possible for the first time to determine if blood was human or from some other animal, a hugely significant development. Hot on the heels of that advance, the Austrian scientist and subsequent Nobel Prize-winner Karl Landsteiner had unlocked the key to ABO blood grouping, which had enormous implications for catching criminals. The innovations were chasing each other with impatient haste.

But all these laboratory miracles were useless without skilled detectives who understood how to process crime scenes and harvest evidence. In England, for example, Scotland Yard was ready at a moment's notice to dispatch experienced murder investigators to every corner of the country, wherever they might be needed. In the vast federal sprawl of America this was not an option. Each state was a law unto itself, and some embraced the new advances more readily than others. Predictably, progress was fastest in the big cities, like New York, Boston and Chicago, where they had the most crime. Here, the men and women in white lab coats soon caught up with, and in many cases overtook, their European counterparts, but across the American hinterland it was a quite different story. When it came to fighting crime, rural jurisdictions such as Orleans County and law officers like Sheriff Bartlett were still fumbling in the forensic dark ages.

And, of course, there was always the political dimension to be considered. On this occasion it came in the form of the impressive bulk of local district attorney (DA) John C. Knickerbocker, aged 49, who drove up to the crime scene shortly after Bartlett arrived. He and the sheriff were close political sidekicks and both had been elected to office on the Republican ticket in the 1913 election. Knickerbocker was a real heavyweight in the political life of Orleans County, and this was his second term as district attorney. Until 1910 he had served as the police justice for Albion and, even after he was elected DA, people still called him Judge Knickerbocker. He had a reputation for fairness and stolidity. He was also astute. And as he listened to Bartlett outline the admittedly sketchy details of the crime, a thread of unease wriggled through him. Phelps was one of the richest farmers hereabouts, a respected pillar of the community; this attack would cause outrage. Knickerbocker's highly tuned political antennae began to twitch. Every fibre in his body cried out that he needed to solve this case at all costs, and he needed to solve it fast.

He and Bartlett worked in tandem, trying to piece together what had happened inside the Phelps house. They began at the kitchen entrance. The outside door had four panes of glass in its upper portion. In the lower right-hand pane – on the right side, slightly above the middle and an inch or two from the framework of the door – was a single bullet hole. After studying the cracked glass, both men entered the kitchen.

The kitchen occupied the north-west corner of the house and was rectangular in shape. Its longest wall – over sixteen feet in length – faced north towards the Benson residence. Bartlett pointed out the lighted lamp, its oil low, almost burnt out, that stood on a stand by the door. He thought – and Knickerbocker agreed – that it had been glowing all night, probably since the attackers had burst in. Jenkins then guided them from the kitchen, through the cavernous dining room that dominated the centre of the house, and into his uncle's ground-floor bedroom. A large bureau had been ransacked, its three drawers yanked out and tossed on the floor, spilling clothes and documents everywhere. Among these papers was a promissory note for $300 from a farmer named Dunkelberger. Because it was worthless as a negotiable asset, the robber or robbers had ignored it. Rather more carelessly, they had also missed Phelps's watch, which still hung on the back of the bedroom door. Not a penny could be found anywhere. Jenkins couldn't put a definite figure on how much the thieves had taken, but he hazarded a guess at several hundred dollars. He confirmed that his uncle, with his miserly distrust of banks, was forever squirrelling banknotes away in various drawers.

What the men next saw – or thought they saw – in this bedroom would forever be a contentious point. Jenkins, testifying later, stated that his uncle's bed, which stood at the far end of the room, against the south wall, appeared not to have been slept in. Apart from some slight creasing on the edge of the bed, possibly made by the old man as he sat down to remove his shoes or trousers, the bedclothes were otherwise unrumpled and the pillow showed no sign of a head imprint. Bartlett remembered no such thing. His evidence on the witness stand was that the bed in Phelps's room *had* been slept in. On the surface, it didn't sound like much of a divergence, but as events unfolded this discrepancy would play a pivotal role in shaping the prosecution's case.

There *was* unanimity over Margaret Wolcott's bedroom, which stood at the rear of the house. According to Jenkins, even before he had grabbed the blankets to comfort his uncle, the bed had obviously been slept in, and Bartlett agreed. Closer inspection suggested that the killer had skipped this room entirely. Beside the bed, laid out neatly on a small nightstand, were Margaret's watch, some rings and a purse containing less than 50 cents.

Slowly a picture began to emerge. It appeared as if, around bed-time, Phelps had been disturbed, either by an intruder or someone knocking at the kitchen door. Grabbing a lamp – the only one in the house – he had gone to investigate. Some kind of struggle had then broken out in the kitchen. Maybe the intruder's intention had been to just threaten Phelps or knock him out with the broken-off mop stick found outside, but the farmer was a tough old bird who knew how to use his fists. Once the cudgel failed in its task, the assailant had opened fire, shooting three times.

Fast asleep in her bed just a few feet away, Margaret Wolcott was jolted awake by the sound of fighting and gunshots. Had she remained where she was and hidden under the bed, perhaps, it's possible the intruder might never have been aware of her presence. But the fight-or-flight instinct screamed out: 'Run!' Trembling in the dark, she had probably waited for an opportunity, then attempted to flee the house in her nightclothes and bare feet. First impressions suggested she had made it to the kitchen door, where a single bullet fired through the window struck her in the heart as she descended the steps. Then, in an almost superhuman feat of strength for such a tiny woman – she stood less than five feet tall – she had staggered across the snow-covered road to the tenant house, a distance of almost 100 yards, where she collapsed on the veranda.

It was a plausible scenario, one that fitted the immediately available evidence, and it was one from which the prosecution refused to deviate when the case came to trial, even though subsequent examination would open up some serious cracks in their argument. For now, though, there were other clues to track down. Bartlett and Knickerbocker moved outside.

The weather that morning didn't seem able to make up its mind; one moment bright and sunny, the next, louring under squally snow showers. Beneath these changeable skies, Bartlett and his deputy, Under-Sheriff J. Scott Porter, circled the house carefully. They stopped by a manure bank beneath Phelps's bedroom window, on the south side of the house. Footprints were clearly visible in the soft surface. They also saw the foot tracks that Jenkins had noted along the driveway; especially those in a snow bank on the east side of the road. Bartlett shouted instructions for these tracks to be covered with a box, and for a blanket to be thrown over the top. Charlie Stielow pitched in with others in carrying out this task. The hope was to preserve the tracks for as long as possible in the fast-melting snow. (Extraordinarily, Bartlett failed to photograph the footprints, settling instead for pressing a piece of paper into one footprint and drawing its outline to give the rough shape and size.) At the same time, Bartlett sent out for a bloodhound to follow the trail.

The investigation was interrupted at 11:00am by the arrival of an ambulance to transport the still-unconscious Phelps to Medina Memorial Hospital, four miles away. The transfer was supervised by Eckerson and Munson, with Bartlett looking on. He waited for the ambulance to leave, then resumed his inquiries.

Most of his time was spent interviewing witnesses. Melvin Jenkins gave a full account of the morning's events, before casting his mind back to the previous evening. He recalled looking out at about 8:00pm and seeing a light in his uncle's dining room. Like most farmers, Jenkins was in the habit of retiring early, and shortly afterwards he had gone to bed. During the night neither he nor his wife Edith, aged 34, nor their teenage maid, Evaline Cromwell, had heard any kind of disturbance. He had arisen at five o'clock and gone to the barn to begin his day's work. The first he had known of the crime had been some time shortly thereafter, when his uncle's newly hired hand burst into the barn with the terrible news.

If Jenkins had little to offer Bartlett, then Erma Fisher was more than ready to take up the slack. She provided an avalanche of evidence – the shots, the screams, the cries for help, rapping at doors, lights flickering in the dark. Bartlett noted it all down carefully. Because Erma's chronology appeared to tally with the doctors' estimate of when Margaret Wolcott had met her death, the Bensons' housekeeper earned for herself a credibility factor that subsequent events would do much to undermine. For now, though, she was undoubtedly the star witness. After leaving Miss Fisher, Bartlett located Knickerbocker and the two men went looking for the German fellow who'd found the bodies.

While the crowds had come from every direction to gawp and to point, Charlie had simply gone about his duties, apparently oblivious to the fuss around him. To some observers, both at the time and later, his oddly self-contained air provided proof of a brutish, uncaring nature. In all probability it would not have occurred to him to behave otherwise. He'd been hired to do a job, and in Charlie Stielow's stunted universe, that meant fulfilling his obligations. One thing is certain; underlying his impassiveness was a gut-wrenching sense of disappointment. He realised that once the dust settled on this tragedy, there would be no future for him at this farm. And that would send him tumbling back to square one. No job, no money, no house. Worst of all, he dreaded what the long-term impact would be on Laura. How many more setbacks could she stand? So, in order to blank out the horrors of the day, and any horrors that might lie ahead, while bodies were being stretchered into ambulances and clues were being processed, Charlie busied himself with mundane farmyard duties such as straining the milk. At lunchtime, though, he was back in his own house when Bartlett and Knickerbocker came calling.

The Stielows and the Greens were gathered in the living room. They weren't used to receiving educated visitors and it showed. They fidgeted, gauche and embarrassed in threadbare clothes that had seen the darning needle too many times to count. Their appearance perfectly matched the rough-hewn furniture that surrounded them. They were dirt-poor and it showed. Tack on their shared air of defensiveness and it was more than enough to arouse suspicions in the two investigators, who reasoned that a roll of stolen bills could make a sizeable difference to lives lived like this. Knickerbocker and Bartlett singled out Charlie first for questioning. They listened to him recount finding the bodies that morning. All the while they sized him up. Then they asked him to account for his activities on the previous day. This proved more difficult for the big farmhand whose powers of recall seemed hazy, and he took some time to gather his thoughts. The answers, when they did come, were mumbled and uncertain, bordering on the incoherent.

He told how the previous night he had finished his chores at the Phelps place around six o'clock, about the time it started snowing and … oh, yeah! Earlier that afternoon, Miss Wolcott had mentioned that a visitor was expected that evening, and she'd asked Charlie if he wanted to come back over and meet him. He had said yes, but before he finished work Miss Wolcott had found him and passed on the news that the meeting would have to be some other time, since the visitor had now begged off.

Investigative ears pricked up at the mention of this mystery visitor. Charlie, though, could offer no clue as to his or her identity, and continued his account. After supper, he had gone to bed around ten o'clock. At some time – he wasn't sure when – he and Nelson had been wakened by the sound of screaming. Bartlett pressed for more information. No, the big man insisted, he'd not heard any shooting, or a woman's voice calling out, or anyone rapping at the door; all he'd heard was two sharp screams. Charlie told how he and Nelson had fumbled their way to the front window and peered out. Neither had seen anything in the pitch blackness. In order to satisfy his curiosity Charlie decided to check the window to the south of the house.

Again he'd seen nothing and had returned to bed, puzzled but not greatly concerned.

Dragging this account out of Charlie Stielow took a long time. His grasp on the English language was ragged at best, full of tangled syntax and odd expressions, while words of more than one syllable only confused him. But the thrust of his story was confirmed by Laura, who fixed the time of the screaming at 10:45pm because she'd checked her bedside clock.

Nelson Green maintained the united front. If anything, his answers were even more hesitant and confused than those of his brother-in-law, leaving Knickerbocker and Bartlett in no doubt that they were dealing with a near mental defective.

Of all the residents in the tenant house, Mary Jane Green was much the most self-assured and assertive. Matriarchal down to her boot heels, she took her duties as Laura's protector very seriously indeed. She explained truculently how her daughter, now in the last month of her pregnancy, needed rest, and plenty of it, and could the two gentlemen please get their questioning over and done with as soon as possible. All she succeeded in doing was raising hackles. Knickerbocker and Bartlett bristled as Mrs Green rattled off her answers with an all-too-obvious lack of patience. Like everyone else, she'd heard two screams, but no shots or pounding on the door.

Bartlett logged all these statements with a thoughtful air. Like many small-town sheriffs he had an inbred parochialism that gave him a visceral distrust of strangers. Also, he rebelled against the notion that such a hideous crime had been committed by someone local. Surely it had to be the work of some out-of-towner? And the Stielows and the Greens certainly fitted the bill. Besides, apart from the domineering mother-in-law, there was a caginess to their answers that irked the lawman. Knickerbocker, too, had picked up on this reticence, and it was he who asked Charlie Stielow, point-blank, if he owned any firearms. After another of those long pauses, the big man shook his head and grunted that he possessed no firearms of any kind.

After exchanging glances – this reply had been unusually hesitant – Knickerbocker and Bartlett left.

Lunchtime came and went without any fresh developments, but early afternoon brought the grim news that everyone had feared and expected – Charles Phelps had died in Medina Memorial Hospital at 1:00pm, without ever regaining consciousness. Bartlett, now dealing with a double homicide, decided to clarify witness statements from the neighbours. It didn't take him long. Apart from the voluble Erma Fisher, who was forever refreshing her memory and her testimony, none of the other witnesses came up with any additional information. Bartlett felt uneasy. Already the pressure was beginning to build.

All afternoon the morbid and the curious continued to pour down Salt Works Road from either end. They came on foot, by horse, by buggy, and a privileged few by car. One estimate put the crowds gathered about the Phelps house at more than 500, all fighting and shoving each other for the best view. Pride of place in the aggression stakes went to the newspaper reporters, some from as far as three counties away, and all desperate for details of what was the most sensational murder case in living memory. In truth, there wasn't much to see or report. Mostly the crowd just stood around and shivered, stamping their feet against the cold. A few had already begun to drift away, when, at six o'clock, just as the light was beginning to fade, a sudden buzz of anticipation thrummed through the crowd. Some began to point excitedly. The source of this sudden interest was the arrival of a local hunter, Charles Scobell, and his bloodhound, a veteran tracker called General Lee.

Dogs have a phenomenal sense of smell – witness the number of murder victims whose bodies have been discovered by the proverbial 'man out walking his dog'– and the bloodhound is the undisputed leader of the olfactory pack. Its long, damp nose is perfectly designed for the business of smelling. Inside is a honeycombed sinus cavity packed with 25 times as many receptors as humans possess. These allow it to detect traces as small as one drop of blood in five quarts of water. Nobody can really quantify how much more sensitive the bloodhound's nose is compared with that of a human, but even the most conservative estimate rates it at 1,000 times superior.

Scobell led General Lee, snuffling, out to the snow bank and gave him the scent of the tracks that had been protected by sacking. The effect was electric. Immediately, the giant dog yanked Scobell into the driveway, up to the kitchen door, then back and forth a few times along the north side of the house. Scobell, an experienced tracker, bent down to examine these prints more closely. Judging from the creases that ran across the soles, he would stake his reputation on the prints having been made by rubber or felt boots. He decided to give the dog its head. But when General Lee began lunging off in the direction of a snow-covered field, Scobell called a temporary halt to proceedings. He yelled for someone to hold the straining dog while he went inside the house for his long boots.

General Lee's energetic bulk made him popular with the bystanders. One of them, a farmhand in dungarees, set down the pail of milk that he carried in each hand to fondle the bloodhound's slavering muzzle. Charlie Stielow had always liked dogs and they liked him. General Lee was no exception.

Scobell reappeared, suitably attired in long boots. This time he tethered General Lee to a leash strapped about his waist, which allowed him to have both arms free should the scent lead them through any thick undergrowth. Alongside Scobell was his partner, B.A. Snoover, and together they let the dog run ahead.

If the scent is strong a bloodhound will follow it on the run, but if the scent is weak or disappears, the dog tends to walk in a circle until the trail is picked up again. Here, General Lee caught a really powerful scent and tugged Scobell in through the kitchen door, across the dining room and into Phelps's bedroom, right up to the bureau. At this spot the dog became hyper-excited.

It required all of Scobell's strength to haul the dog outside to the main road where the scent was first taken. Straight away, General Lee bounded off in a northerly direction, through a break in the fence into a sodden field, then north-east to a small path known as Jenkins Lane. Because this route was taking them away from the crime scene – and possibly to where the killer might be holed up – Scobell halted and suggested to Snoover that they ought to get a law officer to accompany them.

When they returned to the house, Bartlett brushed off their request imperiously, insisting that he needed to remain *in situ* to supervise the crime scene. Nor, for some inexplicable reason, would he allow Porter to accompany the trackers. This was too much for John Stork, the veteran chief of police in neighbouring Medina, who had been present for most of the afternoon. He snorted in disgust, 'If they don't want to go, I will.'[5]

By the light of hand-held oil lanterns, the three men set off after the eager dog. Behind them, scores of enthusiastic spectators joined the chase. The pack pursued General Lee across the field to the Jenkins residence, along a lane, across some ploughed ground, until the dog reached a fence. At this point, General Lee's throaty barking left no doubt that the trail continued on the other side. With a combined effort, the three men heaved the great beast over the fence. Immediately it picked up the scent again, this time to a small creek where the trail went cold. After a couple of false leads, further along – where the creek backed onto the corner of Jenkins's orchard

– General Lee grabbed hold of the scent again. He pulled in an easterly direction, to a point behind the orchard, then north-easterly to a large tree that stood in a plot of land near an electricity transmission line. From there, the dog veered abruptly southwards, and headed right back to the Phelps place.

It was a confusing, circuitous route, one that baffled investigators. Although General Lee continued working the grounds until eleven o'clock that night, nothing further was discovered. After such a promising start, there was no denying the sense of disappointment. The next day's local newspaper captured the gloomy mood: 'The trail had been crossed and recrossed by so many that it was quite impossible for the dog to get a scent ... Sheriff Bartlett said that the efforts of the dog, while interesting, were of no material value.'[6]

The dog handlers left behind them a sombre scene. At the end of day one the inquiry had uncovered no clues, nor any real leads, and when Bartlett and Knickerbocker sat down and compared notes that night, they shared a sense of foreboding. Unless a new witness materialised in the next day or two, this case could slide right into the 'unsolved' file, taking their careers with it. Their major drawback was the absence of any obvious prime suspect.

Unless, of course, that big German fellow in the tenant house had something to hide ...

3

Out Of The Mouths ...

At just after daybreak the next morning, Bartlett and Porter were back at the farmhouse. It was another cold day with flurries of snow in the air. Even though old man winter still had the region firmly in his grasp, the icy wind whipping along Salt Works Road had done nothing to diminish local interest in the tragedy. Once again the rubberneckers were out in force. Car horns honked and horses whinnied excitedly as spectators jostled for the best vantage point of West Shelby's hottest new attraction. As the morning wore on, the worsening crush caused tempers to run high. When some of the more adventurous visitors tried to muscle their way into the house, they found their path blocked by heavily armed deputies who stood on little ceremony in repelling the intruders.

Not everyone along Salt Works Road was preoccupied with the tragedy. That morning Charlie Stielow had awoken at his customary early hour. It was still dark when he drew back the curtain and peered through his front window. Despite the early hour, the crowds were already beginning to swell. With all this commotion, he decided there was no chance of getting any work done around the farm. Good time to run some errands. After making breakfast and checking that Laura was all right – the events of the past 24 hours had sparked fears for her health and that of the unborn baby – he went out to the barn and hitched up his Democrat wagon. Ignoring the reporters who rushed up with a flurry of questions, Charlie whipped the horse into action and threaded his way along the crowded highway. His destination was the heavily mortgaged farm in Wolcottsville. There was still one last load of potatoes that he needed to collect for his family. He would be gone for most of the day.

Over at the murder house, the investigation was humming. As promised, Scobell had returned with General Lee, and good fortune had favoured the experienced tracker. The sharp overnight drop in temperature had preserved the footprints in the snow bank and this was where Scobell recommenced his search. With Porter in close attendance – Bartlett wasn't about to repeat his tactical blunder of the previous evening – General Lee this time lugged his way round to the rear of the Phelps place, then ran excitedly up and down the drive as far as the henhouse in the back yard. The dog's barking brought Bartlett from the house. He directed Scobell to the footprints found beneath Phelps's bedroom window. Scobell thought that these looked very different to the rubber-soled tracks he'd followed the previous night. The hound sniffed around for a few moments then, apparently picking up a scent, headed back out to the main road.

Although the General's inclination was to travel northwards, Bartlett had other ideas. He ordered Scobell to haul the powerful bloodhound towards the tenant house. The crowds parted to let them through. When the dog reached the Stielows' front porch it exhibited no sign of having caught a familiar scent. Similarly, inside the house. With the entire Stielow family, except Charlie, in attendance, the dog snuffled around the living room and bedrooms a couple of times, before padding uninterestedly out of the front door.

Once they were out of earshot, Bartlett took Scobell to one side. He had a question: if Stielow *had* made those footprints beneath Phelps's window, was it possible that the dog could have missed his scent? Scobell shook his head. General Lee was the best tracker he'd known. Rest assured, Scobell said, if Stielow had made those footprints, the dog would have been jumping all over him. Besides, he'd seen Stielow stroking General Lee the previous day, and the dog was acting like he'd just met his best friend.

Bartlett became thoughtful. That worm of unease from the previous night was beginning to wriggle annoyingly as he returned to the farmhouse to continue the search for clues. The only fresh item of interest was an unmade bed in one of the upstairs bedrooms. It had apparently been used by a guest, though how long previously it was impossible to tell. It might have been a couple of nights, it might have been a week or more, depending on the level of domestic fastidiousness. The rest of the search was perfunctory at best. For instance, there is nothing in the record to show that surfaces in the house were examined for fingerprints. This was hardly surprising. Despite recent legal precedents – most notably the Illinois Supreme Court's groundbreaking decision to admit fingerprint evidence in *People vs. Jennings (1911)** – the benefits of fingerprint identification had yet to filter down to many rural jurisdictions, and Orleans County was no exception. Bartlett emerged from the house, scowling. With no obvious clues there, all hopes now were pinned on General Lee. Bartlett told Scobell to give the bloodhound one last run at the tracks in the snow bank.

Just like the night before, the General immediately pulled north, towards the small stream where the trail had petered out previously. Today, though, aided by daylight, the searchers were able to scour the banks of the creek more thoroughly. After a while someone shouted and pointed at the ground. Tracks – male, most likely, judging from the size and the depth – could be seen emerging from the water. Scobell gave the dog his head. With his great, square muzzle scanning the terrain on either side of the scent like a present-day mine detector, General Lee led the trackers across a field to a small residential road that headed south. Before going any further, Porter summoned Bartlett to rejoin the search. A few minutes later the two lawmen, at the head of a sizeable posse, set off down the road. At each house

---

* On 16 February 1912, a Chicago criminal named William Jennings became the first killer in America to be executed as a direct result of fingerprint evidence.

they asked the residents if they had seen anything suspicious. They soon received some interesting news.

First one homeowner, then another, spoke of having seen a young man running from the direction of the creek on the Monday morning between seven and eight o'clock. Even though this sighting was as much as nine hours after the murders were thought to have been committed, the investigators' pulses quickened. Bartlett learned that the young stranger – no older than a teenager – had been heading south, on a course that took him into the Tonawanda Swamp.

Since the Big Tree Treaty of 1797, the Tonawanda – a sprawling expanse of muddy water and scrubby trees, filled with turtles and colonies of great herons – had been home to the Seneca Indian reservation. In that time, the Seneca had seen their original allotment of 300 square miles whittled away by logging and other commercial interests until they retained just a tiny fraction, barely 7,000 acres, but the swamp that remained spilled over the reservation's boundaries, as mysterious and spooky as ever. For a fugitive, the Tonawanda was an ideal place to hide out. Except that this youthful and energetic athlete seemed wholly uninterested in any form of concealment.

From all accounts he'd made no attempt to hide his rapid progress, nor had he attempted to hitch a ride from any passing farmer's wagon. He was also possessed of great stamina and a rather bizarre dress sense, judging from descriptions of his appearance. Witnesses reckoned him to be about eighteen years old, approximately five feet ten inches tall and weighing over twelve stone. He wore yellow-coloured trousers, a blue jacket, tan shoes and a salt-and-pepper golf hat. His shoes and trousers were covered with mud. Despite the inclement weather, he wore no overcoat. According to various observers, he seemed in a great hurry and would run as far as his lungs would carry him, then slow to a walk until he recovered his breath. Then he began running again. In this stop-start fashion he'd crossed the county line and panted his way breathlessly into the town of Alabama. At 10:00am, Bartlett and his posse did likewise. Here, townspeople who'd seen the athletic stranger pointed in the direction of Wheatville in neighbouring Genesee County. The posse resumed its belated chase. At Wheatville, Bartlett called a halt to the endeavour. His jurisdiction had ended at the county line, obliging him to contact the local sheriff's office and ask them to be on the lookout for the mysterious runner, last seen hotfooting it to nearby Oakfield.

Meantime, back at the tenant house, Laura's 34-year-old sister, Olive Smith, arrived. She'd heard the tragic news the previous evening and had walked from her home in Medina to lend support. Just fighting her way through to the Stielows' front door required a Herculean effort. A large scrum of reporters, hungry for quotes from any member of the Stielow clan, had swarmed across the veranda, peering through the curtained windows. Mrs Green, like Horatius on the bridge, had taken up a stance blocking the doorway, fielding every question and acting as the family's spokesperson. She spoke of their distress and emphasised their collective sense of guilt. Had they reacted more positively when they heard the screams, she said, it was possible that they might have been able to assist Miss Wolcott. As it was, they were 'broken-up'[1] over the whole affair. Beyond this, she was saying nothing. Her unbending firmness did the trick. Disappointed, the reporters scattered and went in search of other sources.

Olive, who had watched this scene from the side, waited until the front of the house was clear of visitors, then motioned her mother indoors. The two women spent several minutes in deep conversation. When the tête-à-tête concluded, Olive left, accompanied by her brother Nelson. Olive was moving soon to a new house in the hamlet of Royalton Center, and her brother's muscle would come in handy.

That evening, a single wagon, heavily laden with potatoes, slowly creaked up Salt Works Road from the direction of Wolcottsville. It was getting cold again and Charlie Stielow wanted to be indoors by the fire. His progress was modest, due to the streams of murder house gawpers who'd finally succumbed to the icy wind and the gloom and were now making their way home. Few, if any, of the shivering people hurrying in the opposite direction recognised the wagon-driver.

It had been an exhausting day for Sheriff Bartlett. He'd returned from Wheatville, red-faced from exertion and embarrassment, too. Goddam running man! Almost 48 hours since the killings and thus far the phantom jogger was the only substantive clue that he had uncovered. If it was even a clue. The way Bartlett figured it, the timing was all wrong. If, as seemed likely, the shootings occurred well before midnight on Sunday, why on earth would the killer still be splashing about in some nearby muddy stream more than nine hours later? And why, if he were fleeing a double homicide, would he make no attempt to disguise his erratic progress? No, none of it made any sense. Bartlett knew, deep in his gut, that he'd wasted a valuable day and made a fool of himself into the bargain. Already he sensed he was losing control of this investigation.

Fortunately, Bartlett's deputies had been pursuing other, rather more conventional, investigative leads that day. From early morning they'd been enquiring locally, trying to build up a picture of Phelps's activities in the days and weeks prior to his death, hoping to uncover some kind of motive for the attack. They learned that on the last Thursday of his life, Phelps had visited the Hart Furniture Store in Medina and lavished $29 on a leather chair. The clerk, George E. Gotts, had gulped at the thick roll of bills – five or six hundred bucks, at least – that Phelps had flashed when paying for the chair. After Phelps left, Gotts had remarked to another clerk: 'That old fellow has a wad big enough to choke a cow.'[2] If Phelps was carrying that kind of cash so close to the weekend, the deputies reasoned, it would still have been in his possession on the night of the attack. This shocked no one. Around Medina, it was common knowledge that Phelps kept a goodly stash about the house at all times. And his miserliness was notorious.

This focused attention on all those hired hands rumoured to have been ripped off by Phelps over the years. According to one neighbour: 'If Mr Phelps had never had trouble with his help he would be alive.'[3] Reportedly, one ex-employee who'd fallen out with Phelps over just a couple of dollars had made open threats, growling that 'if Phelps thought more of $2.50 than he did of his life then he'd find out that he wouldn't make anything by it [sic].'[4] Investigators uncovered plenty of former employees with reason to loathe Phelps. Everyone agreed, though, that Phelps's biggest bust-up in recent times had been with Stielow's immediate predecessor at the farm, the Canadian Kirk Tallman. From all accounts, that dispute had turned really mean. And since then, nobody had set eyes on Phelps's former apple-picker. This set Bartlett thinking. As the last grey streaks of 23 March faded into night, the sheriff issued a message to all his deputies – find Tallman.

The next afternoon, at two o'clock, most of West Shelby was gathered at the local Methodist Episcopal church to watch as simple pine coffins bearing the bodies of Charles Phelps and Margaret Wolcott were shouldered slowly into the tiny chapel. The service was conducted by the Reverend Victor Harding. He addressed the overflowing pews, lamenting the brutality and senselessness of the crime, and the dreadful sense of loss that the community was feeling. His words were relayed outside to a crowd that numbered in the hundreds, all of whom stood in reverential silence. When the proprieties were concluded, six sombrely dressed men carried Phelps's coffin out to the waiting hearse. A few paces behind came the coffin that held Margaret Wolcott. Among her bearers was Adelbert Benson. The crowd stood bare-headed as the funeral cortège set off. Its first stop was Mount Pleasant cemetery in Shelby, where Phelps was laid to rest alongside his parents, Giles and Jane. From there, a single hearse bore Margaret Wolcott the few miles to the family plot at Wheatville cemetery, where she joined five other family members, including her father, J. Warren Wolcott, who had been the town constable for Alabama.

Earlier that day, the ten-man Orleans County board of supervisors had convened an extraordinary general meeting. The only item on the hastily compiled agenda was a motion to discuss whether to offer a reward for the capture of the killer. After a lengthy and heated debate, the board concluded that it had no legal basis for authoris-ing a reward, but it did grant Knickerbocker $500 to prosecute the case. Supervisor Albert Martin of Shelby, who'd requested twice that amount, was infuriated by his colleagues' parsimony. Some penny-pinching board members had actually voted to allocate less than $500, causing one prominent local citizen – almost certainly Martin – to growl anonymously to a reporter: 'Human life is cheap in Orleans County.'[5]

Bartlett was equally dismayed. He immediately dictated a letter to the governor's office, asking the state to authorise a $1,000 reward for the arrest and conviction of the person or persons who commit-ted the murders. At a press conference later that afternoon, Bartlett's gloomy demeanour did nothing to inspire confidence. Nor did his words. He wearily admitted that he had no new clues and that if the killer were not caught within the next day or so, he would be obliged to turn the case over to a firm of private detectives. There was still the coroner's inquest, scheduled for the following Friday; that might uncover some new evidence. But he didn't sound hopeful. In the meantime, he intended going to Oakfield. Apparently, there had been more sightings there of that elusive running man.

Someone else who was baffled and grievously hurt by the board's curious decision was Melvin Jenkins. Whereas others just grumbled and moaned, he opted for direct action. On the morning of 25 March, he issued the following statement:

REWARD FOR ARREST OF MURDERER.

I, THE UNDERSIGNED, HEREBY OFFER THE SUM OF $500 FOR THE ARREST AND CONVICTION OF THE PERSON OR PERSONS WHO MURDERED CHAS. B. PHELPS ON THE NIGHT OF SUNDAY, MARCH 21, 1915, IN THE TOWN OF SHELBY, ORLEANS COUNTY, NEW YORK. THIS IN ADDITION TO ANY AMOUNT WHICH MAY BE PAID BY ORLEANS COUNTY OR THE STATE OF NEW YORK FOR THE APPREHENSION OF THE PERPETRATOR OF THE CRIME.

MELVIN JENKINS.[6]

In a community where any farmhand who made $500 a year would have regarded himself as another Rockefeller, there was good reason to hope that Jenkins's reward might loosen any reluctant tongues.

The hotly anticipated inquest opened on Friday 26 March, at the city hall in Medina. At 11:00am the coroner, Dr Edward Munson, gavelled the crowded courtroom to order. Munson, like Knickerbocker a deeply entrenched member of the Republican cabal that ran every aspect of politico-legal life in Orleans County, was highly experienced, having been coroner for more than twenty years, and he did his best to keep the proceedings moving along briskly. After the customary identification of the victims he got down to the serious business at hand. Because blaring news headlines throughout western New York State had catapulted Stielow into the role of star witness, his was the testimony that was most eagerly awaited. When he took the stand, the farmhand was plainly ill at ease and surprised everyone with the halting manner of his responses. For Munson, it was like talking to an infant: only questions phrased in the simplest of terms yielded the clarification that he and the law required. Piece by painful piece, Charlie repeated the story he had told Bartlett: how, on Sunday evening at six o'clock, he had taken the milk into the farmhouse kitchen where Miss Wolcott and Mr Phelps were talking. Shortly afterwards, he had returned to the tenant cottage, dodging the first few flakes of snow. His mother-in-law had prepared supper and he'd sat down to eat with the rest of the family. At some time between nine and ten o'clock he had retired. Munson asked about sleeping arrangements in the tenant house. Charlie struggled with these, but concluded by saying that he and Nelson slept in a room together on the ground floor on the north side of the house.

What happened next? Munson asked.

Charlie replied that some time later he was awakened by two shrill screams.

What time was this?

Around 10:45pm, though he only confirmed the actual time the following day, when Laura told him. Stielow described how he and Nelson got up, dressed partially and looked out of the house to the north. Neither saw anything. He also peered through the glass in the front door. He had no idea whether Miss Wolcott was lying outside his front door at this time, saying only that he did not see her, claiming that from his vantage point the section of veranda where

Miss Wolcott had been found was not in view. Then, still baffled by the unexplained screams, he had checked the south-facing window. Again, he saw nothing. Munson asked Charlie if he had heard any shots. The witness said no.

Munson moved on to the next morning. Charlie described finding Margaret Wolcott's body on the veranda at approximately 5:30am. He called Nelson and told him to cover up the body, then went across to the Phelps house. Munson carefully noted this timeline and then concluded Charlie's testimony by asking him if he owned any weapons. Charlie replied firmly that he had 'never had a revolver or rifle'.[7] He was then excused.

Charlie's performance on the stand, hesitant at times, pedantic at others, won him few friends. A local newspaper, the *Medina Daily Journal*, was especially scathing: 'Charles Stleo [*sic*] ... is a big, stupid appearing German and was inclined to be phlegmatic.'[8]

Nelson Green came next. He looked and sounded awful. A raging toothache had caused his face to swell up alarmingly and his grey eyes reacted vacantly to almost every question, no matter how simply it was phrased. If he understood the seriousness of the situation, then it wasn't apparent to anyone in the courtroom. All they saw was a half-witted youth with an alarming habit of grinning inappropriately as he struggled with the most elementary queries. On one point, though, Green was emphatic: there were 'no weapons at Stielow's house'.[9]

In necessarily laboured fashion, Munson struggled to draw out the circumstances surrounding the discovery of the bodies. Green's face scrunched up in concentration. His first knowledge of the crime, he said, came when Stielow returned from the Jenkins house and told him to cover the body.

Munson looked up sharply. What was that? Green repeated his testimony, which directly contradicted Stielow's earlier statement. Rather than let Green continue, Munson immediately recalled Charlie to the stand. The coroner demanded to know the exact sequence of events on the morning in question. Charlie had the look of a rabbit trapped in headlights. After several seconds' pause, he muttered that he'd made a mistake. Green's chronology was correct. He had gone to the Phelps and Jenkins houses *before* telling his brother-in-law to cover the body.

It was only a minor discrepancy, but the slip did Charlie Stielow no favours whatsoever. Sworn testimony has a merciless knack of amplifying any inconsistency. A genuine mistake, or a careless lie? It would be for others to decide. But one thing was certain; when Charlie Stielow left the stand he did so under a cloud, one that would darken with each passing day.

When Laura, heavily pregnant, took the stand, Munson treated her kindly. Her testimony did add something of interest, though. On the Friday before the murder, two pedlars with a horse and buggy had gone door to door along Salt Works Road. Charlie had got into conversation with them and had traded some old rubber wagon tyres for a few oranges. She'd remembered them particularly because these men were strangers, the first she'd seen since moving into the tenant house. Munson noted the details and told her she could step down.

Spectators in the packed hall stirred restlessly, craning for a better view of Laura as she took her seat alongside Charlie and Nelson. Among the keenest observers was a middle-aged man of medium build, who sat quietly taking notes as each witness testified. With his pen and notepad he could have been mistaken for a reporter, but George W. Newton was a former police officer who now ran the Buffalo-based Byrne's Detective Agency (the name was handily similar to that of the nationally known Burns Detective Agency, and acquired many commissions from unsuspecting clients who mistakenly believed they were hiring the illustrious William J. Burns and his crack team of investigators). Newton had been summoned by Knickerbocker, who was already losing confidence in Bartlett's handling of the inquiry. The DA was desperate for results and Newton was desperate to provide them.

Newton was a throwback to 18th-century England, when, before the days of salaried police officers, law enforcement was largely left to a group known as 'thieftakers'. Some were honest, but theirs was a system open to every kind of corruption. Because thieftakers were paid by results, many simply fabricated evidence to gain a conviction. And when times got tough, some even originated crimes – hiring robbers to carry out a theft, say – then pocketed the reward for recovering the stolen property. The undoubted king of the London thieftakers was Jonathan Wild, an entrepreneurial psychopath who sent a rumoured 120 men to the gallows and pocketed thousands in rewards and bribes, before himself being hanged at Tyburn Tree in 1720.

Newton and his kind were the spiritual descendants of Wild. The 'bonus' culture was hardwired into Newton's makeup, and as he listened to details of the double murder and the ramshackle investigation that had ensued, he metaphorically smacked his lips over the prospect of a fat pay cheque. He absorbed the contradictory and often confusing testimony, but mostly he spent his time sizing up Stielow and Green; particularly the latter. That swollen face looked to Newton as if it had been caused by a fist rather than toothache. Now, why would that be? Newton had his suspicions. For some reason, henceforth the Buffalo private investigator would not budge from a belief that Stielow had recently beaten up his young brother-in-law. And in his book that could only mean one thing. For now, though, he needed to concentrate on other matters – Erma Fisher was about to take the stand.

Unlike the two previous witnesses, the Bensons' housekeeper adored the limelight, obviously intent on milking the occasion for all it was worth. Her answers were rambling and stuffed full of non sequiturs. When asked by Munson how much time had elapsed between the shots and the screams, she replied: 'Five minutes. It doesn't seem as if it was five minutes. It was a short time.'[10] While the court tried to digest this confusing response, Miss Fisher began to elaborate on the statement she had given previously. The embellishment concerned the words allegedly used by Margaret Wolcott as she cried out in the darkness. In her latest version, Fisher explained how Wolcott had sobbed: "'I'm dying, I'm dying.' Every time she said this she would pound on the door with her hands. The last time I heard her she said, "Will, let me in."'

Munson was puzzled by this reference to 'Will.'

Erma put him right. 'She [Miss Wolcott] might have said, "Will you let me in."'[11]

Munson noted this clarification and asked the witness to continue. She added little to what was already known; only that she'd remained watching by the window for several minutes and had then retired to bed. She'd heard nothing more until the next morning, when she was informed of the tragedy.

The medical testimony came next. Doctors Eckerson and George F. Rogan, who had performed the autopsies, confirmed that both victims had died from .22 calibre bullet wounds. Phelps had been struck three times. One bullet had entered his chest on the left side, piercing the lungs and heart; another hit his head behind the left ear, penetrating the brain; and the third passed through the left arm at the wrist. Miss Wolcott had been hit by a single bullet that transfixed the heart.

As the evening shadows lengthened and the inquest inside the city hall wore on, exasperation got the better of Coroner Munson. Plainly unsettled by the some of the contradictions, he again recalled Stielow to the stand. 'Now, let's go through this sequence of events one more time', he wearily said to the witness. Stielow's confusion deepened with every question. Nothing in his life had prepared the illiterate farmhand for such an ordeal. He stuttered, he froze, he stuttered again under Munson's withering inquisition. Eventually, Stielow managed to unscramble his tangled thoughts and confirm that his last statement had been the accurate version: he had asked Nelson to cover the body only *after* he returned from the Phelps and

Jenkins houses. On this unsatisfactory note, Munson adjourned the proceedings to a later, unspecified date.

No one could pretend that Stielow and his brother-in-law had made a good impression on the stand. Mental insufficiency and the handicap of being outsiders – locals were already muttering that no Medina man could have carried out such a heinous crime – was doubly damning for both men. As the city hall slowly cleared, more than a few suspicious stares were cast in the direction of the two farm workers who were surrounded by family members. And no one was staring harder or more thoughtfully than George W. Newton.

4

When First We Practise To Deceive

As Charlie Stielow shepherded his family out of Medina city hall on that chilly March evening, his lugubrious expression gave no indication of the turmoil he was feeling. His gut was churning with worry. Not because of his confusion over the chronology on the morning in question – ominous as it may have appeared, that was a simple memory slip that anyone could have made – no, this was worry of an infinitely more serious kind. For the fact was that Charlie Stielow had lied on the stand. Moreover, he'd done it wilfully, repeatedly and without provocation. What had originated as a simple expedient, designed to protect his family when the investigation first began, had now, during the course of the inquest, escalated into undeniable perjury. For, contrary to his sworn testimony, Stielow *did* own a .22 calibre firearm. In fact, he owned two such weapons, a rifle and a pistol.

He'd purchased the handgun several years previously, when he and his family had lived and worked on the Fayette Day farm in Orangeport, Niagara County. Just behind their living quarters stood a large barn that, come nightfall, served as a temporary refuge for a band of hobos who were sleeping rough. Their presence, with its fighting, drinking and swearing, had terrified Laura. To help assuage her fears, Charlie had bought a .22 calibre revolver, which the family jokingly nicknamed 'Pop Mitchell', for protection and showed her how to fire it. Fortunately, Laura had never needed to use the gun – the hobos moved on – and, since that time, it had lain, half-forgotten, under lock and key among her belongings. Now, though, that pistol had assumed a frightening significance.

Just hours after the inquest ended, Charlie, Laura, and Mary Jane Green gathered around the supper table to mull over this latest turn of events. As always, Mrs Green took the lead. They'd catch the killer soon enough, she said; in the meantime, they needed to ensure that no outsider found out about the gun. That meant stashing it somewhere safe. Laura agreed. Taking a key from her apron pocket, she went upstairs to her bedroom where she unlocked a large wooden trunk. In the bottom, beneath some baby clothes, lay a Young American .22 nickel-plated, seven-shot revolver with black, carved grips on the handle. It had been made by the Harrington and Richardson factory in Worcester, Massachusetts. Laura grabbed the revolver and returned to the kitchen. Charlie was waiting for her. In his hand was a .22 rifle, retrieved from the children's bedroom, where it had been hanging on the wall in plain view, just as it had been when Bartlett searched the house. Laura handed the revolver to Charlie, who took both weapons out to the barn and placed them on a roof beam above the manger. He didn't cover the weapons, just pushed them out of view. Out of sight, out of mind, was his reasoning.

There was just one problem: plenty of people outside the house also knew that Stielow owned firearms. Among these was Olive Smith, hence her appearance at the Stielow household one day after the shootings. She had warned her mother that Charlie should get rid of any firearms he possessed, in case they caused trouble for him. On that occasion Mrs Green had brushed off Olive's concern, saying that Charlie had nothing to do with the crime and therefore nothing to fear. But after Charlie's dismal performance at the inquest, Mrs Green wasn't so sure. Other people, too, were beginning to talk.

On the following Sunday – 28 March – a woman named Mrs Elmer Klutz came knocking at Olive's home at 224 Oak Orchard Street in Medina. The two were old friends and Mrs Klutz brought some disturbing news. Folks in town were talking about nothing else except the double killing, she said, and most reckoned that Charlie knew a whole lot more about the crime than he was letting on. Mrs Klutz, also aware of Charlie's guns, urged Olive to warn her brother-in-law to be on his guard. If he still had any firearms, she said – especially if they were .22 calibre – then he ought to get rid of them, quickly.

Another of Olive's brothers, Raymond Green, aged twenty, was also present at this meeting. He'd attended the local tabernacle that day and Mrs Klutz's account confirmed what he'd been hearing; suspicion against Charlie was definitely mounting. Raymond cast his mind back to Charlie's fancy nickel-plated revolver. He remembered the gun well, because whenever school was out he would stay with Charlie and Laura and they would often shoot the gun for sport. Although he hadn't seen the gun in years, he assumed that Charlie still owned it. Raymond also dimly recalled a .22 calibre rifle that had been purchased by yet another of his siblings and had subsequently passed into Nelson's possession. Since Raymond hadn't seen this rifle in some time, there was a good chance that it, too, was now in Charlie's hands. Olive thanked Mrs Klutz for the warning. Later that night, after their visitor had left, Olive and Raymond discussed this latest development and came up with a plan.

Next morning, while Olive completed the move to her new home in Royalton Center, Raymond set out on foot for the four-mile trek to the tenant house on Salt Works Road. The journey took him an hour and when he arrived at 11:00am the area was pretty much deserted, with just a couple of stragglers passing by every now and then, to point and stare. He was just in time for lunch, which he ate with Charlie, Laura and Mrs Green. During the meal Raymond relayed Mrs Klutz's warning and the gossip that was circulating. He ended by cautioning Charlie to get rid of the guns and offering to take them away for him.

Charlie made his exasperation plain. 'They are all right where they are,'[1] he grouched. But Raymond kept pressing. Finally, Charlie caved in and led his brother-in-law out to the barn. Stubborn to the end, he made Raymond wait while he fed the horse, before deigning to grab the firearms from the beam. Raymond couldn't believe that they hadn't been better hidden. To his eye, at least, they seemed to be in plain view.

While Raymond disassembled the rifle, Charlie found a suitable box in which to conceal the weapons. He grudgingly handed the package to Raymond. For people of such modest means, any type of firearm was too valuable to destroy, and he told Raymond to take good care of the weapons because, when all this fuss had died down, he would want them returned. Then the two men went back indoors. Raymond remained at the tenant house until after dark before setting off on the long walk to Royalton Center; that way he figured there was less likelihood of anyone seeing him carrying a suspicious package. Again, Charlie thought that Raymond was overdoing the caution. But his young brother-in-law wouldn't be swayed.

Two hours of hard walking took Raymond, without incident, to Olive's new home in Royalton Center. He needed to stash the guns somewhere safe. He thought for a moment. There was a suitcase in his bedroom. That would be the perfect hiding place for the rifle and the revolver. After locking the suitcase, Raymond went down for supper. He was hungry; it had been a long day.

———

Someone else who'd been busy lately was District Attorney Knickerbocker. On 27 March, one day after the inquest, he formally ceded control of the investigation to George Newton. The Buffalo private investigator was placed on a retainer of $8 a day (plus expenses), and the same for any agents that he employed. Newton didn't waste any time. As soon as he was on the county payroll, he tracked down the elusive Kirk Tallman and his wife to a farm near Rochester. However, rather than confronting Phelps's former employee, Newton decided to play it cagily. He spoke to the farm owner and arranged for one of his agents to work in the same barn as Tallman. The hope was that the Canadian apple-picker might start blabbing. But it hadn't worked out that way. In fact, everything pointed to Tallman having a cast-iron alibi for the night of the shootings. Newton would have to look elsewhere.

———————

After the initial shock of the Phelps-Wolcott killings wore off, an almost surreal sense of normality settled on the Stielow household. A rare snippet of good news came when Melvin Jenkins asked Charlie to stay on and help out around the farm while Jenkins struggled to untangle his uncle's probate (Phelps had died intestate and things were turning ugly).

In the meantime, Mrs Green continued to move the family members around like chess pieces. Nelson was dispatched permanently to stay with Olive and her husband Frank at their home in Royalton Center; that way he could help out on their smallholding. With Nelson gone, Mrs Green could now devote more time to looking after Laura, who was due to give birth within a matter of weeks. Laura was sick with worry. How on earth were she and Charlie going to cope once all this blew over?

———————

Newton was now in sole charge of the investigation. And it was going nowhere fast. As he'd feared, Tallman's alibi panned out, and it was the same with all the other disgruntled former employees. During that first week no fewer than fourteen names cropped up as possible suspects – some indication of Phelps's disagreeable temper and tight-fisted hiring strategy – but none had proved promising. Plenty of motive, but no one appeared to have had the opportunity to carry out the murder/robbery. Exasperation, or desperation, finally got the better of Newton. In his book, that only left two viable suspects: Stielow and his mother-in-law. Mary Jane Green's belligerence –

unusual at a time when women, especially if poorly educated, were expected to be deferential in the face of their supposed betters – and her obvious domination of the family, had rankled with Newton. He began to speculate. She was sharp-witted; what if she'd masterminded the burglary? That would make more sense. Certainly, he doubted whether that big German lummox would have brains enough to plan and carry out such a robbery on his own.

As the investigation meandered with no visible sign of any progress, on 3 April yet another special meeting of the board of Orleans County supervisors was summoned to discuss the Phelps-Wolcott murders. And this time Supervisor Martin got his way. Only after considerable argument and a split vote – once again a sizeable caucus was against apportioning a single dime – did the board award Knickerbocker another $1,000 to be used to hire more detectives. This fresh funding brought the investigation into sharper focus. Early the following week, Newton decided it was high time he became better acquainted with Charles Stielow. Although he would later claim to have visited the tenant cottage on several previous occasions, Newton's first officially recorded visit came on 7 April, more than two weeks after the crime.

Newton was accompanied by another Byrne's Detective Agency agent, a pocket-sized bruiser named Robert A. Wilson. Stielow was at home when they arrived and the meeting passed off in an amicable spirit, with no hint of confrontation. While Wilson kept Charlie talking, Newton moved about the house, gaining a sense of the layout. He paid special attention to checking angles of view from the various ground floor windows, particularly the window in the front door. It looked directly across to the Phelps house opposite, but, more importantly, Newton reckoned it also afforded a clear view of the veranda where Miss Wolcott had lain dying. He found it impossible to believe that Stielow could have looked through this window and not seen a body. Of course, Newton's observations were carried out in daylight and he did have the considerable benefit of *knowing* that a body had been found on the veranda. In the middle of a moonless night, trying to locate the source of distant screams, any observer might have neglected to check the situation immediately beneath his window. Newton returned to the living room and casually asked Stielow to run through, once again, the sequence of events on the fateful night. Charlie told his familiar story, how he'd been awoken by a scream and had gone to investigate. Then came a shock. According to Newton, Stielow now claimed to have heard several more screams and 'someone rapping at the door, and a woman say that she was dying and asking to be let in'.[2]

If true, this version was radically different to Stielow's inquest testimony – when he'd mentioned nothing about anyone knocking at his door or begging for help – and served only to harden Newton's suspicions. Sensing he was close to a breakthrough, Newton affected a degree of puzzlement, scratching his head and frowning. 'I forget, how many shots did you say you heard?' he asked. Charlie, caught off-guard, thought for a moment, then allegedly replied, 'I don't think I heard more than one.'[3]

Newton studiously avoided glancing at Wilson. Both men, though, had picked up on the discrepancy. (At the inquest Stielow had denied hearing any shots.) Neither said a word. Newton decided it was time to bring the interview to a close. After some more small talk the two men left. As they drove away, Newton was convinced – or so he would later claim – that he had found the killer of Charles Phelps and Margaret Wolcott.

In a small community like Shelby, gossip travelled like wildfire and details of Newton's visit to the Stielow residence soon reached Melvin

Jenkins. Reversing his decision of just a few days earlier, he now went to Charlie, paid him in full for everything that had been agreed with his dead uncle, then announced that his services at the farm were no longer needed. It was another shattering blow. On 13 April, Charlie and his family once again loaded all their belongings onto the wagon and set off for what would be their fourteenth house together. They didn't have far to travel, just a mile down Salt Works Road to another farmer's cottage. But it was probably the most miserable journey of Charlie Stielow's troubled life to date. Once again, adversity had kicked him in the belly. He didn't see how things could get any worse from here.

As Newton hunted for the corroborative evidence that would condemn Stielow, a single nagging thought plagued him: the failure of the bloodhound General Lee to identify Stielow as the source of the suspicious tracks outside the Phelps bedroom window. Newton wondered whether Scobell's relatively recent acquisition of the dog had led to some kind of canine mismanagement. To clarify that point, on 14 April, Newton called on Charles A. Lee, the dog's previous owner. Lee immediately swore an affidavit. It read:

> In my opinion and from my knowledge of bloodhounds and the working of the dog General Lee, he would, if Stielow had made the foot tracks in the snow bank and their footprints alongside of the house (this referring to the south side of the house under Mr. Phelps window) have followed what were known to be Stielow's foot tracks i.e. the track from the Phelps kitchen door across the field to Jenkins' barn. If Stielow held the dog after he had got the scent the dog would have indicated him at once.[4]

Newton gritted his teeth in disappointment. And his frustration grew as Scobell, understandably testy about having his tracking abilities impugned, remained adamant that the tracks he'd followed to the Jenkins property had been made by a rubber boot; he could tell by the creases. When shown a pair of Stielow's size ten boots, leather and so heavily patched on the soles as to be instantly identifiable, Scobell shook his head. No way had these raggedy old boots made the footprints found beneath Phelps's window.

Still smarting from this setback, Newton decided to reinterview all of the main witnesses. What Jenkins and Kohler had to say especially intrigued him. Each reckoned that on the morning in question, Stielow had said that both victims had been shot. Yet, due to the small calibre of the bullets involved, neither person obviously appeared to be the victim of gunshots at the time. Newton wondered how Stielow could have known that – unless his was the hand on the gun?

Over the next week, Newton drove almost every inch of Orleans County, searching for any kind of clue. Although his actual movements have always been shrouded in mystery, at some point during this odyssey he became convinced that he had enough evidence to make his move.

On the afternoon of 20 April, he and Wilson clambered into a car, with a hired chauffeur, Henry Schultz, at the wheel, and drove to the farm in Alabama where Nelson Green was working. They arrived at 5:00pm to discover that Green was tending one of the fields. Newton sent Schultz to fetch him in the automobile. When they returned, Green was bug-eyed with fear. Newton told Schultz to back the car into one of the barns, then ordered his associates back to the farmhouse; he wanted some time alone with the youngster. Wilson and Schultz knew better than to question Newton and adjourned to the farmhouse. The two men stood around smoking for some considerable time. Eventually, Newton emerged from the barn, Green by his side. The youngster was deathly pale. What happened next was crucial to the course of the investigation. According to Newton, in the presence of his deputies, he asked Green: 'Nelson, who killed Mr Phelps and Miss Wolcott?' After a brief pause, Green replied: 'Charlie Stielow ... Stielow shot him and I helped him.'[5] (Oddly enough, Wilson and Schultz both declined to corroborate that this confession was ever made.)

In the meantime, the detectives muscled Green into the car and drove off. Then came a curious diversion. Instead of taking Green to the sheriff's office or the local jail, Newton headed for Orleans House, an upscale hotel in Albion that regularly hosted conventions and staged large banquets. They arrived at 7:00pm and checked into a quiet room. Word was then sent to Bartlett and Knickerbocker, both of whom arrived by automobile. Knickerbocker hefted a typewriter into the room. The strangeness of the venue was unremarked upon – at least in the official documents – and at nine o'clock, Green commenced telling what he knew about the night of the murder. (See appendix 1 for his full confession.)

While Green talked, Newton typed. Progress was painfully slow. The session dragged on until two o'clock the next morning. At this time, worn out and utterly bewildered, Green signed and swore to this statement before Frank W. Buell, the deputy county treasurer and a notary public, in the presence of Knickerbocker, Bartlett, Newton, Wilson and Schultz.

After the tardiness of the previous weeks, the investigation now took on the impetus of a hurricane. At 3:00am, Green was formally arrested and jailed. Within the hour, Bartlett, Porter and Andrew Van Dell, chief of police at Albion, set out in the sheriff's automobile for Stielow's new home on Salt Works Road. Along the way they were joined by Newton and Wilson, in a car driven by Schultz. In tandem, the two vehicles roared off into the early morning light.

It had been a cold night, and Charlie shivered as he ate breakfast in the kitchen. Even though it was well past dawn, the air temperature outside still hovered around freezing. At about 6:00am he heard the sound of a car. He barely had time to glance through a frost-rimmed window before the kitchen door flew open. Newton stormed in and immediately snapped handcuffs on Charlie's thick wrists, yelling that he was under arrest. Then, before the rest of his family even knew what was happening, Charlie was dragged into Bartlett's automobile and driven to the county jail in Albion. The cars arrived there at about 7:00am.

Still wearing the cuffs, Stielow was placed in a cell on the first floor of the jail. The *Rochester Democrat And Chronicle* reported his arrest in excited and inflammatory terms: 'St. Leo [*sic*] is almost 40 years old, in appearance sullen and almost stupid.' It went on to allege that 'St. Leo and Green had planned the robbery together, but that St. Leo did the actual killing.'[6]

To judge from Green's confession, the robbery had been planned with almost military precision. He claimed that he and Stielow had first discussed robbing Phelps as early as 18 March and had finalised their strategy the following evening. On the fateful night, the two would-be burglars had crept over to the Phelps house at about 10:45pm. While Nelson kept watch, Charlie reconnoitred the area between the kitchen door and the henhouse, to see if anyone in the house was still up. Upon his return, he tried the kitchen door, only to find it locked. At this point, Stielow knocked on the door. Two or three minutes later, Phelps opened the door. According to Green, Stielow immediately opened fire, hitting Phelps in the hand. As Phelps fell back into the kitchen, Stielow sprang in and shot him twice more, the last time in the head. The next minute was a blur. Nelson, still standing guard outside, suddenly saw Margaret Wolcott burst through the kitchen door. She got no further than the top step outside the door. Stielow fired once through the kitchen door glass, hitting her in the chest. She staggered back, screaming 'Help! Murder!'[7] Then, said Green, she stumbled across the road to Stielow's doorstep, where she moaned a few times, knocked on the door and then fell silent. A few minutes later, Stielow had emerged from the Phelps house, fumbling through a pocketbook he'd found and saying he thought it contained around $200. The two men had then returned to the tenant house where they faced a barrage of questions from Mary Jane Green about the screaming. Stielow spared his brother-in-law's blushes by saying it was just some woman who had passed by the house. Then, according to Green, everyone had gone to bed and slept soundly!

When told of Green's confession, Charlie Stielow just gaped. He swore that he knew nothing about the murders. But his protests went unheeded. For the next several hours, teams of interrogators, with Newton at the helm, took it in turns to grill the prisoner like he was a slab of beef. Still he refused to buckle. But there were concessions, including an admission that he had lied previously to various investigators. In the presence of several witnesses Stielow now allegedly stated:

1. That on the night of the murder he heard a woman scream and say: 'Charlie, please let me in, I'm dying.'
2. That Mrs Green, awakened by the ruckus, said she thought it must be the woman across the street and that she heard a shot
3. That he saw Miss Wolcott lying dead on his doorstep: 'We all seen her.'
4. That he owned a .22 calibre revolver, which he had given to Raymond Green for safe keeping two weeks previously
5. That he had lied to the coroner's inquest: 'The story that I framed up with my folks for us to tell at the Inquest was a lie, and we all swore to a lie.'[8]
6. Despite every damning disclosure, Charlie Stielow remained unyielding on one point – neither he nor anyone in his family had anything to do with the killings.

All morning he refused to break. At midday, Newton, frustrated by Stielow's unexpected intransigence, switched tactics. Leaving the farmhand to stew in his cell, Newton took off with Wilson by car from the Albion jail. With them was Nelson Green. In his statement, Green had claimed that Stielow buried the pocketbook and the revolver in a manure pile behind the barn, and he was now ready to reveal the hiding place. Interrupting their journey to pick up Melvin Jenkins, the investigators drove to the murder scene. Green pointed out a freshly dug spot in the manure pile. Nothing was found. Allegedly this incensed Green, who said he'd already argued with Stielow over the latter's refusal to hand over Nelson's share of the money. 'Maybe he threw it down the well,'[9] Green said. Jenkins volunteered to climb down the well to inspect it. Again nothing was found.

According to Newton, all of this – the 40-mile round trip to the Phelps house, stopping for Jenkins, the search of the manure pile, the draining and searching of the well and the return trip to Albion – was accomplished in rather less than two hours. Given the slow transportation and the road conditions of the time, such a timeframe stretches credulity to the limit and, perhaps, explains why details of this alleged search of the tenant house never made it into the subsequent trial record.

But maybe there was another reason – Newton couldn't reconcile the chronology. If, as he subsequently claimed, Stielow had already admitted giving the weapons to Raymond Green for safe keeping, Newton would have had no reason to search the manure pile at the tenant house for the revolver. Instead, he could have driven another eight or ten miles to Raymond Green's home and secured the gun. So, either the visit to the tenant house took place much later than Newton stated – local newspapers describe a night-time search of the Phelps property – or Stielow never made the statement attributed to him.

What is certain is that, at 2:00pm, the investigators were back at the Albion jail and grilling Charlie, hard. The interrogation was merciless, all afternoon and into the night. Charlie was frantic with worry. Not just for himself, but for Laura, too. She was in the last few days of her pregnancy; God alone knew what this was doing to her. At 9:00pm, Charlie finally called Sheriff Bartlett and said that he wished to make a statement. It was taken down in narrative form and typed up by Newton. Others present included Porter, Wilson and Knickerbocker. It was the latter who advised Stielow of his rights and confirmed that he did indeed wish to make a statement. During the course of this statement, which lasted long into the night and into the early hours of the next morning, Stielow basically repeated what he'd said earlier in the day. (See appendix 2 for the full statement.) Significantly, he concluded by saying: 'I certainly don't know who committed the murder.'[10]

At the end of this statement, Buell read it back to Stielow, who said it was true. Unable to sign his own name, Stielow made a mark against his printed name to verify the statement's accuracy.

Following this, Charlie was returned to his cell. It was a hectic night in the jailhouse. Shortly afterwards Stielow was disturbed by the sound of scuffling in the corridor. Bartlett had hauled in a drunk and the man was in no mood to come quietly. The two traded blows and epithets for a minute, until Bartlett gained the upper hand and heaved the drunk into an empty cell. Panting hard from his exertions, Bartlett slammed the door shut, yelling triumphantly: 'You son-of-a-bitch, you will tell me who was with you!'[11]

After another chorus of insults at Bartlett's slowly disappearing back, the drunk turned his belligerence on Stielow. He was a big fellow, about the same size as Stielow, but cut from an entirely different stamp, unkempt with rough whiskers and smelling of drink. Once his truculence subsided, he growled that his name was Charley Reynolds, and he'd been arrested on a suspected burglary charge. Like many jailhouse regulars, he felt the need to shoot his mouth off, bragging that burglary was the least of his crimes. Why, once he'd even killed a cop! Charlie, who'd never been around thugs like this, said nothing, just lay down on his bed and tried to sleep. But the other man wouldn't shut up, kept raving all night. Just like a wild man, was Charlie's last thought before he finally drifted off.

At eight o'clock the next morning Stielow sent for Bartlett and said there were parts of his statement that he wanted to clarify. Inexplicably, Bartlett did nothing. Or rather, he left Charlie alone until 3:00pm, at which time the sheriff returned. What was actually said during the course of this conversation remains shrouded in mystery. Later, on the witness stand, Bartlett would give his account of it, and what he had to say was jaw-dropping.

That same afternoon, Stielow had his first contact with legal representation. Mary Jane Green had called at the Medina legal offices of Coe & Harcourt and pleaded with them to defend her boys. Bertram E. Harcourt and his partner, Albert J. Coe, were experienced trial attorneys and warned her that any defence on the capital charge would be expensive and might cost her every penny she had, including her home. She replied, 'They have got to have someone and I want you to act for them.'[12] At Mary Jane's urging, both lawyers visited Raymond Green, who showed them the weapons. Then came lengthy discussions with Stielow and Nelson Green in their cells. Eventually, they returned to Mary Jane with the bad news: in their judgement, both men were guilty as hell and they wanted nothing to do with two such hopeless and financially unattractive cases.

Stielow's woes, meanwhile, were multiplying fast. At 6:00pm, while being moved from one part of the jail to the other, he passed Bartlett's office and saw the sheriff sitting at his desk. What allegedly followed was peculiar. According to Bartlett, Stielow 'put his hands on my shoulder and commenced to cry, and said that he was worried, that there was a big lump in his throat. He said he could put his finger down his throat and touch it and he must tell the truth in order to relieve himself, and it did not seem as though he could stand it another hour.'[13] Bartlett adopted his best avuncular manner: 'Charlie, why don't you tell us the truth?' Stielow thought for a moment, then said: 'If I could only see my wife I could tell the whole thing. She knows more things and I want to see her a minute.'[14] Following this, Stielow was moved to a new cell. Newton, who'd been at the jail all afternoon, took this opportunity to have a huddled conversation in private with the prisoner, a strange tactic that he'd repeatedly used ever since Stielow's arrest. Whatever passed between the two men wasn't overheard by anyone else.

Another couple of hours passed. At 8:00pm, Charlie was wheeled in for a renewed inquisition. Over the next hour or so, he fended off questions from Newton and Bartlett. The onlookers included Wilson and Under-Sheriff Porter. At one point, according to Bartlett, Newton asked the prisoner: 'Charlie, do you want to tell us anything more about the murder?' and Stielow said: 'Not tonight, I'm tired. If I could see my wife I would tell you all.' Newton became more forceful: 'Charlie, who killed Mr. Phelps?' Finally, Stielow broke. In a quiet voice, he murmured: 'I did, I guess you know all about it.'[15]

So here we have an unequivocal admission of guilt, except for one big problem – only Bartlett later recalled hearing the confession. Not Newton, not Wilson, not Porter. In the event, all three declined to testify that this exchange ever took place, isolating the sheriff with the ultra-acute ears. Bartlett's stubborn insistence that he heard the answer to a question that no one remembered asking was so bizarre that it spurred one investigator to later describe this jailhouse encounter as 'the most unique in the criminal history of the State.'[16]

Instead, Charlie was returned to his cell and left there until 8:45 the next morning, 23 April. After being roused he was taken to Porter's bedroom, which was directly over the sheriff's office. There, in the presence of Bartlett, Knickerbocker, Porter and Wilson, the prisoner reportedly announced that he wished to make a second statement (see appendix 3 for the full statement).

Over the next two or three hours, again with Newton at the typewriter, Charlie dictated his version of what had happened on the night of Sunday 21 March. In most respects it echoed Nelson's confession, but there were some important divergences. According to Stielow the robbery had been two days in the planning. Just after dark on the Sunday, Charlie had gone tramping through the snow 'around by the transmission line … to make it appear that the robbers had gone that way, by my footprints.'[17] After this diversionary tactic, he returned to the tenant house where he and Green slept until 10:00pm. At that hour, Stielow grabbed his pistol and the two men set off across the road. A few flakes of snow were falling as they skulked alongside the house, right up to the dining room window, through which they could see Phelps and Wolcott still awake and talking. To kill time, the two would-be burglars lingered by the chicken coop. Eventually, they saw Wolcott retire to her bedroom and Phelps carry the kerosene lamp into his own room. They waited until the light was extinguished, then Stielow grabbed a mop handle he had seen earlier and broke it in two to make a club. He handed the stick to Green, along with his revolver, at the same time urging Green to 'kill the old son-of-a-bitch and the woman, too'.[18]

They knocked at the kitchen door. Moments later, Phelps appeared, clutching the lamp, which he placed on the stand. As soon as the door swung open, Nelson lashed out with the mop handle. The old man staggered but did not fall. Instead he started throwing some punches of his own and 'hollering' at the top of his lungs.[19] Green's response was to open fire. Two bullets sent Phelps crashing to the floor. Green loomed over him and pumped another round into him for good measure. When the two assailants saw that Phelps was grievously injured and unlikely to pose any further problem, they grabbed the lamp and made their way through the dining room, around the large table, to Phelps's bedroom. Just as they were about to enter, behind them Margaret Wolcott dashed from her bedroom, through the dining room and into the kitchen. Both men immediately gave chase. Miss Wolcott had just exited the kitchen, and was pulling the door closed behind her, when Nelson shot her 'through the glass in the kitchen door'.[20]

Then the two men returned to Phelps's bedroom where Green proceeded to rummage through the bureau drawers. Finally, buried beneath some clothing, lay the item he was seeking – Phelps's leather pocketbook. This vanished into Green's jacket. (Later, Stielow was to claim that he and Green quarrelled and that he didn't receive a single cent from the robbery; Green had kept everything.)

Back in the kitchen, Stielow replaced the lamp on the stand and the two men took a closer look at Phelps. 'He's gone, alright,'[21] said Stielow. Only then did it occur to Stielow to check on Margaret Wolcott. Leaving Green inside the Phelps house, he crossed the road and 'into my own driveway, then I heard Miss Wolcott screaming at my front door, and saw her pawing around on my front door, and she kept saying several times, "Charlie, please let me in, I'm dying."'[22]

Once he was satisfied that the ailing woman posed no threat, and would be dead within minutes, Stielow then entered his own house by the back door, slipped through his wife's bedroom and into his own room. A few minutes later he was joined by Green. From there, the two men went into Laura's bedroom where they discussed the night's events with Laura and Mary Jane. Mrs Green said that she'd heard a woman crying aloud just outside the front door. Stielow went to the front door, peered through the window, and said that it looked like Miss Wolcott from across the way, and she was dead. According to Stielow, Mrs Green ordered him not to open the door because 'it might scare my woman' [Laura].[23] After further murmured discussions, the family retired to bed.

The confession was lengthy, detailed and highly incriminating. There was just one problem; Charlie Stielow refused point-blank to sign or make his mark on the statement. He wasn't going to sign anything, he said, because the version that Newton typed out was not an accurate reflection of what he'd said. But he was on his own. Surrounding him in that room were five witnesses, all prepared to swear that the prisoner had made the confession, even if he wouldn't sign it. With those kinds of odds, Knickerbocker knew he had this case all sewn up.

There was a sense of triumph in the jailhouse that afternoon. After a month-long investigation, Newton had solved the most atrocious double homicide in local memory and could now press his claims for the reward. Newspaper coverage was effusive in its praise for Newton's efforts. The reporters were equally florid in their depiction of Stielow as a criminal mastermind, someone who'd donned a pair of leather shoes to carry out the murderous deed, instead of his normal felt boots, and deliberately laid a false trail away from the crime scene. 'It was such a clever ruse that it was generally believed,'[24] said one report. There was one journalistic curiosity, though. Most unusually, the newspapers went to great pains to assure their readers that neither confession had been coerced by 'third-degree' methods. Both culprits, they were informed, had admitted their guilt freely and without pressure.

At 2:45pm, Stielow was finally given some food. Afterwards he was allowed a meeting with Mary Jane Green. When she told him that Nelson was also under arrest, he seemed genuinely puzzled and asked: 'What have they got him for?' Mrs Green replied: 'They took him the same day they took you.'[25] Mary Jane had some other news as well. The day before, Laura had given birth to a baby girl. The new parents decided to call her Irene. Whether Charlie Stielow would live to see his daughter's first birthday was debatable.

5

'That Man From Auburn'

At 4:15pm on Friday 23 April 1915, Charles Stielow, looking haggard and worn and wearing manacles, was led into the porticoed splendour of the Orleans County courthouse at Albion. Built in the Greek Revival style, the lofty, domed building dominated the square on which it stood. In its 50-year existence, the building had staged many dramas, but never before had it witnessed such interest for an arraignment. Every seat in the public gallery was taken. For most spectators it was their first glimpse of the accused. He was dressed in blue dungarees and wore felt boots and a black cap that had seen better days. So had Charlie Stielow, to judge from the comments of reporters. One noted him as being 'flushed and showing indications of fatigue from his long grilling by the police.'[1] He was arraigned before Peace Justice Henry C. Tucker and charged with double murder. Stielow, pale and dazed, seemed utterly bewildered by the whole affair and only brightened up when Justice Tucker told him that he was entitled to be represented by court-appointed counsel. At the judge's direction, Stielow applied for an adjournment until the following Thursday, 29 April. He was then remanded in custody without bail. As reporters surged around Stielow, he denied having made a confession or having murdered Phelps. Looking more confused with every question, he muttered that Green must have done it.

A few minutes later it was Nelson Green's turn. Courtroom observers were astonished by his youthful appearance and the inane grin that seemed permanently fixed in place. The seriousness of his situation had clearly not registered. 'Nineteen years old and half-witted'[2] was the verdict of one reporter. Green was unshackled and allowed to sit down as the same charge of double murder was read out to him. He tried to concentrate on the proceedings, but they might as well have been in a foreign language. Like Stielow, he was granted legal assistance and remanded until the following Thursday.

News of court-appointed counsel came as an enormous relief to the Stielow family. After being rebuffed by Coe & Harcourt, they had despaired of finding anyone willing to take on Charlie's seemingly hopeless case. The lawyer assigned by the court was David A. White from the Albion-based firm of Fluhrer, Reed, Wage & White. White was still only 27 years old and this would be his first capital case. He was born in Medina and received his degree from Cornell University Law School. There wasn't much of him – at university he had coxed the Cornell rowing crew – but he had a restless vigour that more than compensated for any lack of size. Despite his relative youth, he was already a hard-bitten veteran of the local political wars, although being a Democrat in a Republican stronghold like Orleans County damned him to a career of eternal frustration. (White would run for state congress seven times on the Democrat ticket, losing every time.)

When he read the brief, White's heart sank. Jeez, guilty as hell! Maybe he could muster up some kind of plea bargain? But even on that count, he was pessimistic. The chances of any court showing leniency to a self-confessed double murderer were vanishingly slight. Just keeping Charlie Stielow out of the electric chair would require some kind of legal miracle.

By contrast, Green's lawyer was more optimistic. John Clute, a native of Shelby who now practised in Buffalo, had, by his own reckoning, figured in 39 murder trials, though none had aroused this level of fevered interest. Like White, he entertained no doubts as to his client's guilt, but he believed he had a real chance of saving Green's life if he traded on his youth, his malleability and his patent lack of intelligence.

When White interviewed Stielow for the first time on 24 April, he did so without any sense of expectation. At this meeting, Stielow was surprised to see the youthful White; in his confused state, he thought that Coe & Harcourt had agreed to represent him. As tactfully as possible, White explained that they had rejected the case. Charlie grimaced as his new lawyer took out a legal pad and began taking notes. After getting Charlie's version of events on the fateful night, White asked him to outline what had happened since the time of his arrest. The answers he received at first surprised, then outraged him.

Beyond the boundaries of western New York State, the Shelby murders and the arrest of two suspects had received little attention. The world had far graver matters to consider. On 1 May, the rabid anti-German public sentiment, so artfully manipulated by the East coast press, received an unexpected shot in the arm. It came in the form of an advertisement published in several newspapers and purporting to be issued by the German Embassy in Washington DC. It read:

NOTICE!

Travellers intending to embark on the Atlantic voyages are reminded that a state of war exists between Germany and her allies and Great Britain and her allies; that the zone of war includes the waters adjacent to the British Isles; that, in accordance with formal notice given by the Imperial German Government, vessels flying the flag of Great Britain, or any of her allies, are liable to destruction in those waters and that travellers sailing in the war zone on ships of Great Britain or her allies do so at their own risk.

IMPERIAL GERMAN EMBASSY,
Washington, D.C., April 22, 1915.[3]

The threat was unequivocal; not that it worried the Cunard Line agent in Washington. Charles P. Sumner just scoffed. Merely an attempt to unsettle Cunard and the other great shipping lines, was his considered opinion. He pointed out that the war zone only began in British territorial waters, at which point any merchant ships – especially Cunard's luxury liners – would be safeguarded by Royal Navy ships. Sumner declared that the pride of the Cunard fleet, the *Lusitania*, would sail from New York to Glasgow, as scheduled, on 2 May. There would be no kowtowing to German threats. Nor was Sumner alarmed by rumours of U-boat activity off the British coast. 'As for submarines,' he sniffed, 'I have no fear of them whatever.'[4] Right across America, the Hun-bashing now took on a meaner edge. White's task – already monumental – looked virtually impossible.

In the Albion jailhouse, Charley Reynolds had sobered up and was now a changed character. All the braggadocio was gone and he offered a sympathetic ear to Stielow. The two men were in adjoining cells along the corridor and at mealtimes they ate together. In muttered conversations, Reynolds warned Stielow to be on his guard against jailhouse stool pigeons. Trust no one in the slammer, that was his advice. Charlie murmured that other prisoners weren't any bother; no, all his problems emanated from one of the investigators.

'The big fellow, the big detective,' he said [a reference to Newton], 'I like him. He's all right. He gives me cigars and he told me I could go home Sunday.' But he hated and feared Wilson, saying 'that little fellow, he's a son-of-a-bitch. He always wanted to hit me and calls me a liar and a son-of-a-bitch and I don't like him.'[5]

In his monosyllabic way, Charlie went on to explain how the round-the-clock grilling had pushed him to breaking point, so that in the end he'd been prepared to say anything, just to get the persecutors off his back. 'They wanted me to sign the papers,' he told

Reynolds. The other man frowned. 'Why didn't you sign them?' he said.

Charlie's deep blue eyes fixed Reynolds with a guileless stare. 'Because what I said was a lie.'[6]

Reynolds just shrugged; he'd heard it all before.

A couple of days later, Stielow's older brother, August, and his wife, Emma, arrived at the jail. There wasn't much love lost between Charlie and Gus – those open wounds over ownership of the family farm in Royalton Center had never fully healed – and it was Emma who did most of the crying when the Stielows were taken in to see Charlie. Gus knew about the awful charges; now he wanted to hear it from Charlie's own mouth. There was nothing subtle about his approach; he came right out and asked Charlie why he'd killed the couple. Charlie, eyes blazing and suddenly full of tears, grabbed hold of the cell bars and shook them like a madman, yelling repeatedly: 'I did not do it! I did not do it!'[7]

Gus might not have believed his brother – he left soon after and there is no record of him ever visiting Charlie again – but in the next cell, Reynolds had watched the meeting with a curious eye. Something about the spontaneity and sheer animal intensity of Charlie's response gave him pause for thought. Hey, maybe this guy is telling the truth, after all?

Someone untroubled by such doubts was George Newton. But things weren't panning out quite the way he expected. On 25 April, still frustrated by his inability to recover any of the proceeds of the robbery, he and Wilson had driven to the house on Salt Works Road where the Stielow family had taken up temporary residence. In an angry exchange, Newton accused Mary Jane Green of having hidden the money that was stolen, and threatened to arrest her unless she handed it over. But Mary Jane was iron-hard and refused to buckle under Newton's browbeating. In no uncertain terms, she told him to clear off and to come back only when he had some evidence against her. Newton stormed off, fuming.

Newton's next encounter with Mary Jane came at the second arraignment on 29 April. Like all the other Stielow/Green women, she provided moral support as the two prisoners heard the charges read out to them. A few days of decent food and proper sleep had made a world of difference to Charlie and he seemed far less careworn, more aware of what was going on. Nelson, by contrast, had taken his incarceration badly. He looked gaunt and terrified. For the first time, the gravity of his situation appeared to have struck home. His normal hyper-talkativeness was long gone, replaced by an almost catatonic silence as he listened, uncomprehendingly, to what was said. The hearing was brief and, as before, both men were held without bail.

The following day brought yet more turmoil for the Stielow family: another house move. For the second time in as many weeks they wearily packed up their belongings and readied themselves to move, this time back to Mary Jane Green's home in Wolcottsville. They travelled under Newton's lynx-eyed scrutiny. After several days spent observing Stielow and Green at close quarters, Newton was convinced that the two hicks had acted on the orders of the dominant matriarch. An unnamed source – almost certainly Newton – told reporters that day: 'We're doing the humane thing with this old lady by leaving her up there to care for her daughter and the new babe, but we are ready to move … on a moment's notice if she doesn't come across with certain information.'[8] He added that he fully expected the upcoming hearing to contain further evidence against her. Like so many prosecution promises made in this case, it was a prediction that failed to bear fruit.

In truth, the DA's office was far from sanguine about the Shelby killings. Even with the confessions, Knickerbocker felt uneasy, aware that his case was anything but watertight. Despite the fact that Stielow had, allegedly, provided them with a motive – 'I needed the money [to make an overdue payment on the note on my farm]'[9] – thus far Knickerbocker had failed to trace a single cent of the robbery's proceeds, a sum that Jenkins estimated in the hundreds of dollars. What he did have, however, were the firearms. Newton and Wilson had raided Raymond Green's home and recovered the two .22 calibre weapons. Newton examined the handgun with a magnifying glass. After a few minutes, he turned to Wilson and declared triumphantly: 'I think this is the gun that did it.'[10] But Newton was no firearms authority. If Knickerbocker wanted definitive proof that Stielow's revolver had killed Phelps and Wolcott, he would need to enlist the services of a ballistics expert. Fortunately for the DA's office there lived in New York State, not 100 miles distant from Shelby, a forensic science visionary, a genius blessed with such miraculous powers of analysis and observation as to defy belief – or so it was claimed in a self-penned brochure entitled *That Man from Auburn*.

In the early 20th century, copies of this lavishly worded document had landed on the desk of almost every practising attorney in upstate New York. Its author, Albert H. Hamilton – a fussy little man, balding, with wire-rimmed spectacles that gave him an appropriately studious appearance – promised the reader a matchless level of expertise on just about every topic in the forensic science canon. Without any hint of irony Hamilton claimed expertise in chemistry, microscopy, handwriting analysis, ink analysis, typewriting, photography, fingerprints, toxicology, gunshot wounds, revolvers, guns and cartridges, bullet identification, gunpowder, nitroglycerine, dynamite, high explosives, blood and other stains, cause of death, suicide as against homicide, embalming fluids, determination of the distance a firearm was held when discharged, ballistics analysis, and several others. The bombast thundered on and on, finally running out of breath only when it had reached a staggering total of *26 specialities!* Lawyers, both prosecutors and defence counsel alike, who thumbed through the brochure could be excused for gasping in awe. With such a wealth of knowledge on tap, it was little wonder that Hamilton soon found himself in high demand as an expert witness.

Hamilton's introduction to crime-solving had come about in a strange way. After graduating at the age of 26 from the New York City College of Pharmacy in 1885, he had moved from his native Weedsport to Auburn, and there acquired a drugstore at 51 Genesee Street. One day a neighbour, highly distraught, had come by pleading for help. In his arms he held his lifeless pet dog. What, he cried, could have killed his long-time companion? According to Hamilton, when he examined the canine cadaver he detected the presence of poison. Better still, he was later able to track down the culprit who had deliberately administered the toxin. Hamilton didn't record what, if anything, happened to the poisoner – and like so much in Hamilton's background, we have only his word that this incident ever occurred – but it does provide a suitably bizarre introduction to the person destined to become one of the most dangerous men ever to set foot in an American courtroom.

As noted earlier, when it came to forensic science, America was woefully slow at getting out of the blocks. This sluggishness created a vacuum. Courts wanted expert witnesses, but there just weren't enough of them to go around. Hamilton's stroke of genius was to realise that here was a rich mother lode well worth mining. Cue the publication of *That Man From Auburn*. No one ever accused the little druggist (pharmacist) of being bashful. One passage ran:

Expert Hamilton's almost incredible work has solved many mysteries. When Dr A. Conan Doyle conceived his world famous character of Sherlock Holmes, he probably little thought that there was a man in this State who was destined to be almost an exact materialization of the famous detective, both as to methods and to a great extent as to personal appearance.[11]

On one occasion, when a sceptical counsel asked whether he had indeed authored this self-laudatory guff, Hamilton unblushingly pleaded *mea culpa*. Nor was he embarrassed when another of his publications, *Hamilton's Good Health Manual*, was produced in court to gales of laughter, with its extravagant claims for the merits of 'Hamilton's Sarsaparilla', 'Hamilton's Wine-Oil', 'Hamilton's Nerving' and 'Cleopatra's Secret'. The eponymous healer shamelessly admitted that the products were identical, merely retailed under different brand names. Such chicanery inspired one counsel to query how a quack druggist had managed to transform himself into a ballistics expert: 'Did you get your knowledge by shooting out of the back door of your drug store?' Hamilton was ready for him. 'I did not,' he replied loftily. 'I fired bullets into dead bodies in New York City.'[12]

This retort highlights Hamilton's one unquestioned strength: resilience under fire. Even when it became common knowledge along the legal grapevine that his self-ordained expertise varied between the patchy and the non-existent, Hamilton was peerless at deflecting sarcasm. 'He was smart on the stand,' recalled one attorney, 'he always had an answer for them.'[13] A typical example of Hamilton's quick-wittedness came during one case in which opposing counsel, after working himself up into a self-righteous lather, demanded to know whether Hamilton was not just some scientific pedlar, ready to hawk his opinion to the highest bidder. 'No, sir,' Hamilton smiled sweetly. 'Not even when I was working for you.'

Hamilton was a crackerjack witness. Best of all, he understood one fundamental truth: in order to keep cashing those cheques he didn't need to impress the court officials, just the jury. He knew that in the American courtroom at this time a smattering of scientific knowledge went an awfully long way. Especially if that knowledge was couched in appropriately high-falutin' language. Hamilton laid on the fancy terms with a trowel. It might have been gibberish, but it sounded wondrously convincing, and therein lay the secret of his success. When counsel once mistakenly referred to him as 'Doctor' Hamilton, he did nothing to correct the error, and for some considerable time afterwards this falsehood was repeated as fact in several newspapers. Eventually, though, as Hamilton's court appearances increased and opposing attorneys wised up and targeted his spurious medical qualification, Hamilton merely shrugged, saying that he couldn't be held responsible for what others wrote about him.

As his fame widened, Hamilton surrendered the day-to-day running of the drugstore to his son, Robert, and plunged full-time into the thinly populated expert witness industry. By his own admission the transition was highly lucrative. In an era when the average worker counted himself fortunate if he earned $50 per month, Hamilton regularly pocketed twice that amount daily for offering his opinion from the witness stand. Quizzed during one court case about his fees, Hamilton admitted that, in 1909, his income – excluding those all-important 'expenses and disbursements' – was 'a little over $9,000' (approximately $185,000 in modern terms).[14]

Being an expert witness might have paid well, but it was hardly roses all the way; far from it. In 1911, during one bad-tempered suit in which Hamilton sued a newspaper for libel after it alleged that he had tampered with evidence, his witness-stand pomposity so incensed spectators that they chased Hamilton from the courthouse. (Despite this bizarre interlude, the jury awarded Hamilton $2,000, a fraction of the sum he'd earlier rejected in settlement.) By 1915

Hamilton's reputation had spread state-wide and into the office of District Attorney Knickerbocker.

Whether Knickerbocker contacted Hamilton, or vice versa, is unknown, but what is certain is that, by 1 May, the ex-druggist was actively investigating the Shelby murders. On that day, in a room above the sheriff's office in Albion, Hamilton made an examination of the two bullets taken from the body of Phelps, and the bullet that had killed Margaret Wolcott. He also studied Stielow's .22 revolver.

At the same time, he was shown the broken mop handle found at the scene. Hamilton ran a magnifying glass over the stick, and pointed out a pin-sized brownish stain. He asked Knickerbocker if he might remove the section of the handle containing this speck and take it away for chemical analysis. Knickerbocker gave the okay, and Hamilton bagged his sample. That same day, after lunch, Hamilton visited the Phelps house for the first time. He paid special attention to the bullet hole in the glass of the kitchen door.

Hamilton's crucial role in the investigation was emphasised three days later, when the body of Charles Phelps was exhumed at Mount Pleasant cemetery. For some inexplicable reason, during the original autopsy Dr Rogan had neglected to remove all the bullets from Phelps's body. Now, with Bartlett, Porter, Newton and Hamilton looking on, Rogan made an incision in Phelps's left arm and recovered a bullet which he handed to Hamilton for inspection. In conjunction with Newton – the two would stand shoulder-to-shoulder throughout the case – Hamilton studied this bullet closely, before handing it to Bartlett for safe keeping. At the same time, Rogan excised a sliver of skin and a part of the skull from where the bullet had entered the head. These items were also handed to Hamilton for his expert appraisal. Once this was done, Phelps's body was returned to the soil and Hamilton departed for his laboratory in Auburn.

With just days to go before the arraignment hearing, David White's attitude towards his client had undergone a quantum shift. To his ear, at least, Charlie Stielow's protestations of innocence had the ring of truth about them, and the more he learned about how the prosecution had gathered evidence, the stronger that conviction became. On one point Stielow was adamant: at no time had he ever confessed to the killings. The supposed confession, he said, had been cobbled together by Newton and it was stuffed full of lies. And there were other accusations against Newton. These came from John Clute, Nelson Green's attorney. He had uncovered a witness to that murky interlude in the barn, when Nelson had allegedly fingered his brother-in-law as the killer.

Olive Smith's young son, Roy, claimed to have overheard the events in the barn on the day that Nelson was arrested. In an affidavit, he swore that Newton, Wilson and Schultz had thrown Nelson into the automobile, which they then parked behind the barn. Leaving Nelson, trembling, in the custody of the other two men, Newton had gone to a nearby buggy and grabbed a rope. He then marched back to the car, seized Nelson by one arm and thrust the rope in his face, yelling: 'You son-of-a-bitch, if you don't say Stielow did it I will hang you.'[15] According to Roy, Nelson burst into tears and attempted to escape from the vehicle, only to be dragged back. He looked 'awful scared,'[16] said Roy. Some time later, all four men drove off together. This was, of course, a markedly different version of events to that foisted on to the press by Knickerbocker and, if true, meant that Green's confession was worthless. It certainly gave White something to work with.

First, though, he needed to uncover everything about Stielow's ordeal in the Albion jail. He visited the big man in his cell. Stielow spoke slowly. Although he had not actually been beaten, he had been roughed up and threatened with violence during repeated grillings that left him physically and mentally shattered. He'd also been kept hungry. Worst of all, though, was not being allowed to sleep.

Nowadays the effects of sleep deprivation are well documented, but these were the early days of psychological warfare. Even so, ruthless interrogators were quick to learn how to break a man's will without recourse to that old third-degree standby, the rubber truncheon. According to Stielow, Newton had never allowed him a moment's rest. Whenever he tried to sleep, another team of investigators arrived with more questions, more threats. Gradually, exhaustion took hold. Newton's conduct oscillated between the menacing and the mollycoddling. At times he had taunted Stielow about his lack of manliness and challenged him to boxing matches; on other occasions he had put his arm around the big fellow and tried to schmooze him into some kind of damaging admission. 'He said they [the authorities] didn't want me,' Stielow told White, 'they wanted the man that done the shooting,' adding: 'Newton told me I was too good a man to be a farmer all my life,'[17] and that 'he would make some kind of an officer of me.'[18]

Stielow's mangled syntax might have been hard on the ear, but it did contain a 24-carat nugget of truth. For this wasn't the first time that Newton had dangled a job offer in return for a confession! Back in 1904, in Salamanca, NY, when a local wheeler-dealer named John Spry found himself on trial for suborning perjury, George Newton was one of the chief prosecution witnesses, and he'd readily admitted having secured the defendant's confidence by bribing him with the offer of a position as a private detective.* For an unsophisticated farmhand to have invented such a coincidence beggars belief: common sense dictates that Stielow was telling the truth.

Unfortunately, White had no inkling about Newton's dishonest track record when he entered the Albion courthouse on the morning of 6 May for the arraignment. Once again the old building was

---

* On 25 March 1904, Spry was convicted and sentenced to eight years' imprisonment. Twenty months later, he was pardoned by Governor Frank Higgins, who said he had learned that Spry was 'the victim of those conducting the case and that he had been punished enough'.

packed to the rafters, but a palpable sense of disappointment rippled through the spectators when, after White entered a plea of not guilty on behalf of his client, Judge Tucker adjourned Stielow's case hearing until the following week. All was not lost for avid court watchers, however. At 10:35am, Nelson Green was led into the courtroom and his arraignment began.

First on the stand was the coroner, Edward Munson. He described the scene at the house when he arrived, and his testimony was corroborated by the two other doctors who had been in attendance that day. When Munson testified that he had not filed his inquest finding with the county clerk, John Clute asked if the bullets removed from the bodies of Phelps and Miss Wolcott and other exhibits had been filed with the county clerk and was informed that they had not. A court order was granted, giving the defence access to the exhibits.

The final witness was Melvin Jenkins. His only contribution was to testify that he had last visited his uncle about one week prior to the tragedy. At this point, Judge Tucker suspended proceedings until the following morning.

At 10:30 the next morning, Melvin Jenkins was back on the stand. In a change to his earlier testimony, he now claimed to have seen Green *inside* the Phelps home on the morning the murder was discovered. According to Jenkins, Green and Stielow, accompanied by Mary Jane Green, were in the Phelps kitchen with eight, maybe ten neighbours before Phelps was removed to Medina hospital. He also stated that the tracks he had followed – ostensibly those of the murderer – were made by a leather shoe or boot, as the heel print was plainly visible. After this baffling and contradictory performance, Jenkins was allowed to stand down.

There was a murmur in the public galley as Mary Jane Green was sworn in. But spectators were again disappointed. Judge Tucker immediately excused the defendant's mother, ordering her to appear again the following week at Stielow's arraignment.

By far the most significant testimony came from Henry Schultz. He said that he'd been hired on 20 April to drive for Newton, and described how that afternoon he had chauffeured Newton and Wilson to the farm where the defendant was working. 'Green,' he said, 'was called from the field where he was driving a team on a wagon,'[19] and told that they had come about the Shelby murders. Green replied: 'I don't know anything about it. I had nothing to do with it, whatever.'[20] Wilson, stocky and pugnacious, had got in Green's face. 'Well, you have been kind of expecting us, haven't you?' The terrified youngster stammered a yes. After what Schultz described delicately as 'a two-hour conference in the Smith barn',[21] during which time Newton was mostly alone with Green, he saw Newton hand the youngster a lit cigar. It was then suggested to Green that his interests would be best served if he came to Albion to make a statement to the district attorney. It wouldn't take long, he was told; he'd be brought back to Alabama that night.

Once they arrived at Albion, Schultz had sat in on the interview, which lasted from 7:00pm until 2:00am. Clute, who by now had inherited much of White's scepticism about Newton's tactics, demanded to know if Schultz had been promised a share of the $500 reward on offer. The witness replied that the possibility had been mentioned. At the conclusion of Schultz's testimony, Judge Tucker decided that there was sufficient evidence against Green to remand him in custody.

———

That same day – 7 May – dealt a devastating blow to the defence. Wire reports from England, hazy at first and then increasingly detailed, described how, that afternoon, the *Lusitania* had been torpedoed by a German submarine, just ten miles off the south coast of

Ireland. Within twenty minutes the big Cunarder had sunk with the loss of 1,198 lives. Among these were 128 US citizens. The already overheated American press now went into invective overdrive, fulminating against this 'slaughter on the high seas',[22] with the *Journal of Commerce* forecasting that 'the American temper will not indefinitely endure these international outrages'.[23] In Britain and France there were high hopes that, at last, President Wilson would be shaken out of his neutrality torpor and recognise the German threat for what it was: a global danger. As the wave of anti-Hun hostility swept across America from coast to coast, it inevitably washed up against the grubby jail cell in western New York that housed the 'big, stupid appearing German'. For Charlie Stielow, the sinking of the *Lusitania* was more than just a humanitarian tragedy; it was a personal catastrophe.

Despite this development, Knickerbocker was still worried. In order to secure its case against both defendants, the prosecution needed to beef up the ballistics evidence. On the morning of 8 May, one of Bartlett's deputies, John Rice, travelled from Albion to Auburn, carrying with him Stielow's revolver, the three bullets extracted from the body of Phelps, and the single bullet that killed Margaret Wolcott. When Rice arrived at Auburn, Hamilton took charge of the exhibits. As he later put it, they were contained in a 'nice little travelling bag'.[24] Inside, the bullets were further housed in boxes that had been rolled up in paper and tied up with string, while the revolver was wrapped in another newspaper. Hamilton immediately transferred all the exhibits to a tin box, which he locked and then replaced in the travelling bag. A glance at the clock told Hamilton that it was lunchtime. Rice agreed that he was hungry and the two men adjourned for something to eat. As he locked his office door, Hamilton made a point of handing the key to Rice. He did this for two reasons: first, to ensure that the exhibits technically remained in Rice's custody; second, to demonstrate that he had no means of getting back into his office. (Throughout his career, Hamilton was dogged by accusations of evidence tampering.) After a convivial lunch, Hamilton and Rice sauntered back to the office and for the remainder of that afternoon Hamilton photographed all the exhibits. It was evening before he was finished, at which time he returned all the exhibits to Rice, who then set out on his return journey to Albion.

Expenses incurred by journeys such as these ate deeply into the prosecution's budget, and on 10 May, the beleaguered Orleans County supervisors held yet another special meeting in Albion. Knickerbocker had the begging bowl out again. He said that ever since 20 April, at least one, and often four detectives had been working the case flat out. During that time, investigative costs had soared beyond $1,500, mostly on wages, automobiles and travelling expenses. Sour expressions on the board members' faces told Knickerbocker that he was fighting an uphill battle. He assured the panel that county taxpayers were getting value for their money, and that he would secure guilty verdicts of murder in the first degree against Stielow and Green. Knickerbocker clearly made a strong case. After a contentious debate, the board grudgingly voted him an extra $2,000 for detectives and expert witnesses.

One person delighted by this outcome was Albert Hamilton, as he was running all kinds of expensive tests. For this particular case he had donned his ballistics expert hat, comforted by the fact that American firearms analysis was still in its infancy. Considering the availability and ubiquity of firearms within its borders, it is hard to fathom how America could have lagged so far behind Europe in the field of ballistics analysis. But it had. In 1915 the land of the Colt and the Winchester was still fumbling in the dark when it came to matching bullets to guns.

Ever since the end of the 19th century scientists had known that rifling – the spiral grooving etched into a gun barrel to impart spin to a projectile and thereby vastly improve its accuracy – also made firearms identifiable. Each bullet that passes through a gun barrel sustains distinctive scratch marks unique to that barrel. The raised parts of these marks are called 'lands', while the valleys are termed 'grooves', and they are caused by an unavoidable defect in gun barrel construction. After being smooth-bored, the gun barrel blank is reamed to the specification diameter, then rifled. Because the machine tools used to manufacture barrels wear minutely with each succeeding gun, uniformity is a physical impossibility; hence the unique rifled gun barrel.

The realisation that rifling might assist in matching a bullet to a firearm took time to catch hold. In 1900, a groundbreaking article entitled *The Missile and the Weapon* was published in the *Buffalo Medical Journal*. Written by Dr Albert Llewellyn Hall, it dealt with methods of systematically measuring land and groove markings on bullets, the examination of gunpowder residues in barrels of firearms, and the physical changes that take place over time after a weapon is fired. Although Hall would go on to testify at scores of trials, he is nowadays largely forgotten; a shame indeed, for he truly was one of the early pioneers of firearms identification.

Another decade would pass before Victor Balthazard, professor of forensic medicine at the Sorbonne, devised a means of matching bullets to firearms by use of photographs. He made images of bullets fired from the suspected firearm, as well as the reference bullet, then enlarged the photographs so that he could inspect the lands and grooves in microscopic detail.

Hamilton had adopted Balthazard's technique, taking photographs of the Shelby bullets. This was at least a step in the right direction. While testifying at one trial, Hamilton, who had qualified for the defence as a photography expert, had been forced into the embarrassing disclosure that he didn't even own a camera! When it came to bullets, Hamilton was on slightly firmer ground. His first significant firearms case had occurred in 1903, when an elderly

Churchville, New York, hustler named George Anderson Smith was convicted of having shot his wife some six years earlier, then staging a scene to make it look like a bungled burglary. It had taken three trials to finally convict Smith.[*] On that occasion, Hamilton, testifying for the defence, had clashed vehemently with the prosecution ballistics expert – coincidentally, none other than Dr Llewellyn Hall – and had come off second best. The man from Auburn didn't foresee a similar outcome this time around.

While Hamilton pored over his microphotographs, back in Albion the arraignment hearing for Stielow was finally under way. On 12 May, it was Under-Sheriff Porter's turn to take the stand. He performed poorly. His stock response, when questioned about the methods used to obtain statements from Stielow, was a bemused shake of the head, followed by: 'I don't remember.'[25] He *did* recall that the arrest of Stielow on the morning of 21 April was effected by Andrew Van Dell, the Albion police chief. White looked up sharply. Surely Van Dell had no jurisdiction in that part of the county? This prompted a hasty rethink on Porter's part. Ah, yes, he now remembered that he [Porter] had actually made the arrest; Van Dell had only assisted him. When White asked Porter how Stielow had been treated in the jailhouse, he said 'fine'. 'Did he get any food?' asked White. Porter shifted uneasily in his seat. Although Stielow had been arrested at 6:00am, Porter admitted that he had not been fed until three or four o'clock that afternoon. But he did offer the prisoner cigars, though! The crux of Porter's testimony came right at the end. He claimed that on 21 April, in the jail, Stielow had told the detectives and officials that he wanted to go home and see his wife, after which he would reveal all.

Newton's testimony added little to what was already known. He merely said he had interviewed Stielow and Green several times before their arrest. For many listeners, Newton's testimony provided

---

* In 1905, the 78-year-old Smith had his death sentence commuted to life imprisonment.

their first indication of Stielow's illiteracy. This came when Newton confirmed that, because Stielow could not write, he himself had typed out Stielow's statement, and that Stielow had then made a mark on one statement. White demanded clarification: this was the first statement, the one that contained nothing incriminating, right? Newton agreed that it was. And Stielow had refused to 'sign' the second, incriminatory statement? Again Newton replied affirmatively. After this, Judge Tucker adjourned both cases, saying they would be referred to the grand jury.

Outside the court, in conversations with reporters, White outlined his belief that the alleged confessions had been obtained by duress. He claimed that misleading words had been put into Stielow's mouth, that were then typed up and read back to him, but which he was unable to read. White also hammered home the fact that Newton and his cronies had a financial interest in securing convictions, as they hoped to pocket the reward.

The topic of money never strayed far from the front burner. Even before the grand jury met, Knickerbocker was once again pleading before the board of supervisors. On 21 June he admitted that all but $30 of the $3,000 already earmarked had been spent and asked for an additional $1,000. After much grumbling, this figure was knocked down to $600. It was clear that Orleans County was getting mighty tired of the Phelps case and pressure was mounting on Knickerbocker to deliver the 'right' verdict.

That same day, Knickerbocker presented his case to the grand jury. It was overseen by Justice Cuthbert W. Pound, He was a fine choice. By his own admission, Pound had only one interest – the law. Not that he viewed his single-mindedness as any great advantage. Quite the contrary. 'It is the tragedy of my life,' he once said. 'I have no hobbies. I don't play golf. I do not drive a car. I do not play bridge. I do not sing. My life is one-sided and incomplete.'[26] Pound's tunnel vision was Stielow's gain, as the judge demonstrated, right from the outset, his intention to fully safeguard the defendant's interests. He granted White's request to be given access to all of the prosecution's exhibits, and he made clear his unwillingness to brook any kind of courtroom sloppiness. When, for some unknown reason, Erma Fisher failed to appear before the grand jury, Pound blew a judicial fuse and ordered her arrest. It took some time but eventually the Bensons' housekeeper was brought to court and marched into the judge's chambers. Pound gave her such a dressing-down that when Miss Fisher emerged she was red-eyed and dabbing her cheeks with a handkerchief. There was more humiliation to come. Judge Pound insisted that she post a $500 bond to guarantee her appearance as a material witness; either that or stay in jail. Without any hope of being able to personally raise even the 10 per cent deposit usually levied in such instances, Erma Fisher was fortunate in that her employer's son, Adelbert Benson, agreed to stand the bond.[*]

When Erma did finally testify, her evidence was highly charged and typically erratic. In between the tears the alterations came thick and fast. At the inquest, on 26 March, she had sworn that approximately five minutes had elapsed between the shots and the screams. This time around, the interval had shrunk to 'hardly a minute'.[27] Erma's faulty recall was causing all kinds of headaches for the prosecution. Fortunately, they had Newton on hand to shore up their case. He performed smoothly on the stand, especially when White demanded clarification of that incident in the barn when he had, reportedly, threatened to lynch Nelson Green.

'You did not use any threats?'

'I did not, positively.'

'You did not tell him that he would be hung?'

'No, no,' cooed Newton.

'The conversation was in an ordinary tone of voice?'

'Yes.'[28]

---

* On 10 February 1916, Erma Fisher and Adelbert Benson were married.

White's facial expression made plain what he thought of Newton's replies. Now it was up to the grand jury. Their deliberations took just five minutes. In the early evening of 23 June, indictments were returned against both defendants and they were remanded for trial. Knickerbocker told the court that he intended to try the defendants separately and that he would take up the Stielow case first. Outside the courthouse, he repeated his assurance that the big German was destined for the electric chair.

PART II

6

The Trial

Day 1: 12 July 1915

Jury selection for Charles Stielow's trial began in the Albion court-house at 10:00am on 12 July. Considering all the pre-trial publicity, the courtroom was strangely empty. Those few that were in attend-ance stared hard at the defendant. His thin hair was brushed flat and he wore a neatly pressed suit that had been provided by Sheriff Bartlett; he looked in much better shape than he had 83 days earlier when his incarceration began. He stood smartly to attention while Justice Pound read him his rights, then lapsed into a kind of torpor that endured for the remainder of the day. Only occasionally would his deep blue eyes flicker to the pool of more than 150 prospective jurors – all male – who would decide his fate.* They were ferried over in small batches from the Albion House hotel, under the steward-ship of Sheriff Bartlett. Most were farmers and wanted nothing to do with this trial. They had crops in the ground or animals that needed tending, and pleaded to be exempted. Pound was sympathetic and granted most requests. He was less charitable towards one potential juror who asked to be excused because he had 'only one good ear'. The judge growled: 'If you've got one good ear that's better than two poor ones.'[1] Despite this admonition, the man was excused.

The judge's patience was further exercised by a clutch of potential jurors who claimed that deep-seated objections to capital punish-ment would render them incapable of acting according to the evi-

---

* It was 1937 before women in New York State were allowed to serve on juries.

dence. Pound angrily ordered the court clerk to enter all their names in a ledger; that way they would be barred from being called in any future murder trial, thereby saving the county time and money.

Throughout what was a tedious first day, Stielow received regular words of encouragement from Laura and Mrs Green, who were sitting just behind him. Like the defendant, they looked embarrassed and overwhelmed by their surroundings. 'Tired looking little women' was how one report described them.[2] There was little to enliven them. By the end of day one, just two jurors had been empanelled. It was going to be a long process.

Day 3: 14 July 1915

By the third wearisome day of interrogation, a panel of jurors had still not been seated. Weeding out prejudice towards a German-born defendant took time and effort, though not all of the veniremen paraded their bigotry quite as blatantly as David Newman, a farmer from Ridgeway. 'I don't think the defendant would want me to sit if he knew what nationality I was,' he told the court. When Harold S. Blake, Knickerbocker's assistant prosecutor, brought out that Newman had been born in England, Judge Pound intervened. 'Then you don't think you'd be able to sit on a jury to decide the fate of a German?'

'No, I don't believe I would,' retorted Newman, glaring at the defendant.

'You're rather vindictive,' said Pound. 'How long have you lived in this country?'

'Fifty years.'

'Fifty years and still an Englishman?'

'Yes, sir, still an Englishman.' Newman's eyes blazed.

Judge Pound couldn't resist the opportunity, delivering a chorus from Gilbert and Sullivan's *HMS Pinafore*: 'Despite all temptations to belong to other nations, he remains an Englishman.'[3] It was one of the very few light-hearted moments in the entire trial and ended with Newman being excused.

The lengthy process dragged on. Finally, at 4:30pm, after 112 talesmen had been examined, a panel was filled. All but one were farmers. Ten minutes later Knickerbocker rose to his feet and Charles Stielow was ready to stand trial for his life.

There was just enough time for Knickerbocker to make his opening. He presented the state's case calmly at first, gradually ratcheting up the tempo and the volume as he spoke. Stielow, he told the jury, had the means, the motive and the opportunity to carry out the crime. Moreover, in the presence of several witnesses, he had confessed. 'On April 22, during the afternoon,' said Knickerbocker, 'he told the Sheriff he had something to do with the killing of Charles B. Phelps and Miss Wolcott.'[4] The next day, at 6:00pm, '[Stielow] told the Sheriff that he had not been able to sleep the night before, that he was worried ... and that he wanted to tell all about his connection with the commission of the crime.'[5] But the clincher, according to Knickerbocker, came on the morning of 24 April. That was when 'Stielow was asked if he wished to make a further statement ... and he said he did. His statement was taken in narrative form and he confessed as to all that had taken place on the night of March 21 and that Nelson Green shot Phelps three times and Miss Wolcott once and that he and Green ransacked the bureau drawers in Phelps's room and Green stole the money.'[6]

Stielow listened to all this unfold with his customary lack of emotion. Only the occasional clenching of his jaw betrayed any inner turmoil. Some courtroom observers commended him for his stoicism. Others looked on and saw only callousness.

Knickerbocker, meanwhile, was in full stride. 'We will prove to you ... we will prove to you ... we will prove to you,' he repeatedly promised the jury, without once saying exactly what it was that he intended to prove. Finally White's patience snapped. He stood and demanded a mistrial, on grounds that this was the most prejudicial opening he could recall. Predictably, Justice Pound overruled him.

Knickerbocker's opening did include one surprise. He told the jury that on 22 April the authorities took Stielow out of the jail and spirited him off to Sheriff Bartlett's home 'to make certain arrangements in his cell'.[7] In time, the significance of these 'arrangements' would assume considerable importance, but for now the district attorney glossed over the incident and turned his attention to firearms. He promised that 'we will show that 10 or 11 years ago Stielow bought a .22 calibre revolver ... [and that] one week after the murder, Stielow gave this same .22 revolver to his brother-in-law Raymond Green, together with a .22 calibre rifle and that Raymond Green took these 2 guns and hid them in his home at Royalton.'[8]

In conclusion, Knickerbocker took dead aim at Stielow's veracity. Pointing accusingly at the defendant – Knickerbocker was forever punctuating his sentences with theatrical gesticulations – he said: 'On Monday, March 22, Stielow denied to me, in the presence of the sheriff, at his house, that he had any guns, and later in the week he swore that he did not own any guns nor were there any guns on his premises.'[9] Knickerbocker ended confidently: 'I think we will be able to satisfy this jury that the 4 bullets were fired ... from this .22 calibre revolver that Stielow owned.'[10]

On this note, court was adjourned for the day.

Day 4: 15 July 1915

It had been a sticky night and, next morning, a fierce sun blazed down on the Albion courthouse as lines of people waited patiently for the doors to open. Inside, the courtroom was like a cauldron, made hotter still as spectators bickered over the best seats in the public gallery. They were joined that day by two new onlookers; Ethel and Roy Stielow. It was the first time they'd seen their father since the day of his arrest. He hugged them both.

After a few more words from Knickerbocker, the state began calling its witnesses. First on the stand was the photographer who had taken some general shots of the crime scene, followed by a surveyor who had drawn up plans of the Phelps residence in order that the jury might more easily follow the evidence. Then came Melvin Jenkins. Resplendent in a smart blue serge suit, Jenkins began by saying his uncle had kept a pocketbook in the bureau, and that it was now missing. He had last seen the pocketbook about two weeks before the crime. Next, he recounted details of his early morning barn meeting with Stielow: 'He [Stielow] said there was some trouble, that something pretty bad had happened, that Miss Wolcott was lying dead by his door and that my uncle was lying on the kitchen floor.'[11]

Jenkins described the conditions he found at the house. 'The kitchen door was open. My uncle lay on the floor. The door was opened against his body and I went in and raised his head and asked him what had happened and who had done it. He was unable to reply.'[12] Phelps, barefoot and clad in his nightshirt, was lying with his head about six inches from the sink and his feet pointing southwards, towards the door. The lamp stood on a little stand by the door and was still burning, though the oil had run low.

After entering his uncle's bedroom, Jenkins saw the bureau drawers tipped out on the floor. 'Then I went in Miss Wolcott's room and saw she was not there. I took the bedding off her bed and covered my uncle with it.'[13] Jenkins described finding Margaret Wolcott's body lying on the doorstep of the tenant house, her nightdress saturated with blood. Knickerbocker seemed satisfied by this and moved on to the foot tracks in the snow around the house. Jenkins said they showed heel marks and the shape of a shoe.

After a brief recess for lunch, Jenkins resumed his testimony. He thought that the tracks heading from the kitchen door to the henhouse and those straddling the driveway looked identical. He'd also seen about half a dozen barefoot prints leading from the kitchen door. These had petered out quickly because the snow was already melting in the front yard.

It was 2:00pm when White rose to begin his cross-examination. It centred mainly on Phelps's reputation as a notorious miser, reputed to hoard large sums of money about the house. Jenkins conceded that this was the case and that it was well known locally. White also quizzed Jenkins on his uncle's prickly nature, one that had seen him get into several disputes with former employees. Jenkins admitted that his uncle could be awkward. After two hours, filled with plenty of heat and not much light, White said he had no further questions for the witness.

On re-examination, Knickerbocker introduced the kitchen door into evidence and Jenkins confirmed that it came from his uncle's house. It was painted a light grey on the interior side, while the exterior was varnished and grained. The jury leaned forward for a closer view when Knickerbocker pointed out that one of the four panes of glass had a half-inch hole through it, made by the bullet that killed Margaret Wolcott. Jenkins confirmed that during the winter months, Phelps locked and caulked all the house doors, except this one and another into the woodshed. When Jenkins stood down it marked the end of proceedings for the day. A few minutes later Justice Pound was in his automobile, homeward bound for Lockport, some 28 miles distant. The jury members weren't so fortunate; they were sequestered and remained overnight in Albion.

Day 5: 16 July 1915

The next day began dramatically as Sheriff Bartlett marched down the aisle of the Orleans County courthouse, a rifle slung over his shoulder, a revolver in one hand, an ugly-looking club in the other, his pockets stuffed with bullets. He was the custodian of the exhibits, which he handed to Knickerbocker. The DA now attempted to link these items to Stielow. For this he needed the testimony of Raymond Green; no easy matter, if recent events were any indicator.

On 21 May, Stielow's hot-headed young brother-in-law had decided to flee the county. Unfortunately for him, his chosen means of escape was a bicycle. When news of Green's abrupt flight reached Albion, Newton took charge. He jumped in his car and set off in hot pursuit. What followed next wouldn't have looked out of place in one of the Keystone Kops flicks that were at the time packing movie houses right across America, as Green led his pursuers in a two-county chase that reportedly lasted for 30 miles. Newton eventually ran the hard-pedalling fugitive to ground in the town of Alabama. The courts had come down heavily on Green, slapping him with a $5,000 bail bond that they knew he couldn't possibly meet. As a result, since that time Green had been caged at the Albion jail, held as a material witness.

Looking much younger than his 21 years, the slightly built Green took the stand. He had a shock of thick, brown hair and deep blue eyes that peered fearfully out from a tanned face that evinced no hint of his two-month-long incarceration. He gave his evidence nervously, which was understandable. Like everyone in Stielow's extended family, he was a stranger to court proceedings; but his loyalty was beyond question. In between answers he would glance across at his brother-in-law the defendant and more especially his sister, Laura, flashing encouraging smiles as he did so.

Green testified that he'd attended his local church on the Sunday after the murder, after which he stayed overnight at his sister Olive's nearby home. He described how a family friend, Mrs Klutz, came by with her warning about the guns. The next morning he went to Stielow's house, passed on the warning, brought the guns home and hid them. After that, said Green, no one saw the weapons except the two lawyers, Coe and Harcourt. They had merely inspected the guns, but did not disturb either weapon. Green swore that, so far as he was able to judge, the revolver Stielow gave him to keep after the murder was the same revolver that had been in the latter's possession for more than a decade. On cross-examination White made some headway with Green, confirming that it had been Mrs Klutz – and not a Stielow family member – who had suggested hiding the firearms.

Next up was George Harrington, a young farmer who lived south of Gasport. He testified that in 1904 he had traded a .22 revolver to Stielow in return for a single-barrel shotgun. At this point Knickerbocker produced the alleged murder weapon. Harrington examined it closely and said that in size and shape it resembled the gun he traded to Stielow, but too many years had passed for him to swear positively that it was the same gun. On cross-examination, White reinforced these doubts by showing Harrington a revolver similar to the alleged murder weapon. Might not this be the gun you traded to Stielow? he asked. Again Harrington hedged. While he couldn't swear that it wasn't the gun, gut instinct inclined him to think that this second firearm was heavier than the revolver he had traded to Stielow.

As they listened to Harrington's testimony, jury members, court officials and spectators alike fanned themselves in a vain attempt to find some cool air in the stifling courtroom. Outside, the mercury was sizzling in the upper 80s. It was a good time to break for lunch.

When court resumed, attorney John Clute, who was assisting White, approached the bench to say that during the recess one of the jurors had attempted to engage him in conversation. He'd only wanted to discuss the broiling weather, but Clute was worried about possible accusations of jury interference. Justice Pound nodded sagely. The last thing he wanted was a mistrial and, after the resumption, he sternly lectured the jury on their judicial obligations: they must not talk to the attorneys of either side nor permit anyone of their number to talk to them. If they knew of anyone who contravened these instructions, then they should inform him and he would deal with the offender promptly and severely.

With that legal frisson over, it was the turn of Dr Eckerson to take the stand. After describing what he had found at the autopsies he retired without serious cross-examination. There was just enough time for Deputy Sheriff John Rice, the Albion jailer, to give his evidence-in-chief before Justice Pound closed proceedings with the announcement that the court would take the unusual step of sitting on the following day, a Saturday.

Thus far, the prosecution's case had been decidedly skimpy; they had not produced a scrap of evidence to directly link Stielow to the crime. But they were supremely confident that all that would change on the morrow.

Day 6: 17 July 1915

Something else trying hard to change was the weather. An overnight storm had cooled things off somewhat, but only by a few degrees. As White began his cross-examination of Rice, the drone of an electric trolley car rolling along West State Street made its way into the courthouse, adding to the soporific atmosphere. Rice was resolute. He insisted that the defendant had been treated well at all times and had certainly not been subjected to any physical brutality.

Rice was followed by Mrs Winifred Kohler. She testified that when Stielow had called at her house on the morning of the crime, he had definitely used the expression 'they're shot'[14] to describe what had happened to Phelps and Wolcott. Knickerbocker glanced tellingly towards the jurors. This was a point that he was desperate to emphasise; that before any kind of medical examination had been made, Stielow knew how both victims had met their fate. After Mrs Kohler was excused, a couple of minor witnesses came next. Then it was the turn of the prosecution's star turn – Albert H. Hamilton.

Knickerbocker qualified him in the usual way, reeling off Hamilton's impressive roster of self-awarded credentials, a process that took some considerable time. Then 'That Man from Auburn' was ready to earn his fee. He began with his usual assurances, delivering his testimony in an authoritative, well-rehearsed manner that sounded hugely impressive to the unsophisticated jurymen. He explained how he had made microphotographs of all four bullets from the crime scene, and that each showed the same characteristics: five lands and five grooves. The lands were .07 inch wide, and the grooves were .05 inch, making a pair .12 inches wide.

He described how various markings had been transferred to the bullets by imperfections in the barrel of the murder weapon. On the Stielow revolver (Exhibit G.G.), he found 'at the very edge of the muzzle ... 9 abnormal defects'.[15] Well aware that most of the jury earned their living from the soil, Hamilton dropped in a homespun analogy: 'Under the microscope they are like 9 teeth to a saw with the depressions between them.'[16] Hamilton, now well into his stride, needed only occasional prompting from Knickerbocker. What had caused these defects? 'Improper cleaning,'[17] replied Hamilton, that and a build-up of rust and corrosion. And what impact would these defects have on the bullet exiting the barrel? 'A bullet going out under powder would receive a marking of these projections,' said Hamilton. 'That is, a projection would make a depression upon the bullet, a depression in the muzzle would make an elevation upon the bullet.'

Justice Pound requested clarification:

Q. Then these depressions would make a small scratch or scratches, rather, on the surface of the bullet?
A. Yes, sir.
Q. And you found the scratches made by these projections on each one of these bullets, did you?
A. I did.[18]

Q. Mr. Hamilton, were you able to detect these markings on the bullet with the naked eye, or did you do it with the aid of a microscope?

A. First with a microscope and afterwards with the naked eye. Later my attention was called to the bullet that I saw removed from the arm of Mr. Phelps. I compared that with the muzzle defects of Exhibit G.G., and I found the bullet (Exhibit F.F.), which is marked 'from the arm of Charles Phelps' contained these 9 defects that I have minutely described in the other 3 bullets and correspond in their measurements, in their shape, and the location as I have already described.[19]

Knickerbocker must have been delighted with Hamilton's performance; Orleans County and its hard-pressed taxpayers were certainly getting full value for their money. All that was left now was for the DA to deliver the knockout blow. 'Are you able to state with reasonable certainty,' he asked Hamilton, 'whether these four bullets were fired through the same revolver?'

A. Yes, sir.

Q. Are you able to state … whether these 4 bullets were fired from this revolver, Exhibit G.G.?

A. I can.[20]

At this White leapt to his feet. *Objection*! Based on current levels of ballistics analysis, he protested, such an emphatic conclusion was unsustainable. Justice Pound agreed and ordered Hamilton's answer stricken from the record. But the damage was done. The connection between the murder bullets and Stielow's gun had been firmly implanted in the jury's mind; and Hamilton wasn't done yet. He next applied his formidable powers of persuasion to a discussion about the bullet taken from Margaret Wolcott. On inspection he found 'embedded fragments of broken glass, plainly visible under a high-powered microscope'. Once again, Justice Pound took the lead:

Q. Just with the microscope?

A. Just with the microscope.

Q. Fragments?

A. Fragments, really glass dust, although under the microscope they look like crystallized diamonds.

Q. How do you know it was glass dust?

A. Technically, I do not know, until attempting to remove some and test chemically. My present answer is based upon microscopic examination and not upon chemical analysis.[21]

This was too much for White. He was on his feet, objecting once more; demanding that all reference to glass particles on the bullet be struck out, contending that it was merely a guess on Hamilton's part. But this time Justice Pound stood firm, insisting that it was 'more than that. It is evidence with a qualification. The witness would not be positive about the matter until he made a chemical analysis. What he saw had the appearance of glass dust under the microscope.'[22]

Hamilton added that the hole in the kitchen door's window glass was consistent with having been made by the bullet that killed Miss Wolcott. Knickerbocker wanted more: 'Did you make any examination in relation to Exhibit B.B.?'

'The mop handle?' Hamilton said smoothly, eager to iron out any possible confusion for the jury. 'I did.'

'You found under examination something on the mop stick?'

'I did.'

'What was it?'

'Two stains.'[23] There then followed a lengthy description of how Hamilton had examined the stains and how he had concluded that both contained blood.

When White rose to cross-examine he launched the customary opening attack made on expert witnesses everywhere, demanding to know how much Hamilton was being paid for his testimony – in this case '$25 a day and necessary disbursements'[24] – before getting bogged down in a laboured dispute about how exactly marks were transferred from barrel to bullet. Hamilton's answers, frequently interspersed with joking asides, provoked loud laughter in court, so much so that Justice Pound repeatedly had to gavel everyone to silence, reminding them that this wasn't some carnival sideshow, but a deadly serious proceeding. But it was plain to see that the jury had warmed to Hamilton; he seemed like such a regular guy.

However, Hamilton's bonhomie took a sharp downward slide when White asked him to show the jury the photographs he had taken of the bullets. After the photographs had been returned, White peered inquisitively at the images. He looked puzzled. 'Do any of these photographs of the bullet show any markings on them that you have described?'

For the first time, Hamilton shifted uneasily. 'They do not,' he admitted. 'I think in all these cases they are up on the opposite side of the bullet, or else upon one side of the rear.' White handed the photographs to Hamilton, asking him to point out the markings on the bullets. Hamilton could not. 'I can point them out on the bullets themselves,' he offered lamely.

'Did you photograph the other side of these bullets, other than the one side that shows in these photographs?' White asked.

'I did not, I did not even think of it.'

White's face was a picture of incredulity. 'That never occurred to you?'

'No, sir.'

'You didn't think that would have any bearing?'

'No, sir.'

'You wanted to show us the photograph of the smooth side?'

'No, sir.'

'That is all that you did show us, was a photograph of the smooth side.'

'I simply photographed the side that would show the shape of the bullet,'[25] Hamilton muttered weakly.

And there was worse to come. When White picked up the revolver, he peered down its barrel and professed himself unable to see the imperfections that Hamilton had found so illuminating. This prompted an astonishing response from the witness. The gun, he told White, 'had been so constructed that the cylinder fitted tightly against the rear of the barrel, when the hammer is down against the barrel'.[26] So tightly, in fact, that there was no space for any explosive gases to leak from the rear of the weapon. All the gases were therefore emitted from the muzzle as they followed the bullet out. As a by-product of this action, these gases had *filled in* the nine imperfections, making them no longer visible, even under a microscope!

Nowadays such nonsense would be laughed out of court, but such was the state of ballistics ignorance at this time, and such was Hamilton's oily plausibility, that he managed to slide this deception right past opposing counsel, the jury, the judge, everyone.

Thus far White had succeeded admirably in puncturing Hamilton's pomposity, but now his relative inexperience revealed itself in a grave miscalculation. Having earlier objected to Hamilton being allowed to opine that the bullets had definitely been fired from the Stielow gun, White now, for some unaccountable reason, resurrected that very subject: 'Your contention, Mr. Hamilton, is that these marks were caused by passing over and coming in contact with these projections or bulges that you found or observed on this gun?'

Hamilton could hardly believe his good fortune. 'In Exhibit G.G., yes, right,'[27] he stated definitively. So, for the first time, the jury heard admissible expert testimony directly linking Stielow's gun to the killings. Thereafter, White struggled to regain the initiative and Hamilton settled back into his comfortable, well-rehearsed routine. Next day's *Rochester Democrat And Chronicle* captured the general courtroom mood: 'Hamilton made a first-class witness.'[28]

The afternoon was drawing on when the day's final witness, Adelbert Benson, took the stand. He testified to having been awakened at about 11 o'clock on the night of the murder and hearing a noise. It sounded like a rap, he said, pounding the court stenographer's desk with his fist to demonstrate. Benson was still on the stand when Justice Pound halted the day's proceedings. He told the jurors that tomorrow, being Sunday, they might attend church if they wished or meet briefly with their families, all to be performed in the presence of the sheriff or one of his deputies.

At the end of week one, the trial's momentum had definitely swung back in the state's favour. Hamilton had delivered his usual slick performance, and White, after a promising start, had barely laid a glove on him. The wily old campaigner had definitely outgunned his youthful protagonist. But White wasn't done yet. And, at least, the defence had a day off to regroup.

7

Stielow Takes The Stand

Day 7: 19 July 1915

Each day of the trial saw progressively larger crowds flocking to the courthouse and Monday was no exception. When the doors were thrown open hordes of people surged forward, fighting for places in the public gallery. In no time at all the rows of long, light green benches, separated by a rail from the carpeted area reserved for the attorneys and press, were filled to overflowing. Many of the spectators were women, hardly any of whom heeded Justice Pound's warning that much of the testimony might be rather delicate in nature and that any female should feel free to excuse herself if so inclined. In truth, most of the evidence thus far had been decidedly low-key, and anyone looking for titillation wound up sorely disappointed. Adelbert Benson did little to enliven proceedings and was soon stood down.

Then came a surprise. Albert Hamilton had asked to be recalled to the stand. He declared that his previous testimony had contained a mistake. Over the weekend he had mysteriously found a photograph that *did* show the opposing side of the bullets. Justice Pound duly admitted the photo into evidence. Hamilton apologised for the print's poor quality – it was small and very dark – but he insisted that the identifying groove he had mentioned in his previous testimony was now plainly visible.

Further confusion arose when assistant prosecutor Blake handed Hamilton one of the bullets, only to find that, somehow, the bullets had become mixed up in their respective boxes; a blunder further magnified when Blake dropped one of the slugs, thus prompting the undignified spectacle of lawyers and courtroom attendants scurrying around on all fours as they attempted to hunt down the errant bullet. When it was eventually located, Hamilton came to the rescue. With a flourish, he produced his microscope and theatrically examined all the bullets, restoring each to its rightful box. The jury members looked on in obvious awe. 'No one intimated that the mix-up was anything but accidental,'[1] reported one newspaper laconically.

White rose to cross-examine. Over the weekend he'd delved into Hamilton's aforementioned publicity brochure and now he wanted a few clarifications. The witness at first smiled, then grew beet-red in the face as White read aloud extracts from the by now infamous *That Man from Auburn*, with its boasts of scientific omnipotence. Suppressed chuckles, then loud guffaws greeted the extravagant claims and once again Justice Pound threatened to clear the court unless order was restored. Having succeeded in reducing Hamilton to quivering fury, White turned to the newly produced photograph. He squinted theatrically in an effort to discern the alleged groove and had to ask the witness to point it out. Hamilton held out a trembling finger. White looked incredulous. 'You mean … you did not discover *that* on that greatly enlarged photograph [shown to the court on] Saturday?' Hamilton, by now looking decidedly miserable, mumbled: 'I did not discover it until this morning.'[2] Then Hamilton slunk from the stand, leaving Knickerbocker to ponder the wisdom of permitting his disastrous reappearance.

Hamilton did receive qualified support from a Buffalo attorney named Charles Newton – no relation to the private detective – who doubled up as president of the Newton Arms Company and as a frequent contributor on the subject of firearms to *Outdoor Life* magazine. Although Newton felt certain that all four bullets had been fired from the same gun – a weapon, he said, clearly similar in design to Stielow's Young American – he was less confident as to what had caused the markings on the bullets. Manufacturing tool defects might account for some, he thought; others could have resulted from a build-up of rust and corrosion in the barrel, which he noted was heavily contaminated.

This concluded the firearms evidence. A relieved Knickerbocker called Sheriff Bartlett to the stand. Bartlett began by describing the circumstances of Stielow's dawn arrest on 21 April, and how the prisoner had been interrogated until nightfall. Knickerbocker, eager to ward off any suggestions of jailhouse impropriety, quickly hurried the witness on to events of the next day. At 3:00pm, said Bartlett, the defendant had asked to speak with him. 'He said that he wanted to tell the truth about the murder, that the statement he had made to us fellows was a lie, I asked him who did the murder, and he said, "Nelson and I did it, and the minute I seen you drive up in front of my house that morning I know [sic] you had been over to Smith's and that Nelson had squealed and told all that he knew."'[3]

So, here we have it. According to Bartlett, just over 30 hours after being arrested, Stielow confessed. Ordinarily one would expect such a development to cause considerable activity, even jubilation in the Albion jail – after all, this had been a frustrating month-long investigation – but Sheriff Bartlett was obviously made of taciturn stuff. For not only did he fail at the time to summon a stenographer in order that Stielow's confession might be taken down, but he also declined to mention this confession to anyone else until the trial! Without any hint of embarrassment, the sheriff testified that he merely allowed Stielow to return to his cell.

Bartlett further swore that when he interviewed Stielow later that evening, the latter told him that he didn't want to make a statement because he was exhausted, but he would make one the next day. On the 23rd, according to Bartlett, 'Mr. Newton or Mr. Wilson said – Mr. Newton I think – "Charlie, who killed Phelps?" and the defendant answered "I did."'[4]

White's initial cross-examination of Bartlett revealed no hint of the fireworks to come. He began by extracting a grudging admission from the witness that Stielow had been questioned day and night from 7 o'clock on the morning of Wednesday, 21 April, until his arraignment at 4:15pm on Friday. Then White asked Bartlett if, before Stielow made the alleged statements, Newton's fellow detective, Robert Wilson, had squared up to the defendant, asking if he knew how to box, and that when Stielow had answered 'No', Wilson ordered him to stand up and 'show how good' he was.[5] Bartlett denied any recollection of such an incident. Again and again, he insisted that the prisoner had been treated properly at all times.

Convinced that Bartlett was lying through his teeth, White asked the court to have any statement made by Stielow declared inadmissible on the grounds that the defendant's constitutional rights had been ignored. When Justice Pound denied the motion, White dropped a bombshell. He temporarily excused Bartlett and called Charles Stielow to the stand.

A sudden buzz of expectation hummed round the court. The defendant looked as startled as everyone else by this entirely unexpected development. He levered his considerable bulk out of the chair, his face chalky white and his hands trembling visibly as he lumbered to the stand. Justice Pound ruled that Stielow could be called at this unusual juncture to give his account of how the statements had been obtained. Knickerbocker would be allowed to cross-examine at this time, but only on matters relating to the alleged confession.

For most in court, this was their first chance to hear Stielow speak. He did so haltingly and in a tremulous, barely audible voice when White asked him to describe the circumstances of his arrest: 'I was in the house eating breakfast and I see the automobile stop there and I started to go outdoors – and I hadn't got outdoors and they come in the summer kitchen – and they says "You're the fellow we're looking for." And I says, "Wait a minute, I want to get my hat" – and they says "You don't need no hat" – and they took me by the arm and led out to the automobile.'[6]

He continued by saying that Newton had then grabbed him by the throat and screamed, 'You sonofabitch, who killed Phelps?' When Charlie replied that he didn't know, Newton handcuffed him and shoved him into the automobile, where he remained in the custody of Under-Sheriff Porter while Newton and others searched the house. Some time later, they emerged carrying a little square box. Right behind them came Mrs Green, angrily demanding that they return the illegally snatched item. They refused. (The significance of this box, if any, was never divulged.) Stielow said he was then driven to Albion jail. At about 1:00pm, Newton and Wilson entered the cell where he was being held and, while Bartlett and Porter stood some way off, out of earshot, Newton quizzed him about the murder. Charlie insisted that he knew nothing about it. Wilson then began taunting the prisoner, saying he was a pretty big fellow, and asking him if he was a good boxer or fighter. When he said he wasn't, Wilson needled him further: 'Come out on the floor, I'd like to try a round with you.'[7] Stielow turned pleadingly to Newton and insisted that he didn't want to fight. At that point, Newton waved Wilson away and the baiting ceased.

White, like everyone on the jury, struggled to hear Stielow's hushed voice, and he asked him to speak up. Charlie continued: 'Newton asked if I done it, and I says "No." He says, "You're a liar and I can see it right in your eyes." I says, "I am not." He says, "Come on, tell the truth. It'll be too late tomorrow." I says, "I am telling the truth." He says "I know you're not and you know it."'[8]

By now, word had circulated around Albion that Stielow was on the stand, and all through his testimony the old courthouse continued to fill with spectators. Eventually, the public gallery was crammed to overflowing and the court attendants had to bar the doors. A queue snaked along the corridor and down the main courthouse steps, and as one spectator left, another ran forward to claim the vacant space. Those fortunate enough to have a seat craned their sunburnt faces forward to hear, as Stielow told how Newton kept up the jailhouse taunting, sneering that even his folks had said he was guilty. White asked Stielow if Laura had been mentioned. 'Yes,' he replied. 'They said my wife said that I had some guns. I told them it wasn't so.'[9] When he asked for his family to be brought in, so that he could hear these accusations for himself, Newton refused point-blank. Instead, according to Charlie: 'They said that Nelson Green was outside having a good time and I was locked up.'[10]

White then handed the witness to Knickerbocker. He began sedately. He wanted to know more about the defendant's time in the Albion jail. Had anyone actually abused him physically? Stielow said no. How about Wilson? Hadn't the witness exaggerated all this talk of some 'boxing match'? Hesitantly, Stielow replied that Wilson 'wasn't good-natured about it' during the interview, and had dealt with him in 'kind of a rough way'.[11] Whenever Knickerbocker asked a question, Stielow took a long time to answer, a hesitancy that clearly tried the DA's patience. With each question, Knickerbocker's voice gained a decibel until he was leaning in close to the witness, wagging a finger in Stielow's perspiring face, and almost shouting his questions. When Knickerbocker asked if he was scared at any time during the interview, Stielow said: 'I was afraid, yes.'

Knickerbocker feigned astonishment. 'Of whom?'

'Of the whole of them.'[12]

Knickerbocker sprang the trap. But hadn't the witness previously told the court that Sheriff Bartlett had treated him well? Which was it? Stielow was forced to backtrack. He fumbled and stuttered for answers, overwhelmed by the sheer force of Knickerbocker's attack. And then his torment was over. After two hours on the stand, Stielow was allowed to return to his seat next to Laura. Once there, he slumped again into that strange torpor that was his default attitude throughout most of the trial.

Stielow's departure signalled a return to the stand for Sheriff Bartlett and another volley of questions from White. The witness, still patently rattled, angrily denied that the prisoner had ever been

beaten or offered immunity in return for a confession that impli-
cated Green. Bartlett's composure only returned when he described
visiting the Stielow house one day after the murder and asking the
defendant if he had a gun in the house. No, said Stielow, nor had he
ever owned a gun. By Stielow's own subsequent admission, that had
been a lie. And now Bartlett was able to reinforce that lie a hundred
times over. Nothing colours a jury's opinion more than a proven
falsehood. 'Sometimes jurors can forgive a man for his killing,' wrote
the celebrated trial attorney Gerry Spence, 'but they never forgive a
man for lying.'[13] And that was the way it was with Charlie Stielow.
He'd lied out of expediency and, judging by the stonefaced jury, he'd
never get his credibility back.

It had been a long, exhausting day, but there was time for yet more
excitement, as Erma Fisher, still smarting from that humiliating $500
bond, was called to the stand. No one knew quite what to expect and
she didn't disappoint. She told the court how she had been drawn
to the kitchen window by the sound of shots being fired. 'One first,
then two shortly afterwards and then the fourth a little later.'[14] Her
first inclination was that someone was shooting cats. Thinking no
more of it, she returned to bed, only to then hear at least three shrill
screams. She was asked how long elapsed between the shots and the
screams. Her reply was astounding: 'It might have been 20 minutes.'[15]

Knickerbocker blanched. At the coroner's inquest, Erma had
reckoned the delay at five minutes. By the time of the grand jury
this estimate had contracted to 'hardly a minute'. Now she had multiplied the time twenty-fold! Justice Pound, fighting to keep the sarcasm from his voice, attempted to extract a modicum of sense from
the witness:

Q: Yes, it might have been 24 hours, but tell us as near as you can
how long it was?
A: I couldn't tell that.
Q: Couldn't you tell us as near as you can?

A: I just said about 20 minutes.

Q: You said it was 20 minutes after you heard the last shot before you heard the screams?

A: Yes, sir, I should think.

Q: And how long a space of time did it occupy, all these noises that you heard, the shooting, the screaming and rapping?

A: I couldn't tell how long.

Q: About how long?

A: I can't tell.

Q: Just a few minutes? Answer that question, please.

A: It might have been.

Justice Pound's exasperation mounted. 'When you say it might have been ... it might have been an hour, or it might have been two hours, or it might have been all night ... It might have been anything. It is your recollection it was a few minutes from the time that you heard the first shots until the time that you heard the scream?'

A: Yes, sir.

Seemingly oblivious to the confusion she was causing, Miss Fisher floundered on. When asked to describe what else she heard that night, she said: 'I heard the voice of a woman, it sounded like a woman saying, "I am dying, Charlie, open the door, I am dying."'

Q: How many times did you hear that?

A: It might have been two or three times.

Q: And the rapping and screaming was loud enough so you heard it before you opened the window plainly?

A: Yes, sir.[16]

Once again, this was hopelessly at odds with her inquest testimony. Then she had sworn that the woman said: '"I'm dying, I'm dying."

Every time she said this she would pound with her hands. The last time I heard her she said, "Will, let me in."' She might have said, "Will you let me in."'

Q: I thought you said Charlie?
A: No, I said Will. It might have been, 'Will you let me in. I am dying.'

Quite what the jury made of Erma Fisher is unknowable, but as far as the prosecution was concerned, she was an unmitigated disaster. White's cross-examination was brief. With Miss Fisher's unreliability a matter of public record, he had little need to undermine what was left of her tattered credibility.

Day 8: 20 July 1915

Day eight of the trial promised to be crucial, with George Newton scheduled to take the stand. There was just one problem; the witness couldn't be found. Eventually, he was tracked down in another part of the courthouse. He raced through the building, into the courtroom, made his apologies and began. Once in his stride, as expected, he gave his evidence confidently. His suspicions had been aroused from experiments he had performed at the Stielow house regarding the line of sight from the front door window. He found it impossible to believe that, when Stielow looked out of the window, he had not seen Margaret Wolcott's body lying on his doorstep. When he'd tackled the accused on this anomaly, Stielow replied that he had been standing much further back from the window on the night in question. Nor was Newton able to understand how, if Erma Fisher, who lived much further away from the crime scene, heard the gunshots, Stielow did not. The tenant house was of poor construction, with thin walls. On a still night, the sound of gunfire would have been clearly audible.

Newton moved smoothly along. He'd been testifying in courtrooms for years and his experience showed. He told how he and
Wilson had called on Stielow several times, and with each visit the
defendant became increasingly cagey. On 10 April, said Newton,
when he asked Stielow why he wouldn't say anything, the defendant
allegedly replied: 'I guess you know enough now. I won't talk any
more about it.'[17]

Newton's testimony regarding the circumstances surrounding
Stielow's two statements was substantially the same as that of Bartlett
and Porter. He categorically denied swearing at Stielow and laughed
off accusations that Wilson had attempted to fight the defendant.
Stielow, he said, had been contrite right from the first, admitting on
the day of his arrest that he'd lied to the detectives, the district attorney, the sheriff, the coroner, everyone.

Knickerbocker guided Newton expertly through his testimony.
And like the pro that he was, Newton saved the best for last. He told
the jury how, while he was putting paper in the typewriter, preparing
to record Stielow's confession on 23 April, he had asked the big man:
'What did you do it for Charlie?'

'I needed the money for my family,' was Stielow's reply.[18]

Knickerbocker cooed his satisfaction. He now had the prosecutor's classic courtroom hat-trick: the means to carry out the crime
– the .22 calibre pistol; the opportunity – he lived just across the
street; and the motive – he needed money for his family. Although
not required by law to prove motive, all prosecutors in homicide
cases feel far more confident if they can offer the jury a cogent reason why the defendant killed the victim. It just ties up all the loose
ends. When he sat down, Knickerbocker felt confident that he'd just
strapped Charlie Stielow into the electric chair.

But White had other plans. According to one observer, Newton
– previously so cocky – suddenly looked 'very nervous'[19] as White's
cross-examination caught fire. First off came an attack on Newton's
embarrassing non-appearance earlier that day. White speculated

whether this arose from the witness's arrogance – maybe he wasn't particularly interested in the case? Newton angrily denied the imputation. He explained that he'd been using the telephone at the time, as he had not expected to be called so early in the day. Seeing that the witness was getting hot under the collar, White cranked up the provocation. Was this the attitude he adopted during his interrogation of Stielow? 'Not much different, no,'[20] Newton blurted out thoughtlessly. As White piled on the accusations of bullying and third-degree tactics, Newton became ever more heated, vehemently denying either charge, and seemingly oblivious to the impression he was making on the jury.

At this point, with the witness close to boiling point, White switched to the so-called confessions and the fancy language used in them. He plucked an example from Stielow's first statement, where he allegedly said, on finding Phelps lying injured, 'I did not try to assist him or arouse him.' White asked whether the witness thought that an uneducated farmhand like Stielow would use such phraseology? Newton snapped back that he had typed 'substantially' what Stielow had said. White struck with cobra-like swiftness. Was it what Stielow had said, or was it what the witness had said? Newton, although badly flustered, stuck to his guns; these were Stielow's words.

White just scoffed. 'You and your associates weren't willing to accept anything from Stielow except an absolute statement that he committed the crime, were you?'

'We wanted the absolute truth.'[21]

White asked Newton if he had seen Stielow between the time of his last visit to the defendant's home and his arrest. Newton said no.

'You saw him when he went to move?' asked White.

'No.'

'One of your men, one of your *operatives*?'[22] White let the sarcasm drip from his lips. This provoked a thin smile from Newton, who had frequently used the term 'operative' in his direct examination when talking about his associates. Again, he insisted that no one had visited Stielow.

White next dealt with Newton's financial interest in the case. He brought out the fact that Newton and his three associates were employed by the county at a daily rate of $8 each, plus expenses. Newton said that, although he had worked the case since 27 March, his associates' involvement had been far less. So, how about the $500 reward that had been posted? Newton admitted that he knew of the reward. 'If this man is convicted,' said White, 'do you expect to claim the reward?'

'If I am entitled to it, I may be prevailed upon to accept it,' smirked Newton.

'Do you intend to accept it?'

'Yes.'[23]

After a confident start, Newton had deteriorated badly on the stand, oscillating wildly between egotism and nervousness. By the end of his ordeal, he was reduced to staring out of the window and twiddling a pencil, and couldn't get off the stand fast enough. Newton's performance had been a setback for Knickerbocker, but he still had plenty in hand: the two alleged statements. After the lunch recess he read both out in full to a hushed court. Women dabbed at their eyes as Knickerbocker recited: '[We] shot Phelps ... in the head after Phelps was lying on the floor.'[24] Heads in the public gallery swivelled angrily towards the defendant who sat tapping his fingers on his lower lip. Only once did Stielow display any emotion, when Knickerbocker read out a passage that referred to Laura. For a moment Stielow's eyes filled and he fought to hold back the tears. Then the moment passed as quickly as it had arrived, and he fell back into his usual stolid demeanour.

After reading the two statements – the first, non-incriminatory and signed; the second with its alleged confession, left blank – Knickerbocker called a string of witnesses to highlight inconsistencies in Stielow's sworn testimony at the various hearings. Among these were William Pogle and William Warner, who both testified that, when they spoke to Stielow on the morning of the crime, he spoke of hearing groans in the middle of the night and going outside to investigate. Finding nothing, he had returned to bed. Coroner Munson was recalled to read Stielow's inquest statement in which he denied ever having left the house. Like most of the crime scene witnesses, Warner and Pogle were asked to confirm what shoes Stielow had been wearing at the time. Both said felt boots with rubber overshoes, as had the previous witnesses. It was Knickerbocker's contention that the defendant had worn his patched leather boots to commit the crime, and had later changed into the felt boots and rubbers in order to throw off the investigators.

Under-Sheriff Porter was next on the stand. Porter had sharpened up his act since his flaky performance at the arraignment and now gave his evidence in a terse, professional manner. Stielow, he said, had definitely confessed to the murders, despite his stubborn refusal to sign the statement. Another witness to this alleged incident, Frank Buell, the notary public, also swore that Stielow had admitted culpability. Buell said that he'd read back the statement to Stielow and asked him if he wanted to change any part of it, and that the defendant had declined. White struggled with both witnesses. No doubt about it, their combined evidence against Stielow had the ring of authenticity.

Charles Daniels, a former employee of Phelps who had once lived in the tenant house and who, on the morning of the crime, had helped the investigators to cover the foot-tracks with blankets, swore that Stielow told him that the authorities would 'be awfully surprised when they found the man that done that job'.[25] Quite what Stielow had intended by this remained unclear, but it certainly sounded odd. Daniels also claimed that Stielow told him that if he, Stielow, had opened the door that night to see who did the shooting, he and Nelson would have 'gone out and rounded him up and hung him in a tree'.[26]

With this lurid claim to digest, the court adjourned for the day. On the morrow, Knickerbocker was expected to conclude the state's case. Then White would get his chance to put Charlie Stielow's side of the story.

Day 9: 21 July 1915

The broiling weather had finally broken and the temperatures were in the mid-60s when Robert Wilson took the stand the next morning. Like everyone present when the jailhouse statements were taken, Wilson toed the line on the manner of their dictation. In every detail he corroborated what had gone before: the confessions had been freely given, not coerced in any way. As White persisted in his claims of a jailhouse conspiracy, Knickerbocker butted in angrily, even offering to put himself on the stand to refute the accusation. Justice Pound defused what was becoming a distinctly volatile situation, by telling the district attorney that such an unusual step would not be necessary, but White had clearly rattled his opposite number. And when he tackled Wilson on alleged threats made to Stielow, the witness began to back-pedal. While other witnesses had denied hearing any talk of a 'boxing match', Wilson grudgingly admitted asking Stielow if he was 'much of a scrapper',[27] and that the defendant had answered that he 'could not fight a baby'.[28]

Knickerbocker's already dishevelled feathers received another ruffling when he attempted to recall Hamilton to provide evidence about blood allegedly found on a pair of Stielow's shoes. White objected at the top of his lungs. Since no evidence had been introduced to show at what time Stielow had worn these shoes – or even if he had worn the shoes – White argued it was irrelevant. Justice Pound agreed.

At 11:46am the prosecution rested. Over six and a half days – unusually long for a murder trial involving an indigent defendant in the early 20th century – the state's case basically boiled down to two strands: the alleged confession and Hamilton's testimony linking Stielow's gun to the crime. Either one was sufficient to send Charles Frederick Stielow to the electric chair.

Uppermost in White's mind was the need to counter the Hamilton effect. In the desperately unequal contest that exists between state and defendant when it comes to expert witness testimony, White had been granted a modest allowance to fund the entire defence, and that included finding gun experts of his own. The best he could manage was Dr Albert Sly of Buffalo, and, as it turned out, the defence would have been better served if they had found no one at all. At the very last moment Sly suffered a crisis of confidence, taking White to one side in court and whispering that he felt unable to contradict Hamilton's testimony. In all likelihood he didn't relish a grilling at the hands of Knickerbocker. Rather than risk this, White yanked his only ballistics expert, hoping that the conflict between the two prosecution firearms witnesses over how the bullets came to be marked would raise sufficient doubt in the jury's mind. Whatever the motivation, Sly's defection didn't look good.

Stung by this disappointment, White opened by recalling Melvin Jenkins. The prosecution had earlier made a great fuss over some stationery found in Stielow's house, declaring that it had been stolen during the robbery. Jenkins admitted that this wasn't the case. He told how, after cleaning his uncle's house in the days following the murder, he had come across the writing paper and had given it to the defendant.

Next came a string of character witnesses for the defendants. William H. Lee, John C. Rhoades and Albert Pechuman of Wolcottsville, and Herman F. Sauer of Royalton, all testified that they had known Stielow for many years. And in that time he had been a quiet, sober and peaceful citizen who had never once run foul of the law.

It was early afternoon when White called Laura Stielow. A hum ran through the spectators as she strode defiantly through the court. She was tiny, sparrow-like, swallowed up by the witness stand that surrounded her. She had worked on smartening up her appearance for the trial – a wide-brimmed, round hat covered her black hair – but the threadbare clothes told of a life long on hardship and short on money. And she could do nothing to conceal the strain of the past three months, etched deep in her face. White began with a simple question: 'Mrs Stielow, do you know who killed the people across the road?'

'No,'[29] she fired back, large brown eyes flashing and shaking her head with such vehemence that her hat looked in danger of flying off. White asked her to recount what had happened on the night in question. 'We all went to bed about eight o'clock. About eleven o'clock I was awakened by screams. I heard Charlie and Nelson get up and they looked at the front windows.'[30] A few moments later, the men were joined by her mother, and all three took the lamp and went into the kitchen. When Charlie returned he said that he'd also heard two screams, but nothing else. She then fell asleep. 'I got up about eight o'clock the next morning and that was the first I heard anything about the murder and then only when I looked out of the window and saw the crowd around the Phelps home. I did not hear anyone come to or leave our house that night.'[31]

White then handed Laura the Young American revolver and asked if she'd ever seen it before. She held it in her left hand and studied it closely. After a few moments she said that it 'looked like' a gun she had seen before.

'Assuming that it is the gun that you have seen,' asked White, 'can you tell me who it belongs to?'

'It belongs to me,'[32] Laura replied. Charlie had obtained it about ten years beforehand when they worked at Fayette Day farm, because she was worried by the hobos who were sleeping rough in the barn. 'I told him that I wouldn't stay there alone without some fire alarms.'

A titter ran through the courtroom. White smiled kindly. 'You mean firearms?'

'Yes,'[33] Laura said, reddening noticeably. She admitted that her mother told Charlie to remove the gun from the house, in case the authorities found it. The gun, she said, was always kept locked in a trunk. She kept the key in her apron pocket. 'Why did you keep the trunk locked?' asked White. 'What was in it?'

'Baby clothes.'

'Why should you want to keep it locked up on that account?'[34]

Safety reasons, Laura replied; she was worried in case the children found the gun. She had unlocked the trunk and removed the revolver, which she then gave to Charlie, who was holding a rifle. When White showed her the rifle, she said it resembled the one belonging to Charlie, which had hung with a shotgun on an upstairs bedroom wall.

White next produced Charlie's patched leather boots. Laura was certain he hadn't worn them around the time of the murder because he had been wearing felt boots and rubbers due to the snow. She remembered this distinctly because, on the day before the murder, 'I told Ethel to take them [the boots] upstairs.'[35]

Knickerbocker handled the witness gently on cross-examination, but he did undermine her credibility. He quoted from her testimony at previous hearings and highlighted several instances where it differed from her evidence today. She admitted having discussed her testimony with her husband's attorney. White, eager not to have his own reputation traduced, called out: 'What did I tell you to testify about?'

'You told me to tell the truth.'

'And have you?'

'Yes.'

For the most part, Laura's testimony remained unshaken. She had given her evidence clearly and well. Only once did she lose her composure, when she spoke of her three-month-old baby. Then, for just the briefest moment, her voice quivered; otherwise, according to one newspaper, 'She stood the ordeal of examination and cross-examination admirably.'[36] After testifying, she left the stand and resumed her seat next to Charlie.

Laura's mother came next. Mary Jane Green's testimony was a virtual rerun of that provided by Laura, except in two vital areas; she had also heard something fall against the front door, and what sounded like a woman's voice. Asked why her son-in-law did not investigate any further, she replied: 'Charlie said he'd open the door, only he thought it might scare Mrs Stielow if anyone were there.' She also testified that 'before I went back to bed I heard a rig of some kind pass the house.'[37]

As before, Knickerbocker worked hard to undermine the witness's credibility. But Mary Jane Green was frontier tough. Each time Knickerbocker pointed out discrepancies between her testimony today and that at the inquest, she merely said that she couldn't remember what she'd said earlier. There was a testiness to her replies that plainly got under Knickerbocker's skin. In most of the exchanges he came off worst. When he angrily accused the witness of being deliberately obstructive, willing to say anything to save Stielow and Green, she snapped back: 'I want a fair thing done. I don't want them used as dogs.'[38]

Knickerbocker managed a sickly smile and hastily excused the witness. Mary Jane had surprised most of those in court. Some found her jarring, others were quietly impressed. Certainly Knickerbocker had made little headway with her. Her testimony concluded court business for the day. Everyone went home that night buzzing with anticipation. The next morning could be pivotal. That was when Charlie Stielow was scheduled to take the stand again.

Day 10: 22 July 1915

At just after dawn the next day, crowds started gathering on the Albion courthouse steps. Some had journeyed from adjoining counties and many had brought packed lunches, not wishing to miss a minute of what promised to be the most sensational day of the most sensational trial in living memory. The crowds continued to grow right up until the time that Justice Pound gavelled proceedings to order at 9:30am. Every seat in the public gallery had been taken. Fire safety concerns meant that more than 100 spectators were left milling about the halls outside, all denied a glimpse of the accused double killer.

Without any preamble, White called Stielow. Slowly and with great deliberation, he recounted his version of events. He said that, after supper, both he and Green sat around the kitchen of his house. 'I went to bed about eight o'clock. I went to sleep before nine o'clock and was awakened about 10:40pm by a scream. I got out of bed and was about half dressed when I heard the second scream. Nelson and I looked out the windows and through the glass in the door. I saw nothing outside; finally I hollered, "what's wanted, who's there?"'[39] When he didn't receive any reply, Mrs Green, who had also been disturbed by the commotion, told him to lock any doors; she didn't want Laura upset in her present condition. On one point Stielow was emphatic: 'I didn't go out or open the door of the house at all that night.'[40]

White showed Stielow the .22 calibre revolver. Stielow said he hadn't fired it in five or six years, not since he'd lived at George Dale's farm in Royalton. Even then, he'd only fired it for sport, shooting at a target. White didn't tarry over events at the Phelps house on the morning of the crime, most of which were not in dispute, and instead concentrated on what exactly happened when Stielow was arrested and tossed into the Albion jailhouse. Stielow described a litany of non-stop bullying, stretched out over three long days, that wore down his resistance to the point where he was prepared to say practically anything to escape that hellhole. Yet still he wouldn't give the investigators what they wanted. He told how Newton pulled him to one side, out of earshot of Bartlett and Wilson who lingered a little further down the corridor, and said: 'Charlie, if you tell us who killed Mr. Phelps we'll all three hold up our right hand and swear we won't tell a soul.'

'What was your response?' asked White.

'I said I couldn't because I didn't know.' This response had infuriated Newton and triggered a foul-mouthed tirade with accusations that he had killed Phelps. 'I said, "No, sir. I didn't kill him."'[41] Newton had then stormed off. Later, having had time to mull things over and desperate to get back home to his pregnant wife, Charlie had sent for the private detective. Newton again huddled with Stielow in a quiet corner of the jailhouse. 'I says, "Here, Newton, if I said that I done this will that hurt?" He says, "No, sir, it will not. It's the fellow that done the shooting that we're after. We want you home where you belong with your family."'[42]

Sensing that Stielow was close to confessing, Newton had shrewdly decided not to press. Instead he played him like a trout on a line, giving him a few minutes alone to consider his position. Sure enough, a short while later, Stielow summoned Newton once more. This time the detective 'told me that he wanted me to go home, that I was too good a man to be locked up'.

'Did you believe those statements of Newton?' asked White.

'Yes, sir, I did. I believed every word he said.' He then added: 'He also said that if I'd believe him I'd wear diamonds.'[43] At this, the court erupted in uproar. Justice Pound hammered his gavel repeatedly, shouting for order. When the din finally did subside, White asked Stielow why he hadn't signed the second statement. 'Because it wasn't the truth and I didn't feel like signing it.'

'Did you know it wasn't the truth?'

'Yes, sir.'[44]

White asked if, prior to making the first statement, he had been apprised of his constitutional rights? Stielow's blank expression obliged White to rephrase his question in simpler terms. Eventually the mists cleared and Stielow replied: 'I do not remember, the district attorney told me in advance that my statements must be voluntary and that they would not be used against me.' He went on to explain the circumstances surrounding the first statement. 'I can't read or write, but I made my mark on the statement.'

And both of these statements included falsehoods? Why?

Because, said Stielow, 'The detectives wanted me to do it.'[45]

When White sat down, Knickerbocker waited a few moments before beginning. He let the pressure build, then launched his attack, loosing a salvo of quickfire, unrelated questions designed to knock the witness out of his painfully slow stride. He reminded Stielow that originally he said he hadn't heard Margaret Wolcott say anything on the night of the murder.

'Was it because you weren't in the house that you didn't hear it?' asked Knickerbocker.

'No, sir.'

'What did you hear the woman say when you were outdoors?'

'I wasn't outdoors.'

Knickerbocker suddenly grabbed the revolver and rifle and held them aloft. 'Which one of these guns did you take to the Phelps's house that night?'

'I didn't have any of them over there.'[46]

Having notably failed to undermine Stielow's equilibrium, Knickerbocker shifted tack. Why, he asked, if you knew nothing about the murders, did you claim that Nelson Green carried out the shooting? Charlie mused for a moment. 'I kind of thought by the way things were going that he was trying to put it on me, and I was trying to put it on him.'[47]

Charlie's habit of delivering his answers accompanied by a nervous giggle clearly unsettled Knickerbocker. Didn't the witness understand the peril he was in? Charlie's only response was another high-pitched giggle. Knickerbocker asked: 'Do you even know the penalty for first-degree murder?' The witness looked blank and admitted that he did not, though this ignorance may well have been a deliberate subterfuge designed to spare the feelings of his family, all of whom, except baby Irene, were present in court.

A rare amusing moment in what had been an otherwise heavily oppressive trial came when the state attempted to demonstrate that Stielow's illiteracy was all a pretence, that he could write his own signature. The witness admitted giving Melvin Jenkins a receipt that he had signed. 'I had a way to kind of write my name,' he said, smiling sheepishly. 'I don't know whether it was my name or not.'[48] As chuckles broke out in the courtroom, Knickerbocker, who by now was fighting a decidedly rearguard action, produced two notes, both of which bore Stielow's signature. Stielow said that Laura had signed both in his presence. At this point, Knickerbocker handed Stielow a piece of paper and a pencil and asked him to write his name. Laboriously Stielow scrawled something and handed it back. Knickerbocker studied it and professed himself defeated. Which part, he asked, was supposed to read 'Stielow'? The witness conceded that he didn't know.

As the day wore on, the crowds continued to arrive and lines formed outside the courthouse. An early afternoon rainstorm drove some away, but most stayed. Bartlett's deputies struggled to maintain order. Eventually the crush proved so great that a dust-laden loft had to be pressed into service to accommodate the overspill. Almost everyone in Albion, it seemed, wanted to see the life-and-death struggle being played out before them.

Hour after hour, Knickerbocker battered away in remorseless fashion. Stielow readily admitted that he had lied in both statements, but insisted that his testimony today was the absolute truth. He had made the statements because he wanted some respite from a three-day grilling at the hands of tormentors who woke him at all hours. In making this claim, Stielow was merely foreshadowing a defence that would resonate in thousands of courtrooms worldwide from that day to this. But mental bullying didn't fall within Knickerbocker's purview; all he understood was physical aggression. Hence his eagerness to drag from Stielow the admission that he'd never once been beaten. Charlie Stielow wasn't the first, and he certainly wouldn't be the last sleep-deprived prisoner to break under relentless psychological pressure. Judicial history is replete with prisoners making false confessions for this very reason. Knickerbocker's scoffing contempt might have played well with the jury, but the witness's plainly told tale of prolonged mental torture clearly impressed at least one other court official, as we shall see later.

Finally, after five hours on the stand, Stielow's ordeal came to an end. By common consent he'd 'made a much better impression' than on Monday, having held up well to 'a searching cross-examination'.[49] Wearily he trudged back to his chair beside Laura and the two children. Everything now depended on White's closing address.

He spoke for more than three hours with such passion and intensity that several jury members were seen to dab tears away from their eyes. When White mentioned the Stielow children, even Charlie and Laura joined in the weeping. Just about the only ones unaffected were Ethel and Roy themselves. Both had fallen asleep at their parents' side. They didn't hear White as he heaped derision on 'Gun Expert Hamilton', this 'humbug'[50] who hawked his opinion to the highest bidder. But most of White's anger was reserved for the so-called confession. Was it safe, or even just, to convict on the basis of a sleep-deprived statement – unsigned – made by a three-quarter-witted farmhand who'd been subjected to days of bullying and abuse? White pointed at the defendant. The jury had heard this man speak; they'd heard his struggle with even the simplest language. Yet they were being asked to believe that he'd uttered the almost ornate sentences set down in the statements typed up by Newton. It was a farrago, said White, cooked up by investigators motivated by money not justice.

It was generally agreed that White's speech was 'one of the best addresses that has been made before a jury'[51] in Orleans County for many years. Courts were more robust places in those days, and when White finally sank, exhausted, into his chair the clock had moved on to 9:00pm. Justice Pound, in adjourning proceedings for the day, announced that court would resume the following morning at the unusually early time of nine o'clock. To ensure his own attendance at that hour, the judge, for the first time since the trial began, stayed overnight in Albion, rather than commuting to his home in Lockport.

Despite the lateness of the hour, a crowd of over 200 people watched as the defendant was escorted across the square to the local jail. Most would be back the following day to witness what everyone expected to be the climax of this astonishing trial.

Day 11: 23 July 1915

That morning's newspapers recorded a distinct hardening in America's attitude towards Germany following the *Lusitania* tragedy. In a note to the German government, Washington warned that any repetition of illegal acts by German U-boats 'must be regarded by the Government of the United States, when they affect American citizens, as deliberately unfriendly'.[52] This was exceptionally strong diplomatic language. Although President Wilson's isolationist policy was still intact, anti-German feeling was mounting daily and provided a febrile backdrop for Knickerbocker as he rose at the stroke of nine o'clock on Friday morning to make the most important speech of his career. He described the Shelby murders in searing tones that left no one unaffected. He insisted that the confessions made by Stielow were entirely voluntary, the product of a stricken conscience.

And if that were not enough, there was plenty of other incriminating evidence. At six o'clock on the morning after the crime, before anyone had properly established the manner of death, Stielow had told some neighbours that the victims had been shot. How could he have known this?

Knickerbocker upped his argument a gear. Stielow's motive was plain, he said; robbery, made necessary by his family's parlous financial condition. But it was the confessions that spoke loudest of all against the defendant. One alone, that made to Sheriff Bartlett on the day following his arrest, was sufficient to justify Stielow's conviction. Knickerbocker reminded the jury how Bartlett had testified that, while sitting in his office, he answered a call from a cell. Of his own accord, Stielow had then told Bartlett he wanted to make a clean breast of the whole affair; that he'd repeatedly lied to the officers, and that he and Nelson Green had killed Phelps. Could anything be more self-evident?

Piece by excruciating piece, Knickerbocker surgically dissected the divergences between Stielow's previous statements and his testimony here on the witness stand. It was expertly done and sounded utterly damning. Knickerbocker could afford to be gracious to Laura Stielow and her mother. He didn't condemn them for testifying in the manner that they did; they were, he said, merely responding to their natural instincts.

He extended no such mercy to opposing counsel, blasting White for the manner in which he had attacked Hamilton as a 'humbug'. Contrast Hamilton's testimony with Dr Sly's craven performance. He'd examined the gun in Hamilton's presence and yet, at the last minute, he'd flatly refused to testify. 'Do you think if they [the defence] had known that Hamilton's statements were wrong they would not have put their own expert on the stand?'[53]

And then there was that copper-bottomed gift from White. Knickerbocker reminded the jury how defence ineptitude allowed the court to admit Hamilton's opinion that the bullets had been definitely fired from Exhibit G.G., the revolver given by Stielow to Raymond Green shortly after the murder. A bungled defence for a guilty client, said Knickerbocker.

Throughout his closing address Knickerbocker constantly reminded the jury of their duty. Several times he mentioned the death penalty, his voice sinking to a whisper as he leaned over and peered into the eyes of the jurors. At one point he suddenly whirled around and pointed at the defendant. 'Do you think I would try to convict that man if I thought he was innocent?' he roared, his voice shaking with rage. Even his own honour had been impugned by the defence, he said. Such accusations, if made outside a court of law, would render the defamer liable to a charge of criminal libel. But Knickerbocker was prepared to take the high ground because he was speaking for the people, and the people demanded justice. After being on his feet for almost three hours, he built to a terrible crescendo. Standing in the middle of the courtroom, he pointed again at the defendant, and bellowed: 'The evidence in this case shows conclusively that Charles Phelps met his death at the hands of this assassin.'[54]

When Knickerbocker sat down, few doubted that his impressive rhetoric had delivered a knockout punch to the defence. He'd consigned White's speech of the night before to the distant memory banks. All that was left now was Justice Pound's final address to the jury. Few expected any fireworks from that quarter. They were wrong.

Justice Pound's charge to the jury covered two areas: the firearms testimony and the confessions. He alluded to the defensive blunder that had permitted Hamilton to give his opinion – 'for what it's worth'[55] – that the bullets had definitely been fired from the Stielow gun. (It's worth noting that Justice Pound was a 30-year veteran of the New York judicial circuit and would have been familiar with Hamilton's dubious reputation.) 'Of course,' the judge continued, this could only be an opinion because 'he [Hamilton] does not know'[56] whether these bullets were fired from Stielow's gun. Pound warned the jury to view warily the evidence of paid expert witnesses and the testimony of anyone with a vested financial interest in the defendant being convicted. This particularly applied to the testimony of George W. Newton. 'Private detectives,' Pound said, 'have a motive – temptation at least – to make as much of a case as they can, because their compensation depends on the amount of work they do.'[57] It didn't follow that this meant they were not to be believed, but that it was appropriate to 'scrutinize their evidence carefully'.[58]

But it was Stielow's alleged confessions that clearly troubled the judge most. In particular, he was concerned about the evidence given by Sheriff Bartlett. He referred to Bartlett's claim that, on 23 April, Newton, in front of several witnesses, had drawn a confession from the defendant. 'The curious thing about that is,' said the judge, 'that while the statement was made – *if you believe the sheriff* [emphasis added] – in the presence of Newton, Wilson, and Scott Porter, the sheriff is the only person who testifies to that statement made at that time.'[59] Faces hardened around the prosecutorial table as Pound spoke. Thinly veiled accusations of lying against one of the state's major witnesses – especially an elected peace officer – were as unusual as they were damning, and there was more hostility to come as Pound directed his fire on the use of third-degree tactics to coerce prisoners. The judge was no wide-eyed naïf; he knew all about jailhouse beatings and the kinds of psychological tricks that investigators employed to extract confessions. It was his job to explain the law on such evidence. 'If you think that it [the confession] was made under the influence of fear produced by threats, or if you think it was not voluntary,' he told the jury, 'you should reject it *even if it is a true statement*.'[60] This might sound shocking, but Pound had strong legal precedent on his side. In 1897, the US Supreme Court had ruled that, in order to be admissible, a confession had to be free and voluntary, not extracted by any sort of threats or violence, no matter how slight.

Nor could any confession be received in evidence where the prisoner was influenced by any threat or promise.[*]

Pound paused for a moment to let this sink in before proceeding. 'I may say to you now, gentlemen of the jury, that this defendant cannot be convicted by you … unless you are satisfied beyond a reasonable doubt that the second statement made by him … in which he states the circumstances and particulars of the crime, is in substance true.'[61] Everything, he said, hinged on the statement of 23 April; indeed, 'If it were not for that statement, it would be the duty of the court to direct you to render a verdict of acquittal.'[62]

This was remarkable. At a stroke, Justice Pound had dismissed the so-called expert ballistics evidence of Albert Hamilton and that of his colleague Charles Newton: it would have to be the confession or nothing. Whatever complaints might be levelled against numerous prosecution witnesses in Charlie Stielow's trial, there could be no accusation of bias from the bench. At every stage of the trial, Justice Pound conducted proceedings with scrupulous fairness to the defendant.

Now everything rested with the jury. They retired at 1:25pm, and their first course of action was to call for lunch. They broke again for an hour around 6:00pm, for supper. At 8:14pm, with their bellies comfortably full at the county's expense, they sent word that a verdict had been reached. This news sparked a mad scramble for seats in the public gallery, with no one wanting to miss the denouement. Reporters sat, pencils poised, as Justice Pound took his place at the bench and ordered Stielow to his feet. The big farmhand stood erect. A second or so later, the jury room door opened. Slowly, the twelve men filed back in. All wore sombre expressions and few could bring themselves to acknowledge the defendant. They settled awkwardly into their seats and then the jury foreman Mark Porter rose to deliver the verdict.

---

[*] *Bram v. United States,* 168 U.S. 532; 18 S. Ct. 183; 42 L. Ed. 568; 1897

8

The Verdict

A graveyard hush filled the courtroom as the clerk addressed the jury. 'Gentlemen, have you reached a verdict?' Ashen-faced, Mark Porter mumbled an affirmative. He began slowly, 'We find the defendant …' then came a long pause, as if the words were sticking in his dry throat, '… as charged.' There was a moment of confusion, broken by Justice Pound. 'I suppose you mean that you find the defendant guilty as charged in the indictment?' Porter answered: 'We do.'[1]

An orgasmic release of tension swept through the courtroom. Then chaos as reporters dashed for the exits, desperate to file copy with their newspapers. The public gallery, previously frozen, suddenly burst into activity and excited chatter. Judging from the broad smiles, most observers agreed wholeheartedly with the verdict. Hardly surprising, really. It had been a ghastly crime, the kind that cried out for justice, and now the self-confessed killer would have to pay society's price.

Marooned in the midst of all this mayhem, Charlie Stielow stared almost motionless at the jury. Only the muscles of his jaw moved as he slowly ground his teeth together. Then he swayed. A helping hand from a deputy steadied him as he sank into his chair, stupefied. The uproar grew louder and louder. Almost lost in the bedlam, Justice Pound's gavel banged repeatedly in an attempt to restore order. Eventually the din subsided, allowing the judge to speak. He advised the defence that it was customary in capital cases to wait 48 hours before pronouncing sentence, but White, after a brief word with his client, announced that the defence chose to waive that right. Judge Pound studied Stielow and asked if he had anything to say. He murmured no. Then, without frill or comment Justice Pound passed the mandatory sentence for first-degree murder in the state of New York; Charles Stielow would be taken to the state prison at Sing Sing and there, in the week beginning 5 September 1915, he would suffer death by electrocution.

Knickerbocker's triumph was palpable. He sat behind the prosecutor's desk, gathering up his paperwork and basking in the congratulations of colleagues and courtroom officials alike. In the biggest and most expensive trial ever to hit Orleans County, the DA had hit a home run. His political star had never been brighter. Come election time, he was looking at a landslide. Almost unnoticed among the back-slappers and well-wishers, Clute, the attorney for Nelson Green, leant down and breathed something into Knickerbocker's ear. After a moment's consideration, the district attorney motioned Sheriff Bartlett to the table. All three men put their heads together, muttering in low voices. Seconds later, Knickerbocker nodded. This was the cue for Clute to hurry from the fast-emptying courtroom.

Across the aisle, still slumped in his chair, Charlie Stielow looked shell-shocked. His face was bloodless. Only now, for the first time since his ordeal began three months earlier, did the real peril of his situation strike home. When two sheriff's deputies ordered him to stand, he tried and failed, as his nerves and legs gave way. The deputies moved quickly and grabbed hold of his arms, then steered him like a newborn foal on wobbly legs over to the clerk of the court where he gave his personal details. When this ritual was complete, Charlie was shackled and then handcuffed for the first time since the trial began. As he was marched from court, the only crumb of comfort to sustain him was that no family members, not even Laura, had been present to hear his fate. White had anticipated the verdict and, at his urging, all relatives had stayed away in order to spare them any unnecessary grief. Laura was still ensconced in Sheriff Bartlett's home next to the courthouse.

It later emerged that the jury had taken five ballots to reach its decision. Guilt was never an issue – Knickerbocker's case had sounded overwhelming – it was a question of culpability. In the first four ballots, there were ten votes for murder in the first degree and two for the second, no votes being cast for acquittal. On the fifth vote unanimity had been reached.

Outside the courthouse a large crowd surged around Stielow as he was led away on foot. The brutal heatwave of the past few days had given way to pleasantly cool temperatures and the evening shadows were just beginning to lengthen as the big man shuffled awkwardly in his chains across historic Courthouse Square. Ahead of him lay a short walk. There were no jeers, no taunts from the onlookers, just silence as they watched Stielow disappear inside the county jail.

Back at the courthouse, White was doing everything possible to eke out a few precious days of extra life for his client. He begged Justice Pound to delay signing the death warrant until the following Monday, 26 July. This would allow Charlie two more days in the Orleans County jailhouse – enough time to say his goodbyes to immediate family and other relatives – before he was transferred to the death house. White explained that there was very little chance of any family member being able to afford the round trip fare to Sing Sing. Justice Pound, maintaining the scrupulous fairness that he had exhibited throughout the trial, readily agreed.

There was still more court business to be transacted, as the verdict against Stielow had triggered some feverish legal horse-trading. Clute had hotfooted it across to the Albion jailhouse and told Nelson Green the outcome. He made it plain that if he [Green] persisted in pleading not guilty, then he, too, would be doomed to the electric chair. Nelson fought back the tears. All was not lost, though, Clute explained; his discussions with the DA had made it clear that there was a deal to be done. Clute laid out Nelson's meagre list of options. Nelson listened, only half comprehending, and agreed to follow his lawyer's advice.

At 8:50pm, Nelson Green was hustled up the back stairs of the by now almost deserted Albion courthouse and into court. Clute told Justice Pound that he had conferred with Knickerbocker and that Green now wished to change his plea to guilty to second-degree murder. Knickerbocker confirmed that the state was willing to drop the capital charge. He explained that Green was 'mentally and physically weak'[2] and that, in his opinion, he had been entirely dominated by Stielow's more powerful personality. Moreover, he told the judge, Green's plea bargain would spare local taxpayers the cost of another expensive trial.

As news of this latest development got around, the courtroom began, once again, to fill up. Most of the newcomers were reporters and they were just in time to hear Justice Pound address the petrified young defendant. 'You know, Green, what that means, do you? It means that you now and here admit that you and Stielow murdered Charles Phelps and Margaret Wolcott, and that you plead guilty to murder, second degree.'

'Yes, I do,'[3] Green said feebly. Asked if there was anything that he wanted to say, the youngster shook his head. Justice Pound then called upon Knickerbocker to make a brief statement. The district attorney announced publicly for the first time that, on 15 May, Green had made a second confession in which he identified Stielow's .22 calibre revolver as the one used by the condemned man to murder Phelps and Wolcott. It was Green, said Knickerbocker, who first provided the clue that led to Stielow's arrest. Because of this and the defendant's youth, Knickerbocker felt justified in accepting the plea of second-degree murder.

Justice Pound rested his kindly gaze upon the teenager as he sentenced him to between twenty years and life. There was genuine compassion in his voice when he told Green that he loathed passing such a sentence on a young man, but that if he, Green, 'kept a good deportment'[4] he stood a good chance of being released after the minimum tariff. Almost overcome with relief, Nelson Green was then removed to the county jail.

He arrived just in time to witness a truly harrowing scene. When Stielow returned to the cell that had caged him for the past three months, he had collapsed onto his bed in utter dismay. Just minutes later a woman's voice echoed along the stone corridor. Laura was pleading with the deputies for a chance to see her husband. At first they tried to turn her away, but Laura refused to leave. After a minute or so, the guards relented, accompanying Laura to his cell and unlocking the door. Charlie, once again free from his shackles, threw his huge arms around his diminutive wife and hugged her to him. Both dissolved in a flood of tears. Laura's sister Olive, there to provide moral and physical support for her frail sister, looked away, embarrassed to be intruding on such personal grief. Not the guards, though. They were under instructions not to let Stielow out of their sight. At one point, when Laura leant forward to whisper something in her husband's ear, they stepped in to separate the couple, fearing that Laura might pass Charlie either a weapon to help effect an escape or some means of suicide.

After several angst-ridden minutes the guards announced that time was up and Laura was dragged from the cell. As she was being hauled away, Charlie, his tear-streaked face shining, cried out, 'Bring the new baby down so that I can see it before they take me away, will you?'.

'I will, Charlie,'[5] Laura sobbed and then she was gone.

Just along the corridor, Nelson Green listened to these exchanges in shamefaced silence. When he did try to speak to Charlie later on, he got no response. The big man just blanked him. Nelson's anguish seeped out in quiet tears. Making the courtroom confession might have saved his own skin, but it had virtually destroyed any hope of a pardon for his brother-in-law. With an eyewitness to swear that Charlie Stielow gunned down and robbed two helpless victims, he'd fry for sure.

That Friday night Stielow was placed under a double death watch. Two deputies were stationed outside his cell, round the clock. There wasn't much for them to see. At 10:00pm Stielow fell asleep, utterly exhausted by the strain.

He didn't awake until late the next morning, when he was disturbed by the footsteps of a few newsmen on the prowl for some follow-up copy. Stielow glared at them through the cell bars. For the first time there was real anger in his normally timid voice as he protested his innocence. 'There are four fellows here,' he shouted, pointing in the direction of the sheriff's office, 'and I hope God will watch them and do something to them for what they have done to me. I never had anything to do with that job, and if I ever had a penny of Mr. Phelps' money, or saw one, I would give it to the sheriff.'[6]

Repeatedly he insisted that Newton, Bartlett and others had put words in his mouth, bullied and browbeaten him for hours on end, called him a liar and threatened to beat him up. After more than 48 hours of unremitting mental torture, he'd finally cracked and agreed to say something – anything – just to call off the jackals. The reporters duly noted all of this and left. As they filed out of the jailhouse they met Mary Jane Green, who was holding forth in Courthouse Square. She echoed Stielow's words: her boys were innocent, she cried; Nelson had pleaded guilty because that was the only way to save his life and she didn't blame him for that. The trial, from start to finish, had been a frame-up. Few of the reporters showed any interest. The Stielow case was already yesterday's news. Time to move on to the next story.

The next afternoon, Stielow finally got to see his newborn baby. He cradled little Irene in his huge arms. Once again, Laura and the other family members were body-searched, in response to growing fears that the whispered conversation on Friday night might have included plans for suicide. But nothing was found, and the meeting, though packed with gut-wrenching levels of emotion, passed off without incident. As she left, Laura sobbed that this would have to be the final goodbye; there was no money to pay for a car to get the family into town the next day. Charlie understood.

Just after dawn the next morning – Monday 26 July – Stielow was shaken awake by the deputies and told to get dressed. Word had come through that Judge Pound had now signed the death warrant, setting the legal machinery in operation. A breakfast tray was brought to Charlie. One thing that hadn't suffered during his long ordeal was his enormous appetite and he polished off the food with ease. Every mouthful, every movement was scrutinised by at least two officers. After finishing breakfast, he donned his blue serge suit, cuffs were snapped on his wrists, and he was led along the stone corridor. Nelson Green shouted his goodbyes, but Charlie maintained his grim silence. Sandwiched between Porter and another deputy, Michael De Leo, Stielow exited the jailhouse. His eyes blinked in the strong sunlight. Only a few Albion residents were around at this early hour to see the county's most notorious criminal, but, judging from the prisoner's expression, most felt that he seemed mightily relieved to get away from a building and a town that had brought him nothing but sorrow. From the jailhouse it was but a few minutes' walk to the red-brick railroad station. When Charlie reached the platform he jolted upright in surprise – Laura and the three children were waiting for him.

David White had come through once again. Laura told Charlie how White, out of his own pocket, had hired a car to transport the Stielows to the station so that they could share a few more precious moments together. Stielow's body shook with sobs as he kissed each family member goodbye. Then the guard's whistle blew. The deputies pushed Stielow aboard and, seconds later, the 7:15am to Albany steamed slowly out of the station. Laura, damp eyes glistening in the sunlight, watched the train until it disappeared from view. Deep in her broken heart, she was certain she would never see her man alive again.

A few minutes later it was Nelson Green's turn to leave the county jail. He'd always been a supporting player in this tragedy, and his departure was once again largely ignored by any passers-by. Two deputies escorted him to the electric trolley car station. There he boarded an eastbound Buffalo, Lockport & Rochester trolley car for the 30-mile journey to Rochester. From there, he would travel by train to Auburn Prison, aware that he would be middle-aged by the time he got to make the return journey.

As prospects go it wasn't much, but it sure beat Charlie Stielow's immediate future. Editorials in local newspapers were confidently predicting that, now White's court-appointed duties had expired, the German farmhand was doomed. Everyone agreed that White had given it his best shot and had certainly earned every cent of the $500 allotted by the county treasurer to defend Stielow. But this, surely, was the end of the road. In capital cases, a defendant's best chance of an appeal generally lay in claims of misdirection from the bench. Here, though, Justice Pound's conduct of the trial had been impeccable. Indeed, some had grumbled that his final charge to the jury was, if anything, slanted in the defendant's favour. Nor could Stielow expect any kind of succour from Orleans County. The treasury was desperate to wash its hands of an expensive, messy affair that had eaten deep into the county's coffers. As he watched the vast, fruitful fields – the fields where he'd spent all his life – glide past his carriage window, Charlie Stielow was friendless, penniless and bereft of hope. Overriding all else was the grim realisation that, in just over six weeks, he would most likely be dead.

By the time the train reached Syracuse, word had got around that the 'Albion Murderer'[7] was on board, and large crowds thronged the station platform, all eager for a glimpse of the region's most notorious killer. An orderly line filed past his open carriage window, like mourners at a wake viewing the contents of a coffin. Some went back for a second look. In response to a shouted question through the window, asking why he'd committed the murders, Charlie showed a rare dash of annoyance, brandishing his manacled hands angrily and protesting his innocence. Just once his dull eyes glinted, when a reporter asked him to comment on rumours that he might be granted a new trial. But before Charlie could respond, the guards snapped the window shut and ordered the prisoner to keep quiet. Stielow, the indentured servant, someone not given to questioning authority, meekly lapsed back into the sullen silence that he'd brought with him from Albion. Then the train whistle blew and the engine chugged forward. Stielow settled in his seat. He maintained his morose silence all the way to Albany. There, he switched trains for the two-hour final leg of his journey to Sing Sing.

PART III

9

The Big House up the River

In 1685, a wealthy colonial merchant named Frederick Philipse journeyed north from his elegant townhouse in New Amsterdam (later New York City), into what is today Westchester County. He was looking to buy some land. His journey ended just over 30 miles up the Hudson River, on the eastern shoreline of Croton Bay. This was territory that belonged to the Sint Sinck Indians, members of the Wappinger Confederacy. Philipse liked what he saw; good verdant soil and cooling breezes off the river. He convinced the Sint Sinck to sell him a tract of land, and the region soon became popular with wealthy families looking to escape the sweltering summertime bustle of New Amsterdam, but retain the proximity. The region's name always caused a problem. Newcomers, unable to get their tongues around the Indian pronunciation, simply settled for calling it Sing Sing. Official recognition of this linguistic expediency came in 1813 when the village was incorporated under the name of Sing Sing. Perched on the banks of the Hudson River, Sing Sing remained a sleepy village for most of its early life. The big upheaval came in 1824 when the legislature voted to find a suitable site for New York State's third prison. The existing prison in Greenwich Village, called Newgate after its notorious forerunner in London, was no longer fit for purpose and had been earmarked for closure, while the other correctional facility at Auburn was too distant to receive convicted felons from New York City, then, as now, the state's predominant source of prison inmates. A commission headed by Elam Lynds, the warden of Auburn Prison, was charged with finding a suitable location for the new prison. Like Philipse more than a century before him, Lynds was drawn irresistibly to the attractions of Sing Sing, though for entirely different reasons. He zeroed in on the Silver Mine Farm, an abandoned site that overlooked the Hudson, just south-west of the new village. The location fitted Lynds's demanding criteria with room to spare. A nearby quarry would provide the limestone rock to build the prison; the river would provide easy transport to New York City; but, best of all, certainly so far as the legislature was concerned, Lynds reckoned he could build the prison with convict labour drafted in from Auburn, at virtually no cost to the taxpayer. The legislature agreed and appropriated $20,100 to buy the 130-acre site. Lynds was true to his word. By 1828 Sing Sing was finished, under budget, and two years later it was already housing a population of 513 inmates.

Lynds' reward was the plum appointment of Sing Sing's first warden. He ruled his fiefdom with medieval severity. In his cramped view of the universe, a convict had forfeited all rights to be regarded as a human being and Lynds regarded it as his God-given duty to break that man's spirit. To achieve this aim, he imported what was called the 'Auburn System', a carefully designed programme of mental disintegration that many a modern secret police force might have envied. At its core lay total silence. Prisoners were forbidden to talk to anyone. This unbending monasticism even spilled over into the exercise yard, home of the hated 'lockstep'. In this, the inmates were herded into single file, right hand on the shoulder of the man in front, left hand at each man's own side; then the convicts stepped off in unison, raising the right foot high and shuffling with the left. They marched, still in silence, around and around the exercise yard. The lockstep had originally been devised as a means of moving large numbers of convicts from one place to another with minimal control, but Lynds was quick to recognise its mind-numbing potential in day-to-day prison life. Lynds made no pretensions to enlightenment or rehabilitation; he was a whip-carrying enforcer, nothing more. Legislators in Albany were prepared to turn a blind eye to his sadism because the prison always generated a handsome profit. The brutal regime established by Lynds survived him by several decades and guaranteed that for the remainder of the 19th century, Sing Sing's notoriety multiplied exponentially, until, by 1900, the 'big house up the river'[1] had become the most infamous penal institution in America.

For those townspeople who lived within the shadow of the prison, Sing Sing provided mixed blessings. While it offered an excellent source of employment – most of the guards lived nearby – the trade-off came in notoriety. Local manufacturers feared that their goods were tarnished by the prison's reputation, with many potential customers harbouring the misapprehension that 'Made in Sing Sing' meant convict labour. The clamour eventually reached such a pitch that a campaign was initiated to change the village's name. This won executive approval, and on 25 March 1901 the name of the village was officially changed to Ossining.

Still the bellyaching continued. And in 1914 civic unrest focused on the town's railroad station, situated where Main Street met the Hudson. Since so many of the passengers alighting at this station were convicts with one-way tickets, why, angry locals grouched, couldn't the prison have its own dedicated railroad station? That way decent folk would be spared the often raucous spectacle of convicts walking the half-mile that brought them to Sing Sing's formidable gates. Not all locals agreed. For many, the convicts' parade along the banks of the Hudson was a marvellous opportunity to catch a glimpse of the latest headline-maker. Some just stood and stared; others lobbed jeers, giving the display all the trappings of a modern-day bear pit.

There were no crowds clogging the platform on the evening of 26 July 1915 when the train bearing Charlie Stielow steamed to a halt. (Appalling though the double murder was, it had been lightly reported outside western New York State.) There was still plenty of daylight and a strong sun – with a temperature in the 70s – as Stielow climbed down from the train. The two deputies guided their shackled charge through the station and on to Westerly Road. On Stielow's right, the mighty Hudson rolled lazily southwards. Directly ahead – and now just minutes away – lay his destination.

Elam Lynds had intended Sing Sing to look intimidating and he'd certainly succeeded in his mission. Grey and grim, its huge walls punctuated by watchtowers, the building sprawled across a bulge in the river bank that jutted out into the Hudson. Behind the prison, heavily wooded hills stretched skywards. Beyond these, and hidden from view, lay the town of Ossining itself. At the other end of the bulge, a large steam whistle straddled one of the mess halls. Its distinctive shriek, which howled whenever an inmate escaped, reverberated for miles. Few did. For most of Sing Sing's 1,700 inmates, liberty was literally the stuff of dreams.

Deputies Porter and De Leo rapped at the main gate. Their work was nearly done. It was time to deliver their prisoner into the hands of the formidably well-oiled execution machine that was Sing Sing. Since the electric chair was first used at Sing Sing on 7 July 1891, when four killers were executed in one night, 166 men and one woman had entered the death house at Sing Sing.* Of those, 115 had paid the ultimate penalty. On that warm July evening very few would have bet against Charlie Stielow's name being added to that grim list. Once inside the main gates, Stielow stood mutely as Porter and De Leo handed over the formal paperwork. Some quick goodbyes and then they were gone. As the gates clanged shut behind him, Stielow was taken to the prisoner reception area. Here, his clothing and belongings were taken from him and he was handed the plain grey uniform of the death house inmate. Then he was marched into the bathhouse. His handcuffs were unlocked and he was told to get bathed and shaved. With his ablutions over, he dressed and was again manacled before being led through a maze of stone-floored corridors. The clank of doors opening and slamming shut, the

---

* Just five days before Stielow's arrival, Madeline Ferola, 47, who had murdered her lover, had seen her death sentence commuted to life imprisonment. But she had never actually entered the death house. Upon her arrival at Sing Sing in 1914, she had been placed in a former guard's quarters (with fourteen rooms and half a dozen servants) across the road from the main gate. She was transferred to Auburn Prison on 27 July 1915.

monotonous clink, clink, clink of keys that formed the background chorus to every action inside the prison, rattled in his ears as he burrowed deeper into the maze. Eventually, his progress was halted by a great door made from grey steel. It led into a squat, ugly bunker that stood apart from the rest of the prison.

As the door swung open, Stielow squinted to make out what lay beyond. When his eyes had adjusted to the gloom, he got his first sight of Sing Sing's death house. It was actually two rows of cells – seven on the left, eight on the right – that faced each other. Due to recent overcrowding, a second tier of four cells had been built above those on the right. The two main rows of cells were separated by a wide corridor. Along the length of this corridor ran two barriers of heavy wire netting – one on each side – a foot or so in front of the heavily barred cells. These were designed to keep family and attorneys out of arms' reach when they came to visit the inmates. At the far end of the corridor, set high in the wall, a small window looked out over a fifteen-by-fifty-foot exercise yard. This was the only natural light that made its way into the death house. Beneath this window sat a guard. At the near end of the corridor, alongside the door through which Stielow had entered, a second guard lounged on a chair. This dual watch would be maintained 24 hours a day. They both studied the newcomer with curious eyes.

So did the other inmates. As Stielow squeezed his bulk into a tiny cell, a guard handed him some tobacco and a pipe. When the guard asked if he wanted any books, Stielow shook his head. He didn't say that he couldn't read; he didn't have to, the guard just sensed it. As the barred door slammed shut behind him, Stielow took stock of his new surroundings. The cell measured eight feet from front to back, and six across, with most of that space being taken up by the bed. It stank of disinfectant and stale urine, and had white-painted stone walls that were sweaty with condensation. The wooden floor was uneven and the washbowl heavily stained. The whole unit reeked of despair – hot as Hades during the summer; freezing in winter.

At the time of Stielow's arrival, the death house contained 24 prisoners. Since it didn't have enough cells to accommodate them all, the overspill – usually those inmates whose cases were being appealed – were held in another, adjoining unit. Because Stielow's future could be measured in weeks rather than months, he was immediately placed in the death house proper, alongside some of America's most notorious killers. There was Hans Schmidt, the priapic German-born Catholic priest who had butchered his clandestine girlfriend. Another yellow press headline-maker was Oresto Shilitano, a psychotic 23-year-old Italian, dubbed the 'Paper Box Kid', who had blown away two cops when they disturbed him in the act of murdering another gangster. Without his guns Shilitano didn't amount to much, just a small, skinny punk with a pock-marked face that never stopped sneering. But the undoubted star of death row, the man whom the other inmates had unanimously elected their 'captain', occupied the third cell on the left.

If Stielow had seen photographs of former New York police lieutenant Charles Becker in the newspapers, then seeing him in the flesh must have been an unnerving experience. Two spells in the death house had put decades on the 45-year-old ex-New York Police Department cop. He was still tall, but the intimidating bulk that had terrified gangsters and fellow police officers alike was now a distant memory. Fear had chipped away at his muscular body, shrinking him into premature old age. It had been two and a half years since Becker first arrived on the row. Then, his natural air of authority had been unquestioned. It was Becker who had organised daily exercise routines; simple things like getting the guys to reach up and grasp hold of the bars of their cell door, then pull themselves up until their chin was level with their hands, before dropping down again. He drilled them like a sergeant major. Besides looking after his fellow inmates' physical well-being, Becker read aloud to them from newspapers and dime novels. He also mediated in their frequent disputes; his word was final.

But all that charisma had long since disappeared. Seeing Becker slumped on his bed, shrivelled and pale, and surrounded by books and stacks of newspapers, it was hard to believe that he had once been the most feared cop in New York, undisputed ruler of the Tenderloin, a twenty-block hellhole stuffed with brothels and illegal gambling dens. In this part of Manhattan, if you wanted to stay in business, you had to pay off the 'lootenant'. Becker pocketed thousands of dollars annually in kickbacks and protection money. Most Tenderloin veterans paid without quibble, accepting Becker's cut as an unavoidable expense of doing business; others grumbled without pause. One of the noisiest complainers was a short, fat gambler named Herman Rosenthal. He loathed Becker, badmouthing him constantly, always threatening that one day he would blow the whistle on Manhattan's 'millionaire cop'. Most dismissed Rosenthal as a cantankerous blowhard. Then the local grapevine started humming: Rosenthal had arranged a meeting with Charles S. Whitman, the local hotshot district attorney who was spearheading a crusade against police corruption. And, if the rumours were true, the number one item on the agenda was Lieutenant Charles Becker. On 16 July 1912, two days before Rosenthal's scheduled meeting with Whitman, the gambler was gunned down outside the Hotel Metropole on West 43rd Street. Whitman exploded with rage. It didn't matter that Becker's alibi at the time of the murder was unimpeachable; the DA would always believe that Becker had ordered the hit on Rosenthal to save his own neck.

In short order, the gunmen – four in number – were rounded up. Two weeks later, Becker was also arrested on a charge of having ordered the gangland slaying. In October 1912, all five defendants were sentenced to death and shipped off to Sing Sing. Becker still had clout, though, and his legal team put in plenty of hours to keep their client alive. On 24 February 1914 the Court of Appeals decided that the presiding judge in Becker's trial, Justice John W. Goff, had made several erroneous rulings that were inimical to the defendant, and they ordered a retrial. Becker's spell of freedom was brief and punctuated by a grim reminder of what might await him when, on 14 April 1914, the four young gunmen were duly dispatched in the electric chair. The following month, Becker stood trial for a second time. The outcome was utterly predictable and, on 22 May, he was again convicted and subsequently sentenced to death. A triumphant Whitman, who had prosecuted both trials, declared that the verdict 'speaks for itself'.[2]

When Stielow entered death row on that Monday evening, Becker was heaving a huge sigh of relief. He'd just heard that his execution – scheduled for the following Wednesday – had been stayed for 48 hours, to allow his lawyers time to plead for a new trial. Becker's eyes, deep-sunk and surrounded by black circles, stared lifelessly through the bars as Charlie was locked in his cell.

That first night, Stielow received his introduction to the death house rituals. At some point he would have noticed a single door, made from steel and heavily bolted, set deep into the wall immediately adjacent to the cell where Becker lay quaking. It was painted a drab green colour and Charlie learned that it was only ever opened on execution nights. Just a few well-varnished paces beyond it lay another door, this time painted yellow. Once that was opened, you were in the execution chamber. None of the men on death row knew this, because no inmate had ever returned after passing through 'the little green door'.[3] It was where life ended and death began.

As night fell and Stielow lay down on his bed, outside his cell door a single sixteen-candlepower bulb burned constantly. It never went off. The nights were always the worst in the death house. This was when the demons came out to play. Groans and occasional cries echoed in the darkness as tortured minds struggled for the merciful oblivion that sleep would bring. Every newcomer to the row found the first night especially hard. Charlie Stielow found it tougher than most. He knew that, barring a miracle, he had only seven weeks at the most to live.

Breakfast came early, at 7:00am. It had been prepared by two trusties – long term prisoners, usually, who posed no escape threat – in
a small kitchen that adjoined Principal Keeper Frederick Dorner's
office at the end of the death house. The trusties worked their way
along the row, handing over the meals and a mug of coffee with
outstretched arms to the inmates. When the plates were finished,
another trusty collected them.

After breakfast, Dorner visited Stielow and ran through the death
house rules. They were straightforward and unbending: three meals
a day, one brief spell of exercise in the yard between 10:00am and
midday – depending on the weather and the availability of guards – a
bath and shave once a week, and pre-approved visitors twice weekly.
All visitors needed to be screened, to ensure that any warring relatives of the condemned man didn't collide with each other in the
death house.

Charlie absorbed all this as best he could. There was no chance
that he'd be overwhelmed by visitors. His folks were too poor to
make the eight-hour train journey from Medina to Sing Sing, except
maybe right at the end, when all hope had expired. And he sure
wasn't expecting much in the way of legal assistance. All he could do
was wait and stare at the little green door. No one could remember
where the name came from, but no one ever called it anything else.
It was the axis around which everything in the death house pivoted.

As the morning dragged on, Stielow received his next caller, the
Reverend Anthony N. Petersen, who would attend him daily. Sing
Sing went out of its way to cater to every death row inmate's religious
persuasion. Beside the Protestant Petersen there was Rabbi Jacob
Goldstein, while Father William E. Cashin comforted the Catholics.

The final meal of the day was served early, at 3:45pm. After that
there was nothing except tedious monotony, fractured only by the
stomach-churning prospect of what lay ahead.

Later that same day, a guard brought Stielow some extraordinary and wholly unexpected news. Confounding all press predictions, David White had refused to abandon the doomed farmhand, and that morning had filed notice of appeal at the Albion courthouse. A copy had been forwarded to an infuriated Knickerbocker. The very act of appealing meant that the original death sentence would have to be stayed, as the appeal wasn't scheduled to be heard for at least two months.

Charlie Stielow's lease on life had been extended by probably as much as six months. Not everyone in the death house would receive such welcome news.

Next morning – 28 July – at 10:30, the main door of the death house swung open. Deputy Warden Charles Johnson, grim-faced, strode along the silent corridor. Every eye followed his tread. He walked up to Becker's cell and thrust a note through the bars. 'I have some bad news,' he said. 'Your appeal has been denied.' Becker's face, already pale, drained of all colour. 'Denied? Denied?'[4] he kept repeating to himself, as if unable to comprehend what he was hearing. Johnson told him that his new date with death had been set: Friday 30 July at 5:45am, fewer than 48 hours away. For the deeply superstitious Becker, who'd always had a dread of Fridays, the timing could not have been any more ironic.

Now the disgraced former cop's only chance of escaping the electric chair rested in the hands of just one person – the state governor. The omens weren't good. Of the 167 death row inmates in Sing Sing since New York State had switched its method of capital punishment from hanging to the electric chair, only seven had been reprieved by governor's decree. And Becker was fighting even greater odds than that. Because the district attorney who had put him on death row, Charles S. Whitman, was now the governor of New York State.

Like many lawyers, Whitman had ambitions far beyond the courtroom. And in the wake of the Becker conviction – hugely popular with the public – Manhattan's district attorney had set his sights firmly on the Executive Mansion in Albany. Voters adored Whitman. He was vigorous, still only 45 years old, and most important of all, he had nailed New York's dirtiest cop. Such credentials made him a shoo-in for the Republican nomination for the position of state governor. And so it proved. But Whitman's popularity cut right across the political spectrum and on 3 November 1914, the voters handed Whitman a landslide as he ousted the incumbent Martin H. Glynn and surged into Albany. As far as Whitman was concerned, Albany was just the first stop on the career path that he had mapped out for himself. His intention was to follow former New York governors Grover Cleveland and Theodore Roosevelt all the way to 1600 Pennsylvania Avenue, Washington DC. And he wasn't about to let a few quibbles about Charles Becker stand in the way.

The murmurings had begun early. Most centred on the ethical rights or wrongs of the same man both convicting a death row inmate and then deciding whether that person should live or die. Legal scholars declared it to be a situation unprecedented in American history. Displaying the dismissive arrogance that would hallmark his administration, Whitman brushed aside demands that Becker's clemency petition should be reviewed by the lieutenant governor, Edward Schoeneck, and announced that he, Whitman, would have the final say. Bookmakers were giving long odds against the vengeful governor extending mercy. If Becker's conviction had secured the governorship for Whitman, then he was damn sure that Becker's execution would keep him there.

Whitman made his decision known that same night: there would be no reprieve.

Whenever an execution drew near, tensions inside the death house soared with each passing hour. Ordinarily, Becker would have occupied the cell to the immediate left of the green door. This was always reserved for the next person to take that brief walk. The well-rehearsed routine was: exit the cell, walk just a couple of paces, swing left into the short corridor, a few steps and into the death chamber. But on this occasion that cell was occupied by Samuel Haynes. He had originally been scheduled to die on the same morning as Becker, but when Becker won his temporary stay, Haynes was similarly respited. (There was no altruism at work here, just money. This way, rather than pay the executioner twice, the state could escape with paying a single set of expenses for a double execution.) Now Haynes, too, would die on Friday morning. And he was occupying the customary holding cell.

The parallels between Haynes and Stielow were striking. Both were illiterate farmhands and both had been convicted of shooting their employers. On 2 June 1914, Haynes, drunk on rough cider, had, for some reason, gunned down John Harrison and his wife at their farm in Patterson, New York. It was a crime wholly out of keeping with his hitherto blameless background. His culpability was beyond doubt; so was the sentence. In contrast to all the hullabaloo and headlines surrounding Becker's fate, the press had exhibited no interest whatsoever in Haynes. In the eyes of everyone, except the law, he was invisible. In his twelve months on death row, Haynes had received no visitors, no books, no papers, and no lawyer had come to discuss his case. His solitary friend throughout this lonely ordeal was John Lowry, a New York pastor who regularly visited Sing Sing to comfort those convicts without relatives or friends. Haynes asked Lowry if he would accompany him on that last terrible walk. Lowry said yes.

As the final countdown began, two extra guards were drafted into the death house. Their job was to sit in front of the cells housing Becker and Haynes until the time came.

At midnight on the last night of Becker's life, the execution routine swung into action. Large white sheets, more like curtains, were draped over the front of every cell, as a palliative to the inmates' feelings and also to prevent them from witnessing the ritual. According to one death row inmate who lived to tell the tale, Roland B. Molineux, some men lay on the floor to peek under the sheet. If anyone did so tonight, he would have seen Becker sitting on his bed, writing furiously. Unlike before, his cell looked spartan. Earlier that evening Becker's personal belongings – his tobacco, cigarettes and books – had been distributed to the other inmates. Now he was left with just a few sheets of paper and a pen. Enough to fire one last vitriolic blast at Whitman, professing his utter innocence of the crime for which he was about to be executed.

Just a few yards behind Becker's cell, beyond the intervening wall, a short, wiry man with a shiny bald head and dressed in a grey suit had much to occupy his mind. Most days, 45-year-old John W. Hulbert worked as the chief electrician at Auburn Prison, but tonight he had travelled down to Sing Sing in his secondary capacity: state executioner. This would be his first time in charge. The previous executioner, Edward P. Davis, had resigned when the prison board baulked at his demand that they increase his fee of $50 an execution. Hulbert, previously Davis's assistant, stepped into the other man's shoes. It was Davis who had put Becker's alleged hirelings to death. Now it would be Hulbert's turn to flick the switch on the mastermind of the murderous conspiracy. He moved quickly around the room. The death chamber always surprised first-time visitors. Expecting some gloomy medieval dungeon, they found themselves in a room that was light and airy, with white concrete walls and a white-painted ceiling. The chair itself, carved from 300 pounds of light-coloured oak and festooned with leather straps and buckles, stood on a thick rubber mat and was secured to the highly varnished floor by sturdy metal bolts. A few paces to the left of the chair a yellow door opened onto the short corridor that led to the death house. Just in front of the yellow door, and slightly to the left, two rows of wooden pews ran along the side wall. These were for the witnesses. There were always more applications than available seats, but tonight, for Becker's execution, the warden's office had been inundated with requests.

Hulbert inspected every inch of the lethal hardware. He needed to be ultra-cautious. Just 24 hours before the other four Rosenthal killers' date with death, someone – believed to be a prison employee – had taken a hammer to the electric chair's dynamo and smashed it to bits. That attempt to stall the executions had failed; Davis had a new dynamo rushed to the prison from New York City, but it provided clear proof of how Becker's execution had polarised public opinion. Tonight, though, Hulbert found nothing untoward. He examined the heavy, insulated wiring that ran to a wall-mounted control board, the two copper electrodes – one for the head, the other for the leg – and he also made sure that the bucket that stood beside the chair contained an adequate supply of salt water. This would improve the conductivity between copper and flesh. With his meters in place, Hulbert ran one last test of the circuitry. The dynamo whined as he checked the dials. Everything was in order. Now it was just a question of waiting.

Becker's final hours were spent with his own priest, Father James Curry, and the prison chaplain, Father Cashin. He received Holy Communion and, at 5:00am, he was given the last rites of the Catholic Church. In between the prayers and the hymns, Becker had one last request: he pleaded to be executed before Haynes. His reasoning was stark; he didn't want to sit in any chair – not even one hooked up to 2,000 volts of life-sapping energy – that had been occupied 'by a black man'. His wish was granted.

At 5:40am, Dorner reached Becker's cell and told him that the time had come. Becker staggered to his feet and tried to walk, but his legs had turned to mush. Utterly broken, he was propped up like a puppet between two guards and hefted from his cell. His two priests followed, still intoning prayers. From behind the curtains, a few muffled goodbyes echoed along the row.

Four minutes later, the satanic whine of the dynamo seemed to bore right through the death house. Then again. Then once more. For the men cowering behind the white curtains, it was a blood-chilling reminder of what awaited them. A few minutes of silence were followed by the sound of the death chamber door swinging open once more.

It was time for Samuel Haynes to call out his farewells. Unlike Becker, he seemed calm, serene almost, and resigned to his fate. He walked stoically to his doom, fingers wrapped around a Bible. Behind him the little green door clanked shut for the final time that morning.

Outside the main gates a huge crowd had gathered in the dim dawn light to hear news of Becker's demise. New York State hadn't generated this much judicial excitement since Chester Gillette (later fictionalised as Clyde Griffiths in Theodore Dreiser's *An American Tragedy*) went to the chair in Auburn some seven years earlier. Wary guards, armed with rifles, kept the crowds in check. When the formal announcement was made, reporters ran to phone the news of Becker's death to the outside world. Few stayed to hear the Haynes notice.

Inside the death house, it was eerily quiet. Huddled in his cell, behind the white sheet, Charlie Stielow had just endured his first experience of the machinery of state-sponsored death. It was awesome, efficient and the grimmest possible reminder that in a matter of months – maybe a year if the appeals process dragged on – it would be his turn to cry out those last goodbyes and walk those final yards.

10

The Killing Machine

As the twelve official witnesses filed shakily up the wooden staircase that led out of Sing Sing's death chamber and into the still morning light, most were ashen-faced and some still had the stink of burning flesh in their nostrils. Becker had died hard. The straps securing him to the chair had slipped, while a similar mishap affected the poorly secured face mask. In all, it took three jolts of electricity and eight long minutes to kill Becker. To the witnesses it felt more like a year. Most had been shattered by the experience and, as they gulped in refreshing draughts of cool morning air, few paid any attention to a sturdily built middle-aged man who was pacing the prison yard some way off. Had they drawn nearer, they would have seen that the anguish they felt was mirrored in his face.

Thomas Mott Osborne had been the warden at Sing Sing since 1 December 1914, and in that time no fewer than ten inmates had walked 'the final mile'. On each occasion Osborne, an implacable foe of capital punishment, had contrived to absent himself from the prison. Tonight, though, his plans had gone awry and he had been obliged to remain at Sing Sing. Despite this, he had still refused to enter the death chamber, delegating the official duties to his deputy, Charles Johnson.

As the witnesses made their way groggily towards the front gate, Osborne gave them a hard stare. He wondered if any shared his conviction that the state had just executed an innocent man. Like just about everyone else, Osborne accepted that Becker was rotten down to his boot heels – no surprises there because the NYPD was riddled with crooked cops – but gut instinct told him that Becker's murder conviction just didn't smell right. And Osborne wasn't the kind to internalise his doubts. He'd blasted Whitman to anyone who would listen and that meant the press. As a result, seven months into the job as warden and Osborne was already fighting for survival.

Ruffling feathers was nothing new for Osborne. After many years in politics, including a spell as mayor of Auburn, at the age of 54 he was appointed chairman of the New York State Commission on Prison Reform. He immediately hit the headlines with his unconventional methods. To gain some insight into prison life, the flamboyant Osborne contrived to get himself 'sentenced' to a week in Auburn Prison as convict 'Thomas Brown #33,333X'. On his release he published his findings in a book, *Within Prison Walls* (1914). It caused a sensation. Osborne proselytised that no one, not even the most hardened recidivist, was beyond salvation. This idea, which was revolutionary, even heretical in some quarters, had made Osborne one of the most divisive figures in American penology – idealised and loathed in equal measure.

When, in late 1914, the wardenship at Sing Sing fell vacant, Osborne lobbied hard for the post. What gave his job application added piquancy were his highly unusual financial circumstances – he was a multi-millionaire. His Auburn-based family had made a fortune in manufacturing, but Osborne felt called to a life of public service. Opponents argued that it was madness to appoint a rebel like Osborne to such a sensitive post, where his financial muscle would make him virtually unmanageable; but amid a storm of controversy, and against all odds, Osborne landed the job. His immediate boss, Superintendent of Prisons John B. Riley, a protégé of Whitman's, was confident that he could handle this trust-fund dilettante. Except it didn't work out that way. Osborne's reforming zeal was immune to any form of outside meddling. Riley, pushed to the sidelines, fought back viciously. He initiated a whispering campaign that Osborne was coddling the prisoners, that he was hell-bent on establishing a 'Convict Republic'.[1] Osborne, for his part, merely shrugged off the barbs and continued his task of humanising America's most notorious prison.

His most radical innovation was a concept he had helped initiate at Auburn Prison. The Mutual Welfare League (MWL) was a charitably funded organisation that set out to give prisoners a degree of autonomy over their day-to-day life. Convicts could elect delegates to vote on prison matters and even hold *ad hoc* courts to punish transgressors. Under Osborne's auspices, a chapter of the MWL was established at Sing Sing. The League's motto was: 'Do good, make good.'[2] Elam Lynds would have choked on his breakfast.

The MWL's reach was wide-ranging. For instance, on this particular morning, it was the MWL that ensured that Samuel Haynes got a decent burial. Unlike Becker, whose wife was waiting to claim her husband's body,* Haynes had no one to claim his mortal remains. The League had searched high and low for relatives of the condemned man, and when none could be found, it had paid for Haynes to be buried in 'Gallery 25', the little graveyard on a hill by the prison, so called because, originally, there had been 24 cell galleries in the death house itself, and the inmates always referred to the cemetery as 'the final gallery'.

With a simple ceremony, attended by Osborne, Pastor Lowry and few others, Haynes was laid to rest. Afterwards, Osborne walked slowly back to his office and right into the middle of a bureaucratic tempest. It transpired that one of the execution witnesses had been an agent of Riley's called Patrick H. McDonald. Osborne had thought that McDonald was there solely to witness the execution. But Riley had other plans. After the execution, McDonald had toured the prison unsupervised, in a desperate search to dig up any dirt on the warden. Osborne's first intimation of this duplicity came when a convict showed him a letter that McDonald had produced. It had

---

* A silver plate, inscribed 'Murdered July 30, 1915 by Governor Whitman', was torn off Becker's coffin by the police before it proceeded to its final resting place at Woodlawn Cemetery in the Bronx.

been signed by John B. Riley and it authorised McDonald to appropriate any records he saw fit, in order 'that they may be placed on file in this department [New York State Prison Department]'.[3] Worse still, another trusty told Osborne that McDonald had removed a stack of records from the warden's office. Osborne hit the roof. Furious at being duped, he went looking for McDonald. But the agent had left the prison. Osborne rounded up two officers, jumped in his automobile and headed for the train station. They caught up with McDonald on the platform, as he awaited the 10:12 to Albany. Osborne rushed up to him. 'I want those papers which you took from my office,' he panted.

McDonald stood his ground. 'You can't have them,' he said, adding that if the other two men were not present he would give Osborne 'a good licking'.[4] At this, Osborne grabbed hold of McDonald's yellow satchel with its stash of paperwork. McDonald fought back, swinging punches, and had to be restrained until a police officer arrived and he was placed under arrest. Round one had gone to Osborne, who returned the documents to his office where he locked them away in a safe.

Round two was fought later that same day. Whitman blew his top upon hearing how his official representative had been manhandled. He telephoned Sing Sing and ordered Osborne to get himself immediately to Albany. All pretence at civility had vanished. The hitherto private feud between Whitman and Osborne was now an ugly open wound. Speaking later to the press, Whitman delivered a heated and very public dressing-down to Osborne. By contrast, Osborne was much cooler. He told reporters that he had not been asked to resign and had no intention of so doing: 'I told the governor I was a Quaker – ready to turn the other cheek.'[5] By day's end, it was clear that Sing Sing was a powder keg waiting to blow.

That same day, almost 400 miles north-west of Sing Sing, Orleans
County was enduring its own crisis. Just hours after Becker and
Haynes were electrocuted, the board of supervisors had once again
convened in an effort to cure the financial headache that the Shelby
murders had inflicted on the county. The supervisors listened to a
glum report. According to the treasurer, putting Charlie Stielow in
the death house had cost the county approximately $12,000. And the
bills were still flooding in. Detective Newton was leading the money
grab. He'd already disbursed the $3,000 previously allocated to
investigators – this was in addition to the $500 reward that he'd per-
sonally pocketed – and he now presented the county with another
bill for $719.06, boosting the total paid to detectives to $4,219.06.
Everybody wanted a slice of the Stielow pie. Henry Schultz filed a
claim for $114 for his chauffeuring duties, while the Orleans House
hotel requested $124.19 for expenses incurred. Sheriff Bartlett got
in on the act by submitting a bill for $127.65, for summoning jurors
and escorting the prisoners to Auburn and Sing Sing. Hamilton and
Knickerbocker had also freshened up their claims, while the latter
managed to get his associate, Harold S. Blake, on the payroll. The
county treasurer reckoned that these services alone would cost the
beleaguered Orleans County taxpayers an additional $2,000. Such
onerous demands meant that a desperately needed highway improvement scheme would have to be shelved unless the county approved
a special $8,000 bond issue. The meeting broke up with the county
treasurer grumpily announcing that no more Stielow-related bills
would be paid until the November annual meeting.

Over the days and weeks, Charlie Stielow slowly got to grips with
the unvarying routine of the death house. He had no visitors and
very few letters. What correspondence he did receive had to be read
out to him. Most of it originated from David White, whose stalwart

support remained undiminished. He told Charlie that he was trying to uncover new evidence that might lead to a retrial. But with no money and few allies, he was being repeatedly stymied in his hunt for new witnesses. He urged Stielow not to lose heart. Easy enough to say – when you didn't have to spend all day staring at that green door.

It next opened around dawn on 27 August 1915, this time for Karol Draniewicz, a 22-year-old Russian-born lowlife who bossed a New York gang that exploited recent Slav immigrants. Using a group of attractive women as bait, the gang lured labourers to an apartment where they were first drugged, then relieved of their wallets. But Ivan Martysewicz was tougher than most. And when he failed to keel over after downing one of Draniewicz's mind-blowing cocktails, he was shoehorned clumsily into a trunk. It was the slamming of the lid that broke Martysewicz's neck and took Draniewicz to the chair; all for $2 and a cheap watch.

But the Sing Sing death machine hit peak performance one week later, in the early hours of 3 September, when five men were executed with a conveyor-belt efficiency that Henry Ford might have admired. The killings began at 5:00am when Antonio Salemme was strapped into the chair, and ended 61 minutes later with the death of William Perry. In between came Pasquale Venditti, Louis M. Roach and Thomas Tarpey. Tarpey, an English ex-soldier, had marched to the chair at such a pace that Father Cashin struggled to keep up. As the guards fumbled to adjust the chest strap, Tarpey had looked on disdainfully and remarked: 'It's a tough job, boys.'[6] True to tradition, Perry, the only African-American of the five, was executed last. The prison hierarchy saw no point in inflaming racial sensibilities, even under these harrowing circumstances.

Five men executed in one night was not a record – just three years earlier, Sing Sing had resurrected memories of the 18th-century hanging sprees at Tyburn Tree, when seven men were electrocuted in just over an hour – but never again would the 'big house' stage slaughter on such a scale. Osborne, predictably, was nowhere to be seen. At the end of his night's work, executioner John W. Hulbert pocketed 250 bucks and caught the first train back to Auburn, careful as always to dodge the reporters and, more importantly, the photographers. His nerves were never good at the best of times and throughout his career he remained notoriously camera-shy, fearing retribution from a vengeful relative.

———

As the days began to shorten and the thermometer fell, summer's killing frenzy in the death house also cooled off. For the next three months an uneasy hiatus took hold. But Sing Sing never drifted far from the headlines. Osborne, utterly determined to push through his reforms, caused jaws to drop with his announcement that convicts would be allowed to marry. Disbelief escalated to indignant outrage when it emerged that he had placed certain trusties on an unofficial day release scheme (none let him down, all returned to the prison at sundown).

As the press criticism intensified, Osborne took steps to cover his rear end. Shortly after the Becker execution he had fired Charles Johnson and brought in Spencer Miller, Jr. as his deputy warden. Miller, still only 24 years old, had left Columbia University a year earlier, burning with idealistic zeal. He was a wholehearted convert to Osborne's doctrine of inmate rehabilitation and he approached his responsibilities with a Calvinist intensity. Each day he inspected every corridor, kitchen, laundry and lavatory to ensure that standards of cleanliness were being maintained. Part of his route took him through the death house. He came to know all the inmates by their first names, passing each cell door and exchanging a few words with the occupant. Most were hoodlums, a few were slighted lovers, others were men who had simply snapped under pressure.

And then there was Charlie Stielow.

On each visit, Miller found himself spending more and more time outside Stielow's cell. There was something in Stielow's open-faced manner that resonated with Miller. Stielow wasn't tough, like many of the other death house inmates, some of whom actually bragged of the murders they had committed. No, he was almost childlike in his speech and in his insistence that he hadn't committed the crimes for which he'd been sentenced. Miller might have been a rookie, but he was no fool. As any round of Sing Sing's cells would confirm, the prison was full of 'innocent' men, but Stielow's guileless manner held the ring of truth.

When Miller began to quiz Stielow about the Shelby murders, Charlie showed him the stack of letters that White had written to him, handing them shyly through the barred door. The fact that David White had continued the correspondence impressed Miller; most court-appointed lawyers tended to vanish into the ether once a verdict had been delivered. But as White's letters made plain, the Medina attorney had no intention of abandoning Charlie to his fate. Miller familiarised himself with the case. Every time White sent a new letter, Miller would read it out to the grateful Stielow, keeping him up to speed on the current status of his case. Gradually, as the two men talked, the kernel of doubt continued to germinate in Miller's mind.

Eventually, Miller took these misgivings to Osborne. His timing could not have been worse. Osborne's health had collapsed, undermined by the constant sniping from outside. He was exhausted. And on 31 October 1915, citing the need for a complete rest, he took temporary leave of his office and went home to Auburn. In his absence, his friend Professor George W. Kirchway of Columbia University agreed to act as temporary warden.

John B. Riley smelled an opportunity. He immediately accused Osborne of exceeding his authority by taking an unauthorised break and he set in motion plans to oust Osborne permanently from the post. Governor Whitman was his usual cagey self, holding back on giving Riley his wholehearted support, unsure about Osborne's influence in the penal community. The convicts at Sing Sing made no secret of where their sympathies lay. On 3 November they published an open letter to Osborne, praying for his health and an early return to work. But the attacks on Osborne mounted daily. His former deputy, Charles Johnson, bitterly resentful of the way he had been unceremoniously dumped in favour of Miller, added his voice to the chorus of disapproval. By the end of November, Osborne was under siege from all sides.

Miller, meanwhile, had immersed himself in Stielow's predicament and, on 28 November, he brought the condemned prisoner a rare nugget of good news. A letter from White mentioned some tantalising new evidence. According to as yet unnamed witnesses, a stranger had been seen at the Phelps house on the night of the killings, a fact that the prosecution had known and deliberately suppressed. Apparently, an extra place had been set at the breakfast table and the guest room showed signs of recent occupancy. Even more intriguing were vague claims that some hobo currently serving a prison sentence for an unrelated, though similar, crime had been boasting of his involvement in the Shelby murders. White ended on an upbeat note. He intended drafting a motion for a new trial, based on these new revelations. If that failed, all was not lost, he said; there was still the appeal which was scheduled for the new year.

Stielow barely had time to savour these good tidings before a bombshell hit the prison. In early December, press reports announced that the Westchester grand jury was investigating how Sing Sing was being run. Reading the subtext left no doubt that opponents of prison reform had taken dead aim at Osborne. On 13 December, Westchester Assistant District Attorney William J. Fallon brandished a fistful of affidavits sworn by convicts, all of which alleged that Osborne was an 'unfit'[7] person to run Sing Sing. Although the actual detail contained in these affidavits would always remain suspiciously nebulous, Fallon, a brilliant attorney with the ethics of a Tenderloin pimp, leaked enough hints to confirm that Osborne was accused of having had sex with several prison inmates. Suddenly, Osborne's battle for survival took on a whole new dimension.

For Charlie Stielow, though, there were more pressing concerns. The morning of 17 December saw two more cells on death row vacated, as Worthy Tolley and Ludwig Marquardt took their final walk into the unknown. Warden Kirchway had no more stomach for the grisly ritual than did Osborne, and he refused point-blank to attend the executions. So did Miller. The buck finally stopped with Principal Keeper Frederick Dorner. Although no advocate of the death penalty, Dorner had a strong sense of duty. There were no hitches.

In the meantime, White's efforts had borne some fruit. The Court of Appeals had announced that it would hear Stielow's appeal in late January 1916. There would be plenty for White and the appeal court judges to digest; the trial transcript alone ran to more than 1,000 pages.

As Charlie saw in the New Year, he wondered if it would be his last. Every hope was pinned on that appeal. If it failed, there could be only one outcome, as the chances of Whitman extending executive clemency to a convicted double murderer were non-existent. All Stielow could do now was to pray and wait, pray and wait.

For Antonio Ponton, a 28-year-old Puerto Rican law student who had stabbed his girlfriend in a lover's quarrel, the praying and waiting ended on the morning of 7 January. It was just before 5:45am. The witnesses, who had gathered in the warden's office, were being led by Dorner through the sub-zero inky blackness to the death house. Just as Dorner reached the door, a guard came running to say that an inmate in the prison's general population, James Hill, had escaped and clambered onto the prison's roof. Dorner immediately ordered the witnesses back to the warden's office. He then rushed through the death chamber, past a startled Hulbert, and into the cells. Ponton, who had already taken the first steps of what was supposed to be his last walk, was shoved back into his cell and locked down. Understandably, the strain proved too much and Ponton collapsed. He wasn't alone. When news of the unexpected delay reached Hulbert, he also fell in a dead faint. Two doctors rushed forward to attend the ailing executioner. Dorner then left to join the pursuit of Hill. After a rooftop chase that lasted half an hour, Hill was recaptured.

Just minutes later, Sing Sing's death machine swung back into action. The witnesses took their seats in the polished wooden pews. Hulbert, still groggy, resumed his place by the controls and gave a tentative nod of his large, bald head. The door swung open. Ponton was brought in. By this time his shattered nerves had taken away the use of his legs. Two burly guards had to physically carry Ponton into the death chamber like a sack of potatoes. He was strapped into the chair and promptly given three jolts of electricity that ended his misery. After the execution, a quaking Hulbert had to be confined to the prison hospital.

Spencer Miller had witnessed all this activity from outside the death house, his face awash with tears. Many of the witnesses, too, were teetering on the verge of hysteria as they exited the death house. They huddled in a group while Miller sobbed out an impassioned protest against the evils of capital punishment. And then they left.

Within a week, Sing Sing's death house was once again hitting the headlines. On the morning of 13 January, keepers Frank Kagley and Peter Fitzmaurice were making their rounds when they found gangland hoodlum Angelo Leggio hanging from a bedsheet tied to a bar on his door. Just three days beforehand, Leggio's final appeal for a new trial had been turned down. According to the guards, they had seen Leggio apparently asleep on his bed at 5:30am. Just six or seven minutes later, as they made a second pass, they found him hanging from the sheet. For the next twenty minutes the death house resembled a French farce. Because strict prison rules prohibited death house guards from carrying keys, Kagley and Fitzmaurice were unable to

1. Charles Stielow, convicted of double murder and sentenced to the electric chair

2. District Attorney John Knickerbocker, pictured in 1905
for Albion Bar Association

3. Thomas Mott Osborne, warden of Sing Sing and a leading campaigner in the fight to save Stielow

4. Governor Charles S. Whitman on the day of his inauguration, 1 January 1915

5. Grace Humiston, the lawyer who became America's greatest female detective

6. *(below)* Inez Milholland Boissevain, leading the Suffrage Parade in Washington, DC, on 3 March 1913

7. Erwin King: was he a double murderer?

8. Philip O. Gravelle and the comparison microscope that he invented with John H. Fisher

let themselves out of the top security wing. All they could do was bellow at the top of their lungs in the hope that someone would hear. Eventually someone did. But the delay turned farce into tragedy. When the physicians did arrive they worked on Leggio for several minutes with a pulmotor,* but all to no avail. Warden Kirchway told the press: 'Leggio was not crazy, but was depressed when he heard that he could not get a new trial ... we have not found that the keepers were at fault.'[8] As a direct result of this fiasco, Kirchway ordered that death house guards should carry keys on them at all times.

Like most of the population, Osborne could only read about Sing Sing's debacles in the newspapers. He was not just involved in a struggle to save his career and reputation, but he was fighting the very real prospect of becoming a prison convict at the very institution he had run. And this time, there would be no 'get-out-of-jail-free' card to play after one week. Riley and Whitman were going for the jugular. On 17 January, Osborne was formally charged with having given perjured testimony to the Westchester grand jury that was investigating Sing Sing. Already being written off in the press as the 'former warden of Sing Sing',[9] Osborne pleaded not guilty.

A cold, sleety rain was falling in Albany on the morning of 21 January, when White addressed the Court of Appeals, laying out his arguments for a new trial, citing fresh testimony about a mysterious stranger. The judges were not impressed. Neither was Knickerbocker. He argued that justice had been done, had been seen to be done, and that all this shilly-shallying around was a waste of everyone's time

---

* A now obsolete apparatus that worked as a kind of artificial respirator, pumping oxygen into the lungs.

and an unnecessary drain on the already beleaguered taxpayers of Orleans County. Knickerbocker was addressing a reduced panel of judges. Since the Stielow trial, Justice Pound had been elevated to the Court of Appeals, and had, quite properly, recused himself from the court's deliberations. In the event, the court reserved judgement and said it would deliver its decision the following month.

The news was passed to Stielow that night at the prison, and the former farmhand resigned himself to another agonising wait. He had now been incarcerated for nine months and the enforced indolence had added several pounds to his already bulky frame. On the rare occasions when Stielow made it to the exercise yard, his clumsiness had made him a figure of fun to the other inmates, so he had stopped making the effort. The double chin was becoming more noticeable; so too were the ghastly pallor and sunken eyes that seemed to affect all death house inmates. Months spent in the shadow of the electric chair could drain even the strongest constitution.

Someone who knew this better than most was Giuseppe Marendi. Back in February 1914, this low-level thug had shot and killed two Brooklyn police officers during a routine stop and search. For two years his defence team had argued that since neither shooting had been premeditated, he should not have been convicted of first-degree murder. The courts disagreed and now it fell to John W. Hulbert to finish the legal process. On 4 February 1916, Marendi walked to his death. Right to the end, even as he was being buckled into the chair, he protested his innocence. He kept protesting right up until the time the juice hit him.

Marendi was the twelfth person in just six months that Stielow had seen shuffle off to his doom. Every time a cell became vacant, another condemned inmate was moved in from the holding cells in the punishment block that were still being used to ease death row overcrowding.

There was not long to wait until the conveyor belt inched along another notch. On 18 February time finally ran out for Hans

Schmidt, 33, the German-born Catholic priest and former medical student who had turned his hand to abortion, counterfeiting and murder (see chapter 9). His story was incredible. In September 1913, Schmidt had slashed the throat of 21-year-old Anna Aumüller, whom he had 'married' in a bizarre self-conducted ceremony. Anna's crime had been to fall pregnant. Drawing on his medical training, Schmidt then reduced Anna to handy-sized chunks that he lobbed into the Hudson. Culpability wasn't an issue, just his sanity. At his first trial, the jury voted 10–2 for conviction, with the holdouts convinced that Schmidt was a raving lunatic. A second jury was less charitable and he was sentenced to the electric chair. Eighteen months in the death house did nothing to dilute his formidable powers of self-delusion. In a statement issued just before his execution, he excoriated the system that had brought him to this end, saying 'I happen to be the victim this time,' adding his hope that his 'judicial murder will help to abolish executions, for not one-third of the men who have been in the death chamber with me, including Becker, were guilty of murder.'[10]

In the parlance of the death house, Schmidt 'died game'. After napping for three hours, he sprang to his feet when the time came and strode confidently from his cell. Just before leaving the death house, he called back to the twenty remaining inmates, hidden behind the white sheets, 'Goodbye, boys.'[11] They answered faintly.

There were seventeen official witnesses on hand to watch Schmidt die. Since taking over from Osborne, Kirchway had adopted a policy of banning reporters from all executions, but the press clamour surrounding Schmidt – the only priest ever executed in the US – forced him to relax the rule. As the guards steered Schmidt towards the chair, those present were treated to another of his homilies. 'Gentlemen, I ask forgiveness of those whom I have offended or scandalised. I forgive all who have injured me,' he intoned, before sitting down, quickly and unaided, placing his arms neatly in place so that the straps could be tightened. As the helmet containing the electrode was lowered over his head, the sermon droned on: 'My last word is to say goodbye to my dear old mother.'[12] He spoke no more. Hulbert's lever crunched over, the dynamo began to whine, and one of the most extraordinary killers in American history was silenced.

Inside his cell, Stielow reached for the German Bible that had been his constant companion during his time on the row. Although he had never been a particularly religious man, like many in his position he was now clutching at every available straw. The next 72 hours would be the worst of his time behind bars. All he could do was wait, knowing that on the following Monday his fate would be announced. White was confident that he'd presented a strong case. Now it was up to the Court of Appeals in Albany. Their decision, released on 22 February, was terse to the point of derision: 'From an examination of the record, it is inconceivable that the jury could have rendered any other verdict.'[13] Judges Bartlett, Hiscock, Collin, Cuddeback, Hogan and Seabury were unanimous in their verdict: conviction and sentence were upheld.

Stielow got the news that night in his cell. It was a crushing blow. Worse still, a new death warrant had already been made out. He would go to the electric chair on the morning of Friday 14 April.

11

Mrs Humiston Lends A Hand

Spencer Miller wasn't the only Sing Sing staff officer with grave doubts about Charlie Stielow's guilt. During his time on death row, the dull-witted farmhand had also impressed the guards with his simple sincerity. They liked the way he didn't make waves, didn't get involved in fights or arguments, didn't brag about his crimes, and generally spent most days slumped on the bed in his cell, just staring off vacantly into space. Even the harshest of all juries – his fellow inmates – just couldn't picture him as a cold-blooded double murderer. One, Joseph Hanel, a 36-year-old butler who'd supplemented his wages by killing and robbing his elderly employer, Mrs Julia Heilner, even shared his doubts with Miller. 'Boss, I know there isn't a chance in the world of me beating the chair, but they shouldn't be let crown that Dutchman [Stielow] [*sic*],' he said. 'He didn't kill those folks they say he did any more than you did.'

'What makes you say that, Joe?' Miller asked.

'Because I know it,' Hanel replied. 'Everyone here knows it ... You can't fool the men in here very much. They are pretty wise guys in some things. They know this fellow is in wrong ... You ought to get busy and try and save him.'[1]

Miller agreed. But at this juncture, personal impressions counted for naught; what Stielow desperately needed was fresh evidence. And that was in perilously short supply. Also, the clock was ticking. There were now fewer than six weeks until his execution date.

Each day Revd Petersen called to offer whatever solace he could. Like all the religious advisers at Sing Sing, Petersen stressed the concept of redemption; a crime confessed was a crime expiated in the eyes of the Lord. Problem was, Charlie refused to budge from his insistence that he was innocent. Instead, he repeated details of the harrowing interrogation he'd suffered at the hands of Newton and his cronies, and how they'd tricked him into making that spurious confession. As Charlie expanded on his plight, Petersen's concern mounted. Finally, he went to Miller, only to discover that he was preaching to the choir; Sing Sing's assistant warden was already convinced that Charlie was an innocent man.

Which is more than could be said about Walter Watson. This 41-year-old delivery driver swore that his wasn't the hand on the carving knife that halted the life of his estranged wife, Elizabeth, at their home in Brooklyn on 26 March 1915. Considering that his son, Thomas, had witnessed the whole grisly business, Watson's denials struggled for credibility. Thomas had also helped the police in their efforts to track down his murderous father. At his trial, Watson could only sit and fume as his own son condemned him to the chair. On his lawyer's advice, he chose not to give evidence on his own behalf. Since his conviction he'd been more than making up for that silence. It didn't do him any good.

On 3 March 1916, still bemoaning the injustice of it all, Watson walked those final few yards. His protestations continued right up until the final moment. 'I am innocent! Heaven help us. I am innocent!'[2] he cried as the death mask was clamped on his head. As was customary nowadays, Dorner was in charge of the execution protocol. Warden Kirchway had once again absented himself from the prison.

There was a poignant end to the night's grim proceedings. After Watson's body was removed from the chair and carried to the makeshift morgue that adjoined the death chamber to await autopsy, Father Cashin reached inside his cassock for an envelope that Watson had given him at the last moment, together with a request that it not be opened until he was dead. Inside was a note that read: 'This envelope contains a flower from my dear wife's grave. Please bury it with me and let it be on my breast. It is a token of remembrance of my wife, whom I always loved. May our souls rest in peace.'[3] Cashin complied with the dead man's final wish.

Watson's execution, the fourteenth since Stielow had been housed on death row, marked a sharp raising of the stakes for the German farmhand. There was now no one standing between him and the electric chair.

On 15 March, the 'Save Stielow' campaign received a boost when Justice Arthur S. Tompkins, sitting in the Supreme Court at White Plains, New York threw out the perjury charge against Osborne. Having heard the case by the district attorney of Westchester County, Tompkins ruled that Osborne need not present evidence to establish his innocence. 'I direct a verdict of acquittal,' said the judge, 'and dismiss the indictment.' Handclapping, foot stamping and cheering broke out among the spectators. Kirchway, one of those present at the court hearing, couldn't mask his delight at the verdict. Asked for his reaction, he laughed and said: 'Well, I'm afraid I'll lose my job soon.'[4]

But Osborne wasn't out of the woods just yet. There was still another charge on the docket, accusing him of neglect of duty and 'unnatural and unlawful acts'.[5] A hearing was set for 10 April, just four days before Charlie Stielow was scheduled to die.

In the meantime, Revd Petersen had been putting pen to paper. In March he wrote to David White, expressing his belief that Stielow was innocent and offering his services in any way to help the cause. White, isolated in Orleans County and grateful to have been thrown a lifeline, immediately contacted Petersen, thanking him and explaining his relative inexperience in such matters. Petersen informed him that Miller was also pulling strings, and that he'd spoken to John Lowry, the veteran New York pastor who was well known to all the death row inmates. Lowry had a Fifth Avenue address and he had contacts. These included the Humanitarian Cult (HC). Membership of the 250-strong New York-based Cult required just two qualifications; a big heart and nerves of steel. It had been founded by a lawyer named Mischa Appelbaum with the twin goals of helping the underprivileged and abolishing capital punishment. Appelbaum, who was constantly being bombarded by requests for assistance, told Lowry that he would examine the Stielow case but made no promises.

Like most political activists, Appelbaum ran a pragmatic eye over the case, to gauge the amount of publicity the HC could extract from the situation. The answer, he decided, was considerable. What it required was a high-profile campaign to save Charlie Stielow's life. And for that he needed someone, preferably a lawyer, who knew how to exploit the press to the Cult's best advantage. There were several attorneys affiliated with the Humanitarian Cult; all were earnest and steadfast, but none had the kind of moxie that Appelbaum was after. He needed a dyed-in-the-wool headline-maker. Appelbaum began a desperate search for someone who fitted the bill.

As the days passed, with little movement in Stielow's situation, tension began to mount. Crunch time came on 10 April, when White travelled to Albany to argue before Whitman that Stielow deserved a new trial. Whitman just shrugged. The courts, he said, had settled this case definitively; as for White's so-called new evidence, well, most of it came from Stielow's own family, and they could hardly be expected to be impartial witnesses, could they? White pleaded for a stay of three months, promising more revelations to come. Eventually, Whitman did agree to review the case in depth, but White left the meeting disillusioned and riddled with despair. The only bright spot on an otherwise gloomy horizon was Whitman's decision to delay Stielow's execution for five days, to 19 April. It wasn't much, but at this stage every extra hour was precious.

Miller, too, was feeling the strain. His conversations with Charlie were becoming ever longer and more intense. But the big man was fading fast. As his life came to be measured more in hours than weeks, Charlie slumped into a slough of depression. His child-like mind couldn't understand why the Orleans County politico-legal machine was so desperate to kill him. On 18 April, fewer than 24 hours before his intended execution, he pleaded with Miller, vehemently denying that he had ever confessed to any murder.

When Miller left this meeting he had to choke back the emotion that welled up in his throat. Stielow exhibited a sincerity that overcame his lack of eloquence. Like most who ended up on death row, Stielow was poor and ill-educated and couldn't even read the documentation that was authorising his death. As Miller dried his tears outside the death house, he realised that the time had come for desperate action.

Putting his own career on the line, Miller went to the phone and placed a call to the governor's mansion in Albany. Whitman was startled by Miller's impassioned intervention; after all, pleas for clemency in capital cases from the deputy warden of Sing Sing were not common occurrences. To his credit, Whitman set aside his long-running animosity towards the hated Osborne and gave Miller a full hearing. But the sly old fox wasn't being entirely altruistic. In the background, his political antennae were twitching like rabbit ears. The surge in popularity he had expected following Becker's execution had failed to materialise. Indeed, the first murmurings of doubt regarding Becker's guilt had begun to surface, along with whispers that Whitman had knowingly scapegoated a crooked cop for political ends. Suddenly the road to the White House was looking a lot rockier. All of which may or may not have influenced Whitman's shock announcement that he was issuing a 60-day stay of execution, to allow Stielow's defence team time to produce this rumoured new evidence.

When Miller took the news to Stielow that night, cheers echoed all through the death house, the way they always did whenever anyone cheated the chair, even if only temporarily. Two weeks later, Miller took heart from the revelation that Sydney Walsh, the Sing Sing inmate who'd made the allegations of immorality against Osborne, had abruptly retracted all of his claims. Osborne would be back at the helm within days.

Delighted though he was with the prospect of Osborne's return, Miller knew this was but one step in the struggle to save Stielow from the chair. He needed someone to review the evidence in the case, to uncover some way that Stielow could get a new trial, and that meant hiring a lawyer with plenty of experience in death penalty cases. By his own admission, White was a novice in this, the ultimate game of legal brinkmanship; but Miller had already spotted a possibility. Some time earlier, a death house inmate named Gennaro Mazielo began receiving regular visits from a lawyer determined to save his life. This in itself was unusual; indigent inmates often had no legal representation at all after sentence of death had been pronounced. But what really piqued Miller's curiosity was the fact that this particular attorney was a tall, supremely elegant woman with an abundance of thick, dark hair. Fashionably attired females were not a common sight in the death house and she'd stuck in Miller's memory. He wondered if she might take on the Stielow case.

———

By the middle of 1916, Grace Humiston was on her second marriage and her fifth career. By the standards of the time, and given her privileged upbringing, her résumé was colourful, to say the least. In 1903, at the age of 34, this sloe-eyed daughter of a property magnate had graduated from New York University's Evening Law School, one of just twelve women that year to acquire a degree in law. Her reasons for reading the law were twofold: first, her father needed every scrap of help he could muster with his sprawling real estate empire. Over the course of his 70 years, A. Judson Winterton had amassed a sizeable property portfolio on the Upper West Side, but now the first knockings of dementia were being heard; without strong legal guidance he would be carved up by his cutthroat business rivals. There was just one problem: Judson hated lawyers, didn't trust 'em an inch. Which is where Grace came in. Why didn't she attend college and obtain the necessary degree, she said; that way she could act as her father's proxy?

Grace's second reason for wanting to immerse herself in work was even more personal: she was getting over a bad marriage. In 1895, after a brief spell as a schoolteacher, she had married a socially prominent doctor named Henry Forrest Quackenbos. Whatever charms Quackenbos possessed – obviously considerable, judging from the fact that Grace was his fourth wife and he was still only 25 – soon faded as Grace realised that she was ill-suited to the confines of late Victorian matrimony and the marriage fizzled out. She had no interest in the things that well-brought-up New York socialites were supposed to be interested in, and when the chance came to study the law she jumped at it. Sadly, within a year of her 1903 graduation, Grace's heart was ripped in two when first her mother, and then her beloved father died.

This dual tragedy devastated the young woman. Something snapped inside her and she descended into a deep, dark well of despair. In keeping with the times she wore heavy mourning clothes, black with a long veil, but there was no statute of limitations on Grace's grief, and for the remainder of her life she would wear only black or the darkest purple she could find.

With both parents dead and a shrivelled marriage to forget, Grace threw herself into the practice of law. After a year clerking with the Legal Aid Society, she branched out on her own, establishing the

People's Law Firm at 10 Bible House, Astor Place. The intention was to provide New York's huddled masses with affordable access to the legal system. Within a month she had a caseload that ran to three figures. Her clients came from every corner of lower New York. Hungarians, Italians, Austrians, Jews who'd escaped the savage pogroms in Russia, Armenians, Greeks, even the occasional Egyptian, all showed up to consult the kindly woman lawyer whom many were already calling 'sister' or 'mother' from her habitual black attire and the unvarying dark veil. For each case that Grace took on – and she needed to be selective because the line outside her door often snaked around the block – she assessed what she thought was a fair fee. The sums ranged from $1 on up, according to the means of the client. Whatever the fee, there would be no stinting on service. As Grace put it, she was in business to provide 'St Regis law at Mills Hotel prices'.[6]*

Mostly she handled domestic skirmishes – runaway husbands, battered wives, sweatshop bosses, grasping loan sharks, bullying landlords, that kind of thing. But in 1906 Grace's life changed irrevocably when she became involved in the fight to save a young illiterate Italian immigrant named Antoinette Tolla from the gallows. The way Antoinette told it, she had merely been defending her honour when she had shot a neighbour, Joseph Sonta, as he tried to rape her in her New Jersey home. The court didn't see it that way and condemned her to hang. Grace didn't just save Antoinette from the gallows, she also got her sentence commuted to just seven years; the first time under New Jersey law that any death row inmate had seen their sentence reduced to a term of years rather than life imprisonment.

Because female lawyers in New York at this time were scarcer than snowballs in August, this success brought Grace an avalanche of glowing press coverage. She made great copy and she adored

---

* Mills Hotels, founded by the Californian banker and philanthropist Darius Ogden Mills, offered inexpensive overnight lodgings to 'poor gentlemen'. By contrast, the St Regis, owned by John Jacob Astor, was one of New York's grandest and most fashionable hotels.

publicity. And later in 1906 New York's yellow (tabloid) press went haywire again, when Grace declared war on working conditions in parts of the South. Distraught relatives had come to her, begging her to find missing relatives who'd disappeared into the network of lumber and turpentine camps that stretched across Dixie from Florida to Arkansas. Rumours hinted at virtual concentration camps run by brutal guards and fed on a diet of slave labour from the north. Grace didn't wait for any evidence; she jumped right into the public arena with her accusations and caused a sensation. Then she disappeared. She surfaced a few weeks later, having journeyed south, undercover, to find out first-hand if the rumours were true. It was worse than she thought. Illiterate immigrants in New York were being gulled into signing contracts of employment that gave them no more rights than pre-Civil War cottonpickers. The abusive system, known as peonage, made headlines all through 1906, and so did Grace's part in the exposé. The power brokers in Washington DC, too, began to notice this extraordinary woman. They acted fast.

On 1 November 1906, just over three years after leaving law school as an anonymous graduate, Grace made history by becoming the first woman to be appointed to the rank of special assistant US district attorney, with responsibility for investigating the lumber camps. An awestruck leader writer in the *Washington Times* described her as 'the most distinguished woman lawyer in America'.[7]

But Grace had seriously underestimated her opposition. The camp owners – organised, vengeful and exceptionally well-financed – were disciples of the philosophical school that regarded any kind of federal meddling as the work of the devil. Thus began a brutal campaign against the Yankee lawyer with the long black veil. It lasted until 1910 and proved horribly effective. Denounced in Congress and viciously libelled by the Dixie press, Grace was forced to endure one courtroom humiliation after another as southern juries refused to convict the labour camp bosses she had indicted.

In the end, worn out by the metaphorical sniping from the press and the actual sniping of would-be assassins – she had once come under gunfire while riding a train in Florida – Grace turned her back on the law, and for the next few years lived the life of the wealthy divorcée. She visited Egypt and Israel, and sailed from one end of the Mediterranean to the other. Even on this sabbatical, her finely attuned sense of moral outrage was never far from the surface. At stopovers along the way, she wired telegrams to Washington, claiming that in every European seaport she'd found agents of the southern labour camps, ready to pay the fares of anyone willing to emigrate to the United States. Angry locals told Grace that, once there, their relatives simply disappeared into the work camps. But nobody in Washington was listening and frustration eventually led her to abandon her pursuit of the crooked labour bosses.

While on her travels in 1911, she married for a second time, this time to a fellow lawyer, Howard Humiston, who was four years her junior. The ceremony took place in Lima, Peru. When Grace's ship docked at New York harbour on 17 June 1912, she had a new husband and a new-found desire for matrimonial bliss. But the old restlessness was still as strong as ever. Within a couple of years, she had taken an apartment at 20 Fifth Avenue, just a few doors along from Pastor Lowry, and was once again providing legal assistance to the needy and the desperate. Men like Gennaro Mazielo. And then came her meeting in the death house with Spencer Miller.

Miller filled Grace in on the background to the case, then escorted her to see Stielow, whose cell was directly below that of Mazielo's. She spoke briefly to Stielow. His speech, she noticed, was halting and vague, and he had an air of innocent docility entirely alien to most death house inmates. At the meeting's end Grace made no promises, either to Stielow or Miller; her first duty, she explained, was to Mazielo. To this end, she had enlisted the assistance of Warden Kirchway. On 31 May he wrote a letter to Governor Whitman, stating his belief that Mazielo should be reprieved. It was clear to anyone who studied the case, said Kirchway, that Mazielo had acted in self-defence.

While Whitman pondered the contents of Kirchway's letter, the next day Sing Sing's death house readied itself for yet another celebrity habitué. At the age of 28, Arthur Waite, a New York dentist, had decided to enhance his precarious financial standing by poisoning his wife's wealthy parents. He made no great attempt to cover his crime and did not seem greatly concerned when arrested and charged with double murder. Asked why he wanted to kill his in-laws, Waite looked mockingly at his inquisitor and riposted: 'For their money!'[8] He was sentenced to death on the morning of 1 June 1916 and his train journey to Sing Sing was packed with reporters. Waite, a psychopathic solipsist who revelled in the limelight, held court in the smoking car, laughing and joking about his predicament. 'I had no sympathy for my victims,' he said airily, 'and I want no sympathy for myself.'[9] Waite reached Sing Sing at 1:00pm.

Within an hour, the debonair dentist had bathed and exchanged his fashionable clothes for prison grey. Then convict number 67,281 was led away to join the eighteen other inmates in the death house. When told by a guard that two men were scheduled to be executed the next morning, Waite expressed envy, sighing that he wished it was him. His initiation into the death ritual was quick. At midnight, the sheets were draped across the cell doors and the process began.

In the grey light of dawn the next morning, Roy Champlain and Giovanni Supe made that lonely walk into the death chamber. Waite seemed genuinely unconcerned, bored even, as the grim events unfolded outside his cell, but another inmate, Oresto Shilitano, went berserk. The Paper Box Kid (see chapter 9) smashed his porcelain wash basin with a stool, beat against the bars of his cell and made the prison ring with his hideous cries. Frederick Dorner and Keepers Bullard and Nichols finally overpowered him while a prison doctor injected the half-crazed prisoner with a sedative.

Throughout the ruckus Charlie Stielow had remained quiet in his cell. His mind was elsewhere. His new date with the chair was only two weeks away.

———————

David White was still doing everything humanly possible to extend Charlie's fragile lease on life. He returned to the Court of Appeals and argued that Stielow's diminished mental capacity made it manifestly clear that his so-called statements had been fabricated. His plea obviously impressed the court. In order to give themselves time to examine this argument, the court announced, on 7 June, that Stielow had been granted an extra one-month stay of execution.

Within the next couple of days, White received more encouraging news from Miller. Dr Frederick Parsons, a psychiatrist at Hudson River State Hospital in Poughkeepsie who also practised at Sing Sing, had, at Miller's request, examined Stielow to ascertain his mental capabilities. From the tests he administered, Parsons concluded that Stielow had the reasoning power of a child of seven. 'He's little more than a clod of earth,'[10] was Parsons's blunt analysis. More significantly, though, was his finding that Stielow's rudimentary vocabulary barely extended to 150 words. This posed problems for the state, because the two statements allegedly made by Stielow contained no fewer than 369 different words. Clearly, if Parsons was correct – and his was a highly subjective and controversial opinion – Stielow could not have made the statements attributed to him.

But White had uncovered some even stronger evidence – a new witness. Nona M. Gleason was a Medina stenographer who had worked with the team that grilled Stielow round-the-clock. She was now prepared to swear that Newton had boasted of how Stielow – 'the biggest boob I know'[11] – had been fooled into confessing and blaming it on Green. She also confirmed Stielow's claim that Newton had offered to make him a deputy sheriff if he would only confess, 'and he swallowed it,'[12] Newton had chortled to Miss Gleason.

On 13 June White presented Gleason's affidavit and Dr Parsons's report to Justice Charles E. Wheeler in Buffalo. After a long and considered hearing, Justice Wheeler granted an application directing Knickerbocker to appear at a special session of the state Supreme Court to show cause why, in light of this fresh evidence, a new trial should not be granted to Stielow. Knickerbocker was not best pleased by the decision.

Nowadays, many US death row inmates receive daily medication to calm their raging fears. (Bizarrely, some states actually force prisoners to take anti-psychotic medicine in order that they be mentally fit to be executed.) As a result, the death house is often the most tranquil facility in the prison, with little of the internecine warfare that can wreak such havoc among the general prison population. In 1916, inmates received nothing. As a result, Sing Sing's death house was always like a simmering volcano. At any time it could blow. On the morning of 22 June, it did just that.

Ever since Oresto Shilitano's breakdown, the 23-year-old hoodlum had been closely monitored by the prison's medical staff. They couldn't decide whether he was genuinely deranged or just faking it in an attempt to cheat the chair. Kid gloves, though, were the order of the day, and the ailing prisoner was extended privileges not normally granted to death row inmates. For instance, when, early on the morning of 22 June, he asked if he might be allowed to stretch his legs in the corridor that ran between the cells, Keepers Ernest Bullard and Daniel McCarthy granted the request. As soon as Shilitano's cell door was open, he shoved a revolver into McCarthy's belly and demanded his keys. Kirchway's humanitarian gesture of a few weeks earlier, in allowing death house guards to carry keys, had backfired in the worst possible way. McCarthy responded by pushing the pistol to one side and grappling with Shilitano. Bullard, who had been standing some distance away, began shouting for help. All hell broke loose. The inmates were yelling at the tops of their lungs, rattling tin mugs on their cell door bars. Then two shots rang out. Bullard reached the mortally wounded McCarthy just as Shilitano was levering the keys from his pocket. Shilitano spun round and fired twice more, hitting Bullard twice in the arm. Shilitano then unlocked the death house door that led into the prison yard and took off. By now the alarm had been raised and guards came running from all directions. All they found was a pile of clothing by the outer fence. Apparently, Shilitano had scaled the eleven-foot wall with the aid of a suspiciously convenient bench, stripped naked, ran towards the river, then plunged into the always-chilly Hudson and struck out for the opposite shore. It would have been some swim – two and a half miles – but just minutes later he abandoned the attempt and dragged himself back to the bank, close to the railroad tracks. Behind him the steam whistle screeched out its warning as Shilitano ran off in the direction of Ossining.

This escape resurrected memories of the night of 20 April 1893, when Thomas Pallister and Frank W. Roehl also broke out of Sing Sing's death house after overpowering their guards. On that occasion they got clean away from the prison and remained at liberty for over two weeks until their bodies, both bearing bullet wounds, were dragged from the Hudson. The official story was that Roehl had shot Pallister and then committed suicide; others, though, reckoned that some locals had taken matters into their own hands.

Whatever happened to Pallister and Roehl, Sing Sing's top brass was in no mood to let Shilitano lead them a merry dance for long. And he didn't. In fact, two hours after fleeing the prison, the exhausted and frozen Shilitano staggered, still stark naked, into Ossining Hospital, asked a nurse if she would call the prison, then sat down and awaited the guards' arrival. He was escorted back to the death house. Apparently a getaway car, organised by Shilitano's mob boss father and waiting on the other side of the Hudson, had fled when the steam whistle blew.

Eight days later, Shilitano was put to death in the electric chair. In his final minutes he called Spencer Miller to his cell and told him that, contrary to official suspicion, the gun had not been smuggled into the prison just days before by his sister – female visitors to the death house were never searched – but that he'd inherited it from a former death row inmate, Vincenzo Campanelli, who had been executed the previous year. According to Shilitano, he had waited until all hope was gone before attempting his escape. Miller didn't believe Shilitano for one moment. Nor did anyone else familiar with Shilitano's gangland relatives.

Just 48 hours before Shilitano went to the chair, a rare glint of sunlight had permeated the death house gloom. Gennaro Mazielo learned that Grace Humiston's efforts on his behalf had borne the sweetest fruit. Following a letter from the Court of Appeals, in which the court stated that, in their view, Mazielo was guilty of second-degree murder at worst, Governor Whitman had commuted Mazielo's death sentence to life imprisonment. Miller, delighted and relieved, immediately contacted Grace, who assured him that she would devote her undivided efforts to the Stielow case.

She needed to be quick. Because the big man had just received a shattering setback. Despite White's valiant efforts, Justice Wheeler had denied the motion for a new trial, on grounds that the stenographer's testimony, even if it were admissible, would not have affected the verdict. The court had also rescheduled Stielow's time of dying. According to press reports the new execution date was 4 July. Once again Charlie Stielow knew that the next time the little green door opened, it would be for him.

On the morning of 4 July, most Orleans County residents woke up believing that Charlie Stielow had finally paid his debt to society. Indeed, some newspapers actually reported that Stielow had been electrocuted at Sing Sing that morning. But they were wrong. There had been a mix-up over the death warrant. Initially, press reports stated that Stielow would die on 4 July, but closer scrutiny of the warrant showed that the four-week stay of execution granted by Whitman did not expire until the week beginning 10 July. News of this hitch infuriated Knickerbocker, Bartlett and all those in Orleans County who were desperately anxious for the Stielow debacle to be consigned to history. The delay condemned them to another ten days of annoyance, as Stielow's new date with death was set for Friday 14 July.

The delay might have frustrated Knickerbocker *et al*, but it gave enormous hope to the pro-Stielow campaign. By now, the ground-swell of support was gathering momentum. Not only were high-ranking staff members at Sing Sing – including temporary warden Kirchway – declaring Charlie Stielow's innocence, but other influential organisations such as the Women's Federation of Buffalo and members of the State Prison Commission were adding their voices to the cause.

Much the most significant development, though, had come three days earlier, when Grace Humiston travelled to Albany to pick up Stielow's appeal record; all 1,450 pages of it. Spencer Miller had arranged for her to see the dossier and, over the next four days, Grace scarcely left her apartment, as she waded through the reams of trial testimony and affidavits. Like the original trial judge, she concluded that everything hinged on Stielow's alleged confession. And to her ears, at least, that confession stank like week-old fish. She recalled the mumbling inmate she had interviewed at Sing Sing – someone 'floored by any question but the most elementary one',[1] as she later put it – and found it impossible to imagine him having dictated a confession of such verbal complexity. It just didn't ring true. And there was something else. Buried deep in the pile of affidavits and witness statements was mention of an unnamed pedlar who had visited the Phelps house on the day of the murder. She wondered why this avenue of investigation had been ignored by the prosecution. Four days of intensive study convinced Grace that Charlie Stielow had, indeed, been the victim of a grave miscarriage of justice. She reached for the phone. In her heyday she'd always provided great copy for the press, much of it on the record and highly detailed. Now it was time to call in a few favours.

Before July 1916, few outside of western New York State had heard of the Phelps/Wolcott killings; what caused a sensation in Orleans County created barely a ripple in New York City. But all that was about to change. Gotham's perennially warring heavyweights of yellow journalism, William Randolph Hearst, publisher of the *Evening Journal*, and his arch-rival Joseph Pulitzer who ran *The World*, both recognised the circulation-boosting value of a juicy murder. Where they differed was in approach. Hearst preferred his cases larded with sex; Pulitzer, on the other hand, instinctively sided with the underdog.

When Pulitzer died in 1911, and his sons assumed control, *The World's* liberal instincts remained intact, and it was their chief reporter, Louis Seibold, who first latched on to the Stielow story and decided to follow it up. (In the summer of 1916, Hearst was too busy flaying the British Empire and her lackeys, for causing all that bloodshed on the fields of Flanders, to worry about some hick homicide.) Seibold hired a private eye whom he'd used before, Thomas

O'Grady, an ex-cop from Buffalo. Coincidentally, O'Grady had been at the Phelps house on the day after the killings. He'd gone there, sniffing the wind for a possible job, only to be appalled by the shambolic crime scene. Like many big-city cops he was deeply contemptuous of his rural counterparts; in his experience, most small-town sheriffs couldn't find their own backsides with both hands! Didn't surprise him in the least that the Stielow case had gone sour. Now he had a chance to help set things right and to pocket some serious cash from a major newspaper. He wouldn't have the field all to himself, though; Grace Humiston, too, had decided to take a closer look and had bought a train ticket for Orleans County.

After months of battling alone, David White was now recruiting legal allies from every direction. Besides Appelbaum at the Humanitarian Cult, suddenly another prominent New York anti-capital punishment campaigner, Stuart M. Kohn of the Public Defender Association, was added to the Stielow fold. It was Kohn who sharpened the legal focus. But everyone in the team recognised that most of their hopes rested on what Grace Humiston could uncover.

She travelled every corner of Orleans County in her search for new evidence. A decade earlier she had travelled the labour camps of Florida and Alabama, posing as a magazine writer, and seeing for herself the grisly working conditions that indentured employees were subjected to. On this occasion, in Orleans County, she didn't need to rely on a disguise – there were no belligerent camp owners ready to pump a bullet into her brain or feed her to alligators – she just needed someone prepared to talk. But word had filtered out that some fancy 'lady lawyer' from New York City was sticking her nose into the county's business, and doors were slammed shut in Grace's face when she started asking awkward questions. But there was the occasional chink in the wall of silence. William Pogle, Phelps's neighbour and one of the first to enter the murder house on the morning of the crime, told Grace that he'd seen dishes and silverware on the breakfast table and three chairs set. Another neighbour, Wallace Moone, backed up Pogle's claim. He saw obvious signs – a half-burnt cigar and ash on the floor – of someone having recently used the spare room upstairs. Yet he knew for a fact that ever since Phelps hired Stielow, this room had remain unused. Like Pogle, he'd wondered if maybe a third person had stayed at the house on the fateful night. However, when they raised these inconsistencies to the investigators at the time, they were just brushed aside like annoying mosquitoes. Early on, both men sensed that Newton had already targeted Stielow and Green and wasn't interested in any awkward facts that might get between him and the reward money.

Someone else prepared to talk to Grace was Newton's chauffeur, Henry Schultz. Grace's ears pricked up when Schultz expressed misgivings about the way Newton had cornered a terrified Nelson Green in the barn. She began writing fast.

A few days later, Grace also interviewed Charlie's daughter Ethel Stielow. The youngster was old well beyond her fourteen years, and she swore an affidavit to the effect that her father had remained indoors all night. Even as Grace took this statement, she was smart enough to question its value as evidence. First, there was the close family tie to overcome; then, was it really likely that Ethel would have remained awake all night and would therefore be in a position to provide such an assurance?

As the days of July counted down, Grace's buoyancy began to flag. Although she forwarded every statement, every affidavit to Kohn and White to arm them in the legal battle ahead, gut instinct told her that it wouldn't be enough. No, she needed something far, far stronger if Charlie Stielow were to avoid his date with the electric chair.

The hammer blow came on Wednesday 12 July. That was the day Governor Whitman announced his final decision – there would be no last-minute pardon for Charlie Stielow. He would die at 6:00am on Friday 14 July.

On Thursday 13 July, Stielow's legal team converged on Buffalo to argue before Justice George W. Cole that Charlie deserved a new trial on grounds of newly discovered evidence. In truth, there wasn't that much, just a slight shifting of testimony from Adelbert Benson over the gunshots he heard, the doubts expressed by Pogle and Moone, and Ethel's sworn statement that her father had not left the house all night. But there was also Henry Schultz's affidavit. And it was this evidence that intrigued Justice Cole. Schultz's hitherto untold version of that notorious barn incident, when Newton had allegedly threatened to lynch the terrified Green, perplexed the judge. Why, if it were true, had Schultz not mentioned this before? And, if it were false, what did Schultz hope to gain from this claim? Justice Cole pondered the dilemma over supper. Finally his mind was made up. There was enough in Schultz's story, he decided, to warrant a closer look. He asked the telephone operator to put him through to the governor's office in Albany.

Whitman was flabbergasted by the unexpected call. *Damn Stielow case; why the hell couldn't it just go away?* Dutifully, he listened as Justice Cole opined that a brief respite would aid the course of justice and permit the court to further examine claims for a new trial. Whitman, infuriated by the delay, but mindful of the backlash over Becker, gritted his teeth and issued the temporary reprieve that Cole ordered.

That Thursday evening, just ten hours before he was scheduled to die in the electric chair, Charlie Stielow learned that his lease on life had been extended by another two weeks. The news sparked off another gale of raucous cheering from the other inmates as the big farmhand was escorted back to his old cell. Charlie, embarrassed more than anything, just fell to his knees and went right on praying.

The emotional turmoil that affected just about everyone associated with the Stielow case – defence and prosecution alike – had largely bypassed George Newton. He was too busy counting his money. Since his triumph in the Stielow case, the boss of Byrne's Detective Agency had seen his professional reputation and his bank balance both soar. Each day brought new clients to his Buffalo office, all eager for the region's most famous detective to solve their problems. The dowager aunt who arrived in early July with her sobbing niece was a typical example. Obviously very well-heeled, from the cut of her clothes, Miss Wintergreen overcame her initial embarrassment and whispered that she would like Newton to investigate, er ... a rather delicate matter. Discretion guaranteed, promised Newton, and the woman began to elaborate. Her tearful niece, Marion Clark from Baltimore, was engaged to marry a Mr J.W. Wallace of that city. Unfortunately, Wallace's premarital conduct was a trifle relaxed and he had been seen entering a New York hotel with 'a Southern society girl'.[2] Despite his insistence that the meeting had been entirely innocuous, Wallace was now the target of a vicious blackmail ring. If news of the extortion attempt became public knowledge, said Miss Wintergreen, her poor niece would be humiliated and socially ostracised, ruining her chances of any kind of marriage. Newton gave a knowing nod; in the early 20th century, this kind of hotel blackmail was commonplace in big cities like New York. Miss Wintergreen wondered if Newton would investigate to establish the truth of the situation? Sure, said the detective, and a hefty retainer changed hands. Plus expenses, of course. With the money burning a large hole in his pocket, Newton caught the first train for New York City.

He didn't have far to walk when he exited Grand Central Station. Right across the street stood the plush Belmont Hotel – at 28 storeys, the tallest hotel building in New York – and this was where Newton took a room. Over the next few days, he submitted a string of telephone reports to the anguished Miss Wintergreen. Newton told how he had tracked down the blackmailer and scared the bejeezus out of him. Although he doubted that she would have any further trouble from that quarter, he intended sticking around in New York for a few more days, just to be sure. However, something in Newton's slick assurances grated on the matronly aunt and she asked if he would mind clarifying matters with her New York lawyer. Sensing a certain hesitation in her tone, and deeply worried that the golden goose was about to stop laying, Newton agreed. An appointment was made and shortly thereafter Newton presented himself to an attorney named Welch, at his offices at 80 Maiden Lane in Lower Manhattan. Welch, too, expressed scepticism about the intelligence that Newton had supposedly gathered and asked the private eye to enlarge on the methods he had employed. Newton wasn't fazed at all. Puffing out his chest, he outlined his various techniques, throwing in the Stielow case as an example. This was a shrewd move, since Stielow's ordeal was just beginning to make headlines in Manhattan. Welch, obviously impressed, asked Newton to continue. Flexibility, the detective insisted, that was the key; for instance, he boasted that he had treated Stielow's interrogation like it was a game.

Welch frowned. 'I don't quite understand what you mean.'

'Well, you see, that was part of my method. I wanted to get him all excited and worked up, thinking we had the real murderers. I told him a whole lot of things about this and that, made a lot of motions, got him all excited, had my two men with me and at the psychological moment, when I had him all worked up with excitement, I rushed at him, grabbed him, shook him, and threw him against the wall and said, "Charlie, who murdered old man Phelps?" and repeated this several times.'

'Did you hit him?' asked Welch.

'Well, not very hard. Charlie said "I don't know." I rushed at him again and grabbed him by the throat and said, "You sonofabitch, who killed Mr Phelps?" He answered, "I don't know. I don't know." I grabbed him again and said, "Come along with me." … Three of us went at Charlie all night long with hammer and tongs. I finally told him that if he would tell me that Nelson shot Phelps I would let him go home to his wife, who was about to be confined. But after he made these admissions before my men, I notified the District Attorney, and the Sheriff and called in the County Treasurer, before whom he made a full confession. We then got Nelson, used Stielow's confession against Nelson and worked the two of them against one another. Nelson said that he held old man Phelps while Charlie shot him.' Newton chortled and slapped his thigh delightedly.

Welch was clearly impressed. 'My God, that was a clever piece of work. Your rushing a man like you did at the psychological moment practically scared the confession out of him. How do you account for that?'

'Well, you see, Mr Welch, that was the master mind over the weaker victim,'[3] smirked Newton, confident that he had salvaged the situation and ensured the continuation of Miss Wintergreen's lucrative retainer.

Newton's smugness evaporated within seconds. Unbeknownst to him, the conversation in Welch's office had been picked up by a concealed Dictograph[*] and transmitted to the next room, where a stenographer was transcribing every damning word. For in truth, there was no aunt, no niece, no upcoming marriage and no blackmail plot. It had all been a subterfuge, carefully fashioned by Grace Humiston. As the 'aunt', Grace had been very ably assisted by a young Buffalo lawyer named Charlotte E. Cunnean; while the New York attorney, 'Mr Welch', was none other than Stuart M. Kohn.

---

[*] The Dictograph was a highly sensitive microphone that transmitted sounds to an earpiece worn by the listener.

And it was Kohn who now decided that the time had come to confront Newton. He called out to his assistants in the next room. Newton, confused at first, blanched as the stenographer, complete with headphones and dictation pad, entered the office. His mouth opened and shut silently a couple of times as he realised how he had been duped. Then he burst into tears. Moments later, with breathtaking temerity he looked up at Kohn and meekly announced that he was prepared to forgo the remainder of his fee – but perhaps Kohn could advance him $75 so that he might return to Buffalo? Kohn sent him packing.

The plan had worked to perfection. Newton had been exposed as a duplicitous thug who'd pummelled Charlie Stielow to the point of mental collapse, until the farmhand had bent to his will. Later that day, after phoning Grace and Spencer Miller with the good news, Kohn read over Newton's transcribed admission and permitted himself a glow of triumph. This was the clincher. He was now convinced that, legally and morally, New York State owed Charlie Stielow a new trial.

Kohn wasn't the only person celebrating good news that night. Thomas Mott Osborne, too, was riding the crest of a wave. Just a month earlier, his time in the wilderness had concluded in spectacular fashion when all immorality charges against him were thrown out, after the convict who'd made the allegation admitted that it was all a pack of lies. Whitman and Riley had been utterly routed. All their attempts to depose Osborne had crumbled to dust. On 6 July, a terse press release from the governor's mansion in Albany announced Osborne would be reinstated as warden of Sing Sing. Spencer Miller was delighted, calling the decision 'a triumph for decency and common sense'.[4]

Osborne's triumph peaked on 16 July when he returned to Sing Sing in a carnival atmosphere. As his automobile drew up at the north gate, about 1,600 prisoners cheered themselves hoarse in welcoming him back. Joining in the celebration were approximately 500 townspeople from Ossining who thronged the hill behind the prison. As Osborne entered the main gates, a marching band struck up and a long line of prisoners waved banners paying tribute to Osborne and Kirchway. One read: 'With Tom and the Dean both on the job/What care we for the political mob?' Osborne joked about the prison's regime during Kirchway's tenure, saying: 'I have repeatedly heard, since I have been away from here, that under the Welfare League plan men are treated too leniently, and you may find me a little stricter.'[5] There was plenty of laughter and back-slapping before Osborne made his way through the crowd and into his office.

On this high note, Osborne resumed control of Sing Sing. At the back of his mind, though, was the troubling knowledge that one of his first official tasks would be to arrange the execution of Charles Frederick Stielow.

Kohn was determined that that day would never come. He had rushed to Buffalo with a transcript of Newton's confession and on 19 July, alongside White, he pleaded with Justice Cole to allow a new trial. The judge was unconvinced. 'Suppose a new trial were granted,' he said, 'how could you hope to use his [Newton's] Dictographic evidence? Isn't it a fact that it is not evidence, that you could not so introduce it?'

'I would never use the Dictograph evidence,' Kohn admitted. 'But if the facts are true here, then the trial judge should have known of them, the district attorney should have known of them. The evidence concerns the admissibility of the confession. It is significant that Newton says his work was the triumph of the master mind over the weak one. It is important as newly discovered evidence showing that the confession was illegally obtained.'[6]

Cole wasn't buying it. 'If Newton did not take the stand you couldn't use it [the Dictographic evidence]. It would be hearsay only. Isn't that right?'

Knickerbocker, who'd been present throughout, smiled his agreement. Besides, the district attorney had ammunition of his own: an affidavit sworn by Newton, denying that he'd ever made the statement attributed to him in Kohn's office.

'The facts are true, your honour,' Kohn said. 'It shows how Newton preyed on Stielow's mind until he controlled every move and thought. I am convinced that in court Newton wouldn't have the nerve to take the stand to deny this report of his conversation with me. This shows that the whole confession was vitiated.'[7] In corroboration he offered an affidavit sworn by Stielow, to the effect that he had been coerced and threatened into making the disputed confession.

Justice Cole shrugged. It wasn't looking good for White and Kohn. Forced onto the back foot, they made a panicky application for a writ of habeas corpus. They urged that Justice Cole would take a very different view of the case if he personally heard Stielow speak. Knickerbocker's disdain was palpable. 'If Stielow didn't do the murder,' he said, 'then Green had nothing to do with it. Why then not make a fight also for Green? That's what strikes me as absurd about this proceeding.'

'We are interested right now in saving Stielow's life. He is due to go to the electric chair,' replied Kohn, adding caustically, 'It would be regrettable to find the real murderer after Stielow had been executed.'[8]

Justice Cole denied the habeas corpus writ, saying he could find no reason to remove Stielow from Sing Sing to Buffalo. Nor was he impressed by a belated affidavit from Nelson Green. During his time behind bars, Green had never once claimed that he'd been framed – until he was visited by the Stielow defence team. Under their probing, he now swore that he, too, had been terrorised into making his confession. At the end of a long hearing, Justice Cole announced that he was reserving his decision on a possible retrial until the following week.

While White and Kohn squared off against Knickerbocker, outside on the wide courthouse steps Grace was handling the press. Beneath a blistering sun, she told reporters: 'We are going to get the real murderer. I am firmly convinced of Stielow's innocence.'[9]

One week later, on the morning of 26 July, the State Supreme Court was packed to hear Justice Cole deliver his decision. He dealt with the issues, point by point. Regarding Stielow's affidavit, he said that it 'contains no statement of any newly discovered fact. It relates to the identical matter to which he testified and which was fully litigated at the trial.'[10]

He next turned to Newton's Dictograph interview. 'I do not undertake to determine where the truth lies with respect to that interview, but shall consider the effects of this interview as if it were truly stated by Mr Kohn and the stenographer. The inherent defect in these affidavits is that the evidence is purely hearsay. It could not be used in another trial unless Newton were sworn, and then it could be used only to impeach him by contradicting him.' Therefore, he decided, its evidentiary value was nil.

As for Nelson Green, the fact that he had confessed to the crime 'in all its revolting detail' caused Justice Cole to reject Green's affidavit out of hand, calling it 'a tissue of falsehood in its entirety'.[11] In conclusion, Justice Cole found nothing in this application to show that full and fair justice was not done to the defendant or that Stielow was not guilty beyond reasonable doubt. For that reason, he was refusing the application for a new trial.

It was a devastating setback. And it only served to widen a rift that had already opened up in the defence team. Grace had been incandescent at the earlier court hearing, blaming White and Kohn for what she deemed to be a lacklustre presentation. Afterwards, in private, she declared her intention of going to Albany to further demand a writ of habeas corpus. White and Kohn looked at her askance, and Kohn shook his head. 'I have a reputation to take care of, Mrs Humiston,' he said. 'There is no court before which Stielow can be brought.'

'There is the great court of humanity and justice,'[12] Grace retorted. She'd always been big on oratorical flourishes, but Kohn was speaking no more than the truth. One year to the day after Charlie Stielow first set foot in the death house, and after three stays of execution, once by appeal and twice by respite from Whitman, he'd finally reached the end of the legal line. That evening, Spencer Miller gave Charlie the terrible news: his execution was set for 6:00am on Saturday 29 July. For the second time that month, his life expectancy could be measured in hours rather than days.

Events now gathered pace. On the evening of 27 July, the HC held a hastily arranged meeting at the Delmar Theater on Medina's Main Street. An estimated 600 people packed into the stuffy little auditorium to hear Mischa Appelbaum, the Cult's leader, open the speeches. The state was executing someone with a child's mentality, he shrilled in his excitable manner, and urged everyone present to sign the petition that Stuart Kohn would present to Governor Whitman. Then Grace took the floor. She began by asking how many of those present knew Stielow personally? Barely half a dozen raised their hands. She thanked everyone for attending, anyway, and then hit her stride. Throughout her career, Grace Humiston held a low opinion of police officers, and the investigation of the Shelby murders had done nothing to change her mind. She lambasted the detectives for their shoddy processing of the crime scene, asking why no one had dusted for fingerprints, and if they had, why was such evidence not introduced into testimony? With the crowd warming to her, Grace suddenly held aloft a letter written by Ethel Stielow to her father. In a quavering voice she read it aloud: 'We hope to hear some good news from you may have a new trial and be let come home and have your freedom and liberty again, as you are innocent [*sic*]. We all know you were not out of the house that night and God knows it as well as we do and may our prayers of that which we ask of Him. God be with us till we meet again.' Grace showed the crowd the 50 'kisses' at the end of the letter, beneath which was written: 'May these be a bless-ing to your heart.'[13] By the time Grace finished, many in the crowd were visibly moved – which was the point, after all – but she wasn't done yet. With a dramatic flourish worthy of Sarah Bernhardt, she suddenly whirled round and pointed at a small group of people – a woman and two children – sitting at the side of the stage. Grace's voice crescendoed: 'There is the little girl who wrote this letter. Stand up and tell these people your story.'[14]

Ethel Stielow climbed nervously to her feet. Alongside her, blush-ing wildly, sat Laura Stielow. Her face betrayed a mix of pride and gaunt-faced exhaustion. Next to her sat her son, Roy. A hum of antic-ipation buzzed round the auditorium; until that moment few had known that Stielow's family was present.

All eyes were trained on little Ethel Stielow as she walked deter-minedly to the centre of the stage. Sallow-faced from the strain, cheeks pinched and eyes blinking behind heavy spectacles, she began quietly but gained confidence with every word. 'I know papa is innocent. That night we were around. Someone was at the door, hollering they were murdered. I heard my father ask grandma if he should open the door. Grandma said no, they might kill mama. I heard Nelson Green talk also. So that's why I know my papa is inno-cent. The person hollering at the door was Miss Margaret Wolcott,

Phelps's housekeeper, who had dragged herself across the snow to ask for help, and was found at the Stielow door the next morning.'[15]

It was good theatre, but bad law. Ethel's determination to help her father was understandable and hopelessly skewed. Each version she now offered of the night's events differed slightly from the ones given before. In terms of credibility, she was beginning to echo Erma Fisher. Although Ethel performed a major-league feat of heartstring-tugging, centre stage that night was grabbed by a woman, yet another lawyer, whose personal magnetism electrified everybody present. This was not unexpected.

Inez Milholland was born to the limelight. Still only 29 years old, she had already lived the lives of ten women. In her teens at Vassar College, New York, this daughter of a wealthy newspaperman had been a champion athlete in track and field, while her stunning dark looks and beautifully modulated voice lit up countless productions of the dramatic society. But she was no mere powder-puff; she was whip-crack smart, with a rebellious streak wider than the Grand Canyon. Most of this energy was channelled into the fight for women's suffrage. When the college refused permission for her to hold a rally in the campus chapel, Inez switched the venue to an adjoining graveyard at night (making sure that there were plenty of reporters in attendance). The university president retaliated by suspending her. After graduating in 1909, she became a labour lawyer and contributed to a fiery socialist journal called *The Masses*. But universal suffrage was the cause closest to her heart and she became a head-line speaker for the radical National Woman's Party. On 3 March 1913, one day before President Woodrow Wilson's inauguration, it was Inez Milholland who stole the Washington DC headlines as she led the Suffrage Parade through the nation's capital. Draped in flowing white robes and astride a white charger – half Joan of Arc, half Renaissance goddess – she led protesters through an often hostile, jeering crowd. At every step of the way she mugged unashamedly for the cameras. This knack for high-profile posturing led some fellow suffragists to vote her 'the most beautiful, intellectual, all-around woman of the future'.[16] Others weren't so sure. They resented Inez's haughty, self-aggrandising air and dubbed her 'Lady Milholland'.[17]

Not that she gave a damn. She might have been a political fire-brand, but she was also pragmatic (her job applications generally included a glamorous photograph of herself). Use what you've got, might have been Inez's motto, and it seemed to work. One of her former lovers, the handsome magazine publisher Max Eastman, besotted after an 'exalted week' in her company, always referred to her as 'my Amazon'.[18] In June 1913 she married a wealthy Dutch importer named Eugen Jan Boissevain after a whirlwind shipboard romance. Theirs was a highly unusual union, particularly for those strait-laced times. Both espoused a belief in 'free love', and each had a formidable disregard for fidelity; what bound them together was an unquenchable political commitment. In 1915 Inez secured creden-tials as a war correspondent for a Canadian newspaper and sailed for Europe, renewing her affair with the inventor Guglielmo Marconi, whom she'd bedded a decade earlier. He helped secure her entry into Italy. There, she began reporting the war, but the strident pacifism of her articles so incensed the Italian government that they kicked her out. She returned briefly to America. In December of that year, she joined other pacifists on Henry Ford's ill-fated peace mission aboard the steamship *Oscar II*, bound for Europe with the intent of keeping America out of the war. It was a tough itinerary, one that ate deep into her always-frail health. Making things worse were the constant battles with her fellow travellers over what she perceived as their undemo-cratic procedures. Disgusted with the bickering, she returned to the United States, where she resumed her connections with the National Association for the Advancement of Colored People (NAACP), took part in a garment workers' strike in New York, and immersed herself in the Humanitarian Cult. It was through them that she heard about Charlie Stielow.

At the meeting in Medina, Inez Boissevain drew on all of her dramatic skills to win over the audience. She used the bluntest possible language. 'My point is this – here is a man with the mind of a child, a semi-idiot, whom they want to kill. It is monstrous! The law was framed to apply to grown men, not to men who are less than a third developed. Is it fair or just or Christian to put him to death?' Then came a dagger aimed right at the heart of Governor Whitman: 'When we remember the use that has been made in the past of convictions as stepping stones to political advancement and when we remember that election time is near, it behoves us to be doubly cautious. We must take care that only the principles of abstract justice are allowed free play and not those of political expediency. Society is the better, the kinder for the distillation of the milk of human kindness. The worst that can happen is that a murderer should receive life imprisonment instead of death and that happens often enough, especially with rich murderers. But let not a cripple be put to death, and possibly an innocent man.'[19]

When Inez sank, exhausted, into her chair the theatre erupted in thunderous cheers. It was her densely argued plea, delivered without frill or ornamentation – in contrast to Appelbaum's strident hectoring – that urged swathes of the audience into surging forward to add their names to a petition to save Stielow. More than 500 signatures were collected. After the hall emptied, the Stielow family was driven away for their first ever night's stay in a hotel. All were dressed in their best summer finery as they sat down for a meal at the Hart Hotel. Little Roy seemed particularly proud of the silver clasp pin that held his tie in place.

Grace had no time to eat. When she arrived at the hotel a long-distance phone call came through. The caller gave her name as Emma Voorhees and said that she lived in Friendship, a small town in Allegany County. She told Grace that on 27 March, five days after the Shelby shootings, a hobo had come to her house, begging for food. He was muddy, wet and very dirty, with some unidentifiable dark spots on his threadbare light grey suit. The kindly Mrs Voorhees told him to wash up at the sink while she got the coffee brewing.

After gulping down some much-needed food, the hobo compared Mrs Voorhees's hospitality with that doled out to him recently by a farmer whom he called Charles. He claimed that, after carrying out some work for Charles, he'd asked the old tightwad for some money. The farmer had turned to his housekeeper and said, 'Margaret, give him some.'[20] Whereupon the housekeeper had derisively tossed him a quarter. The incident had slipped Mrs Voorhees's mind until she read about the appeals for Stielow. She now wondered if it might have some significance.

Grace was in a rush. With time so short, she urged Mrs Voorhees to put this information in a letter and mail it to the Ten Eyck Hotel in Albany, where she was headed, by special delivery. The woman agreed. When Grace passed along this development to the rest of the team, it sparked only apathy. Too little, too late was the general consensus. With their spirits dragging, the entire Stielow defence team headed for Albany to lobby Whitman the following day. Laura and the kids would travel with them. Before leaving Medina that night, Appelbaum took Laura to one side and pressed $41.20 into her hand. The money had been raised by Stielow's fellow prisoners at Sing Sing. If the legal efforts failed, this money would at least allow Laura and her two children to travel to Sing Sing to say their final farewells. It would be the first time any family member had seen him since his incarceration at Sing Sing – and most probably the last.

13

The Longest Night

At daybreak on Thursday 28 July, Charlie Stielow began readying himself for his last 24 hours on earth. Just after breakfast, guards began the execution-day ritual. First, they took Stielow to the bath-house and ordered him to scrub down. There was no privacy; he was scrutinised every second. After he had dried himself and looked for his clothes, he saw that his previous prison grey uniform had been taken away. The fresh underwear – rough white cotton and prison-sewn – looked familiar enough but the rest of the garb was different. There was a black, loose-fitting canvas outfit of trousers and a kind of blouse, cut low at the neck. Underneath was a grey cotton shirt, and black slippers completed the outfit. These would be the clothes that he would die in.

Stielow had already been moved to the holding cell, directly along-side the green door. His old cell was then sluiced from top to bottom with water and its bars scoured with antiseptic, in readiness for the next inmate. Earlier that morning, while he was absent, a team of guards had bundled up his meagre possessions, ready to be shared out among his fellow inmates after he was dead. As always, the hot-test item was his tobacco, the eternal currency of prisons worldwide. That, and his pipe, would make for rich barter when the time came. There wasn't much else; just his German Bible, a few photographs, and a handful of letters that he couldn't even read. When Charlie returned from the bath house he walked slowly past the other prison-ers. Some tried to shake his hand, only to be thwarted by the guards, but everyone wished him well. Being Charlie, he just nodded in that embarrassed way of his, and kept on walking. Then he was locked in the holding cell. Apart from a simple oak bed, it was bare. Between now and six o'clock the following morning, he would be watched for every minute. Much of that time would be spent in the presence of Revd Petersen. And the chaplain would be there tomorrow morning, to accompany him on that lonely walk into oblivion.

While Charlie Stielow prepared himself for death, just over 100 miles away in Albany, his defence team was making a last-ditch attempt to save his life. The morning had brought bright sunny weather and bitter disappointment. Before breakfast, Grace checked with the front desk at the Ten Eyck only to learn that the promised letter had not arrived. Suspecting that she had been the victim of a cruel hoax, she nevertheless agreed to wait at the hotel while White and Appelbaum led the delegation to see Governor Whitman.

Nothing could have prepared Laura Stielow for this day, as she shepherded her two children up the long driveway to the governor's Executive Mansion in Albany. Never before had the farm girl from western New York seen anything so grand. Built in 1856 on Eagle Street, high on a hill with views out to the Hudson, the rambling, brick-built house was designed to be impressive and didn't fail in its mission. It had been the official residence of the governor since 1877 (the first governor to live there, Samuel J. Tilden, had rented the house for two years before that date). With its gabled roof, turrets and sweeping balconies, the building might have been plucked from the pages of a Grimm Brothers fairytale. At another time its grandeur might have overpowered Laura, but she wasn't about to be cowed. She was there to plead for her man's life. She followed White and Appelbaum through the sweeping porch and into the foyer. A few minutes later they were escorted into the governor's office.

Whitman greeted them cordially. Besides a clutch of affidavits, the lawyers had mainly pinned their hopes on Ethel being able to extract a little humanity from the governor. Like her mother, the fourteen-year-old was not overawed by the experience. For the umpteenth time she told how her father had never left the house that night and therefore could not have been the killer. Whitman listened sympathetically, but was unmoved. 'This is not new evidence,' he said when Ethel had finished. 'It is merely corroborative.' As gently as he could, he told Laura that he felt unable to interfere with the law's course. Numb with shock and flooding tears, the Stielow family stumbled, broken, from the governor's office. An HC representative was waiting to guide them towards the train station where they would catch a train to Ossining.

Whitman waited until the Stielow family was out of earshot, then unleashed a fearsome barrage on White and Appelbaum. He derided them as 'sentimentalists', adding: 'This man has had every chance … I am satisfied that the man is guilty … Three of the best judges in the state – Pound, Wheeler and Cole – have passed on the case. They have gone carefully into the merits of the case and I am content to rest upon their conclusions.'[1]

The sheer forcefulness of Whitman's rejection knocked every ounce of wind from the Stielow defence team's sails. White, in particular, was ashen with disbelief; he'd convinced himself that popular feeling had swung to their side. It was time to regroup. At a hasty conference outside the Executive Mansion, Appelbaum, Inez and Kohn agreed to head back to New York City and their many contacts in the legal profession. Grace, meanwhile, volunteered to stay in Albany. White would remain with her, helping to draft letters to Whitman in hopes of gaining a last-minute reprieve. As the group of five separated, no one needed to check his or her watch. They all knew that, most likely, this time tomorrow Charlie Stielow would be dead.

The train carrying the Stielow family steamed into Ossining railroad station in the early afternoon. This wasn't like the Becker execution; there were no gawping crowds thronging the platform to monitor the comings and goings, no gangs of reporters and cameramen. The station was almost deserted as Laura and her children alighted from the train. Arrangements had been made for them to check into the Weskora Hotel, a four-storey wooden building that straddled the junction of Broadway and Route 9. After cleaning themselves up there, they set off on their sad procession to the prison, less than a mile distant.

Last visits on death row were always a harrowing experience for everyone involved; the guards, the inmates, the condemned man, but mostly for the family. Usually it fell to the condemned man to comfort distraught relatives, rather than the other way around. The prison, with its pungent smells and strange noises, the incessant clanking of keys as doors were opened then locked again, was an utterly alien world to Laura. When she finally reached the death house it was the first time she had seen her husband in over a year and she could scarcely believe the transformation. His natural bulk, reined in by years of hard farm work, had ballooned to nearly eighteen stone of blubbery fat; while his hands, normally calloused from handling the heavy machinery, were now soft and doughy. Like every other long-term inmate on the row he sported a 'Sing Sing suntan' that had left his face the colour of cold porridge. He and Laura spoke through the twin barricades of bars and wire netting. When they tried to hug each other, the guards moved in quickly. Since the Shilitano fiasco four weeks previously, no one was taking any chances that a female visitor might smuggle a weapon into the death house. Laura told Charlie that the lawyers were still continuing the fight, but he just grunted. Like most condemned men in the final hours, he'd become resigned to his fate, lethargic almost. The tear-drenched meeting was conducted within the hearing of the other inmates. Even at this most intimate and desperate of moments there was no privacy. It was early evening when Principal Keeper Dorner signalled to Laura that it was time to leave and ushered her away. She left sobbing. Charlie cried out his goodbyes. One final slamming of the door and she was gone.

Outside the prison, a small clutch of reporters surrounded Laura as she exited the main gate. Red-eyed and ghostly white, she sobbed: 'He's innocent and I'll swear to the truth of it till my dying day.'[2] Then she and the kids trudged slowly back to the Weskora Hotel. In fewer than twelve hours, when the law had taken its course, Laura would return to Sing Sing to claim her husband's body, then she would go back to Orleans Country to try to repair her family's shattered existence, knowing that nothing could ever be the same again.

Meanwhile, in Albany, Grace Humiston's temper was wearing perilously thin. She and White had hand-delivered two letters to Whitman and the governor had answered neither. Finally, her patience snapped. She stormed round to the Executive Mansion and demanded to see the governor in person. An assistant told her that Whitman wasn't present, but she was quite welcome to wait. To save precious minutes, Grace called a stenographer and dictated a version of what Mrs Voorhees had said on the phone the previous night. The assistant promised that Whitman would read it as soon as he returned. After three fruitless hours, during which Whitman still didn't show, Grace angrily returned to the Ten Eyck hotel. Never before had she lost a client to the electric chair, but all that looked set to change.

Inside the death house, it was nightfall when Osborne made his final call. As he did with all the convicts who were about to die, the warden shook Charlie's hand. And, of course, like always, he told Charlie not to lose hope. Charlie muttered his thanks. And then Osborne left. As was his usual custom on execution nights, he intended to spend the night away from the prison.

With the clock moving inexorably on, Charlie was served his final meal: chicken and potatoes, followed by a slice of strawberry short-cake. He picked at it uninterestedly. As he did so the clock ticked past midnight. Charlie Stielow now had fewer than six hours to live.

———

At 30 minutes past midnight, an open-topped roadster threaded its way through Manhattan's still-crowded streets, until it came wheezing to a halt outside a West Harlem brownstone. The occupants, Inez, Kohn and Appelbaum, tumbled out. All were in sorry shape, running on adrenaline and nothing else. Following Whitman's rejection, they had driven through the night at breakneck pace, 150 miles from Albany. They checked the address: 335 Convent Street. Right place. They reached up and knocked on the door.

Justice Charles L. Guy did not approve of being disturbed in the middle of the night, not even in life-and-death cases. Grudgingly, he admitted the lawyers. An enthusiastic and active Democrat, Guy was the team's best – make that only – shot of gaining a stay of execution at such a late hour. Since his elevation to the New York Supreme Court in November 1906, Guy had established a reputation for liberal views on women's suffrage and he was a staunch opponent of capital punishment.

Appelbaum reached inside his briefcase and handed Guy a huge bundle of case papers and affidavits, all designed to demonstrate Stielow's innocence. The document stack ran to more than 1,000 pages. Guy blinked as he realised the enormity of the task ahead of him. With the clock shifting round to 1:00am, the judge made himself a pot of coffee and settled in for the long haul.

At about the same time, Grace reached the Ten Eyck Hotel. She entered wearily, only to be summoned by the front desk clerk. He handed her a letter. She tore it open. It was from Emma Voorhees and it contained much the same story that she had told over the phone. Except there was one big difference. A name. In the course of their investigations the Stielow defence team had kept hearing about a mysterious pedlar who'd been seen in the vicinity of the Phelps house in the days before the shooting. Now here was an actual name to flesh out the rumours. Grace immediately rushed back to the Executive Mansion. This time, Whitman was at home. Grace handed the letter to his secretary, William E. Orr, and demanded that he take it to the governor. Orr said he would see what he could do.

Charlie left most of his last meal. After the guards cleared away the tray, he was joined in his cell by Revd Petersen. He would accompany Charlie on those last few yards. For now, though, he was there to provide a grain of comfort, no matter how small.

Every word that passed between them was overheard by a guard posted just outside the cell. Since the Shilitano shootings, security in the death house had been beefed up on execution nights. Not that anyone expected the big German to make any trouble. He hadn't caused a moment's bother to anyone in the twelve months that he'd been in Sing Sing, and no one was expecting any fuss tonight.

Petersen had performed this grim ritual numerous times before and it never got any easier. Perched on the edge of the narrow bed, he laid a reassuring hand on Stielow's broad shoulder, while simultaneously fiddling with the leather-bound Bible, notepad and pencil resting on his lap. Most condemned men felt the need to make some kind of final statement, often to unload their conscience, sometimes to vent one last bilious blast at the world, and he was always ready to document their words. Invariably these found their way to a hungry media. For the tabloids down in New York City, death house final testaments – especially last-minute confessions – were money in the bank, adding thousands to the circulation. Petersen didn't give a jot about news-stand sales; tonight all he cared about was giving Charles Stielow some kind of public voice, no matter how belated.

Like just about everyone else at Sing Sing, from the warden on down, Petersen was convinced that the state was about to execute an innocent man. He found it impossible to picture this overgrown child as a callous double murderer. Most death house newcomers bellowed their innocence when they first arrived, but in Petersen's experience the protestations slowly fizzled out as the hopelessness of their situation sank in and they became resigned to their fate. Not Charlie, though. His quiet insistence that he was the blameless victim of a frame-up hadn't wavered an inch from day one. At times he'd struggled to articulate his anger, because words and Charlie Stielow were uneasy companions, but when it came to consistency and heartfelt resolution the big guy had it in spades.

His last testament was rambling and, at times, almost incoherent, but it was shot through with simple honesty. 'Mr. Petersen, it is an awful thing for an innocent man who don't know one thing about who committed the crime,' he began. 'I don't see how they can do such work and take an innocent man's life. If I had been a man of low class – but I never did any crime and was never arrested for any crime before. Isn't it an awful thing to go for someone else? I have got no idea of who the one is. If I was guilty I could go willingly to the chair like a man, but I'm going to the chair innocent.'[3]

Petersen believed him.

A few yards away, just beyond the intervening wall, the man who would end Charlie Stielow's life was carrying out his final tests. John Hulbert's nerves, always shaky on execution nights, were jangling hard as the hour drew near. In the Midwest, a brutal heatwave, with temperatures soaring to 104°F, had claimed more than 200 lives, but at Sing Sing the temperature was in the comfortable mid-60s as Hulbert tested the chair. It worked fine.

At that moment, 35 miles further on down the Hudson, Justice Guy was toiling right through the night. The mountain of case papers was even more complex than he'd feared. Like all the other justices who reviewed the case, he could find no hint of reversible error; in fact, the original trial judge, Cuthbert Pound, had clearly bent over backwards to be fair to Stielow. Everything, therefore, depended on the reputed new evidence. Guy scrutinised it closely. Or as closely as time would allow, for the pile of documents seemed never-ending. Another pot of coffee was called for.

Grace Humiston didn't have long to wait for her answer. Within a matter of minutes, Orr had returned. His grim face told the story as he handed over the letter and informed her that the governor, though regretful, did not intend to intervene. Realising that any further argument was pointless, Grace left the Executive Mansion and went searching for a phone. She asked the operator to find her the number of a Mr Justice Guy, in Manhattan.

The death house ritual rumbled on. Just after the white curtains had been lowered over the cell doors, there was the clinking of keys and the main death house door swung open. Two men entered. One was a guard, the other a grizzled old con named Henry Dorsch. Back in June 1899, the yellow press had dubbed Dorsch the 'Brooklyn Wife

Slayer' when he'd shot his estranged 36-year-old wife, Annie, four times before turning the gun on himself. He was thwarted in his suicide bid only because a neighbour had grappled with him (the bullet passed through his cheek). At his trial, the reason for Annie's defection from the marital home was made abundantly clear. One year earlier, the German-born Dorsch had stolen his wife's life savings of $1,500 and blown the lot on high living. Understandably miffed, Annie left him. Her punishment was four bullets in the head. Dorsch's luck held at his trial. He caught a lenient DA and somehow dodged the electric chair, being given a life sentence. Throughout his trial he'd barely said a word, remaining sullen and silent. Once behind bars, the former brickyard labourer discovered a hitherto unsuspected talent as a barber and for the past seventeen years Dorsch had been cutting hair inside Sing Sing. Part of the job spec meant that every time someone got to take that final walk, they did so sporting Dorsch's trademark tonsure.

Stielow was ordered to turn the back of his head towards the cell door. Dorsch worked quickly. One hand held a brush full of shaving foam, the other a cutthroat razor. He daubed a saucer-sized glob of foam on the crown of Stielow's head, and began scraping with the blade. Although the guards weren't expecting any trouble from Stielow, both had positioned themselves strategically, lest the big guy decide to grab hold of the razor and start slicing everyone up like salami.

Dorsch had seen it all before, more times than he could remember. He always did a good job. Just enough bare skin so that the guards could get a good tight contact with the electrode; not enough to really humiliate the poor sap in his final moments. Three flicks with the razor were all it took. He towelled off the top of Stielow's head, then motioned towards his leg.

Stielow dutifully rolled up the slit trouser leg. A quick swipe with the foam just below the knee, another pass with the razor and Dorsch was done. After gathering the scraps of hair, he stood up and wiped the razor clean on the grimy towel. Without a word, he nodded to one of the guards, who steered him out of the impossibly cramped cell. A quick clink of keys and both men disappeared as fast as they had arrived, their footsteps fading into the distance.

When Dorsch left the death house, Charlie Stielow had just two hours to live.

Just eight blocks away, in her room at the Weskora Hotel, Laura was sobbing helplessly. She hugged her children tight to her, certain she would never see their father alive again.

———————

Justice Guy took the call from Grace and listened closely as she read out the contents of the Voorhees letter. She begged for a stay of execution long enough to allow her to catch a train to New York, so that she could show him the letter in person. Guy promised to consider the letter and returned to his burdensome duties.

The hands on the clock were showing 5:00am when Justice Guy finally summoned the three lawyers to his study. It had been an exhausting night for everyone. Guy declared himself overwhelmed by the sheer amount of documentation; it was impossible for him to review it all in time. For that reason, he said he was issuing a stay of execution until 11:00pm that night, one hour before the death warrant expired. By that time, he would render his final decision. Appelbaum, Inez and Kohn could scarcely believe their ears. Guy wrote out the appropriate writ and handed it to Kohn, who set off immediately for Sing Sing. He had one hour in which to drive 35 miles. For this reason, Guy took the highly unusual step of phoning the prison personally. Nowadays, we take the reliability of telecommunications for granted. In 1916 things were very different. Breaks in telephone lines were commonplace. Anything – a storm, an out-of-control vehicle slamming into a telegraph pole, or just shoddy workmanship – could be enough to put a line out of action for hours, sometimes days at a time.

Fortunately, there was no such service interruption tonight and, at a few minutes past five, Guy got through to Sing Sing and Principal Keeper Dorner. He instructed Dorner to halt the execution until 11:00pm, and said that a writ to that effect would be at the prison inside the hour. Dorner was in a quandary. He had never heard Guy's voice before and had no idea if this call was genuine or the work of some prankster.* When Dorner began to hedge, Guy handed the phone to Appelbaum, whom Dorner *had* met. Appelbaum vouched for the caller's identity and confirmed that the stay was legally binding.

Dorner heaved a huge sigh of relief. His first duty was to tell the official witnesses who had already assembled in the warden's office to return that night at 10:30pm. Then he set off for the death house.

Charles Stielow was just 40 minutes away from taking his seat in the electric chair when Dorner burst into the death house. The big man listened, bewildered, as Dorner told him what had happened.

'Thank heaven,' gasped Charlie. 'I hope they can do something for me.'4 Loud cheers resonated along the row as the sheets were taken down and the other inmates joined in the rejoicing. In all the excitement Charlie asked, almost apologetically, if someone could please tell Laura. A messenger was sent to the Weskora Hotel to pass on the good news. Laura immediately dressed the children and all three ran to the prison.

---

* On 1 October 1903, a telegram purporting to be from the President of the United States was received at Clinton Prison at Dannemora, New York, ordering that the impending execution of three brothers named Van Wormer be stayed. The prison authorities agreed that the telegram was a forgery and 30 minutes later the execution went ahead.

Without the invention of the telephone, Charlie Stielow would have been dead at a few minutes past 6:00am. On the journey to Sing Sing, Kohn's car, exhausted from covering just about every corner of western New York State in the past week, broke down repeatedly and it was eight o'clock before he reached the prison.

In the meantime, Grace, clutching the Voorhees letter, had reached Manhattan and Justice Guy's office at 51 Chambers Street. Guy thought that the letter, taken in isolation, was hardly conclusive proof of anything. Similarly with Ethel's testimony; that might easily be dismissed as that of a well-meaning daughter desperate to save her father. As for the business of the alleged extra place setting at the breakfast table, well, who was to say what the jury would have made of that evidence? But the cumulative impact of all these points did impress Guy. He agreed to hear further representations from the lawyer who knew the case best of all, David White.

It was late afternoon when White, who had been up all night lobbying in Albany, reached New York. He made immediately for Justice Guy's office and at 6:00pm, he began pleading for his client's life.

He based his plea chiefly upon three affidavits. The first, by White himself, averred that, during his trial, Stielow was so overawed by the magisterial might of the proceedings that he was too scared to describe the circumstances under which he'd made the incriminating statement relied upon so heavily by the state. The second affidavit concerned the Dictograph evidence against Newton. But it was the third affidavit that really focused Guy's attention. Admittedly, it was vague, but if it contained just a glimmer of truth, then it demanded further exploration. It concerned an unnamed new witness who claimed to have seen two pedlars in the vicinity of the Phelps house on the evening of the murder. It was further rumoured that, after the killings, both pedlars had been unusually flush with money. When Guy studied this affidavit, in conjunction with the Voorhees letter, it flagged definite questions in his mind.

But the clincher for Justice Guy was Charlie's purported confession. White had cited the psychiatrist's view that someone with
Stielow's limited vocabulary was incapable of dictating such a
sophisticated statement. Guy agreed. He'd worked in the law for 34
years and harboured no illusions about the kind of jailhouse tactics
employed to extract confessions from exhausted prisoners. Stielow's
three-day nightmare, thought Guy, was downright unconscionable.

At just before 7:00pm the judge decided that he'd read and
heard enough. He grabbed the phone and asked to be put through
to Sing Sing. Once again he spoke to Dorner, this time to say that
he'd extended the stay of execution until 24 August at the earliest.
He stated that he had directed Knickerbocker to appear before the
State Supreme Court in Rochester, on 23 August, to show cause why
Stielow should not have a new trial. Asked later by reporters why
he had stayed the execution, Guy singled out Stielow's 'confession':
'When I saw that paper I did not believe that Stielow ever made it. I
believe it was a case of too much "third-degree."'[5]

Some of the official witnesses had remained at the prison all day,
and they now heard Dorner tell them that their presence would definitely not now be required. At least not tonight. Then he hurried to
the death house. Laura was still there when the head keeper arrived.
'I've good news, Charlie,' beamed Dorner, unlocking the cell and
letting Laura in. 'Judge Guy has given you three more weeks to get
a new trial.' Charlie, stunned, just looked at him vacantly. Dorner
repeated, 'You get another chance for a new trial.'

Laura almost fainted into her husband's arms. Charlie squeezed
her tightly. 'Thank God,' he whispered. 'This is a great thing for me
and my family.'[6] As the couple embraced, the other inmates banged
cups on the bars and added their approving cheers. Then Charlie
Stielow did something he hadn't done since entering the death house
twelve months earlier: he wept.

14

A New Suspect

When Sing Sing's electric chair was finally mothballed in 1963, it had been in use for more than 70 years and had claimed 614 victims. During that time no one had ever been snatched from its clutches at such a late hour as Charlie Stielow. It was not the kind of record that anyone wanted. And his keepers were especially thankful. One explained their sense of collective relief, saying: 'They feel as you would expect them to feel if they had to strap a big, scared baby into the chair.'[1] Another guard, a veteran of several executions, had reportedly asked to be relieved of his duties, because he would 'not help put Stielow to death for $10,000.'[2]

Not everyone was overjoyed. In Orleans County, news of Stielow's reprieve had caused outrage, triggering a fresh round of recriminations, with most of the bile being heaped on Knickerbocker. He was still getting it in the neck from a near-bankrupt county treasury, and now he faced the embarrassment of yet another expensive court appearance. When people find themselves cornered, they either fight or throw in the towel. Whatever else might be said about Knickerbocker, he was no quitter; let the paymasters bitch all they wanted, he was going to fight this case right down to the wire.

Saving Charlie Stielow might have been an undoubted triumph; but it was only a temporary respite and his defence team still had a huge mountain to climb. Grace, who never thrived in a 'team player' situation, decided to strike out on her own. Within hours of the temporary reprieve being issued, she was *en route* to Auburn Prison.

In his time behind bars, Nelson Green had become the forgotten man in this case. Indeed, many in the Stielow camp seriously questioned whether Grace should even bother with him at all, since it was Nelson's plea of guilty that had virtually doomed Stielow's chances of obtaining a reprieve. But Grace had got wind of a new development – Erma Fisher Benson had changed her mind once again.

In the weeks preceding Stielow's scheduled execution, Mrs Benson had confided to a local preacher that she had not told the entire truth at either the inquest, the grand jury or the trial. As a direct consequence of these revelations, on 13 July 1916 the Revd Frank J. Millman swore an affidavit to the effect that Mrs Benson told him 'that on the night of the murder she was sick and consequently walking round the house, when she heard two shots and she called Mr. Benson, and he opened the window to ascertain what the trouble was, and he saw two men passing by his house coming from the direction of the Phelps houses and going in a northerly direction'.[3]

Considering Erma Benson's erratic track record, it was difficult to gauge how much credence to afford this statement, but, in studying the case papers, Grace remembered Charlie mentioning that, on the day of the shootings, a pedlar had called at the Phelps place. Like so much of what Charlie had to say, this had been entirely ignored by the prosecution. Even White had missed it. Now, as she passed through the gate at Auburn Prison, Grace was curious to learn what Nelson Green recalled about that fateful day.

Like just about everyone who met Nelson, she found it difficult to communicate with the young man. Sometimes catatonic, other times jabbering wildly – his alarming mental state on arrival at Auburn had led to his hospitalisation – any conversation with him was guaranteed to be chaotic, but out of that chaos one fact emerged: Nelson *had* seen a pedlar call at the Phelps place on the day in question. Furthermore, he'd also heard the man speak. However, even Grace was utterly astounded by what the youngster had to say next. Nelson was like an excited infant. Not only had he heard the voice, he burbled, but the person he heard speaking was currently doing time for armed robbery, *in this very prison!*

Grace sat dumbfounded. This sounded too incredible for words; no novelist would have dared invent such a coincidence. But Nelson wouldn't be swayed. He insisted that the pedlar, named Clarence O'Connell, had been in Orleans County at the time of the shootings, since when he'd been jailed for an unrelated, though similar, crime. Grace hurried immediately to the office of Warden Charles F. Rattigan. He checked the records and confirmed that Clarence O'Connell, 25, was indeed an inmate, eight months into a possible nine-year prison term. Grace asked Rattigan if she might speak with him. The warden made no objection.

O'Connell limped painfully into the interview room – the legacy of a bullet to the knee sustained accidentally during the bungled robbery that landed him behind bars. He glowered at the chic-looking lady who sat demurely at the table before him. Grace invited him to sit and explained the purpose of her visit. Just moments into what she had to say, he butted in crudely: 'Has King been squealing?'[4]

'King?' Grace feigned puzzlement but inside must have been fizzing – *because King was the name that had cropped up in the Voorhees letter!*

Without being asked, O'Connell unleashed a venomous diatribe against his former partner. Erwin King was a worthless sonofabitch with the instincts of a rattlesnake, he snarled. Grace decided to play it cool. Long experience of loosening tongues had taught her that in such volatile and potentially rewarding situations, silence was often the greatest ally. Just let the other guy do the talking, that was her favoured tactic. And once O'Connell started blabbing he found it hard to stop.

Clarence O'Connell was born in 1891 and for most of his life he had inhabited the Lockport and Medina area, scuffling from one hobo camp to another. His father, an itinerant gambler, had vanished years beforehand, leaving his mother, Lydia, to hook up with whomsoever was available. For several years she'd bedded down with another swamp angel, Frank Hartnuff, and during this time

O'Connell had taken his surrogate father's name, especially if he was in trouble with the law, which was pretty much all the time. At the age of eight, he and a gang of young tearaways were arrested for breaking into a store in Herkhimer, just south of Utica. Four years later he was caught acting suspiciously in a rail freight yard in the Mohawk Valley and was hauled, kicking and swearing, back to his mother, who promised to straighten him out.

When he was in his early teens, his mother dumped Hartnuff and transferred her affections to a hulking fellow named Erwin King, a horse trader and junkman who was always looking to hustle a buck by any means possible. O'Connell clearly took to his new 'pa' – despite the 30-year age discrepancy – and over the next decade the two men tramped the back roads of south-western New York State and the northern counties of Pennsylvania, robbing chicken coops and raiding horse barns in between occasional bouts of honest employment. Along the way, O'Connell acquired a wife and a couple of kids, and together the rag-taggle bunch maintained a gypsy-like existence, trudging from one camp to another.

The autumn of 1914 found them making camp at Five Mile Valley, just outside Allegany; King and Lydia in one tent, O'Connell and his family occupying another. By day they went knocking at people's doors, looking to buy and sell any kind of junk. By night they robbed houses.

On 24 September 1914, O'Connell asked King to hitch up the wagon, murmuring that he had some business in Allegany. Although King suspected what form this business might take, he knew better than to ask any questions. After the two men separated in Allegany, O'Connell continued on to Salamanca where he reportedly met up with two brothers, Roy and John Hall. The third leg of O'Connell's journey took him another 22 miles by horse and wagon to the hamlet of Bowen. At some time between 10:00 and 11:00pm, a general storekeeper there, named Louis H. Brown, was closing up shop when two men burst in and ordered him to hand over his money. Brown set aside his advancing years and started laying into the two robbers with his fists. O'Connell panicked, yanked out a pistol and began spraying bullets around. One of the slugs hit Brown and he fell to the floor, seriously but not fatally injured. Somehow, during the fracas, O'Connell took a bullet to the knee.

Much later that night O'Connell returned, limping, to Five Mile Valley camp and told King what had happened. They cleaned up the wound as best they could, then O'Connell began getting his alibi straight, just in case the law came calling. Not that this was likely. The bungled robbery had taken place 40 miles away and, with their kind of nomadic lifestyle, there was little chance of connecting O'Connell to the Bowen raid. And so it proved.

Just over three weeks later, on 15 October 1914, the King and O'Connell clans broke camp and moved further north to Delevan, Cattaraugus County. Here they rode out the worst of winter. This was alien territory to King and early February 1915 found him itching for his more traditional haunts. He left alone for Lockport and was joined a few days later by Lydia. Just over a month later, on 4 March, O'Connell put his wife and children on the train to Lockport, while he followed on by horse and wagon, arriving the next day. For whatever reason things didn't work out at Lockport and, two days later, both families moved to Shelby Basin. At first they stayed with friends, but more upheaval was in store.

On 14 March, after ten years of hustling, drinking, loving and fighting, King and Lydia had their final bust-up. That afternoon, King left Shelby Basin and made his way to Knowlesville, about seven miles from Albion, where he found work with Frank Montondo, the proprietor of the Barge View Hotel.

Next morning, O'Connell and his family drove their wagon to the house of Charles Laskey, who lived in the town of Barre, south-east of Medina, and about twelve miles from the Phelps farmhouse.

Six days later Charles Phelps and Margaret Wolcott were murdered.

As Grace Humiston listened to O'Connell she struggled to suppress her excitement. Although O'Connell mentioned the Shelby murders in vague, ambiguous terms, he clearly knew a whole lot more than he was divulging. And it was also pikestaff plain that something had occurred to make him very bitter towards King. He kept dropping sly hints that King was in some way involved in the Phelps-Wolcott killings. Eventually Grace came right out and posed the question: 'Do you think King committed the murder?'

'I wouldn't be surprised, it would be just like him.'[5]

Grace still couldn't figure out O'Connell's animosity towards King. And then she learned that O'Connell's surprise arrest for the eight-month-old Bowen robbery had come smack in the middle of the Stielow trial. Coincidence? Maybe, but like most experienced investigators Grace distrusted happenstance. She wondered if the timing was significant. O'Connell growled that – for reasons he would not reveal – John Hall's wife had broken the hobos' code of silence and ratted him out. Still, this didn't explain O'Connell's hatred of King. Especially when, at O'Connell's trial in November 1915, King had taken the witness stand and sworn that, at 10:00pm on the night of the robbery, O'Connell had been in his tent at the Five Mile Valley camp, and that he saw him again at five or six o'clock the next morning.

It should have been an impregnable alibi, except that O'Connell suddenly decided to make a full confession. For some reason the sanctuary of a prison cell suddenly seemed mighty appealing. Because of this confession, the judge exercised leniency, sentencing O'Connell to between four-and-a-half and nine years for first degree assault.

Grace wanted to know more about the elusive Erwin King. 'Would he do the shooting?'

O'Connell just sneered. 'King wouldn't do the shooting himself if he could help it. He would get somebody to do it for him.'[6]

All this time, O'Connell's anger had been building. Now it boiled over. He glared across the table at Grace and loudly swore that Roy Hall, who'd also been arrested for the Bowen robbery, was entirely innocent. How'd he know? Because his accomplice on the night in question was none other than Erwin King! Furthermore, King was the sonofabitch who'd accidentally shot him in the knee!

Grace understood how the convict game was played. She'd never bought into that garbage about 'honour among thieves'. In her considerable experience of the underworld it was dog eat dog. Now was the time, she thought, to press home the advantage. Coolly she asked O'Connell if he knew King's current whereabouts.

'I know right where to look for him,' said O'Connell, 'I would go right to Hank Burr's in Buffalo.'[7]

Grace asked for the address and O'Connell duly provided it. Once outside the prison, Grace rushed to find a telephone. Thomas O'Grady, who was still on *The World*'s payroll and had chipped in from time to time with information useful to the Stielow campaign, listened carefully to what Grace had to say and noted Burr's address in Buffalo. He promised to look into it immediately.

When O'Grady questioned Hank Burr, all he would say was that King had left some time before. Last he'd heard, the pedlar was working somewhere down around Warsaw, in Wyoming County. O'Grady got back in touch with Grace, passed on the news, and received the go-ahead to continue his investigations.

Among the death house inmates who had cheered Charlie Stielow's reprieve the loudest was Allen Bradford, a 29-year-old Harlem apartment fireman who'd spent his final pay cheque of $7 on a .38 calibre pistol and then pumped four rounds into his estranged wife. The shots had been fired at such close range that the victim's blouse had caught fire as the explosive gases belched from the barrel. Then

Bradford had calmly gone outside onto West 71st Street, fired the last remaining bullet into the air, tossed the empty gun onto the ground and waited to be arrested. He told the first officer on the scene: 'I had good reasons for shooting her.'[8] The reason, it transpired, was that his wife had failed to invite him to a party. On 28 January 1916, Bradford was sentenced to death. Just over six months later, on 4 August, it was his turn to find out what lay beyond the little green door. There were no last-minute reprieves, no relatives to say goodbye or to grieve his passing. He died alone.

Over the next days and weeks, O'Grady combed a string of hot, dusty towns, hunting for the mysterious Erwin King. He finally hit paydirt in Little Valley, Cattaraugus County, where the local sheriff, Charles B. Nichols, reckoned he might have a lead. On Tuesday 8 August, the two men drove to the town of Pavilion, in the far south-eastern corner of Genesee County. Erwin King was doing odd jobs in a hotel when O'Grady and Nichols finally caught up with him. King was a big man, over six feet tall, with a bronzed face and thick iron-grey hair, and his deep-set eyes stared out from beneath bushy grey eyebrows at the two men before him. The grizzled old swamp angel didn't seem unusually alarmed by their presence, until Nichols announced that he was under arrest for involvement in the Bowen robbery. King blew his top. Goddamit! He'd been 40 miles away at the time of the crime, and that bastard O'Connell knew it! Nichols told him to save it for the judge, and heaved King into the local lock-up. At no time did anyone mention the Stielow case.

That night Grace arrived in Pavilion and began questioning King. She did so in the most oblique of terms, never once revealing her genuine purpose. For his part, King had cooled down since his earlier outburst and was much calmer, affable even.

Early next morning King was taken by automobile to Buffalo. In the car with him were Grace, O'Grady and Nichols. Along the way the talk dealt with the Bowen robbery. King maintained his innocence and denied ever having carried a gun. Not his style, he said, adding that whenever he went housebreaking, he always carried a club. The three investigators exchanged looks; the autopsy revealed that Phelps had been clubbed about the head before being shot. Only now did Grace casually slip the Shelby shootings into the conversation. King conceded that he'd heard about the killings, eyes sinking just that bit deeper into his head: this was his first inkling that there might be more to this arrest than just the Bowen robbery. For the remainder of the journey he clammed up tight. After a night in the Buffalo cells, King was on the road again, this time to Little Valley jail and a charge of complicity in the Bowen robbery. He pleaded not guilty.

That same night, Nichols and O'Grady questioned King further, this time about the Shelby murders. Grace sat in on the interview. King stonewalled all of their efforts. Then Emma Voorhees was brought in. King glanced up as Mrs Voorhees walked in and quickly lowered his head. She took one look at King and nodded, identifying him as the hobo who had called at her house just days after the crime. King just shrugged. He denied ever having been down round Friendship way, and he sure as hell had never seen this woman before.

Having made little headway, Nichols and O'Grady decided to give themselves some breathing space. They called a break and left to ask the sheriff's wife if she would prepare supper for the prisoner. This left Grace alone with King. It was time for a different strategy. She took out the farewell letter that Ethel Stielow had written to her father in the death house and read it aloud. King's lips tightened as he turned and lowered his head. 'He didn't say anything at that time,' Grace said later, 'but I could see that he was thinking deeply about something.'[9] When Mrs Nichols brought in the supper, King ate in silence. Later, after the dirty dishes had been cleared away, King remained unusually quiet. Then, suddenly, out of the blue, he looked up at Grace and blurted out: 'Stielow didn't kill old man Phelps or the woman. I did.'

Grace stiffened. 'Will you repeat that before a witness?'

'Yes.'[10]

Grace called for Mrs Nichols to return and King repeated his admission. Then Grace, aware that without further corroboration King's confession could be worthless, began phoning around for credible witnesses. Within minutes she had rounded up a well-respected local lawyer, Surrogate (later county judge) George H. Larkin, together with Nichols, O'Grady and some others. She also located a stenographer, Miss Martha Hughes. As the group assembled, King studied them and then turned to Grace. 'I guess it's right that I should tell them,' he said. Grace nodded. King composed himself. 'I'll tell you just how it happened.'[11]

Surrogate Larkin extended every kind of warning to King. 'Do you know what this statement you are making is?'

'Yes.'

'Do you know what it might mean?'

'I do not know whether it will be the electric chair or a life sentence.'

'Knowing that this might mean the electric chair for you, will you still make this statement?'

'Yes, sir. I have got to the stage where I do not care.'

'Has anyone promised you any reward for this?'

'No, sir.'

'Have you had anything to drink today?'

'Not a drop.'

'When was the last time?'

'Day before yesterday at Charley Fisher's hotel in Batavia.'

'Are you ready to make a statement as to the Phelps murder at Shelby?'

'Yes, sir.'

Again, Larkin repeated his warning. 'Now, Mr King, I want to warn you again that what you say here may result in the electric chair for you.'

'Yes, sir.'[12]

King then proceeded to make a second statement. It, together with his first statement to Grace, was widely and disparately reported in the press. In essence, the gist of King's confession ran as follows:

I was in Medina, NY, March 21, 1915. I met Clarence O'Connell there. I had known him well and had been in deals with him. He asked me if I wanted some easy money. He said he had a place framed. I told him I would go with him. We drove out of town at night and stopped by a barn. I knew the place as old man Phelps's as soon as we drove up there.

I found a broomstick handle, and when Phelps came to the door I knocked him down with it. Then O'Connell and I went inside. The broom handle was the only weapon I had. O'Connell had a gun. A bedroom door opened and a woman in her night clothes came out. She saw Phelps on the floor and O'Connell and me and she yelled and ran out through the door. O'Connell shot through the door and hit her as she ran.

O'Connell ransacked the bureau drawers and pulled out a roll of bills. He said he would give me half. He peeled off $100 and gave it to me. That was all I got. The old man began to squirm around on the floor and O'Connell shot him three times. I was sore at O'Connell and would not go away with him. He got into the buggy and drove off. I walked back through the woods and fields, and early next morning got a ride with a man driving to Akron, where I caught a train and made a getaway. I did not know Phelps or the woman was dead until I read it in the newspapers a few days later.

Significantly, King did not repeat the sentence in which he took sole blame, but what he did say filled eight typewritten pages, each of which he signed in the presence of the witnesses. Grace wasted no time in finding a telephone.

It was Warden Osborne who took the call. He listened closely as Grace dictated the details of King's confession. When he replaced the receiver, Osborne summoned Miller and together the two men headed across the prison yard to the death house. They made straight for Charlie's cell. Hurried activity of any kind was unusual in the death house and the other inmates, sensing that something was up, pressed themselves against the cell-bars as they strained to hear what was happening.

Charlie levered himself clumsily up off his bed when he saw the two men standing there. Osborne let Miller do the talking. Miller, smiling broadly, explained to Charlie that someone else had confessed to the double murder. For a moment there was a blank stare as Charlie struggled to take it in. He swayed for a moment as if about to faint. Then his fingers gripped the iron bars to steady himself. Beneath the bushy moustache, his mouth twitched perceptibly and then his eyes grew big and bright. All he could mumble was: 'That's – that's fine.' When he tried to push his hand through the bars in an effort to shake the deputy warden's hand, Miller had to gulp back his emotion. As he put it to reporters later, 'Did you ever have a big Newfoundland dog gratefully paw you for feeding him a scrap? Well, that's how the big fellow put out his hand.'[13] Miller told Charlie that it might take a month or two before the legal formalities could be completed. 'Well, I've been in prison a year now,' Stielow mumbled, 'and I guess I can stand another month.'[14] Then he began weeping.

There was the usual chorus of cheering from the other inmates, all eager to grab hold of any scrap of good news. Then came a truly surreal moment. Since returning to the prison, Osborne had decided that, on special occasions, death row inmates should be allowed to listen to phonograph recordings. He figured it was good for morale. This was one of those occasions. As the phonograph cranked out a scratchy two-step, some of the prisoners began dancing in their cells.

Their makeshift partners had been fashioned from clothes stuffed with a pillow and blankets. A kind of hysterical euphoria took hold. Laughter, unnaturally loud and mighty rare in such surroundings, echoed along the flagstones as the prisoners pirouetted in their cramped quarters. Charlie didn't join them in the dance. He merely watched from his bed. Every now and then a smile flickered across his rubbery, plump face. That, too, was a first.

15

Startling Confession

The next day – 11 August 1916 – a jubilant press conference was held at the Little Valley jailhouse. Reporters poured in from around the state, on the trail of what was now the hottest crime story to hit this region in decades. Most of the Stielow defence team were in attendance but all eyes were on just one man – Erwin King. All his life he'd been a bum, scuffling around on the edges of society; now he was the undisputed centre of attention and determined to soak up every last drop. Earlier that day he had been arraigned on the Bowen robbery charge, and remanded for examination by the grand jury. The ordeal had not sapped his bonhomie or desire to please. When one reporter asked how he came to confess to the Shelby murders, he said: 'On our way from Buffalo in the automobile we all got to talking the matter over and I thought that it was no more than right to tell them about it.' He laughed off suggestions that his confession had been obtained by third-degree methods. And he had nothing but good things to say about his jailers. 'They treated me like a king',[1] he guffawed, evidently pleased at his own punning humour. Then he was returned to the cells.

In his wake, the lawyers fielded questions from the press. Kohn declared that 'even the hardest judge in the world'[2] couldn't now refuse to grant Stielow a new trial. But behind the bravado and the rhetoric, Kohn was anxious. What if King had cooked up this story just to gain revenge against his erstwhile buddy? Kohn pondered this because he couldn't work out why O'Connell would have revealed King's whereabouts if he [O'Connell] himself had been involved in the Shelby shootings.

Sheriff Nichols also interjected a note of caution. When asked if King would now be charged with murder, he said: 'Not yet. You see this is Mrs Humiston's case. He is being held for the time being on the warrant charging him with assault in the first degree.'[3]

By common consent, the hero of the hour was Grace Humiston. White, modest as always, took his customary back seat and lavished praise on his associate. 'Mrs Humiston, who has worked untiringly for months on this case, is a wonderful investigator ... her purpose is honest and her methods are honourable.'[4]

In the midst of all this mutual back-slapping, Mischa Appelbaum was purring like a satisfied cat. On the day before Stielow's intended execution, he had stood in Whitman's office like a naughty schoolboy, smarting as the governor lambasted him for his bleeding-heart gullibility. Now it was payback time. In a wire to Whitman – made public, of course – the head of the Humanitarian Cult wrote: 'Hasten to inform you that real murderer in Stielow case has confessed, proving Stielow innocent and proving that we are true humanitarians and not sentimentalists as indicated by you when we asked for a reprieve.'[5]

When news of King's confession reached the Executive Mansion, it was greeted with an ominous silence. No comment, was all the governor's secretary would say. But later in the day came the official announcement that Whitman had confirmed Justice Guy's decision and had scheduled an extraordinary special term of the State Supreme Court at Rochester on 23 August, to hear Stielow's motion for a new trial.

The press, meanwhile, had really got behind Stielow. A report in *The World* applauded this latest development 'which will save him, undoubtedly, from death at the hands of the State'. The paper confidently forecast that Stielow's release 'is now inevitable'.[6]

Such predictions sparked spluttering outrage in Orleans County, where the reaction to King's confession ranged from disbelief to outright fury. An awful lot of time, money and political capital had been invested in securing the Stielow conviction; a reversal was unthinkable. Those with most to lose presented a united front. Sheriff Bartlett, blustery and mean, expressed open scepticism about King's confession. 'Anyone who has been reading the papers could tell this sort of a story,'[7] he said. When pressed, however, he glumly conceded that charges would be preferred against King, if and when he reached the Albion jail.

District attorney Knickerbocker was more defiant. 'I see nothing in the alleged confession of King to change my opinion of Stielow's guilt,' he said. 'King's confession does not check up with the facts of the case.'[8] He also questioned Justice Guy's legal authority to issue a stay.

When Knickerbocker's comments were relayed to Guy he was sanguine to the point of iciness. 'In granting the stay I acted within my judicial power and upon evidence that made me doubt Stielow's guilt,' he said. 'When it comes to a question of human life and a possible miscarriage of justice on one side and judicial etiquette on the other, judicial etiquette has to step aside. If the King confession is true, the people should rejoice that judicial etiquette was thrown aside in this case.'[9]

But the Orleans County politico-legal machine was determined not to let the Stielow defence team gain the upper hand. Knickerbocker, his assistant prosecutor Harold Blake, Bartlett and Newton set off by car for Little Valley. They needed to hear the confession direct from King's mouth, not filtered through some political pressure group suffering from an overactive agenda. When they arrived at Little Valley, Grace was waiting for them. It was the first time that either Knickerbocker or Bartlett had met their joint nemesis. A pace or two behind, Newton couldn't make that claim. He glared malevolently at the woman – 'Miss Wintergreen' – who'd so thoroughly duped him less than a month previously, and he was thirsting for revenge. Knickerbocker, too, was in no mood for niceties. He demanded that Grace hand over King's original confession. She told him to go to hell. Grace knew that the Orleans County cabal facing her today had been squeezed into the tightest of corners; in such circumstances – given their dubious track record – it would be all too easy for the confession to mysteriously disappear. Besides, as she told Knickerbocker, she was not the attorney of record in the case; priority over the confession rested with the Supreme Court, when it heard arguments on 23 August.

Knickerbocker fought to control his temper: 'If I am to take any action in this affair, I must have the original confession.'[10] Grace continued her needling. How come, she asked, he was so desperate to get his hands on the original confession, when all he needed to do was walk into King's cell and ask the man himself? Knickerbocker stood tight-lipped while Grace smiled sweetly. As a token of her rather strained goodwill, she did offer Knickerbocker a sight of the carbon copies of the confession. Knickerbocker snatched them from her grasp and began reading. He pointed out accusingly that the sheets had been mixed up: which was the second copy?

Grace, dark eyes flashing, sorted the papers into order and thrust them back at Knickerbocker. With tensions threatening to boil over at any moment, Surrogate Larkin stepped in as peacemaker. 'Well, settle it this way,' he soothed. 'Mrs Humiston retains the original to give to the court. Let us take this copy, read it over page by page to King and have him sign each sheet.'[11] Grace and Knickerbocker grudgingly agreed to this arrangement and then exchanged the frostiest of public handshakes. Having been thoroughly bested by the busybody from the big city – for this was how Grace Humiston was now depicted in Orleans County – Knickerbocker then demanded to see the prisoner.

King was waiting in his cell. As Knickerbocker and Bartlett approached, he didn't show any hint of alarm. A lifetime of dealing with irate lawmen had given him an enviable calm in such situations. Nor was he prepared to let them mar his enjoyment of his new-found celebrity. When Knickerbocker held out the typewritten confession, King admitted, in the presence of witnesses, that it was truthful and had been made voluntarily. At Larkin's suggestion, King then signed each carbon copy. When Knickerbocker emerged from the interview, he looked utterly crestfallen and much of his confrontational demeanour had evaporated. Despite this, he couldn't resist yet another cheap shot, telling reporters: 'If King had a hand in the Phelps murder, then I am convinced that Stielow was with him.' Then came a pivotal announcement. 'There is no other revolver in the country that could have done the job except Stielow's and that's been established beyond question.'[12] For the first time – in his public utterances at least – Knickerbocker had betrayed an element of doubt over the state's blinkered reliance on Stielow's disputed confession. He was now hedging his bets. If any embarrassing chinks were discovered in the statement, Knickerbocker still had Hamilton's ballistics testimony as his ace-in-the-hole. He concluded by saying: 'However, I am going to make the closest investigation of King's story. I want to see the O'Connell story also, which I understand was made at Auburn. This story will be thoroughly sifted.'[13]

After further consultations, Bartlett then asked Nichols for custody of the prisoner. Nichols, only too happy to offload a jailhouse liability who was causing him nothing but grief, readily agreed. Grace was horrified. She demanded that a charge of murder be laid against King immediately. Nichols shook his head. He had no jurisdiction in this matter, he explained; any murder charges would have to wait until the prisoner reached Albion. Bartlett nodded agreement. Grace still wasn't happy. She asked Nichols to hold off for just a few minutes, while she hurried to speak with the jailer who had guarded King during his interview with Knickerbocker and Bartlett. He confirmed that King had repeated his confession and, what's more, the prisoner had made it plain that he was greatly relieved to unburden himself; it had been a great weight off his mind. This satisfied Grace, who returned to the office, checked that she had the original confession, said her goodbyes and then made her way, accompanied by White, towards the railroad station. Her destination was New York City, where she would map out the Stielow campaign's future strategy.

Knickerbocker watched Grace leave and nodded for Bartlett to fetch the prisoner. At 2:30pm, King was loaded into the back seat of a touring car, between Knickerbocker and a grim-faced Newton, while Bartlett and Blake sat up front. King obviously thought it was all a hoot, grinning and waving at the press pack. He didn't seem to have a care in the world.

Which is more than could be said for Grace Humiston and David White, who were standing some way off, unnoticed in the shadows. They'd still been in deep conversation when Knickerbocker's party hurriedly exited the jail. As they watched the car speed away on its four-hour journey to Albion, the two lawyers exchanged uneasy expressions. White, especially, was worried. He didn't trust Newton an inch.

It was almost sundown when the automobile carrying King arrived back in Orleans County, and King's arrival was bitterly received. He was notorious throughout the county's legal circles, and Irving L'Hommedieu, a Medina lawyer who was also chairman of the local Republican Party and who knew the pedlar from way back, said of him: 'He'd swear he shot President Lincoln, if you got after him in the right way.' Even so, L'Hommedieu's scorn was tinged with obvious concern as he continued: 'The county officials have worked very faithfully to establish the truth in this case and most of us are puzzled to understand this latest turn in the case.'[14] As understatements go, this was top drawer; for in truth, certain local residents were trembling like leaves in a high wind over what Erwin King might say.

The next morning, Charlie Stielow was taken to a room in Sing Sing, where Inez Boissevain and Stuart Kohn were waiting for him.

Stielow mumbled his gratitude, then did his best to concentrate as Kohn explained that the battle was not fully won yet; there were still some legal skirmishes to fight. But even so, the hard miles had been run; Kohn was confident that common sense would prevail and that Charlie would be a free man in a matter of weeks. When Charlie enquired about the confession, Kohn replied that he didn't have it with him – Grace was not letting it out of her sight and she was in New York – he was therefore unable to discuss it in depth. Over the course of an hour, Kohn and Boissevain talked and Charlie listened. Just before the meeting drew to a close, Kohn raised the topic of possible compensation for his ordeal. Charlie wasn't interested. 'I don't want money or anything else,' he said. 'I just want to go back to my wife and children.'[15]

For Grace the stopover in New York was just that, a brief interlude in what had become an almost impossibly hectic schedule. After several meetings the next day with members of the Humanitarian Cult, she returned to her apartment on Fifth Avenue to catch up on some much-needed rest. Dawn the next day saw her on the road again. This time it was to Sing Sing, and her chance to meet Stielow, to discuss every detail in King's confession. Spencer Miller also sat in on the conversation. He paid special attention when Grace produced three photographs and showed them to Stielow. She asked if he recognised anyone. The big man nodded. Yeah, he'd seen the one in the middle before – by the Phelps house in the days before the shootings. Grace smiled at Miller: Charlie had picked out King; the other two photographs were of detectives. When Grace told Charlie that King had recognised him as someone who used to drink in a local saloon, Charlie was puzzled. While admitting that he had frequented the bar in question, he couldn't recall having seen King there.

When Grace left Sing Sing around lunchtime she was joined by White, and together they headed north for Auburn. Although it was late when they arrived, they hurried to the prison to interview O'Connell, only to find themselves crudely rebuffed.

Warden Rattigan wasn't letting anyone – lawyers, press, anyone – get close to the man who overnight had become the prison's most notorious inmate. Nor would Rattigan allow them any contact with Nelson Green, since neither was his lawyer of record. Rattigan was more tractable when it came to the other prisoners. And they were only too willing to talk. While Grace and White took depositions, various inmates claimed that, early on, O'Connell had dropped some sizeable hints about his involvement with the Shelby shootings. All that changed after news came through of King's treachery. By all accounts, O'Connell had blown his top – blithely ignoring the fact that it was his loose talk that had led authorities to King in the first place – and was now vehemently denying any involvement in the killings. Perhaps the most telling admission came from one con who told Grace that on the morning of Stielow's scheduled execution on 28 July – and believing Stielow to be dead – O'Connell had seemed especially relieved, sighing that a great weight had been taken off his mind. Grace desperately wanted to confront O'Connell with this claim, but Rattigan wouldn't budge.

The affidavits were good, but not great. Jailhouse snitches have a lot to gain by ratting out other inmates and, without being able to tackle O'Connell directly, there was no way that Grace and White could test the other inmates' claims.

It was late when they left the prison and White accompanied Grace back to her hotel, before he returned to New York City. Both had a niggling sense of frustration at Rattigan's intransigence. But that was nothing compared to what awaited them when they reached Grace's hotel. The clerk at the front desk handed Grace a telegram, and what it contained threatened to blow the 'Save Stielow' campaign clear out of the water.

16

Knickerbocker Fights Back

All that Sunday, rumours had swirled around Albion that something big was about to break. The activity had begun shortly after dawn, when Knickerbocker, Newton and Bartlett took off by car. After driving through West Shelby, they headed east to a string of camps used by horse traders in the summer and spring. Patently, they were searching for someone or something; but who or what? Every inch of their journey was tracked by a posse of newspapermen. At no point did Knickerbocker seem fazed by their presence, but throughout the day his frustration built palpably. During one impromptu press conference, he angrily reminded everyone that 'there is no revolver in the country but Stielow's that could have killed Mr Phelps and Miss Wolcott'.[1] It was 10:00pm when Knickerbocker, Bartlett and Newton returned to the Albion jailhouse and, judging from their sour expressions, the day had not panned out well.

King, who had been snoozing contentedly in his cell, was roughly shaken awake. What happened next is not documented, but, within minutes, the jailhouse was humming with activity. Knickerbocker conducted everything by telephone. First, he summoned a panel of five local citizens to act as witnesses to a statement that King intended making. Then he called Mabel Ryan, a Medina-based stenographer, and told her to get to the jailhouse as soon as possible. The sight of the assistant prosecutor Harold Blake rushing to the local railroad station alerted reporters to the fact that something was up. It was Blake who met Miss Ryan when the Medina train arrived and whisked her back to the jailhouse. All journalistic eyes then turned to a fourth-storey window where the curtains were being hurriedly drawn. Inside the smoky room, King was surrounded by grim-faced men and one slightly bemused woman. He talked almost non-stop. He finally ran out of things to say at 1:15am, at which point Miss Ryan dashed over to the court where she transcribed the statement. When she was done, the document was returned to the jailhouse.

At 2:35am, Knickerbocker emerged from the jailhouse, beaming fit to bust – *Erwin King had repudiated his confession!*

The reporters were almost too stunned to write as Knickerbocker continued: 'I have carefully, diligently, and calmly investigated the truth of the statements made to Mrs Grace Humiston at Little Valley by Erwin King ... and unhesitatingly say that I have ascertained that the same are false and untrue and that King had no connection in any way, manner or form with the murders.'[2] When the inevitable barrage of questions came, Knickerbocker fended them off expertly. All he would say was that neither he nor Newton – nor indeed any official of Orleans County – had been present when King dictated the retraction. The DA might have concealed his participation, but few listening had any doubt that King's refutation had been scripted by John Cole Knickerbocker.

News of King's repudiation hit the Stielow defence team like a thunderbolt. Without the confession, there was no chance of obtaining a second trial, and without that second trial Charles Stielow was, once again, doomed. In New York, Grace and White had no doubt as to what had provoked King's change of heart. They'd seen the junk dealer climb into the car alongside Newton at Little Valley. That had set alarm bells clanging. But neither had expected a *volte-face* of quite such dynamic proportions. Only now did they fully appreciate the malevolence and force of Knickerbocker's single-minded determination.

Before leaving for Albion, Grace and White summoned a press conference, eager to get their shots in while the press was still making up its mind how to handle this extraordinary development. White went first. He dismissed King's retraction as 'ridiculous', the product of self-interested meddling by the Orleans County district attorney. 'He [Knickerbocker] came to Little Valley, Cattaraugus County, with Sheriff Bartlett, and that detective, Newton, whose methods were exposed in New York, and they took King away from Sheriff Nichols … after assuring Nichols that District Attorney Knickerbocker would file a charge of murder against King.'[3] With the reporters scribbling flat-out, White piled on the insinuations. 'Instead of taking King by train they took him the entire distance from Little Valley to Albion, 110 miles, by automobile.'[4] What, he mused, had happened on that journey to make King change his mind?

Grace also fanned the conspiracy flames. 'We are very much surprised that Mr. Knickerbocker still employs the services of Newton,' she said, adding her belief that the detective had been hired 'to use third-degree methods on King to get him to change his confession.'[5]

And then there was the question of legality; had Knickerbocker's cabal acted within the law? 'They took King out of a neutral county and brought him here for Detective George Newton to handle,' said White. 'We are anxious to find out whether they abducted King or arrested him.'[6] With this tantalising question left dangling in the air, Grace and White departed for Albion.

When White's comments reached Knickerbocker, he scoffed at any hint of abduction. He also refused to publish King's statement. 'That will be done before the court where it belongs,' he said. 'King himself is absolutely willing to appear on that occasion and tell all that there is to the transaction.'[7] Despite the mauling he'd recently suffered at the hands of the 'Save Stielow' campaign, Knickerbocker chose not to lash out in retaliation. Instead, he opted for an impressive display of sanctimonious grandstanding. 'I could make criticism of the methods ... in which a wicked attempt has been made to prevent the administration of justice, but I believe I have a higher duty to the public at the present time.' He continued in this windy fashion for some while, concluding: 'My obligation is to ... secure the final determination of this controversy, the only rightful conclusion of which is the enforcement of the judgment of conviction which the courts have rendered against the defendant, Charles Frederick Stielow.'[8]

There was one flash of anger when a reporter asked Knickerbocker for his response to accusations that it was jailhouse muscle that had refreshed King's memory. The questioning had been rigorous but fair, he said heatedly, and, throughout, King had consistently failed to provide answers that fitted the facts of the crime. 'King does not know whether Mr Phelps was struck once or a dozen times over the head,' Knickerbocker snapped. 'There should be no question in the minds of the public that the authorities of Orleans County were attempting only to ascertain nothing but the truth.'[9]

In the space of just 48 hours Charlie Stielow had experienced polar extremes of emotion; soaring elation followed by a headlong plunge into a pit of black despair. He slumped on the bed in his cell, head in hands. From along the row came words of encouragement from the other prisoners. Charlie was popular, and there wasn't a man in the death house who didn't share his anguish. That premature promise of an early release had now disintegrated to dust. In Sing Sing's long and tempestuous history, no other condemned prisoner had been subjected to such an emotional rollercoaster. Don't lose hope, Charlie, they cried from behind their bars. But the big German couldn't hear them; he was too busy praying.

Over the next two days, the standoff in Albion turned increasingly bitter, with both sides desperate to extract the maximum leverage from the situation. Grace attacked Knickerbocker for his mulishness. 'If Mr Knickerbocker is at all familiar with the facts of the case,' she told the *Buffalo Express*, 'he must be convinced after a 10 minute talk with King that the man is telling the truth.'[10] She also, for the first time, released a full copy of King's Little Valley statement. It added nothing to what was already known.

Knickerbocker's retaliation was blunt. 'I can only say that within half an hour after he left Little Valley for Albion, King told Sheriff Bartlett, alone, that the statement was a lie.'[11] (Quite how King, who was sitting in the back of the car, and Bartlett, in the front passenger seat, managed this discreet *tête à tête* was something that Knickerbocker failed to explain. Also, it stretched the bounds of credulity to breaking point to imagine that Knickerbocker would have sat on such a revelation for 48 hours before informing the press.) Mindful that much of the Stielow defence strategy revolved around accusations of official brutality, Knickerbocker stressed that Newton 'never applied any so-called third-degree methods on the way over, at the jail here or at any other time.' Indeed, said Knickerbocker, Newton had scarcely seen King since they'd arrived back at Albion and had pointedly absented himself from the room when King dictated his confession. Next came a bilious attack on Stielow's supporters. 'Infamy, dishonour and chicanery' were just some of the tactics they had employed to thwart the will of Orleans County. The courts had spoken, said Knickerbocker, and it was time 'to carry out the judgment of the court against the murderer of Phelps'. The DA's peroration rose to an ominous finale: '[I] will not cease until Stielow, the murderer, is punished.'[12]

And the best way of guaranteeing this outcome, Knickerbocker decided, lay in blocking every attempt by the Stielow defence team to interview King. He declared the junk dealer off-limits, saying he would remain in custody as a material witness until the Rochester hearing. And now it was Knickerbocker's turn to play hardball over affidavits, refusing to let Stielow's lawyers see King's repudiation.

All of this was for public consumption. Knickerbocker, an old-school politician, knew that when it came to inflicting serious damage on an opponent, nothing beat a finely-tuned smear campaign. He got busy. A steady drip of disinformation found its way into the press with much of it aimed squarely at the person Knickerbocker feared most – Grace Humiston.

According to a member of the five-man panel present when King made his retraction, King alleged that Grace had offered him half of the Stielow campaign's $6,000 war chest if he would confess to the crime. Furthermore, Mrs Humiston had sweetened the deal by saying she had 'fixed' it with Governor Whitman and that if he [King] confessed, he would 'not be locked up a great while'.[13]

Grace reacted angrily to this 'malicious, absurd, evil lie'. White, too, described the allegation as 'false'.[14] (Surrogate Larkin, present when the affidavit was taken, also confirmed that no such bribe had been offered.) When Grace telephoned Knickerbocker and demanded an apology, he slammed down the receiver on her. She immediately tried again. This time another voice answered and told her that 'Mr. Knickerbocker has stepped out'.

Grace took her complaints to a delighted press. 'My treatment at the hands of the Orleans County officials has been lacking of all professional courtesy,'[15] she said. 'The same illegal influences which wrung a false confession ... from Stielow have been used to secure this repudiation from Erwin King.'[16]

Although Knickerbocker was determined to keep King away from Stielow's supporters, he certainly didn't extend this embargo to members of the fourth estate. In a chain of press interviews, King expanded on the reasons for his spurious confession. 'All I told her [Mrs Humiston] was just what I read in the papers. And that is all that I know about it.'[17] He claimed to have been strong-armed into a car by Stielow's lawyers and then spirited away. 'When we got out of the city, Mrs Humiston and O'Grady began to talk about the Stielow case and I told them I thought they had the right man ... At Little Valley, after dinner, I was alone all afternoon in the jail hall with Mrs Humiston and she kept talking and talking.'[18] Then came the $3,000 bribe attempt, coupled with the promise of a short prison term.

Apparently, while King was dictating the retraction, Thomas A. Kirby, one of the five witnesses, had asked him: 'Didn't you appreciate that you were confessing to the crime of murder?'

'Yes, sir,' King replied. 'But through the promises they were making ... I did not think there would be anything to it. If I could get as much money as they were talking about, I thought I would be willing to be locked up a little while.'[19]

Next day, King elaborated further with the press. 'The Little Valley story was all a damn lie. I wish I had never seen again that gang down there.'[20] And for the first time he now claimed to have an unimpeachable alibi for the time of the shootings. On the night in question, he said, he had been working as a porter in a Knowlesville hotel, ten miles away from the crime scene. According to Knickerbocker, who rarely left King's side during these press conferences, Newton was currently seeking witnesses to corroborate King's alibi.

News that Newton was back on the Orleans County payroll led David White to demand that the county treasurer submit an accounting of all payments to the private detective since this case began.

In the meantime, the mudslinging got sharper. On 15 August, one of Knickerbocker's cohorts threatened that Mrs Humiston 'would be in jail if she wasn't a little more careful'.[21]

But the press had made up its own mind and was now beginning to smell blood. Across the state, editorials accused Knickerbocker of professional cowardice, not daring to test this new evidence in a court of law. Orleans County, too, was fast losing patience with Knickerbocker, unable to stomach the embarrassing paradox of a public prosecutor suddenly turning quasi public defender.* Discontented murmurs in the Republican Party burst into an open revolt, with many former allies refusing to sign Knickerbocker's primary petition for re-election. Knickerbocker got wind of these defections while he was in Auburn interviewing O'Connell. (The results of this meeting were never made public.) There had been hate mail too, with one anonymous writer warning Knickerbocker 'to watch yourself'. Another stated baldly: 'If King is not guilty, you and Newton are'.[22] Both letters, Knickerbocker pointed out contemptuously, had been mailed in New York City. It was a bad situation, no two ways about it, but the DA was confident he could still pull through. He cranked up his image of a courageous man under fire, a small-town David trying to slay the federal Goliath.

But the heartaches kept on coming for Knickerbocker. The four people named by King as witnesses to his presence at the Barge View Hotel in Knowlesville from around 10:00pm on the night of the murders were proving understandably hazy in their recollection of the fifteen-month-old events. The hotel owner, Frank Montondo, after discussing it with his wife, conceded that King might have been present, 'but I can't say so definitely. I have no recollections of that particular night.' Neither did Harry Horn, a local farmer. 'There wasn't anything about that night to fix it in my mind,' he said. King also claimed that an art dealer, Patrick A. Grimes, had delivered a picture to the hotel early the next morning. When questioned, Grimes recalled making the delivery but added: 'I don't know whether it was a Monday. It might have been another day.'[23] The only witness absolutely certain of the timings was a fellow hotel employee named Frank Stevens. He didn't have to rely on his memory. His wife was a meticulous diarist and her journal recorded that, at 11:00pm on the night in question, Stevens had been eating supper at the home of his in-laws who lived in Albion. If this was accurate – and Stevens had

---

* America's first public defender's office had been established in California in 1914.

no reason to doubt it – he could not have been at Knowlesville at 10:00pm, as King had claimed.

Despite these setbacks, Knickerbocker refused to acknowledge that King's alibi was blown. He continued to blame all his woes on those interfering outsiders, especially that damn 'woman lawyer', Grace Humiston. When Knickerbocker heard that Grace had returned to Albion after trying, unsuccessfully, to find a judge ready to remove King from Bartlett's custody, he sneered: 'Again I am hearing complaints that Mrs Humiston has been denied the privilege of seeing Erwin King. As far as I am concerned she may see King any time … and talk her own head and his off if she cares to.'[24]

But all wasn't lost for Knickerbocker. He still had important law enforcement allies and they were beginning to close ranks around him. When Grace contacted Sheriff Nichols and asked him to demand that King be returned to Cattaraugus County, the sheriff refused point-blank: 'Nor will I do anything else to embarrass the Orleans County authorities.'[25] Furious and frustrated, Grace returned to western New York to obtain fresh affidavits from King's alleged alibi witnesses.

The game of legal cat and mouse continued. On 19 August, Knickerbocker once again visited O'Connell in Auburn Prison. He also interviewed several other inmates. As before, full details of these conversations were not divulged, but afterwards Knickerbocker announced triumphantly that O'Connell also had a complete alibi for the time of the murders. Apparently, O'Connell had been boarding with a couple named Laskey who lived in Barre, twelve miles away from the crime scene.

But when the Stielow lawyers contacted Charles and Clara Laskey, they got an entirely different story. Each swore an affidavit that O'Connell was absent from their house with a buggy on the night of the murders, and had not returned until the early hours. Furthermore, the next morning O'Connell had talked freely about the murders, before news of the tragedy was widely available.

Hot on the heels of the Laskey statements, Inez Boissevain interviewed Laura Stielow. With a husband on death row, and reliant on handouts to feed herself and her kids, Laura was frantic, ready to say anything, and it showed in a new affidavit that she swore. 'On the night of the murder ... a light rig or Democrat wagon drove up to our house about 10 o'clock. "Hello, is Tallman here," somebody in the wagon asked. Charlie said, "No, no more." The man in the rig said, "Hello, Charlie, is that you? Does old man Phelps live across the road yet?" Charlie said "yes." Both my husband and myself had known O'Connell at Wolcottsville and it was him. We recognized his voice. There was a man in the rig with O'Connell. Charlie went out to the rig and then returned to the house.'[26] Laura's eagerness to help her husband was wholly understandable, but it did beg the question – why had she not mentioned this crucial incident before?

Confident that they had crushed King's alibi and added a new suspect to the mix, the Stielow defence team went hunting for fresh witnesses. But the calendar was catching up on them. On 23 August they travelled to Rochester for the special hearing, and pleaded with Justice Adolph J. Rodenback for a continuance. Knickerbocker, unsurprisingly, wanted no more delay. But there wasn't the same iron-hard implacability to his argument. In fact, for the first time, he showed signs of a shift in attitude, a definite softening. 'If Stielow is innocent, I don't want him punished,' he told the judge. 'If King is guilty we want to know that ... We have nothing to cover up. We want to arrive only at the truth.'[27] Rodenback agreed and adjourned the case until 27 September.

For Stielow the decision brought at least another precious month of life; for Knickerbocker the delay provided some much-needed manoeuvring room. The Laskeys' affidavits had eviscerated O'Connell's alibi, which is why, on 24 August, Knickerbocker and his colleagues met the Laskeys and deposed them. After a lengthy locked-doors interview, both retracted their earlier affidavits and now swore that O'Connell *had* been in their house when the Shelby shootings took place. Yet another of Knickerbocker's secret conferences had paid off.

The next day Knickerbocker was back in Albion. Before a special meeting of the Orleans County board of supervisors, he pleaded for an extra $1,500 to pay for additional detective services. He faced an uphill battle. The review demanded by White showed that the Stielow case had already cost about $22,000, or about one dollar per capita for the county. Knickerbocker's investigation was bleeding the county dry and the purse strings were getting tighter by the day. Nobody could understand why the district attorney was blowing all this taxpayer cash on a campaign to prove two men innocent; surely that wasn't his job? Frothing with rage and only after much heated argument, the board reluctantly agreed to stump up another $1,000.

Meanwhile, in the death house the grim procession continued. On the morning of 1 September, two more men shouted their goodbyes and then walked to their deaths. Their executions were doubly poignant for Stielow. The first to die was Charlie's best buddy on the row, Joe Hanel, who had murdered his employer on 23 April 1915 by crushing her head with a beer bottle and then made off with a handful of money. The testimony of expert witnesses, so damning in the Stielow trial, had also figured prominently in the case against Hanel. This time, though, the testimony was rock-solid. Fingerprint evidence had first been admitted in an American murder trial fewer than five years earlier,* and it had been Hanel's thumbprint, found on the broken bottle, that linked him indisputably to the crime.

The second killer, Jan Trybus, 33, an Austrian-born weaver, had also killed in the furtherance of theft when, on 17 October 1915, he had broken into the Batavia home of Jacob Schoenberg and battered

---

* *People v. Jennings*, 252 Ill. 534; 96 N.E. 1077; 1911 Ill

him to death in his bed, before jumping out of the bedroom window empty-handed. As robberies go it was brainless – Trybus had been blind drunk – and he was easily identified by the victim's son, who had been sleeping in the same bedroom as his father. At his trial, Trybus's defence was that his confession had been beaten out of him by the arresting officer. Found guilty and sentenced to death, Trybus appealed. In the event, the Court of Appeals, while deploring the arresting officer's roughhouse tactics in obtaining a confession – '[he] deserves the severest censure'[28] – felt that his conduct had not materially affected the outcome of the trial. A little-known curiosity is that the officer in question was none other than Thomas O'Grady – the same Thomas O'Grady who was now working so diligently on the Stielow case.

As the two men were led to their doom, Charlie Stielow huddled in his cell behind the white curtain and murmured his goodbyes. He took Hanel's death especially hard. The two men had shared time in the exercise yard and had conversed in German. One was a callous killer, no doubt; the other, a bewildered innocent. But the row incubates strange friendships. Most were brief. In his fourteen months on death row, Charlie had heard 21 men disappear through that green door and not one had ever come back. Only by a matter of minutes had he himself avoided the same fate. But how much longer could his defence team keep pulling rabbits out of the legal hat?

17

Special Hearing in Rochester

Survival of an entirely different kind was preoccupying District Attorney Knickerbocker. The Stielow case had turned into a monstrous albatross draped across his shoulders and, with nominations for re-election just a few weeks away, Republican voters in Orleans County were deserting the incumbent in droves. But Knickerbocker wasn't done yet. In a last desperate bid to staunch the haemorrhaging, the DA injected fresh toxin into his war on the hated Mrs Humiston. A string of anonymous quotes began appearing in the press, heavy with hints that 'the woman lawyer' – the term had become a pejorative in parts of Orleans County – was a publicity hog, interested only in lining her own pockets.

Grace, who'd been catching this kind of flak for most of her working life, wasted no time in firing back. 'I have not received a cent for my services in the case and shall not accept a cent,' she said. 'I am paying all my own expenses. I am simply doing what I can to save an innocent man from execution.'[1]

In the past, in Florida, Grace had literally dodged bullets to get the job done; a few words, no matter how untrue or hurtful, weren't going to stop her now. She kept on pestering for permission to interview King, who was still being held, incommunicado, in the Albion jailhouse. After a week of stalling, Sheriff Bartlett ran out of excuses and, on 11 September, Grace finally got to meet the garrulous vagabond. Oddly enough, King seemed delighted to see her. He jumped to his feet and pumped her hand warmly when she entered the room. 'Why haven't you come to see me?' he asked. 'I have been expecting you for three weeks.'[2]

As Grace outlined the difficulties she'd experienced in obtaining access, she had to choose her words carefully because Bartlett had refused to leave the room. He informed Grace that he wasn't prepared to let her interview the prisoner unsupervised unless King sanctioned it. When Grace asked King, he squirmed uncomfortably in his chair and gave a sullen shake of his head. 'I don't want to talk with anybody privately. I've got nothing to say.' Then he added, 'I talked too much at Little Valley. I wouldn't have said so much there if it hadn't been for the promises Mrs Humiston made to me.'

This was too much for Grace. She erupted. 'Do you mean to say, King, that I offered you money?' King recoiled and turned away as Grace bored in. 'Look me in the eye, King, and say that I offered you money.'

King, after a sly look at the sheriff, muttered, 'Yes, you did.'[3]

From that point it was obvious that the interview was over. Bartlett, hard-pressed to keep the gloating grin off his face, quickly herded Grace from the jail. Outside, she was encircled by newsmen. 'It was exactly what I expected,' she said angrily. 'He [King] merely repeated the accusation which he has been taught, parrot-wise.'[4] Grace then stormed off, shouting back to the reporters that she was going to Barre, to interview the Laskeys.

Minutes later, King was wheeled out by Bartlett to give his version of the meeting. 'I don't hold it against Mrs Humiston,' he said. 'She has been mighty nice to me.' When a reporter queried his association with Clarence O'Connell, King just scowled and spat his contempt. 'O'Connell is a roughneck. I haven't any use for the man.'[5] Question time over, King retreated to the sanctuary of his jailhouse cell.

An hour or so later, Grace met the Laskeys. Both were horribly nervous. Clearly, something or someone had spooked them. In their original affidavit they swore that, on the night of the murders, O'Connell had been absent with a horse and buggy, and that, on his return, he had shot the horse using a .22 firearm. Although informed by investigators that when the horse's head was exhumed, no bullet traces could be found, the Laskeys insisted that O'Connell *had* shot the animal. Their recent change of heart had come about, they said, as a direct result of Knickerbocker's harassment; he had terrorised them into signing new affidavits. Grace sympathised with the nervous couple. 'The Laskeys seemed scared to death,'[6] she said later. According to Grace, neither Charles nor Clara Laskey had any idea what was contained in the affidavits that Knickerbocker forced them to sign.

By this stage of their investigation, the Stielow defence team had amassed more than 50 affidavits. Most were window-dressing, but a couple were rock-solid. Two reporters, G. Stuart Berrill of the *Buffalo Evening News* and Raymond C. Myer of the *Buffalo Times*, had interviewed King while he was in the Little Valley jail and, during the course of these conversations, he had admitted the Shelby murders. When asked by Berrill why he had confessed, King replied that it was 'the manly thing to do'.[7] The two affidavits confirmed that, even after Knickerbocker had cornered King at Little Valley, the latter was still admitting his involvement in the killings. Only after that infamous car drive to Albion did his story change.

Newspaper revelations such as these rang the death knell for Knickerbocker's political career. Editorials state-wide, harsher by the day, expressed concerns about the over-zealous nature of a prosecution fixated more on retribution than justice. Even though the embattled Orleans County authorities put on a united front and still adamantly refused to acknowledge that any impropriety had taken place, local Republican Party members were out for blood. They wanted vengeance on the man they blamed for all their expensive woes. Their chance came on 20 September. In the election for nomination on the Republican ticket for district attorney, Knickerbocker was trounced by William Munson,* losing by more than 200 votes. This finished off Knickerbocker for good; never again would he hold

---

* Son of Coroner Edward Munson.

public office. The *Auburn Citizen* captured the mood of general dismay with the disgraced district attorney: 'His apparent interest in proving the innocence of Erwin King … caused many Republicans to feel disgust.'[8] Bartlett, too, was tossed on the political scrapheap that same day; another victim of the Stielow debacle.

Despite this humiliation – or, perhaps, because of it – Knickerbocker refused to temper his chosen role of avenging angel. He was determined to execute Charlie Stielow, whatever the cost, and was prepared to adopt any strategy to achieve that aim. According to *The World*, clandestine political pressure was being brought to bear to expedite O'Connell's release from Auburn. There were no names, of course, but obviously someone wanted O'Connell out of prison and out of contact. At the newspaper's request, the judge who had imprisoned O'Connell for the Bowen robbery, Thomas H. Dowd, checked his trial record. Buried deep in the densely worded document was a paragraph revealing that, after his conviction, O'Connell had signed a confession, implicating King and exonerating his co-defendant Roy Hall, who was subsequently convicted. Oddly enough, the authorities had never acted on this information. Curious reporters wondered why.

On 27 September 1916, the hotly anticipated special term of the Supreme Court in Rochester finally got under way. Laura Stielow, her gaunt face hidden behind a dark veil, and her two oldest children, Ethel and Roy, had travelled over for the hearing. They joined the dozens of other spectators who were squeezed into the crowded public gallery. In what was expected to be a complicated hearing, long on legal arguments, the Stielow defence team had enlisted the assistance of James W. Osborne and Arthur E. Sutherland, two experienced appeal attorneys. This was a shrewd move. For all their crusading efforts, Grace and Stuart Kohn recognised their own shortcomings when it came to navigating the tricky waters of appellate law. They were gut-instinct advocates, fuelled more by passion than legal precedent. As for David White – the person who more than anyone else had kept Stielow alive – a lack of experience at this rarefied level convinced him to remain on the sidelines. With the case now reaching critical mass legally, this was no time to let ego intervene.

Someone who couldn't be there was Inez Milholland Boissevain. There were just too many calls on her time. As a poster girl for the suffragist movement, she was a hot-ticket item and had signed up for a lengthy West Coast speaking tour. Friends were worried. In recent weeks her always-fragile health had declined precipitously. Inez just shrugged off their concerns – mortality was for mere mortals.

Charlie Stielow was also not present. On a day that promised plenty of high drama, it was very much like *Hamlet* without the prince. For this reason, James Osborne requested that Stielow – this '"poor simple boob" as Newton called him'[9] – be brought from Sing Sing in order that the court might gauge his mental capacity. Justice Rodenback curtly denied the motion.

This ruling jolted the defence back on its heels. They'd set great store by showing Stielow's mental insufficiency; now, they were left with just the circumstances of his arrest and the dubious firearms evidence. Osborne suppressed his disappointment and began vigorously. 'Stielow's confession is the most diabolical fraud ever perpetrated on the public,'[10] he boomed, adding, 'I have been a DA for many years and know the third-degree methods. The three-day ordeal that Stielow underwent rivalled the methods of persecution in Russia and Mexico.'[11] The blame, he decided, could be laid squarely at the door of George W. Newton. It was Newton who had browbeaten Stielow into first loosening his tongue; it was Newton who dangled the offer of immunity that led to the unsigned confession; and it was Newton who profited directly from Stielow's conviction.

Then Osborne unleashed a brand new eye-opener as he revealed, for the first time, more evidence of prosecutorial malfeasance.

Orleans County officials 'even put a Dictograph in his [Stielow's] cell to steal the little confidential talks he had with his counsel.[12]' Not until much later would the full extent of this impropriety be made public. For now, it was just another detail in a litany of misconduct by the prosecution.

The firearms evidence was handled by Sutherland. He had himself been a justice on the State Supreme Court from 1910 to 1913, until resigning to resume private practice, and as a long-time veteran of the Second Circuit he was very familiar with the excesses of Albert H. Hamilton. He began by brandishing affidavits from Dr G.A. Herman Kellner and Max Poser, employees of the Rochester-based opticals giant Bausch & Lomb, that directly contradicted Hamilton's testimony regarding the photographs of the bullets allegedly fired from Stielow's gun. According to this new evidence, the scratches that Hamilton claimed to have seen simply did not exist. This is the testimony of impartial scientists, said Sutherland, '… not the mongering testimony of paid experts sold to the highest bidder.'[13] When the state countered that Hamilton's evidence was irrefutable, Sutherland introduced half a dozen affidavits from attorneys who swore that they would not believe Hamilton 'under any circumstances'.[14]

Knickerbocker might have been a lame-duck district attorney, but there was nothing remotely lame about his opening address. It was focused and very sarcastic. He speculated as to why the defence had neglected to raise the issue of King's confession. Osborne interjected. Such a move was futile, he said; if questioned about the confession, King could merely plead the Fifth Amendment against self-incrimination. Although the Stielow team fully intended to quiz King about the circumstances of the crime, they realised that the confession was off-limits.

Knickerbocker rolled his eyes. But this hearing, he taunted, had been convened to decide whether enough new evidence existed to warrant a retrial: thus far he'd heard nothing new. 'Stielow is guilty beyond a doubt. Everything in the case points to it … The prosecution is here to search out the truth,' he told the court, before piously adding, 'I am not bloodthirsty or ambitious.'[15] He challenged the opposition to show anything in the record to indicate that Stielow had not received a fair trial. Complaints about Stielow's confession were old hat; also, the defence had pointedly declined to contradict Hamilton's testimony when the opportunity presented itself at trial. So why are we here? Is it because of the Laskeys? Well, their numerous affidavits had been so contradictory as to be utterly worthless. And, while on the topic of affidavits, Knickerbocker marvelled at the improvement in Stielow's language skills since he'd been imprisoned in Sing Sing. For someone with an alleged vocabulary of 150 words, his most recent affidavit, dictated to White, contained no fewer than 245 words. 'Evidently Stielow's vocabulary is increasing,'[16] Knickerbocker remarked acidly.

The prosecution's biggest oratorical gun was undoubtedly Thomas A. Kirby. He was an old-school attorney, long on rhetorical flourish, and he certainly gave full value for money as he addressed Justice Rodenback. 'Whether a man shall live, or whether a man shall die is the issue that is before your honour. This is a great question and one that must be given great consideration. But, there is also another question that deserves as much recognition by your honour, and that is the administration of justice. Justice, not only for the man but for the people.' Kirby attacked Justice Guy's order staying the execution: 'If the law had been obeyed, as it should have been, this man would have been executed.'[17]

An already eventful opening day now delivered an even more sensational development. Sheriff Bartlett, looking decidedly sheepish, slunk into court with news that the Laskeys – Clara and Charles, along with their twenty-year-old son, Frank – had apparently fled the country in the early hours of that morning. Bartlett professed to have just learned of this defection from Frank's brother, Clarence, who'd brought word that his missing relatives were holed up in Canada 'where no lawyers could find them'.[18] Their mysterious disappearing act certainly did Charlie Stielow no favours and, on this ominous note, proceedings for the day came to an end.

The next day began where the previous day left off: another missing witness. This time it was the stenographer, Nona Gleason – who claimed to have overheard Newton bragging about how he had browbeaten Stielow into confessing – who had inexplicably vanished. Osborne just threw up his hands in exasperation and wearily protested. This was a travesty. Justice Rodenback shared his outrage and ordered Bartlett to find the missing woman. As Bartlett hurried from the court it was hard to escape the conclusion that, for whatever reason – and the defence lawyers had a pretty good idea of what that reason might be – several vital witnesses were suddenly running scared.

But not Erwin King. As he waited outside the courthouse, the hearing's undisputed star witness even managed to make light of his predicament, joking to reporters that after his release he expected to be elected mayor of Akron. King's good humour didn't accompany him to the stand. He proved to be a moody, intractable witness. When Justice Rodenback asked him a few general questions about the Phelps farm, King professed utter ignorance of the place, its location, its interior, everything. Such obduracy temporarily threw the judge, who yielded the questioning to Osborne. It was time for the gloves to come off and Osborne waded in like a street fighter. 'Were you quite frank with the Court when you said you didn't know the location of the farm?'

'I didn't know where it was then, I don't know where it is now,' growled King. Osborne took a moment and then produced the witness's signed statement made at Little Valley, which clearly demonstrated knowledge of the farm's location.

'Did you make a truthful answer to this statement?'

'I don't know where it is,' King persisted.

'Come now, that won't do. Have you a reason for evading my question?'

'No.'

'Then answer it.'

After what seemed like an age, King mumbled, 'I don't think I said it.'

When Osborne pressed him on whether he knew that he was making a sworn statement at Little Valley, King replied that he 'wasn't asked to put my hand up or nothing, and I wasn't asked to kiss any book'.

'They just asked if it was the truth?'

'I said "yes." That's all the swearing there was.'[19]

Later in King's testimony, the defence gained two invaluable admissions. The first came when, after a barrage of questions, King grudgingly conceded that his first words on being arrested at Little Valley were: 'Has O'Connell been saying anything?'[20] The second concerned King's activities in the immediate aftermath of the killings. He admitted that two days after the murders he left West Shelby and thereafter changed his address every few days until he was eventually run to ground. Even by King's peripatetic standards this was unusually nomadic behaviour. After a bruising session, the hobo limped off the stand.

Rodenback, plainly disenchanted with King's wearisome ambiguities, perked up perceptibly when Stuart Kohn began giving his evidence. Rodenback listened closely to the account of Newton's swaggering performance in his office, which had been captured by a Dictograph. The judge requested clarification of Newton's claim that he had grabbed Stielow by the throat and bullied him into submission until his will was destroyed. Kohn was only too happy to provide this. The conclusion of Kohn's testimony marked the end of the witnesses.

Saturday was set aside for closing submissions. Once again the prosecution put its trust in the colourful Kirby. He didn't disappoint, launching an extraordinary attack on New York City political activists – he made 'these persons from beyond the Harlem'* sound like invaders from another planet – who had impugned the justice system in Orleans County and slighted his fellow citizens' reputation. Sarcasm and venom, it all came alike to Kirby. 'Throughout the land the impression prevails that Stielow has been submitted to the worst kind of torture. That his very soul had been torn out until relief was had in a confession that dispatched him straight to the electric chair.' Kirby now really began to hit his stride: 'I challenge those people who have come into this case harmless and honest as a sunbeam, as they claim, to furnish one iota of proof that the rights and privileges of Charles Stielow ... had not been protected to the uttermost degree by this district attorney whose sworn duty it is to see that justice is done.'[21]

Next, to vitiate defence claims that Stielow had been brainwashed into making untrue statements, Kirby made the telling point that Stielow had lied repeatedly at the inquest, long before he was ever taken into custody. At this, Justice Rodenback looked up sharply and asked for the inquest transcript to be included among the briefs he intended to read before making his decision. Hearts around the defence table sank just a little at this development. Kirby next turned his fire on Justice Guy. He cried that, in granting Stielow the last-minute stay, Guy had exceeded his authority by overriding the Court of Appeals and Governor Whitman. As for King's alleged confession, Kirby dismissed that out of hand. Evidence gathered by the district attorney proved that King was not guilty of the Shelby murders. His confession just hadn't withstood close inspection, and 'when King's confession fails ... the whole fabric of the defence falls with it'.[22] Kirby ended powerfully: 'The fact that Nelson Green pleaded guilty when arraigned, sealed his fate – and the fate of Stielow.'[23]

Kirby had made an undeniably strong case, one that the defence would struggle to counter. It was Sutherland who led the charge.

---

* A reference to the Harlem River, the narrow strait that separates Manhattan from the Bronx.

Predictably, he saw Justice Guy not as an interfering villain, but as a hero in shining armour. 'We must thank Justice Guy for his ready action in staying the sentence ... He acted for the citizens of this state who know that this man was innocent.'[24] As Sutherland built up a head of steam, his appeals became ever more strident. 'I ask your Honour, when you write your decision in this case to be strong upon one thing – the question of immunity ... Let us stop this damnable practice of turning private detectives upon men held in jail charged with crimes. Let us put an end to it forever.'[25]

Then, with a display of hammy dramatics that might have been plucked from some vaudeville matinée, Sutherland wheeled theatrically around and strode to the desk where a rather startled Knickerbocker was sitting. 'I am coming to you brother Knickerbocker, six feet in the air, with red blood in my body and I say to you that if you really believe Erwin King had nothing to do with this murder, then I honour you for refusing to prosecute him. If I was district attorney, I would do the same thing.' Drawing back, Sutherland extended a welcoming arm. 'And now Mr Knickerbocker I ask you to come with me. I ask you to agree with me that if a private detective, working under you, gave a promise of immunity to a poor wretch, you should stand by that promise. I would stand by it in spite of all the public sentiment that could be raised against me ... We don't ask you to turn Stielow free. We simply ask that in view of all the things that have arrived in this case we go over it again to settle ... just where the truth lies.'[26]

Sutherland's plea had pushed all the right emotional buttons, but had it been enough? There was nothing on Justice Rodenback's face to indicate which way he was leaning. He merely announced that he was reserving his decision and would have an answer at some time in the next week or two. It was now a question of waiting.

Someone without that luxury was Thomas Bambrick. Convicted of slaying police officer George Dapping, who had been shot during a gangland fight at a Manhattan gambling house on 24 September 1915, Bambrick had never wavered from his claim that he was the victim of mistaken identity and there were many who believed him, including Warden Osborne and Spencer Miller. On 6 October, Osborne took his concerns to a meeting of prominent New York businessmen, saying: 'It is almost as certain that Bambrick is innocent as that the sun will rise tomorrow.'[27] His passion persuaded 50 of the audience, including Theodore N. Vail, president of telecommunications company AT&T, to put their signatures to a last-minute petition pleading for clemency. But getting mercy for a convicted cop killer proved impossible. Whitman was deaf to all pleas. Just a few hours after Osborne's speech, on 7 October at 5:45am, Bambrick set out coolly on his last brief walk. Hulbert was waiting for him. As with the Becker execution there was a hitch, when the connections on the helmet malfunctioned, but three high-voltage blasts of alternating current were enough to overcome any mechanical flaw. Nine minutes after he entered the death chamber, Bambrick's lifeless body was removed from the chair.

Twenty-four hours later, Osborne quit as warden of Sing Sing. His reign there had been brief and humiliating, and for that he blamed just one man – Charles Whitman. Osborne's letter of resignation was astonishing. In it, he openly accused the governor of conspiring 'in the shameful attacks made upon me in Westchester County', and of breaking 'every promise he ever made to me, both before and after he took office'.[28] It was a stunning attack on an elected public official, but Osborne was in no mood for diplomacy. He blistered Whitman as a vengeful ogre, determined to keep prisons and prisoners rooted in the 19th century, and his refusal to issue even a stay of execution for Bambrick was the final straw. Osborne announced that his resignation would take effect from 16 October. In the final section of his resignation letter, Osborne unloaded on the governor with both barrels: 'But I do so desire to influence the future, so far as I may, to the end that no man so weak as yourself, so shifty, so selfish, so false, so cruel, may be trusted with further power.'[29]

Whitman let the news of Osborne's resignation just bounce off his bulky shoulders, declaring himself 'much surprised, as I supposed that he was devoted to his work and anxious to remain in it'. Then, pausing just long enough to plant his tongue firmly in his cheek, he added: 'Warden Osborne has had the support of the Administration from the first.'[30]

It was widely assumed that Spencer Miller would step into the warden's shoes, but the young idealist had no appetite for such a precarious and thankless post. Instead, he tendered his own resignation to take up a position as Osborne's personal secretary. This joint defection – as sudden as it was surprising – sent shockwaves through the New York penal system. The news hit Charlie Stielow hard and heaped even more pressure on the outcome of Rodenback's judicial review.

Just three days later, on 11 October, all parties reconvened at the courthouse in Rochester to hear Justice Rodenback's decision. His honour, a man of rare and welcome judicial brevity, said that the affidavits had raised just five main questions:

1. The defects and marking on the bullets
2. The condition of the defendant's mind
3. The threats and acts of intimidation
4. The alleged promises of immunity
5. King's confession.

He dealt with each point in turn. 'It is incredible that the defendant's expert examined the revolver and bullets ... and did not take the stand. It is more reasonable to assume that he found what the State's experts described, and for that reason did not testify.'[31] As for the defendant's allegedly subnormal state of mind, this, he felt, had been greatly exaggerated. 'His testimony upon the trial shows not only that he was shrewd, but skilful in answering the questions put to him.'[32]

It had not started well for the Stielow defence team, and each judicial utterance from the bench only further blackened their collective mood. Allegations of intimidation and third-degree tactics had been introduced at the trial and rejected by the jury, and Rodenback was not minded to second-guess the jury at this stage. Also, he found nothing in the original trial transcript to prove that Stielow had at any time been offered immunity and, for that reason, he was disinclined to regard such claims now. His dismissal of Erwin King was withering: 'The confession of King is only valuable as a psychological study.'

He concluded briskly. Nine judges, he said, had considered the case and none had found fault with the trial procedure. 'A new trial should not be granted merely to give the defendant an opportunity to discredit his confession, which the court believes to be a true statement of the material facts of the homicide ... The motion, therefore, is denied.'[33]

The summary terseness of Rodenback's rejection poleaxed the Stielow campaign. They had entered this hearing convinced that enough fresh evidence had been uncovered to warrant a new trial, only to have that belief brushed contemptuously aside.

Across the court, Knickerbocker's expression of grim satisfaction said it all. Vindication at last. The voters might have rejected him, but now he could return to a lucrative private practice, comforted by the knowledge that, in his darkest hour, every court in New York had backed him.

Charlie Stielow received the news in his cell that night. What went through his mind cannot be imagined. He had spent fifteen months with his life dangling by a wire. Now that wire had been three parts severed. It wouldn't take much more to sever it completely. He reached for the German Bible that had been his constant companion during his time on the row.

On 15 October, one day earlier than planned, Osborne and Miller took their leave of Sing Sing. In a moving, raucous ceremony, the convicts cheered from their cell windows as the two men made their way to the front gate. Charlie Stielow, denied access to a window in the death house, couldn't add his own cheers to the departure, but nobody felt the loss greater than he. Without Osborne – and especially Miller – he would already be lying in Gallery 25, already half-forgotten. The debt he owed them was unrepayable. When both men had come to say their goodbyes to Stielow, they'd shaken his hand and assured him that their departure would in no way affect their efforts to save him. But they were now outsiders. At a stroke, the condemned man had lost his two strongest allies within the prison system.

Two days later, Stielow heard that the Court of Appeals had set his resentencing date for one week hence. The following day, Knickerbocker announced that he had petitioned for King's release from jail. The junkman immediately vanished.

October was a black month for the Stielow campaign. On 23 October, just 48 hours before the resentencing hearing, Inez Milholland Boissevain was addressing a large suffragist crowd in Los Angeles and had reached the climax of her speech, crying out: 'President Wilson, how long must women wait for liberty?'[34] when she suddenly collapsed, struck down by the pernicious anaemia that had stalked her for years. After fifteen minutes of medical attention she regained consciousness and insisted on finishing her speech, before being rushed to hospital. Compared to others in the Stielow case, Boissevain's role had been peripheral, but she had charisma and hers was the personality that the press latched on to. While her highly burnished ego might have jarred with some in the suffragist movement, there can be no doubt that it served Charlie Stielow well. And right now he needed every scrap of help he could muster.

On the afternoon of 25 October, a palpable sense of gloom filled the Assembly Chambers at the Court of Appeals in Albany, as Stielow, handcuffed between two prison guards, was brought in. One of the guards unlocked the cuffs and Charlie took his seat alongside Stuart Kohn. He looked up at the bench, which was filled with a row of black-robed judges. Across the courtroom, Knickerbocker studied Stielow's every movement. After one more quick glance at the man he had been hounding for a year and a half, the DA rose and made his motion for the resentencing. Chief Judge Willard Bartlett then spoke. 'Mr Stielow, stand up. Is there any reason why this court should not pass upon the time for the execution of the judgment against you?'

Stielow pulled himself clumsily to his feet. After a bewildering pause he said in a barely audible voice, 'I did not do this thing.' His plump cheeks quivered and his face flushed as he fought to find the words. 'I was forced to say what I did.' Another pause. 'I was not out of the house at all that night.' He paused once more. This time the hesitation lasted for several seconds. Finally, the words came falteringly. 'I don't just know of any more I can say.' Then he turned to Kohn and whispered, 'You had better do the talking.'

Kohn was on his feet immediately: 'I have only one request to make, and that is that the court fix a time of execution at as far distant a time as possible.'[35] Bartlett saw no reason to object and set the date for the week of 11 December 1916. This was now the fourth time that Charlie Stielow had been sentenced to death. Judge Bartlett ordered the court to remain seated while Stielow was led from the room. Just before the cuffs were snapped on his wrists, Stielow paused and extended his hands in a helpless gesture towards Kohn. 'I wish I could tell you what I mean,' he said. 'But I can't.'[36] He was then led away.

In a corridor outside, Charlie spoke briefly with Kohn, who assured him that the fight would go on. Then Charlie was taken immediately to the railroad station where he and his guards boarded an afternoon train for Ossining. There were now no more legal avenues open to Charlie Stielow, nothing to block his path to the electric chair.

18

Reprieve!

The courts might have failed Charlie Stielow, but elsewhere his plight was whipping up a firestorm of protest. Proof that his battle for life had now moved beyond uneasy newspaper editorials and into the public consciousness came in Poughkeepsie, New York, in the late autumn of 1916, when the Collingwood Opera House began showing a movie called *The Celebrated Stielow Case*, a short one-reeler that depicted the condemned man's tribulations. For just 25 cents, patrons could digest what the publicity release called 'The most astounding murder mystery in the history of New York State.'[1] Members of the New York State Board of Charities and Corrections were invited to attend. It is unclear whether any took up the invitation.

Also, as promised, Thomas Mott Osborne and Spencer Miller had not abandoned the fight. Even before the bitterly disappointing Rochester setback, both men were hitting the 'Save Stielow' campaign trail. They shamelessly exploited all of their media contacts, as well as shouting themselves hoarse at public meetings, in order to spread the message of an innocent man rotting on death row. In a long-distance phone call to *The World* – such technical marvels were still worthy of comment – Miller reaffirmed their joint determination to continue the fight. 'Stielow is innocent and we will not give up our efforts to save him. His conviction stands simply because of the existing laws of new evidence, which should be revised at once … Our only hope now is having King come forward and affirm that his confession was the truth. I do not believe all hope for Stielow is gone.'[2]

Five days later, on 17 October, at a meeting of the Humanitarian Cult at Carnegie Hall, Miller led the roster of distinguished speakers, all of whom pleaded for a commutation of Stielow's sentence. The next night it was Osborne's turn. His venue was the Cooper Union in downtown Manhattan and 3,000 people had crammed through its doors. Another 2,000 thronging the sidewalks outside, unable to gain admittance, heard the audience bay approval as Osborne tore into Whitman for his refusal to reprieve Stielow. According to Osborne, the governor was a blinkered bureaucrat, someone prepared to execute an innocent man rather than admit the law's fallibility. He urged everyone present to sign a petition, begging for Stielow's life.

With no more legal options open to the Stielow defence team, all hopes were now pinned on one last clemency plea to Whitman. The governor was in buoyant mood. On 7 November, in the state elections, he had been returned to office, defeating his rival, Samuel Seabury, by almost 150,000 votes. But his track record on clemency pleas did not inspire optimism. Although Whitman had commuted some sentences since taking office, every successful application had included a recommendation for mercy from the prosecuting district attorney; and the chances of Knickerbocker appending his signature to such a request were about as likely as the sun rising in the west.

Elsewhere, away from the glare of media and legal scrutiny, a different kind of battle for Stielow's life was still being fought. On 12 November, a team of private detectives, armed with an arrest warrant, raided a farm at Lyndonville, a village eight miles north of Medina. Erwin King was astonished by their arrival. Ever since Rochester, he had kept on the move, dodging from place to place, eventually holing up at the farm of his cousin, Peter King. When King heard he was under arrest, he blanched. When told that the warrant was for perjuring himself at the trial of Clarence O'Connell, his grizzled features creased in a sigh of relief, and he quickly wiped away the salt tears that had dampened his stubbly cheeks. He just shrugged when the detectives explained that he was being taken to police HQ at Buffalo, where he would be held overnight, pending his transfer to Little Valley the following day.

That evening, in his cell, King was visited by one of the arresting officers and told to empty out his pockets. Among the items recovered was a slip of paper. On it was written 'Knickerbocker & Blake, 88 Main Street, Albion, NY.' King made no attempt to conceal the piece of paper. Indeed, he seemed to find some merriment in its discovery, chortling that 'Old Knick will drop dead when he finds out they have got me.' The detective, feigning puzzlement, decided to give King his head. Chatty as always, the hobo explained: 'When I was discharged from the Albion Jail after the hearing before Rodenback, Knickerbocker, Kirby and Blake talked to me in Knickerbocker's office and told me to keep out in the country until this thing blew over.' The detective studied the slip of paper and asked how King had come by it. 'Knickerbocker had Blake write that address on that paper,' King replied, 'and told me if they bothered me again to let them know at once and he would take care of me.'[3]

King then asked the detective to telephone Knickerbocker and inform him that he was once more in custody and being taken to Little Valley. On one point King was adamant; he wanted Knickerbocker, and no one else, to defend him. The detective agreed. He left with the slip of paper, saying he needed it in order to give the telephone operator the correct address when he placed the call. He never did make that call. Instead, he had the slip of paper photographed, waited a few minutes, then returned it to the unsuspecting prisoner.

Next morning, King was taken to Little Valley jail. Later that day in his cell, out of sight of the guards, King scrawled out a letter to his cousin, Peter King, in Lyndonville. An inmate in the adjoining cell, who had been held overnight and was scheduled for release that day, agreed to smuggle the letter out of the jail. Unbeknown to King, the 'inmate' was a plant; yet another detective. The letter is reproduced as written, without corrections:

November 13, 1916.

Dear Friend peat I am Down in Little Valley Held For purgery December 4 i don't think this Will B much. I wish you would get to Knickerbocker and tell him to go to Kearney at Akron and tell him to tell Kearney to say no if they go to him and ask him if i left a Wallet there and some stuff to say no as they say he has told O Grady so and it may go hard with me if he has told it Knickerbocker will do this for me i done what he wanted me to do for him and he told me he would do it for me.

Erwin King.

This was legal dynamite! If Knickerbocker had offered King some kind of *quid pro quo* in return for perjured testimony, then not only was the district attorney facing almost certain disbarment, but possibly criminal charges as well. And yet, curiously enough, the incendiary content of this and subsequent letters written by King was withheld from Stielow's legal team. Instead, it remained a closely guarded secret for the time being, hoarded by another faction deeply involved in the battle to save Charlie Stielow. The Pulitzer family, proprietors of *The World*, had a ton of money and reporter time invested in the Stielow case and it was they who had planted the private detective in the jailhouse. They were determined to extract the maximum commercial advantage from King's indiscretions,* and if that meant keeping everyone else in the dark, then so be it. First, though, they needed to ensure that King's channels of communication were kept open. A few bucks in the right pocket meant that the Little Valley jailers gladly provided an ever-changing series of temporary prisoners, all of whom agreed to smuggle King's correspondence out to the private detectives.

When King didn't hear anything back from Knickerbocker, his panic levels soared, helped along by a string of false rumours planted

---

* In a heavily expurgated form – all references to Knickerbocker were deleted for libel reasons – these letters finally saw the light of day in *The World* on 10 May 1918.

by the private detectives, who said that some scared folks were beginning to blab about King's involvement in the Shelby shootings. On 15 November, King penned a desperate letter to a fellow roughneck named Joseph Kinnie:*

> November 15, 1916.
> Friend Joe Kinnie I hear that you have Been squealing on me. Know you know that if you tell on me it would Bee the way that they would send me to the Chare. You know what i said to you at parkers Livery. Know one knows But you and you Can save me from the Chare.
> > Erwin King.

That same day King's patience with Knickerbocker finally gave way and he dashed off another letter:

> November 15, 1916.
> Dear friend Knickerbocker i wish you would go to Kearney (Kinnie) and tell him to keep still and tell Kinnie to say i said Nothing to him a Bout the wallet or who got it. You had Better see misis O Connell. Tell her to say that she gave it to me and that it was not the phelps pocket Book for it wood Bee Just as Bad for Claranse as for me. For god sake do this nick and save me.
> > Erwin King.

While King fretted, events moved on. The very next day, it was announced that no fewer than nine of the jurors who convicted Stielow had now signed a petition to Whitman begging for clemency. Such agitation only fuelled the mounting public pressure on Stielow's behalf. Letters began pouring into the governor's mansion at Albany. Each day's mail delivery brought new ammunition for the fight. It was an unprecedented situation. Never before had the plight

---

* 'Kinnie' was Joseph Kinnie, with whom King had shared a bunk at Parker's Livery Stable at Albion on the night of the murders.

of an impoverished prisoner aroused such passion in New York. Normally, this kind of reaction was reserved for well-heeled defendants like Harry Thaw, Albert Patrick and Roland Molineux, rich men accused of murder, and all able to hire an army of lawyers to fight their cause. Eighteen months earlier Charles Frederick Stielow had been unknown and penniless; now he was the most notorious and controversial prisoner in the New York penal system. The clamour grew deafening. Finally, Whitman could ignore the pressure no longer. In a press release, he announced that, on 29 November, he would entertain final representations on Stielow's behalf.

Knickerbocker couldn't believe his ears. With just days remaining of his tenure as district attorney, he was determined to leave office on a high note, and that meant Charlie Stielow frying in the electric chair. Now he faced yet more humiliation. And, always in the background, there was the ticking time-bomb that was Erwin King, who by now was becoming ever more exercised over Knickerbocker's continued silence. He made his anxiety painfully apparent in yet another letter to his cousin, Peter King:

> November 17, 1916.
>
> Dear friend peat Did you get my Letter and did you go to Albion or what did you Doo if you went to Albion. Did you see Knickerbocker. And what Did he say or intend to do for me Know they have got me if Kinnie squeals on me a Bout the phelps case and i sead to him.
>
> Erwin King.

King might not have been making any headway with Knickerbocker, but he was about to get another visitor. On 18 November, Stuart Kohn arrived at the Little Valley jail and, once again, pleaded with King to clear his conscience and confess. Kohn failed in his mission; however his visit clearly unsettled the prisoner, who sat down the next day and scrawled yet another letter. The address on the envelope read: 'M.B. Curby, Albion, NY', but it was undoubtedly intended for

Thomas A. Kirby, who had assisted Knickerbocker at the Rochester hearing. It read:

> Sunday 19.
> Friend Curby I Would like to Have you come out here for I have somethings to tell you. Mr. Kon [Kohn] was here to see me.
>
> Erwin King.[4]

With no reply forthcoming – like its predecessors, this letter never reached its destination – King must have sensed that nobody in the Orleans County legal machine wanted anything to do with him. He was right.

———

On 25 November, Inez Milholland Boissevain died. She had been hospitalised in Los Angeles since her collapse five weeks earlier, and not even two blood transfusions could save her. Reportedly, just before her final moments, she awoke and asked her father, John Milholland, for the latest news about Stielow. He lied and told her that the governor had promised to grant clemency. By all accounts her beautiful features then reposed themselves in an attitude of quiet satisfaction. The end came fifteen minutes later. She was just 30 years old.

News of Inez's death cast a dreadful shadow over the Stielow campaign. Grace Humiston, especially, was deeply affected. Although she and Inez came from different ends of the political spectrum – Grace was never an ardent suffragist – both were united in a desire to fight for the underdog. They'd even discussed going into partnership – 'I thought we would make a good team,'[5] Grace later reflected sadly – and now that dream had died.

A gloomy mood hung over the Stielow team as it gathered for the clemency hearing at the governor's mansion on 29 November.

Everyone sensed that this was the court of last resort. Kohn said as much in a subdued opening, telling Whitman that if this round failed, the defence would abandon its fight to save Stielow. His colleagues groaned inwardly. This was a major miscalculation, tantamount to a poker player showing his hand at the start of a pot, and drew a fusillade of glares from the other defence lawyers. Kohn reddened and tried to make amends. But the hole he'd already dug only got deeper, as he blurted out: 'I know positively and personally that King and O'Connell are the murderers, but I can't make it public at this time.' Whitman, quick as a flash and visibly annoyed by Kohn's overwrought outburst, snapped back: 'But you should make this public. It is your duty to do it and you shall make it public now.'[6]

Appalled by Kohn's ruinous opening, James. W. Osborne quickly intervened: 'This is not possible,' he said soothingly, waving Kohn back to his seat. 'We have facts to substantiate it, but thought this hearing might be adjourned until we could be fully prepared.'[7] Whitman would not budge. There would be no more adjournments, no more motions, no more affidavits, no more vague claims of 'fact'; today was Charlie Stielow's final roll of the dice.

The main submission was handled by Arthur Sutherland. In his eagerness to impugn the prosecution at every step, Sutherland reached impressive levels of indignation as he told how a stool pigeon had been placed in an adjoining cell to overhear confidential conversations between Stielow and his lawyer. Whitman, still bristling from Kohn's earlier indiscretion, said: 'Oh, I know that was not proper, but I don't think what you are saying is material –'

Sutherland interrupted: 'I believe a man in authority who has given a pledge of immunity to a weak-minded creature, who is in jeopardy –'

Now it was Whitman's turn to butt in: 'Why was he in jeopardy? Do you admit he was guilty?'

'No, I am not discussing a legal but a moral question.'

'Do you admit his guilt?'

'I do not,' retorted Sutherland. 'I assert as a matter of public morals you should not send this man to his death if he was induced to confess his guilt by someone who promised him immunity.'[8]

Whitman pulled a face. Where was the evidence that such an offer had been made? Sutherland spluttered helplessly. He knew he wasn't going to win this point and withdrew.

Next up was Grace Humiston. She was not a gifted courtroom performer – most of her victories were won on the streets – but she spoke clearly and well as she outlined the circumstances surrounding the acquisition of King's confession. She obviously made a good impression on Whitman, who listened closely, intrigued by the details of Knickerbocker's jailhouse shenanigans. When Grace sat down, there was a definite sense that she had clawed back at least some of the ground lost by previous counsel. Now it would be left to Osborne to make the final plea for Stielow's life.

Even by the rather more relaxed standards of that era, Osborne had a lively courtroom manner – he once famously resolved a disputed legal point by punching out opposing counsel – and he could be hugely theatrical. He began rationally enough, saying: 'There are a great mass of people in this State who quiver at the thought that you are going to turn on the current to electrocute Stielow.' But it quickly became all too much for the excitable Osborne, who loudly proclaimed: 'The birds won't sing any more for me if this man is electrocuted. I won't enjoy poetry any more, nor will I be able to enjoy the theatre.'[9] Whitman's icy stare brought Osborne back to earth. Hurriedly setting aside his own future cultural well-being, the lawyer retreated to safer ground. 'This man Stielow is very deficient in intellect. His confession was obtained by questionable methods. There is a very grave doubt in the minds of many people about his [guilt].'[10] He ended by saying that surely, with the weight of so much public opinion, the governor could see his way to commute Stielow's sentence to life imprisonment, the same as that being served by Nelson Green?

No! No! No! argued Knickerbocker. This might be his valedictory address as district attorney, but surrender wasn't on the agenda. He waved a petition signed by the supervisors of Orleans County, urging Whitman to allow the law to take its course. He vigorously rebutted every argument raised by the defence; he denied that any offer of immunity had been made to induce the confession; he refuted all allegations of third-degree tactics; and he repeatedly and emphatically hammered home the importance of Hamilton's firearms evidence. Stielow's gun had been the murder weapon, that fact was undeniable. Rather needlessly, in the circumstances, he concluded by declaring his utter opposition to any form of clemency.

With the lawyers finished, Whitman spent several minutes reviewing what he thought were the salient points. There was little in his manner or his words to comfort the defence. Every pronouncement sounded horribly ominous. He'd heard or read nothing, he said, to prove that the alleged promise of immunity had been made with Knickerbocker's connivance or approval. Nor did he set much store by defence contentions that Stielow was a mental defective. At his trial, said Whitman, the defendant had answered all questions cleverly and well. Whitman declared himself in accord with all ten judges who had considered the Stielow case: there was nothing, legally, to warrant any intervention. The courts had given careful consideration to every detail of the Stielow case with the exception of the inadmissible evidence regarding the confession of King, an omission he now promised to rectify. He ended by saying that he would announce his decision on 3 December.

The hearing had lasted four hours. And then it was over. Although Kohn had undoubtedly jumped the gun with his emotional declaration that, if this clemency appeal failed, there would be no more attempts to save Stielow's life – Grace Humiston and others had travelled too far to settle for such a soft option – everyone left the governor's mansion knowing full well that if Whitman refused to intervene, keeping Charles Stielow out of the electric chair would be virtually impossible.

As expected, the Humanitarian Cult's battery of lawyers showed no signs of weakening resolve. They were determined to keep Erwin King front and centre stage, and, to this end, petitioned to have him recommitted to the Little Valley jail. But State Supreme Court Justice Harry L. Taylor, sitting in Buffalo, quashed that hope. On 1 December, he decided that the three lawyers who were asking as 'friends of the court' to have King's bail fixed at an unfeasibly high sum were 'acting in the interests of Stielow and that their main purpose is to have King incarcerated so that he may be questioned further regarding the killing of Phelps in Orleans County'.[11] This was bad law, Justice Taylor reasoned, and he ordered that King be released on his own recognisance. The pedlar couldn't get out of court fast enough.

Sunday 3 December 1916 was probably the longest and most difficult day of Governor Whitman's political career. The Becker execution had hit him hard. Lauded for nailing the corrupt cop, he'd then been castigated for signing away his life; and even though Whitman had since been re-elected with an increased majority, he sensed that his dreams of the White House were still balanced on a knife-edge. Everything now hinged on making the right – at least in the public mind – decision. All day long he wrestled with his conscience. Afternoon came and went. Darkness fell. A crowd of reporters, smoking and looking anxious – they had deadlines to meet – jammed the lobby. And still there was no word from the governor. Finally, Whitman was ready. The governor, looking drawn and haggard, read from a lengthy, prepared address.

'No other criminal case, where clemency has been asked, has perplexed and distressed me as has this,' said Whitman. 'The crime, of which the defendant has been convicted, is one of the most atrocious in the history of the State … The intense feeling against the perpetrators of the crime in the community where it was committed is natural and justified.

'I realize that a Governor who interferes with a judgment of the courts of this state, without good and sufficient cause, is himself committing a lawless act.'

What Whitman said next drove a dagger right through the heart of the Stielow camp. 'I believe that Stielow is guilty. Perhaps never, in the history of New York, has a man been afforded greater opportunity to establish his innocence, if that be possible. Twelve jurors and ten judges have passed upon this case without one dissenting opinion, indicated or expressed. The situation, however, so far as I am able to learn, is unprecedented.

'Another man, under sanctity of an oath, with all the solemnity possible under the conditions, has confessed that he and not Stielow committed the crime … To be sure, the King confession has been repudiated and so has the Stielow confession, without which Stielow could not have been convicted.

'I believe that King's confession is a lie. I cannot escape the conviction, however, in the light of all that has been presented to me and which was not before me when I denied the last application for clemency after I had granted three reprieves, that there is a possibility, perhaps more than a possibility, that this defendant is not guilty.

'The procedure in the courts has been correct, the action of the judges on motions for a new trial has been absolutely right. The King confession, uncorroborated and repudiated by himself, could not be introduced under our rules of evidence, as has been very clearly set forth by Justice Rodenback, but I believe, and I speak from years of experience in the trial of criminal cases, that no jury in this country would have convicted Stielow of murder in the first degree with the King confession before it.'

Slowly, Whitman delivered the denouement. 'I commute the sentence of the court to imprisonment for life.'[12]

After seventeen gut-wrenching months of living in the shadow of the electric chair – and once coming within minutes of extinction – Charles Stielow's lease on life had been extended indefinitely. Inside the Executive Mansion, the response to Whitman's statement was polarised. While frantic reporters rushed off to meet deadlines, Stielow's lawyers, ashen-faced and exhausted, stood half-dazed, just staring blankly at each other. Then the celebrations, the back-slapping began. Someone ran to call Sing Sing.

Governmental aides later revealed that, in reaching his decision, Whitman had dwelt again and again on the mysterious disappearance of the Laskeys. That had been the clincher. Although his statement didn't mention the Laskeys, Whitman was certain that they had been scared into hiding by certain interested parties, in one last desperate bid to bury the truth of the Shelby shootings forever.

———

Charlie Stielow was lying on his bed when the news was brought to him by acting warden Dr Calvin Derrick. It took a moment for its import to sink in. And then the big man broke down and wept. All the emotion came gushing out in wracking sobs. Charlie's relief was shared by the other inmates, who shouted their congratulations. Good news was a rare commodity in the death house: great news came along once, maybe twice a year and everyone wanted a slice of the pie. While men cheered and metal cups were rattled on the cell bars, Derrick explained to Charlie that he could do nothing about transferring him into the general prison population until the official documentation arrived. Charlie, wiping the tears from his fat, fleshy cheeks, didn't give two hoots about that. After all he'd been through, what was one more night?

Laura, who was staying with friends in West Shelby, got the news late that night. She also received a telegram from Mischa Appelbaum: 'Am authorized by some of the Humanitarian Cult to furnish you with the means to educate your children and also to see to it that you are not in want. Please come to New York at my expense, so I can make necessary arrangements.'[13] As events unfolded, it became clear that this was a promise easily made and just as easily forgotten, but for now, Laura and the rest of her family were just too overjoyed, too relieved to even consider the future. All that mattered was that her husband and the father of her children had been delivered from the threat of imminent death.

Newspapers right across the state were lavish in their compliments for Whitman's bravery. The *Albany Evening Journal* captured the general mood with an editorial that said: 'Governor Whitman's decision … reveals commendable ability and readiness to see and appreciate the difference between personal conviction and absolute certainty.'[14] The *Buffalo Express*, while applauding Whitman for his action, argued that commutation should not mark the final word in the Stielow saga: 'We look for more efforts to secure his pardon.'[15] Not everyone was pleased. The *New York Times* counselled caution, hinting darkly that Stielow had been merely a tool of anti-death penalty campaigners, and branding his commutation 'highly unsatisfactory'.[16]

Unsatisfactory or not, on 6 December the paperwork was complete and Charlie Stielow said goodbye to the death house for the final time. Arthur Waite, the debonair and deadly dentist who'd grown especially fond of Stielow, led the other inmates in wishing him well, while Stielow said what he could, which wasn't much.* Stielow shook every inmate by the hand. As he gazed upon their hollowed-out faces and forced smiles, he did so with a heavy heart. Even in a place like the death house, friendships form, and he knew that most of the well-wishers were ghosts-in-waiting. There was nothing more to say. It was time to go.

No sooner had the door clanged shut behind Charlie Stielow than a bidding war broke out on the right to occupy his 'lucky' cell. Most of the inmates were convinced it had some magical properties that would keep them from the chair. History doesn't record who landed the jackpot in this death house lottery.

By coincidence, that same day marked the arrival at Sing Sing of a new warden. William H. Moyer had plenty of experience in running tough prisons, having notched up twelve years as warden of the Atlanta Federal Penitentiary. A former teacher, he had switched to penology in his late thirties, and since that time had earned a reputation for severity, tempered with fairness. Although drafted in to 'stiffen the administration of Sing Sing',[17] he would continue many of Osborne's reforms.

One of his first duties was deciding what to do with Charlie Stielow. He decided to transfer him to a squad of prison 'rookies', to give him time to acclimatise to life as an ordinary prisoner. Inevitably Stielow's arrival into the prison's general population triggered a series of nudges and stares from the other cons, all eager to point out the man who'd cheated the chair and become a Sing Sing legend. Charlie, typically, eschewed any kind of notoriety; he just wanted to be left alone. As he bunked down on his bed that night, he did so with his emotions in turmoil. Although grateful beyond measure to have been snatched from the shadow of the chair, ahead lay the stomach-churning reality of knowing that he would spend the rest of his life behind bars for a crime that he did not commit.

---

* Waite was executed on 24 May 1917.

PART IV

19

Governor Orders Investigation

After darkness fell on the evening of Tuesday 30 January 1917, a scene unfolded outside the Executive Mansion in Albany that might have been lifted from the pages of some spy novel. A car swept in through the main gates, pulled up alongside the building, its rear door swung open and a bewildered-looking, shabbily dressed man was pushed, shivering, out into the icy night air. Before he could fully get his bearings, he was hustled up some steps and in through a side door. No one who wasn't authorised to be present saw him enter and no one would see him leave. The visit had been arranged under conditions of great secrecy and the weather had played its part. A cold front, heavy with snow, had come roaring in from Canada, plunging temperatures into the low teens Fahrenheit and sending the newspapermen who usually covered the mansion beat scurrying, either to the bars or else to their homes.

Governor Whitman was sitting behind a large cherrywood desk in his office when Erwin King shuffled in. Behind the governor, blinds covered the windows to keep out any prying eyes. The wall to his right was lined with leather-bound law books. He fixed King with a penetrating stare. Alongside King stood Sheriff Nichols from Cattaraugus County, looking every bit as nervous and disorientated as his prisoner. His orders had been brief: the governor wants to see King – get him to Albany, fast, and don't breathe a word to anyone. The directive had arrived without any warning. Nichols couldn't imagine why the governor was suddenly so keen to interview King. Like everyone else, he'd assumed that the commutation of Stielow's death sentence had marked the end of this bizarre saga. All this cloak-and-dagger stuff unnerved him.

Indeed, so top secret was this meeting that its existence was not even acknowledged until the *Auburn Citizen* ran the story more than a year later, on 9 May 1918. According to the paper, the following exchange was quoted 'on the best of authority' – journalistic code-speak for the governor himself.

Whitman let King stew in silence for several seconds – a holdover from his days as a prosecutor – then spoke abruptly. 'Sit down, King. I want to talk to you about this case. When did you get out of jail?'

King, panicky and caught off-guard, mumbled some response about Little Valley. Whitman rephrased his question. 'When did you get out of the *Albion* jail?'

King told him.

'When did you see Mr. Knickerbocker last?' asked the governor.

'I don't know.'

'Have you communicated with him since you were in jail?'

'No.'

'Write him any letters?'

At first, King replied in the negative, only to backtrack just moments later. 'Yes, but he didn't get them.'

'How did you know he did not get them?'

'I saw him one day in Albion for about five minutes and he told me.'

Whitman pounced. 'I thought you told me you didn't see anybody?'

This rattled King. He garbled something about having a forgetful memory. Whitman didn't bother to hide his contempt as King prevaricated. Moments later the governor reached for a small pile of letters that lay on his desk and fanned them out before King's incredulous eyes. The hobo gulped back his disbelief as he studied the very letters that he had written while being held in Little Valley jail. At long last, *The World* had forwarded the letters to Whitman and their effect on the governor was volcanic. Knickerbocker's duplicity had stunned Whitman; lies, suppression of evidence, perverting the course of justice, the list of malfeasance seemed endless. Whitman was boiling like a cauldron as he glared across the desk at King, fighting hard to keep his rage under control.

King crumbled beneath Whitman's onslaught, as the questions were fired at him like bullets. All of the glib cockiness was gone, supplanted by the cold, clammy knowledge that soon – no, make that *very soon* – he might be sweating his turn in a cell on death row. His spluttering denials eventually petered out and he admitted authorship of the letters. Once this was done, after a few more questions he was bundled out of the Executive Mansion as secretly as he had arrived, and driven back to Little Valley jail.

After a night's sleep, Whitman had decided on his next step. The subsequent 48 hours were spent finalising the details, then came a press announcement: he had appointed former Onondaga County district attorney George H. Bond to head up a commission that would investigate every aspect of the Stielow case. To cloak Bond in the proper authority, Whitman made him a special deputy attorney general.

Whitman's shock announcement, unprecedented in a capital case, caught everyone off-guard. In Orleans County it caused jaw-dropping incredulity that quickly metamorphosed into blind fury. Taxpayers there had been beaten into the ground by the financial burden of the Stielow case – lawyers' bills and other charges were still flooding in – and now yet more expense loomed on the horizon. In reality, county doom-mongers hugely exaggerated the financial impact of Whitman's decision. As the governor made clear in his announcement, all of the commission's expenses would be borne by the state, a fact that was conveniently overlooked by the Orleans County press, leaving most locals convinced that, once again, Albany's clunking fist had crushed the little guy.

There was also a chorus of angry complaints about the man chosen to head the commission, George H. Bond. What chance of a fair
shake could the county expect from someone who just happened to
be a law partner of the state's lieutenant governor, Edward Schoeneck?
It was all too buddy-buddy.

Actually, there was good reason to expect that Bond would be
more than sympathetic to the hard-pressed residents of Orleans
County. By his own admission, he was deeply sceptical about the
need for a commission, saying: 'After I had carefully read and studied
the record of the trial itself my opinion was that Stielow was guilty.'[1]
But the 43-year-old Syracuse-based lawyer promised to banish any
preconceptions. 'I am going after the facts and the truth regarding the Phelps-Wolcott murder,' he told his local newspaper. 'Facts,
truth, justice – those are the big things.'[2]

Whitman had gauged the public mood well. The announcement
of the commission and Bond's appointment rode a rising tide of popular opinion in favour of Stielow. Another movie, called *The People
vs. John Doe*, had opened at the Broadway Theater in New York, and
had played to packed houses. Although a composite of several cases,
the core of the script centred on the Stielow case, with its depiction
of someone convicted on dubious evidence. Critics mocked the film
as nothing more than a heavy-handed polemic against capital punishment. Whatever its philosophical shortcomings, the movie – the
second in just a few months to feature Stielow's ordeal – helped keep
the farmhand's name in the public eye.*

On 9 March 1917, Governor Whitman signed an appropriation
bill for $25,000 to cover the expense of the special investigator 'in
order that the state may settle for all time the guilt or innocence of a
man who is now under sentence of life imprisonment for murder.'[3]

With the funds in place, Bond got to work. Item number one on
the agenda: interview Stielow. In late January, Charlie had been one

---

* In 1919, the movie director D.W. Griffith would also work elements of Stielow's
ordeal into *The Mother and the Law*.

of a batch of 40 long-term inmates transferred from Sing Sing to Auburn Prison, a move that reunited him with Nelson Green, whom he had not seen since three days after the trial. It also meant he would now get to rub shoulders with the prisoner believed by many to have fired the gun in the Shelby murders – Clarence O'Connell.

Over that summer, Bond would interview Stielow several times, but their first meeting was crucial to the commission's outcome. The big-city lawyer saw before him a slow-witted, poorly educated man, surprisingly free from bitterness, and it occurred to Bond that maybe Stielow's lack of rancour was inspired by a sense of profound relief at having escaped the electric chair. Everything in the trial transcript pointed to Stielow's guilt, Bond was sure of that, and he wondered if the big fellow was now ready to make a clean breast of it. Writing later, Bond described how he endeavoured to make the prisoner confess.

'Stielow,' said Bond, 'nothing more can happen to you. You have everything to gain and nothing to lose by telling the truth. If you are guilty of this murder and will confess it to me, you will save the expense of this investigation and in that way you will perform a service to the State. I will write that into my report, with my recommendation, and it may aid you in obtaining some commutation of your sentence. If on the other hand you are guilty and you don't tell of it now and I find it out, I will write that in my report and it will stand against you always.'[4]

Bond explained later that his offer to Stielow hadn't been couched in such precise terms, only that this conveyed the meaning of his message. Had he employed any fancy legal language all he would have received in return was a vacant stare. He realised that Stielow's lack of mental acuity had not been overstated; everything had to be phrased in the simplest words possible. Still, he managed to convey his meaning. Charlie Stielow, made aware that giving the 'right' answer might shave a few years off his life sentence, simply shook his head. 'I did not do it,' he said. 'And if I said I did, it would be a lie.'[5]

The straightforward disingenuousness of Stielow's reply made a deep impression on Bond. For the first time, he wondered if he – like so many others who came face-to-face with the big farmhand – might have made a mistake.

———————

The Stielow defence team had fallen into three distinct camps. There were those like Mischa Appelbaum, who were bitterly opposed to the death penalty and, to some extent, used Charlie as a pawn in their political game. Others – Inez Milholland Boissevain among them – took the view that Charlie was probably guilty but mentally insufficient, and should therefore not face execution. And then there were the likes of David White and Grace Humiston who believed unflinchingly in Stielow's innocence and vowed to continue the fight to free him and Nelson Green. But they were running out of leads. Grace was also increasingly sidetracked by other issues. After half a dozen years of bland domesticity, the Stielow crusade had reinvigorated her campaigning zeal, and the spring of 1917 found her involved in yet another sensational murder case.

On the afternoon of 13 February 1917, a pretty seventeen-year-old high school senior named Ruth Cruger had vanished in Manhattan. She was last seen going to collect a pair of ice skates she had left for sharpening at a motorcycle store on West 127th Street. Each year, hundreds of young women went missing in New York City. Most did so of their own volition. Some eloped; some wanted to break the shackles of convention and make their own way in the world; some simply went off the rails; an unknown number ended up in brothels or working the streets. The detectives who investigated Ruth's disappearance were confident that she fell into one of these categories. Ruth's well-to-do family was appalled by such smug complacency and incensed by what they considered to be a decidedly lacklustre police investigation. (Officers had searched the motorcycle store perfunctorily, found nothing, and left.) When, over the next few days, several witnesses came forward to say that a young woman matching Ruth's description had climbed into a cab outside the motorcycle store, detectives just yawned. This merely confirmed their suspicions. Since no body had been found, they ruled out homicide as an option, and were eager to close the case. By their lights, Ruth was just another 'good girl gone bad'; happened all the time. The running battle between Ruth's family and the police festered until early April, at which point the family contacted Grace Humiston. After Stielow's miraculous escape from the electric chair, Grace was once again a tabloid favourite, and she jumped at the chance of investigating yet another headline-maker. Her commitment to the Cruger case meant that she was only able to render peripheral assistance to Bond as he pursued his investigation.

But he had uncovered two strong allies in the newly elected district attorney for Orleans County, William Munson, and its new sheriff, Isaac Swart. Politically, both were trapped in no man's land. On the one hand, the Orleans County Republican Party machine was desperate to wash its hands of Charles Frederick Stielow, but Munson and Swart had been elected on a ticket of cleaning house. And that meant a complete break with the past. Bravely, both men ignored local prejudice and rendered every assistance to Bond whenever he came calling.

Someone else in urgent need of a helping hand was Laura Stielow, by now the forgotten victim in this tragedy. She and the kids had paid a terrible price for bearing the Stielow name. After the trial they were shunned as pariahs. By early 1916, vicious gossip and iron-hard stares had driven them out of their home and into adjoining Niagara County and the hamlet of Gasport. Thereafter life was one constant round of hardship and hunger. When news of Charlie's commutation came through, Laura, although overjoyed, saw no change in her miserable circumstances. Mischa Appelbaum's windy promises of help – targeted more at the press than the Stielows – failed to materialise, leaving Laura stranded on her own with three youngsters. When winter hit there was no money for new clothes; they had to rely on hand-me-downs and Laura's skill with a needle and thread. At times, their bellies groaned from a lack of food. In March 1917, a faint glimmer of hope suddenly appeared. A farmer in Salamanca, Cattaraugus County had advertised for a housekeeper. Laura got the job but it didn't last long. For reasons that can only be guessed at – the suspicion lingers that the boss expected more than mere domestic duties – Laura quit abruptly and shooed her three children out of the door. For a few weeks they subsisted on the charity of kindly neighbours, until, penniless and close to starving, Laura was forced to throw herself on the mercy of the local superintendent of the poor, Willis P. Kysor. His response was brutal and uncompromising: taxpayers in Cattaraugus County wanted nothing to do with the notorious Stielow family. After three weeks of being shunted around like refugees, on the morning of 7 April, Laura and her kids were dumped on a train at Dayton and shipped back to Gasport, where relatives had promised to take them in.

If any other passengers on the northbound train recognised the infamous Stielows, chances are they didn't pay much attention. They had something else, far more important, to occupy their minds. All talk was of the sensational news from Washington. Just the previous day, at 3:12am, the House of Representatives, by a vote of 373 to 50, had adopted a resolution legitimising hostilities between the United States and the Imperial German Government. At around midday, the bill passed the Senate without a hitch. That afternoon, at a little after one o'clock, President Woodrow Wilson put his signature to the resolution. After three years and 246 days of hostilities, the United States finally declared war on Germany.

At 43 years of age, Bond was too old for the draft – initially it was restricted to men between nineteen and 25 years – leaving him to continue his task without official hindrance. Just as well, really; because he had been handed a truly Herculean task. Collating all the details from more than 1,450 pages of evidence would require more than one brain and one pair of hands. Bond needed assistance from someone he could trust implicitly. It came in the shadowy form of a 51-year-old lawyer and former government investigator named Charles E. Waite. Most unusually for an attorney, Waite had a deep-seated aversion to publicity, particularly when it came to photographs (there are no images of this secretive man in existence, according to the *New York Times*). He was the perfect foil to Bond; incisive and industrious, discreet to the point of invisibility.

Together, the two men set about re-examining every scrap of evidence that had been introduced in the original trial. First, they concentrated on Stielow's unsigned 'confession'. What they discovered was a statement wholly lacking in any single new fact about the murders; everything it contained was an artful reworking of information already in the public domain. And they noticed something even more curious – the entire story was riddled with factual errors. One of the most glaring arose from Stielow's assertion that, after sneaking across to the Phelps house at around 10:00pm and seeing that Phelps and Wolcott were still awake, he decided to lay a false trail by tramping up to Jenkins's barn and down the transmission line. Then, after returning to the Phelps house to discover that the occupants had still not retired, he skulked behind the barn out the back. Yet when that area was searched the next morning, investigators saw no marks in the virgin snow. If Stielow had been hiding behind the barn, any footprints he left should have been as visible as those found in the driveway or on the road.

Details of the break-in itself also sounded phoney. According to Stielow in this 'confession', at approximately 10:45pm, he and Green knocked at the kitchen door. As soon as Phelps opened the door, Green burst in, struck him a blow with the broken mop handle, then shot him three times. With Phelps mortally wounded on the kitchen floor, both men made for the old man's bedroom where he was rumoured to stash his money. They had just crossed the dining room and entered the bedroom when Margaret Wolcott suddenly burst from her room behind them and ran into the kitchen. They chased after her, circling the large table and chairs that filled the central portion of the dining room, and into the kitchen. As she exited through the kitchen door and pulled it shut behind her, Green fired once through the glass, wounding her fatally. Then, without giving their second victim another thought, the two men began ransacking Phelps's bedroom. Setting aside the intrinsic flaw in this story – that Stielow and Green would have been surprised by Wolcott's presence when both knew that she was in the house and had only recently retired – this version of events threw up another major inconsistency.

When Bond and Waite visited the Phelps house, they made careful measurements, the most significant of which showed that the bullet hole in the kitchen door window was exactly three feet and eight-and-a-half inches from the bottom of the door. Now, since Margaret Wolcott had been shot under the left arm and through the heart, by a bullet that continued on a level path through her body, it followed that she and her killer were standing on the same level when the fatal bullet was shot. But Wolcott was very short, a fraction under five feet tall. If she had been standing outside the kitchen door when she was struck – as noted in Stielow's statement – the vertical distance from the first step to the line of the bullet through the glass was four feet and one inch. This meant the bullet would have entered her body somewhere in the vicinity of the shoulder. If she had been standing on the second step – some four inches lower – the bullet would have entered her head. If she had been standing on the ground – a further nine inches down – the bullet would have passed over her head by one or two inches. Simple physics proved that Margaret Wolcott could not possibly have been shot in the manner that Stielow described. This flash of detective brilliance by Bond and Waite wouldn't have disgraced an episode of modern crime drama *CSI*.

The kitchen door posed another serious problem: it opened inward and away from the entrance to the dining room. This also made a nonsense of Stielow's confession. In it, he stated that Miss Wolcott had fled through the kitchen door and pulled it behind her when Green opened fire. Since the shot that killed Miss Wolcott had been fired at right angles to the glass, this meant that the gunman had to be positioned directly in front of the door when he fired. And yet, according to Stielow, Green was standing in the entrance to the dining room when he fired. Had he been so, any shot he fired would have struck the glass obliquely, at an angle of approximately 45 degrees and careered harmlessly off into the darkness. Again, the physical evidence did not square with Stielow's account. When Bond and Waite studied the angles in the kitchen, they concluded that, most likely, the killer had been searching an unused room that adjoined the kitchen to the rear, when he heard Wolcott trying to make her escape. He ran back into the kitchen and fired while she was still standing on the kitchen floor, in the act of pulling the door to with her left hand. The bullet had passed through the glass and entered her body.

Had David White been granted sufficient funds, he might have been able to ascertain all of this, but he had been operating on a shoestring. The state had outspent him by a ratio of 50:1; there was no money in the defence fund to pay for the kind of detailed analysis that Bond and Waite carried out on the Phelps house.

Setting aside the physical impossibility of much that Stielow had alleged, Bond and Waite turned next to the sheer number of illogicalities that littered the confession. For instance, was it really likely that Stielow and Green had set out, undisguised, to rob their employer? To swallow this argument, one would have to believe that they deliberately planned this break-in with murder in mind. Either that, or else face certain identification.

A second oddity was that, after shooting Margaret Wolcott, neither man bothered to check if she'd actually been struck by the bullet. Instead, they merely carried on looting the house. According to Stielow, the next time he saw Miss Wolcott was several minutes later, when he returned to his house to find the stricken woman lying on his doorstep, gasping, 'Charlie, please let me in, I'm dying.'[6]

This raised another red flag for the two investigators: why on earth would Miss Wolcott run to the house of the very men who had shot her? Even in her terror-stricken state, she must have recognised Stielow and Green, yet still she sought safety in their house. Again, this didn't make any sense.

And there was the conundrum of Miss Wolcott's alleged cries for help. Was it really possible, Bond asked Dr Otto H. Schultze, a medical examiner with the Homicide Bureau of the New York City district attorney's office, for a slightly built woman to run more than 90 yards with a bullet in her heart, beat on a door, and cry out in a voice loud enough to be heard in the Benson household, some 130 yards away? Schultze conceded the possibility of her staggering this distance – there are numerous well-documented accounts of people performing quite extraordinary physical feats while mortally wounded – but he thought that, in this instance, the massive haemorrhaging that Miss Wolcott suffered, which caused her lungs to flood with blood, would have stifled any cries for help. She might have screamed twice or three times immediately after being struck, he theorised, but he scotched any claims that her pleas for help could have been heard several minutes after the shooting. By that time she would have been dead.

Another crime scene anomaly that baffled both investigators was why, if Stielow and Green were the killers, they had permitted Phelps to live. Even with three bullets in him, he might possibly recover and identify his assailants. So why not finish him off?

Also, why had Stielow and Green made no attempt to flee the scene of the crime, knowing that they would be obvious suspects? Instead, they had simply strolled back across the road and climbed into bed, just waiting for the murders to be discovered.

And, finally, what had happened to the money? Why was it that neither the pocketbook nor a single cent was ever found in the possession of either Stielow and Green, or their families?

The more Bond and Waite studied the confession, the angrier they became. They were long past the sceptical stage; both were united in their view – namely, that the unsigned statement upon which the state had relied to send Charles Stielow to the death house was a patchwork of lies, stitched together by a team of crooked investigators, to fit the available facts as they saw them. But, as we have seen, most of what Stielow was forced to say, or reputed to have said, was either physically impossible or so absurd as to defy belief.

Both Bond and Waite kept their findings under wraps, glad to be far from the glare of newspaper scrutiny. Not that the press was greatly interested in Charlie Stielow any more. Since his commutation, he'd faded from the headlines and rarely rated a mention, even on the inside pages. All of which suited Bond fine. That meant there were no reporters on hand when he travelled to Buffalo on 27 April 1917, and there met Charley Reynolds. Bond had tracked down the 'wild man' who, two years earlier, had been thrown into the Albion jail alongside Stielow on the night after his arrest (see chapter 4). Except that Reynolds was no drunk, and Reynolds was not his real name. In reality, Charles Sparacino was a Buffalo cop, and back in 1915 he'd been a private detective on the payroll of George W. Newton, planted in the jailhouse to pump Stielow for information.

Conscience and the confessional box had combined to get the better of Sparacino. After agonising with his priest, Sparacino had approached the Buffalo police chief, John Martin, and revealed his part in an underhanded scheme to 'rope'[7] Charlie Stielow. Martin, deeply troubled by the admission, had ordered his junior officer to set the record straight. Sparacino told Bond that he'd spent fourteen days in the Albion jailhouse and, during that time, Stielow had never admitted any guilt. Quite the contrary, he had repeatedly stressed his entire innocence. In an ironic touch, Sparacino revealed that even the unwitting David White had attempted to enlist Sparacino's assistance while he was behind bars, asking him to prevail on Stielow to tell him (White) the absolute truth. Sparacino promised to do what he could. He told Stielow that a lawyer 'was like a priest', and that he could confess anything to his lawyer without it going any further. But Stielow was adamant. 'I have told the lawyer everything,' he said. 'If I told him I done it I would tell a lie.'[8]

Bond was impressed. Sparacino's story confirmed his own favourable impression of Stielow's honesty, but it was what Sparacino said next that really piqued the lawyer's curiosity. In recent months rumours had surfaced of a concealed Dictograph being used to record some of Stielow's jailhouse conversations. Sparacino admitted that the stories were true. Moreover, he revealed that the covert surveillance had lasted no fewer than 85 days – right up to 24 July, the day after Stielow's conviction – and that not once during this period had the prisoner admitted any part in the killings. Even when he met with Nelson Green on 18 May – the first time they had been together since their arrest – neither man said anything inculpatory. Unsurprisingly, this Dictograph transcript never found its way into the trial record, nor was its existence ever made known to the defence.

As Bond returned to New York, a single question dominated his thinking: if Knickerbocker really did have a solid confession, why had he felt the need to place a stool pigeon in with Stielow, and why bother recording all his jailhouse conversations over nearly three months? Only one answer made sense to Bond: the district attorney knew that the Stielow confession was shaky and he was scraping around to find some kind of back-up. It didn't arrive, but Knickerbocker got lucky. Despite Judge Pound's scepticism about the confession, the jury had swallowed it whole. Hardly surprising then, thought Bond, that in his recent pronouncements, Knickerbocker had pointedly distanced himself from the confession, choosing instead to trumpet the importance of the firearms evidence. It was Stielow's .22 handgun and his alone, Knickerbocker told the Rochester hearing, that had been the instrument of death. Hadn't 'Gun Expert Hamilton' testified that the 'nine abnormal defects that looked like nine teeth to a saw'[9] that he'd found in the barrel of Stielow's gun would reproduce markings upon a bullet exactly like the markings which Hamilton claimed to have found on the bullets taken from the bodies of Phelps and Wolcott?

Bond and Waite now decided to put that theory under the microscope. It was time to reappraise the evidence of 'That Man From Auburn' – Albert H. Hamilton.

20

Hamilton Exposed as a Fraud

Bond and Waite scrutinised every word that Hamilton had uttered while on the witness stand. While under oath, the Auburn pharmacist had sworn that the four bullets recovered from the crime scene were '.22 calibre, rim fire, U.M.C. short, black powder, obsolete cartridge bullets,' and that, by obsolete, he meant that 'they were on sale from 7 to 10 or 12 years ago, and are not now in the open market except when found in collections'.[1] Hamilton had prefaced this by stating that he had, over a period of several years, collected more than 25,000 cartridges of various calibres, and had determined that the four bullets had been purchased about eight years previously because they were of a type peculiar to the Union Metallic Cartridge Company (UMC). He also claimed to have some of these bullets in his possession, saying that he'd purchased them in approximately 1908.

This was the Hamilton version. But would it stand up to scrutiny? Bond first set about testing Hamilton's claim that these bullets were deucedly difficult to find. He made his own efforts to locate UMC cartridges manufactured between 1907 and 1909 and came up empty-handed. This prompted a visit to the UMC factory in Bridgeport, Connecticut, where the company's chief ballistics engineer, William Morgan Thomas, told him that, prior to 1909, black powder cartridges and smokeless powder lubricated cartridges were the only cartridges containing soft lead bullets that UMC manufactured. When Bond handed Thomas the four bullets recovered from the crime scene, the engineer studied them closely and told Bond to wait for a few minutes. He returned a short while later with a box of UMC bullets manufactured in 1908. In every respect – calibre, weight of lead, and the number of grains of black power – they were identical to the bullets fired into the bodies of Phelps and Wolcott. Bond paid for the box and left.

While Bond was in Connecticut, Waite had been hunting down recognised experts in the field of firearms identification. This was tricky. Rather than rely on professional expert witnesses who might be tempted to shade their evidence to suit the needs of their pay-master, he took the devil's advocate route and restricted his search to police officers, working on the assumption that they were unlikely to be prejudiced in favour of any accused person. The obvious starting place was the New York Police Department and here the top fire-arms experts were Captain William A. Jones of the Third Branch of the Detective Bureau and Sergeant Harry F. Butts. Bond and Waite met the two police officers on 14 May 1917 at the Third Branch, a three-storey building at 219 East 116th Street. Also present were the pathologist, Dr Otto Schultze, and Lieutenant James A. Faurot, Chief Inspector of the New York Detective Bureau and the country's fore-most fingerprint expert. Faurot was a leading light in the campaign to put American crime investigation on the same kind of scientific footing as that enjoyed in Europe.

As a preliminary, Detective Butts fired several bullets from a variety of both expensive and cheap .22 and .38 calibre revolvers, to show the witnesses how each gun left its own unique 'fingerprint' on every bullet that it fired. He used the preferred method of bullet retrieval at the time; firing into three or four bales of cotton batting (wadding used for quilts). This caused minimal damage to the bullet and enabled a clear view of any markings. When examined under a microscope, none of the markings made on the random bullets bore the slightest resemblance to those found on Exhibit D.D. – the bullet taken from Phelps's chest.

At the time of this test, the Stielow gun (Exhibit G.G.) was in exactly the same physical condition as when it was handed to Bond in March 1917. When Bond gave the gun to Jones, he ordered that its physical condition not be altered in any way – by means of cleaning, for example – except by the passage of the bullet through the barrel. Before Jones and Butts began their tests, Bond read out the following extract from Hamilton's trial testimony: 'I noticed that this particular Exhibit G.G. had been so constructed that the cylinder fitted tightly against the rear of the barrel, when the hammer is down against the barrel. There is no opening. The explosion of gases does not leak out in the rear, and this particular gun causes the explosion of gases all to emit from the muzzle and follow the bullet out.'[2]

Both officers expressed surprise. The Young American .22 was not an expensive, high-precision weapon – far from it – and they seriously doubted that it had been manufactured to the tolerances necessary to confirm Hamilton's testimony. They devised a simple test. After loading one of the UMC bullets into the Stielow gun, Butts folded a piece of paper and laid it over the cylinder. Then he test-fired the weapon. Not only did enough gas escape from around the cylinder to scorch the paper, but the back-flame was so great that it actually ignited the paper. Not for the last time, Hamilton's testimony had been shown to be false. The witnesses all examined the paper closely and each appended his initials to what was left of the burnt sheet to confirm the test's authenticity.

So if the non-existent explosive gases hadn't filled in those 'nine abnormal defects'[3] that Hamilton purportedly found at the muzzle of Stielow's gun, then what had? Hamilton, again, had provided an answer. Just before the Rochester hearing, he'd sworn a fresh affidavit for the prosecution, attributing this mysterious metamorphosis to the use of soft lead bullets. He explained that, as the test bullets left the muzzle of the Stielow gun, the lead in the bullet had expanded, thus filling in 'the rust depressions,'[4] and rendering them invisible. Not an uncommon side effect of soft lead bullets, he added airily, drawing on his experience of hundreds of test firings. It was hokum, of course, and when Butts and Jones read this they just shook their heads in disbelief.

The test bullet was then examined closely. Even to the naked eye it bore not the slightest resemblance, either in size or markings, to the reference bullet that had been removed from Phelps's body. After being marked with a letter 'A' on its base, the bullet was stored in a specially prepared box.

The next day everyone was back at Third Branch. Out of fairness to Hamilton, Bond decided to reconfigure the method of testing. Two weeks earlier he had met Hamilton for the first time and, during this interview, Bond asked what method he had used to recover his test bullets. Hamilton replied that he always packed a pail about three quarters full of cotton batting, and then filled the pail with water. In order to replicate as closely as possible the conditions used by Hamilton, Bond asked Jones that the remainder of the bullets be test-fired into a similar combination of water and cotton. Jones duly packed a pail half-full with cotton, then filled the remainder of the pail with water to within two inches of the top. Butts fired a shot into the pail of water. The bullet was recovered from about the middle part of the cotton. Microscopic examination revealed markings on it identical to those of the bullet fired the previous day. This latest bullet was marked with a letter 'C' and placed in a specially prepared box.

Only now – with two test bullets safely stored – did Bond give permission for the gun to be cleaned. Captain Jones handled this part of the test. He passed four small flannel wads through the barrel. Each wad was numbered and placed in a box. Jones frowned when he saw the accumulation of sediment that the cleanings had removed. He and Butts were of the same mind; before yesterday, no shot had been fired through this gun barrel for at least three, probably four or more years. It was just too dirty. This finding was critical. At a stroke, it ripped the heart out of Hamilton's testimony. Two years earlier at the trial, Hamilton swore that he had carried out test firings with

Stielow's gun. But the physical evidence lying on the flannel wads branded him a liar – *he hadn't fired the gun, at all!* Although it was only opinion and not verifiable fact, by Jones's reckoning, nobody had fired the Stielow gun since 1914 at the very latest.

Bond next asked to see what difference the cleaning had upon a test bullet. A third UMC cartridge was fired under identical conditions to those previously described. When recovered it was an exact replica of the two previous bullets in terms of markings, except that the roughness present in the markings of the first bullet and, to a lesser degree, in the second bullet did not exist in this final bullet, due to the polished condition of the barrel. This third bullet was marked with a letter 'G' on its base and stored safely in a box.

When the tests were completed, Jones and Butts, who between them had more than 30 years' experience in firearms analysis, were emphatic: none of the bullets fired from the Stielow gun bore the slightest resemblance to Exhibit D.D. – the bullet taken from Phelps's chest – which was used as the reference bullet. Their conclusion? Stielow's .22 Young American was definitely not the murder weapon.

Bond and Waite were grim-faced. Hamilton had long been notorious as a glib huckster, but these tests now damned him as a deliberate perjurer, someone prepared to conspire in the murder of an innocent man. And his evidence had been crucial. Bond recalled Judge Pound's warning to the jury that Stielow could only be convicted if they believed his confession; nothing else mattered, said the judge, not even Hamilton's evidence. But Bond had also been a lawyer long enough to realise the impact that expert witness testimony had on the average juror. He also knew just how persuasive Hamilton could be when on the stand. Judge Pound's admonition to the jury to disregard Hamilton's evidence was all well and good, but once that expert testimony was in, it required a rare form of detachment – one possessed by few jurors, certainly at that time – to disregard it completely. In this context, Bond found it impossible to believe a jury made up of eleven farmers and a single tradesman, as Stielow's had been, would not have been swayed by Hamilton's lethal evidence.

With the firing tests finished, Bond gathered up the bullets and shipped them to Max Poser at Bausch & Lomb in Rochester, with a request that Poser make microphotographs for the grand jury investigation into Stielow's conviction that Bond now believed was inevitable. He and Waite took some time to step back and reassess their position. The ballistics evidence, allied to already grave doubts about the confession, now convinced them that Stielow was no murderer, just a hapless dupe who'd been railroaded to the brink of the electric chair. But both men reckoned that in order to clear Stielow's name beyond any shadow of doubt, they needed to track down the real killer. There was, of course, only one place to start. Ten days after the firearms tests were complete, Bond travelled to the Little Valley jail, and there had his first meeting with Erwin King.

King was still being held on perjury charges related to the Bowen robbery. He wasn't alone. Just a few cells along, in an adjoining wing, was Clarence O'Connell. Although O'Connell had been transferred from Auburn on 1 May, pending a potential retrial for the Hall brothers, at no time had he ever come into contact with his erstwhile partner.

Bond's first interview with King went well. The prisoner seemed relaxed and didn't baulk when Bond asked him to repeat, in as near the same words as possible, the confession he'd made to Grace Humiston on 11 August 1916. King began smoothly. Too smoothly, Bond thought. It all sounded very well-rehearsed. Bond noticed that King used the same type of phraseology he'd adopted in making his retraction on 13 August. It took the form of either prefacing his statements with 'I told her', or else interjecting comments such as 'that was what I told her'.[5] A typical example came when he described meeting

O'Connell, as arranged, in Medina on the night of the shootings: 'We went and got a rig and started at Center Street towards Shelby Basin, and I told her [Grace Humiston], he had a quart of whisky and we drank quite freely of it.'[6]

When King finished, Bond read the statement back to the prisoner, who initialled each page before signing and swearing to the document. Once this was done, Bond asked King to recount the events that preceded the retraction. King commenced by describing the notorious automobile journey from Little Valley to Albion and his various conversations with the other passengers. On arrival in Albion, he said, he was taken before a committee of citizens and there, in the presence of a stenographer, he made the unprompted retraction. As before, when King concluded, the statement was immediately read over to him and he initialled each page and signed and swore to it. With these statements in his case, Bond left.

He next saw King on Wednesday 30 May. During this interview, he asked the prisoner to account roughly for his movements from the time of his arrival in Lockport in January 1915. King did this – showing suspiciously enviable powers of recall – setting out in great detail his movements covering each day from 8 March until Tuesday 23 March 1915, two days after the shootings. Once again, he signed and swore to the statement.

Forty-eight hours later, Bond was back. This time his questions were far more pointed. He asked King to repeat, in detail, his movements day by day from the time of his arrival at the Barge View Hotel on 14 March. The interrogation dragged on long into the night and finally halted at 11:45pm, when King was given a break and taken back to his cell. Next morning, at half past eight, the questioning resumed. This time, Bond demanded an account of King's actions from 23 March 1915 until the day of his confession in Little Valley jail in August 1916.

Everything that had gone before between Bond and the prisoner had been building towards this incident – King's confession to Grace

Humiston. At the time, Grace had been mauled by the press – most notably in and around Orleans County – with barely veiled accusations that she had offered him $3,000 and the promise of a light prison sentence in return for a confession. Bond asked for a full account of Grace's involvement. To his credit, King complied. Every word he said was taken down in longhand, with Bond prompting at every turn, 'Well, was there anything further that Mrs Humiston said?' or 'Did Mrs Humiston say anything more?'[7] At no time did King accuse Grace of impropriety. He had made the confession to her freely and without any kind of bribe or coercion.

As Bond read through King's various statements and affidavits, little inconsistencies began to appear. He probably read more into some of these than was really there. Ask anyone to account, over several long, exhausting interviews, for their movements and anomalies will occur. Indeed, modern investigators are trained to be suspicious of statements that repeat, parrot-fashion, an identical string of facts. Such uniformity smacks of being learnt, not remembered. Setting that caveat aside, though, Bond noted that most discrepancies came to light when he compared King's statements with those made by O'Connell. On certain dates, especially around the time of the murders and lasting up until the time of O'Connell's arrest in July 1915, each man told radically different stories of certain days' events.

Bond hounded King over these inconsistencies. Each day he returned, wanting to clarify this, or corroborate that. Gradually, King's cocky manner, originally so assured, began to seep away. The week-long war of attrition came to an end on 7 June.

It was about 2:30pm when Bond arrived at the jail. By this time, King was thoroughly fed up of answering questions and he'd become morose and uncooperative. Still, Bond would not give him a moment's peace. Finally, at a little after five o'clock, King suddenly looked up at Bond and said: 'Come back after supper and I will tell you the truth.'[8] At 6:30pm, Bond returned. Over the next 30 minutes the two men talked. It wasn't inquisitorial, more like a chat between old friends. Finally, with an air of utter resignation, King looked up at Bond and said simply: 'Me and O'Connell did this deed.'[9]

Bond, a solid professional right down to his wingtip shoes, didn't betray a flicker of emotion. He calmly advised King of his rights, saying that anything he might say would be used in evidence against him. Did he understand? The other man nodded. Then Bond stood up and said: 'King, just raise your right hand. Do you solemnly swear that the statement you are about to make in regard to the murder of Charles B. Phelps and Margaret Wolcott, and which is given voluntarily by you without promise of reward, or without any offer of immunity, will be the truth, the whole truth and nothing but the truth, so help you God?'

King's answer was 'Yes, sir.'[10]

He held nothing back. And this confession was infinitely more detailed than that given to Surrogate Larkin the previous August. It contained facts that Bond had already corroborated and which he knew to be indisputable. King went into the motive for the crime, all the incidents that precipitated the planning of the crime, as well as explaining in great detail exactly how it had been carried out, how much he'd received – $100 – and how he'd disposed of it.

Most significant of all, he gave an entirely plausible account of how the robbery had unfolded. This was no spur-of-the-moment burglary; Phelps had been targeted deliberately. He was reputed to be one of the wealthiest farmers around, an old miser who kept hundreds stashed in the house, and the thieves were expecting a good haul. Both King and O'Connell were drinking hard as they drove their rig to Shelby, and they were still guzzling whisky as they made the final leg of their journey, on foot, down Salt Works Road. When they reached the house, they peeked through a window and saw Phelps sitting alone in the dining room. From this, they assumed that he was the sole occupant of the house. Without waiting another moment, they knocked at the kitchen door. Phelps appeared almost instantly and demanded to know what they wanted. When O'Connell tried to push past him into the kitchen, the old man started swinging punches. O'Connell immediately shot him down. Both drink-befuddled robbers entered the house and were still in the kitchen when, to their utter astonishment, Margaret Wolcott suddenly dashed from the dining room and tried to escape through the kitchen door. Neither had known she was in the house. She had just dodged past Phelps's body and made it to the doorway, and was pulling the door behind her, when O'Connell, standing at the east side of the kitchen, fired at her through the glass in the door.

Bond stopped King at this point. He said that, according to prosecutors at Stielow's trial, Miss Wolcott had run out of the door and was standing outside the house before the shot was fired. King shook his head. No, it didn't happen that way. He insisted that Margaret Wolcott was still standing on the kitchen floor, and was in the act of pulling the kitchen door away from Phelps's body to close it when O'Connell fired. This statement, of course, was hugely significant. Without any prompting whatsoever, King had given an account of the shooting that accorded in every way with the physical evidence.

King went on. Miss Wolcott, he said, had screamed once as she ran out the door. They ran out after her and watched her stagger across the snowy road, but after the single scream, she made no further noise, and they saw her collapse on the porch of the house opposite. Both men stumbled after her and saw that she was dead. Hearing no sound and seeing no light in that property, they returned to the Phelps house. It was O'Connell who found the money and divided up the spoils. They left immediately and hurried down the driveway into the road and turned north, walking past the Benson household and on to Shelby, where O'Connell had left his rig.

Bond immediately recalled Erma Fisher Benson's latest affidavit, sworn before the Revd Frank J. Millman, in which she stated that her now husband, Adelbert, had seen two men coming from the direction of the Phelps place. King's story appeared to offer direct corroboration of Erma's statement, for what that was worth.

King continued. After securing their rig, the two killers left Shelby, drove east to Shelby Center, and took the road towards Millville. When they reached the road that led north to Knowlesville, King left O'Connell and returned to Knowlesville, sneaking back through a window into his room in the Barge View Hotel, the same way that he had left it earlier that evening when he was supposed to have retired for the night. O'Connell, meanwhile, drove on to the Laskeys' place, reaching there in the middle of the night, as they had stated originally.

When King finished talking, he sighed heavily, looked up at Bond and for the first time a flicker of relief lightened his solemn, stubbly face. He described it as feeling as if 'a great load had been lifted from him'.[11] In his time as a prosecutor Bond had seen many men confess to dreadful crimes, and he was well used to the reaction.

Bond immediately went and told O'Connell of his partner's confession. The younger man didn't bat an eyelid. He didn't even flinch when told that he would be charged with wilful murder. Instead, he listened in silence as Bond told him that he needed to explain his whereabouts on the night of 21 March 1915. O'Connell coolly denied being with King, or having played any part in the double killing. He insisted that he was at home ill, but that apart from the Laskeys and his wife, there was no one who could testify as to his whereabouts. Over several interviews, O'Connell demonstrated that he was made of much tougher stuff than King, even compiling a diary that attempted to account for every day between the Shelby killings and his arrest for the Bowen robbery. None of it worked. First the Laskeys, then even his wife refused to corroborate his alibi.

As previously noted, almost all of the work carried out by Bond and Waite throughout the spring and early summer of 1917 went unnoticed by the press. Most were too concerned with the ongoing Ruth Cruger saga, which had exploded into a worldwide sensation when a party of searchers, led by Grace Humiston, started to dig up the basement of the motorcycle store where she was last seen alive.

On 16 June, they found Ruth's body.[*] Grace had succeeded where the NYPD had failed, and she was, once again, fêted as the most celebrated and certainly the most newsworthy female lawyer in America. Snowed under by demands on her time, she became even more marginalised by the Stielow campaign. As a result, the woman who'd uncovered much of the evidence that kept Stielow out of the electric chair was not even aware of just how much progress the commission had made.

By the autumn of that year, Bond and Waite had it all: an analysis that revealed the worthlessness of Stielow's unsigned confession; a total demolition of the ballistics evidence that had proved so damaging to Stielow at his trial; King's damning letters from jail; evidence of blatant prosecutorial misconduct; proof of suppressed evidence; and, best of all, a confession that conformed in every detail with the known circumstances of the double murder. It had taken months of laborious effort, cross-checking facts, sifting truth from lies, and, perhaps the hardest part of all, setting aside their own prejudices. The two men, Bond particularly, had begun this investigation in the belief that the courts had got it right and that Charlie Stielow was guilty of murder. Now, they were convinced that a monstrous conspiracy had almost sent an innocent man to the electric chair. It was time to set right this flagrant miscarriage of justice. In November, Bond felt confident enough to publicly announce that he was putting his findings before a grand jury.

---

[*] The store's owner, Alfredo Cocchi, had fled to his native Italy shortly after Ruth's disappearance. Italy refused to extradite Cocchi to the US, but did try him for the murder. On 29 October 1920, he was imprisoned for 27 years.

21

Grand Jury Dashes Hopes

Predictably, Bond's announcement did not exactly thrill most residents of Orleans County. They were incandescent. So furious, in fact, that Bond decided on a peace-making mission. On 11 December 1917 – one night before the grand jury was scheduled to sit – he accepted an invitation by the Orleans County bar to attend a dinner at the Alert Club in Medina. Bond was at his emollient best, schmoozing with Knickerbocker and Blake from the prosecution team. David White was there, too, along with Judge Wesley C. Dudley, who would be presiding over the grand jury. Dudley, like Bond, was an out-of-towner and both guests were treated like royalty. Over dinner, followed by brandy, port and cigars, Bond explained exactly what his role in the investigation had been. He clarified the reasons behind the grand jury, and repeatedly emphasised the fact that no part of the expense of the investigation was to fall upon the county. It was to be a state-funded operation from start to finish. He urged everyone, regardless of personal involvement or conviction, to suspend judgement in connection with any matter that he intended to present to the grand jury. The audience response, by Bond's account, was very favourable. He had been very pleasantly surprised by the conviviality of his welcome. It certainly went some way towards ameliorating the atrocious weather outside that greeted him when he left and tried to make his precarious way to Albion.

A huge blizzard had dumped a foot or more of snow right across western New York, cutting off the roads to Buffalo, paralysing the trolley system and making any kind of travel treacherous. With temperatures plunging to sub-zero Fahrenheit, it was the worst storm of the winter thus far. But Bond's post-prandial good humour refused to be dislodged by anything so trivial as a howling blizzard. No, that dislocation occurred the next morning when he read a copy of the *Medina Daily Journal*, the county's most powerful local newspaper.

Its proprietor, Milton J. Whedon – law partner of Irving L'Hommedieu, the state senator and local Republican powerbroker who had figured prominently in the fight to electrocute Stielow – ran an editorial blasting the grand jury and declaring that the county was 'sick of this fiasco promoted by a lot of half bakes from New York'.[1] Whedon followed this with dire (and wholly inaccurate) predictions that Orleans County was 'in for another financial slaughter,' maybe as much as '$40,000 or $50,000 more of expense,' adding: 'It is to be hoped that the raid on the Treasury will be frustrated in some way.'[2]

As Bond read this, his blood boiled. He didn't mind the backstabbing – hell, he was a lawyer, that went with the territory – but what he loathed was such an egregious attempt to manipulate the legal process. Bond knew that, in all likelihood, most of the grand jurors would have digested these distortions over breakfast, and he could only speculate angrily on the impact that such inflammatory nonsense would have on their verdict.

All through that first day in the Albion courthouse, Bond sensed a hardening of local attitude against him. Gone was the clubbable hospitality of the previous evening; in its place, an obvious and implacable determination to do whatever was necessary to keep Stielow in prison. Bond felt a chill in the pit of his stomach when he learned that two prospective grand jurors had been members of the original panel that indicted Stielow and Green. However, both men assured him that they harboured no prejudice and would weigh the fresh evidence impartially. Choosing a jury took most of the first day, and it was decided to end the proceedings early so that people could make their way home in the dreadful weather.

Next morning, Erwin King was brought to the courthouse. He arrived looking downcast and much scrawnier than hitherto. His already sombre expression darkened as he was formally charged with the murder of Charles Phelps and Margaret Wolcott. At the direction of Judge Dudley, a plea of not guilty was entered on his behalf. After having signed a waiver of immunity, the pedlar entered the grand jury room, yelling back to the assembled reporters: 'I'll tell them everything.'[3]

And he did. His story didn't vary one jot from the version he had given Bond on 7 June. Despite being offered every chance to change his story, King continued to insist that he and O'Connell had carried out the robbery, that O'Connell had wielded the gun, and that Stielow and Green knew absolutely nothing about the crime. Also, there had been no truth in the retraction secured by former district attorney Knickerbocker; that had been a total fabrication. The jurors studied King hard. And, in fairness to them, it was difficult to know what to believe. King was obviously a man who lied as easily as drawing breath, but did that make him a killer or an accomplice to murder? If so, was this latest version the whole truth? Or was he one of those bizarre individuals who feel compelled to make false confessions? One of the jurymen tried to get inside King's mind with a series of questions.

'You know pretty well if what you told us … is true, if you were indicted here and tried regularly, that you would have to go to the electric chair. Do you want to die?'

'No, I don't want to. No man wants to die.'

'You know that will send you there?'

'Yes, sir.'

'What is your case at the present time? Supposing we indict you and you are tried?'

'I am going to plead guilty, sir.'

'Stielow is going clear and you are going to take his place?'

'Yes, sir.'[4]

It was a quite remarkable exchange. Even if most in the jury box did regard King as a pathological liar, what manner of man would perjure himself into the electric chair? King's testimony left plenty of jurors shaking their heads in bafflement.

There was less confusion when the Laskeys took the stand. Finally their day in court had come and what they said delighted Bond. Between them, they destroyed O'Connell's claimed alibi, saying he had not returned until 4:00am, a time they'd especially noted because of the racket he'd made in coming in. Even more damning were all those comments about the Shelby shootings that O'Connell had made to them over the breakfast table, just hours after they occurred and before the details were public knowledge.

The Laskeys were followed by Charles Sparacino and details of his fruitless fourteen-day jailhouse odyssey as a stool pigeon. No matter how much he pumped Stielow for information about the murders, he told the jury, the answer was always the same: 'I didn't do it.'[5] Each day, while in custody, Sparacino had filed a report on that day's happenings, either to Sheriff Bartlett or Under-Sheriff Porter. He also revealed how Sheriff Bartlett had manhandled Stielow on several occasions, with the intent of frightening him into making further admissions. None of this had worked, said Sparacino; Stielow refused to buckle.

Thomas Fogarty, of Buffalo, testified next. Fogarty was a private detective hired by O'Grady, and it was he who had arranged the conduit for King's incriminating letters from Little Valley, intended for Knickerbocker and others, to reach the Pulitzer family. The originals of these letters were offered in evidence. Bond shone a deliberate and very penetrating light on Knickerbocker's role in this whole murky episode, showing how the DA had wilfully attempted to obstruct the law, colluding with others to keep King away from interfering lawyers and reporters.

In Bond's view, the most important evidence at this grand jury hearing, aside from King's confession, was that given by Max Poser. The scientist from Bausch & Lomb made an impressive witness. He had brought his microphotographs of the murder bullets and the bullets fired from Stielow's gun. Better still, he had blown up the images – five for each bullet – onto slides that were then projected onto a screen measuring two feet square. This allowed the jurors to see every groove, every line, every imperfection on the bullets in the minutest detail. It was the precursor of things to come. Nowadays, such demonstrations in court are commonplace, even expected; but in rural New York State, in the early 20th century, this was a revolutionary development. Speaking in clear, simple language, Poser explained just how the photographs were made, as well as outlining the basic principles of bullet identification. He showed the jury members how slides of the Stielow gun bullets all showed exactly the same markings, so as to be identical. Then he compared these slides with images of the Phelps bullet, Exhibit D.D. Even to an untutored eye, the differences were glaringly obvious. Most important of all, there were absolutely no signs of the nine identifying scratches that Hamilton claimed to have found. If they were discernible on Hamilton's photographs, said Poser, they certainly should have been visible on these enlargements. There was nothing. Bond next read out Hamilton's dual explanation of how these scratches came to be filled in, first by explosive gases and then by the expansion of soft lead from the bullets as they exited the muzzle. Poser, not a firearms expert, declined to offer any opinion on such outlandish claims. His speciality, he said, was imagery, and the photographs he had taken didn't lie: the bullets that killed Phelps were not fired from Stielow's gun.

Unfortunately, the grand jury never heard from Albert Hamilton. There is no record that he was subpoenaed and he certainly didn't testify. Staying away was undoubtedly a smart move. Had he attempted to defend his trial testimony, not only would his already shaky reputation have crumbled to dust, but he would also have faced the very real possibility of leaving the court in handcuffs, to face charges of perjury.

Someone else who'd tried hard to wriggle through the legal net – though with less success than Hamilton – was Nona Gleason, who'd originally sworn an affidavit revealing Newton's admission that he'd duped the gullible Stielow into making damaging statements against himself. Miss Gleason was no stranger to the legal process. In 1909 she'd been awarded the astronomical sum of $20,000 for injuries sustained in alighting from a train – the largest civil verdict in Orleans County history up to that time – and since then she'd acted as court stenographer, but she patently wanted nothing to do with this hearing. She made her displeasure obvious to Bond from the outset, insisting that she'd been misquoted in the affidavit. Bond blinked his disbelief. He hadn't expected this. And when he began to question the witness's integrity and motives, she climbed on her high horse. 'Mr Bond,' she said archly, 'I have lived in Medina since I was two years old, I have been in public life for fifteen years in Medina, in politics and affairs, and no one would say I would tell an untruth.'

'The fact is,' Bond pushed, 'Mr White does say that you said this.'

'That is true … I was very indignant at the time and called Mr White's attention to it.' She primly added that she saw no reason why she had been called before the grand jury.

Bond was incredulous. 'I gave you the reason, because Mr White made an affidavit.'

'Yes, and it was very unkind. I had used every effort I could to befriend him. I tried my best to have Mr White appointed to defend Stielow and I succeeded.'[6] She explained that her position in the law offices of L'Hommedieu & Whedon meant that she was privy to all kinds of confidential discussions. Her own reputation, and that of her employer, would be jeopardised if the perception grew that private conversations between lawyer and client were liable to become public knowledge.

In the face of such intractability, Bond was helpless and he released Miss Gleason from the stand. Despite this startling and totally unexpected *volte-face*, Bond was still confident that he'd presented more than enough evidence to warrant an indictment against King, hence his announcement on Friday afternoon that he would call no further witnesses.

At this point, the grand jury was expected to retire and consider its verdict. But there was a shock in store. Instead, foreman R.W. Bamber rose and requested that they be allowed to see certain portions of the Stielow trial transcript relating to his alleged confession. He further requested that other witnesses, including Melvin Jenkins, Laura Stielow, Mary Jane Green and Howard Kohler, be subpoenaed to give evidence. Somewhat taken aback by this development, but powerless to overrule the grand jury, Judge Dudley announced that, to allow time for the witnesses to be summoned, the proceedings would be adjourned until 10:00am the following Monday, 17 December.

For Bond the day had ended on a decidedly low note. Instead of the expected indictment, he was facing another weekend of uncertainty. Still, he wasn't too downbeat. He and Waite knew they had presented a compelling case, and they confidently expected that this business would be settled on Monday at the latest. Over the weekend, it was agreed that these unexpected witnesses would be questioned by the new district attorney, William Munson. This was a shrewd move. It made the grand jury seem less like some Albany-imposed Star Chamber and more of a home-grown investigation. Besides, Bond had no doubts about Munson's integrity. Thus far, the new DA had been utterly forthright in his dealings; unlike several others in Orleans County that Bond could mention.

The weekend brought more heavy snow. It drifted in the lanes and highways, making the roads to Albion almost impassable, except on foot. Still, it wasn't enough to stop three generations of Stielow womenfolk. Despite her slight build and advancing years, Mary Jane

Green trudged five miles through deep snow to reach the courthouse. At her side were her daughter, Laura, and grandchild, Ethel. The journey had obviously been arduous. All three showed clear signs of exhaustion as, breath billowing in the frigid air, they mounted the steps that led into the courthouse.

A few moments later they were followed into the building by Howard Kohler and Melvin Jenkins. Both men were immediately collared by George Newton and his partner, Wilson. While curious reporters observed from a distance, the four men huddled together for one of those ultra-discreet chats that Newton so favoured. All weekend the Albion rumour mill had been grinding non-stop, with whispers that efforts were afoot to influence, even scupper the grand jury. Sneaky little assignations such as these did nothing to allay those suspicions. For the watching reporters, Newton's tactics were doubly frustrating. Unlike a criminal trial, grand jury hearings are always heard *in camera* (not in open court). The need to file a readable report of the day's events compels journalists to rely on contacts, leaks and the occasional supposition. That was what made these whispered conversations so intriguing. What exactly was Newton cooking up?

Whatever did transpire in the corridors outside clearly had little effect on Howard Kohler. His testimony was, in substance, the same as that he had given at the trial. When questioned as to Stielow's appearance on the morning of 22 March 1915, Kohler testified that he 'did not notice anything out of the ordinary in Stielow's appearance and he notified me in a straightforward manner'.[7] Stielow, he said, did not seem to be overexcited that morning. Kohler was also asked about the condition of Phelps's bed. Had the bed been slept in? 'Well, the bed was open. Evidently the covers had been thrown back and if I remember right the pillow was not much mussed up as if he had laid down.'[8]

When Jenkins testified he, too, recalled the bed as having not been slept it. This was crucial: because Stielow's alleged confession said

that he and Green had waited several minutes after the bedroom light
had gone out before knocking at the kitchen door. If this were true,
logic would suggest that Phelps had climbed fully into bed before
getting up. Clearly this didn't accord with the joint recollection of
Kohler and Jenkins. By contrast, King's version of events, given to
the grand jury, did fit the testimony of the neighbours. According to
King, he had seen Phelps through the dining room window, sitting
alone at the table and dressed in a shirt and long johns. King had
then crept back to where O'Connell was waiting and the two men
knocked on the kitchen door. Moments later, Phelps appeared, still
wearing the same clothes.

Thus far, Jenkins' testimony had helped Stielow. Then came a
hammer blow. At the original trial in July 1915, Jenkins had described
Stielow's appearance on the morning of the crime as 'nervous …
[and] excited'.[9] Now, he told the grand jury that, on the morning in
question, Stielow 'had a guilty look on his face, but I cannot swear
to it'.[10]

This was the first time that Jenkins had mentioned anything
about 'guilty looks', and it temporarily blindsided Munson. Bond and
Waite exchanged quick glances, each wondering if this was a product
of Newton's earlier coaching. Munson recovered well, though. 'You
did not attach enough importance to these guilty looks to follow it
up any?'[11]

Jenkins replied that he had not.

There was nothing new in the testimony of Laura Stielow and
Mary Jane Green, leaving the impression that the grand jury merely
wanted to gauge their honesty and integrity, and the day's proceedings drew to a weary close with the promise of still more witnesses
for the following day.

George W. Newton had a confident air as he strode into the grand jury room on the morning of 18 December. Although Knickerbocker had notionally been in charge of the investigation into the Shelby killings, it had been Newton who masterminded the strategy. His had been the hand on the tiller, and his was the bank account that saw the fattest increase from the conviction of Charlie Stielow. Before testifying in front of the grand jury, Newton signed a waiver of immunity; an indication that he didn't fear or expect to be prosecuted. He began by stating that he had suspected Stielow from the outset. His reason? Nelson Green's swollen jaw at the inquest. Nothing – not even Bond's withering sarcasm – could shift Newton from his stated belief that this swelling had resulted from a Stielow haymaker. Newton insisted that his conduct throughout the investigation had been fair and impartial, utterly devoid of any force or third-degree brutality. As Newton moved onto his account of the farmyard interview that prompted Green's confession on 20–21 April, his recall became ever more rose-tinted. There had been nothing heavy-handed about the interview's conduct, no coercion at all, just a spontaneous unburdening of Green's conscience. According to Newton, when he, Schultz and Wilson had arrived at the Smith farm, it was Green who said he didn't want to talk in front of Newton's sidekicks. He'd readily agreed when Newton suggested that they could 'step over there by the barn door'[12] to talk more privately, just the first of what Bond would later deride as Newton's infamous 'secret talks'[13] that had proved so productive for the prosecution. During the course of this conversation, Nelson insisted that he didn't kill Phelps. When Newton asked him to amplify this remark, the youngster said: 'Stielow did [the killings].' Newton then asked 'Did you help him?',[14] to which Green said yes.

Newton's avuncular side then took hold. He wrapped a reassuring arm around the teenager's shoulder. 'That is what I want to know,' he said soothingly. 'Will you come out here and tell these men what you have told me?' Green agreed. 'We went outside and he did tell them Stielow and he committed the crime.'[15] It was all very cosy and civilised, and a million miles away from wild threats of alleged lynching. But it didn't take long for the jury to see the other, darker side of Newton's character. The detective was serene while reciting a rehearsed monologue; less so when bombarded by a string of awkward questions.

As soon as Bond began quizzing him on discrepancies between his trial evidence and the testimony he was giving today, Newton's composure disintegrated. He acted like a cornered animal. He'd done nothing wrong, he snarled. He believed Green's confession then, and he believed it now! Reporters in the corridor outside had their ears pressed to the door as the exchanges turned decidedly combustible. Angry, muffled voices were all they heard as Newton repeatedly roared out his denials of any wrongdoing.

When Newton's torment ended for the day, he staggered, white-faced, from the court showing 'unmistakable evidence of having undergone a severe examination,'[16] according to one report. And his agonies weren't over yet. Next morning he was back on the stand for a repeat dose of Bond's merciless inquisition.

This time around Newton was asked to explain the circumstances surrounding the dictation of Stielow's alleged confession. Again, his answers were confusing and, to Bond's eye at least, he was making a poor impression on the jury. He seemed especially muddled over exactly when Stielow first said that he heard Margaret Wolcott moaning outside his door. At the trial, Newton testified that Stielow had made this claim to him on 7 April. Here – some 32 months later – Newton suddenly recalled that Stielow had actually told him this on 21 April. Even the grand jury foreman Bamber was confused and asked the witness for clarification.

In Newton's latest version, on the early morning or afternoon of the day that Stielow was arrested, he admitted that his testimony to the coroner's inquest 'was a lie, that he framed up the story for Mrs Green and Nelson ... that he did hear those noises, that he heard the woman's screams at night.'[17] Stielow, he said, had 'looked out of the window, and saw Miss Wolcott lying there and that ... [he] heard someone rapping at the front door and crying 'Charlie, I am dying, let me in.' He said they all heard her and that they, Mrs Green and Nelson and he, saw Miss Wolcott lying in front of his door.'[18]

As Bond listened to Newton's testimony, twisting this way and that, his disgust was palpable. Newton, he was sure, had been the driving force in the conspiracy to frame Charlie Stielow. His performance before the grand jury now exposed him as a serial liar, prepared to say just about anything in order to justify his illegal activity. Newton's 'absolute disregard for facts'[19] – as Bond later put it – typified the lax manner in which the witness gave his evidence at every stage of the hearing. Once again, Newton left the stand looking much the worse for wear. Bond had turned him inside out and Newton was uncomfortably aware that his future now rested in the hands of the grand jury. Depending on their verdict, he could soon be facing a charge of perjury and a lengthy prison term. Little wonder then that, as Newton left the court, 'he wore a very serious countenance'.[20] Another report was less charitable: 'He plainly showed the effects of the grilling when he left the courthouse.'[21] Perhaps wisely in the circumstances, two of Newton's underlings, Robert A. Wilson and Melvin Gorman, having seen the beating dished out to their boss, refused to sign waivers of immunity and were thus barred from giving evidence.

In stark contrast to Newton, Bond was beaming broadly when he exited the grand jury room just a minute later. He'd made Sheriff Bartlett jump through hoops in his efforts to explain how, in a crowded room, he was the only person to hear Stielow 'confess' to the murders. The sheriff, embarrassed and confrontational by turns, just could not account for it. His dismal performance, Bond felt, had all but sealed the indictment against King. There had been some grandstanding at the end – a few shots fired from Stielow's pistol in front of the jury, to demonstrate the difference between the markings on these bullets and those extracted from the murder victims – but that was just the icing on the evidentiary cake. Bond knew that everything hinged on the so-called confession. Eliminate that, as Judge Pound had said at the original trial, and there was no case against Stielow. Bond made sure that the grand jury members took this advice with them as court recessed for the day. That evening, as Bond returned to his hotel, he wore the contented expression of a man satisfied with a job well done. All the evidence had been presented; it was now up to the grand jury.

***

After an eight-day hearing – much longer than expected – on 21 December the grand jury was ready to deliver its verdict. At 2:10pm the 21-man jury filed solemnly back into the courtroom. Unlike a trial jury, unanimity was not required to reach a verdict; a simple majority would do. When Judge Dudley asked the jury for its decision, foreman Bamber rose and announced that the jury had found 'nothing to report your honour'.[22]

Bond looked thunderstruck. Waite, too, was horrified. Seven months of meticulous investigation had been tossed in the garbage can. Despite King's confession; the demolition of O'Connell's alibi; the worthlessness of Hamilton's ballistics testimony; the absurdity of Stielow's unsigned confession when judged against the physical facts; the covert Dictograph record in which Newton admitted that 'the three of us went at him [Stielow] all night, hammer and tongs'[23] during an interrogation; and strong evidence of perjury on the part of Newton, Bartlett and others, Bond had been unable to overcome that most implacable of all courtroom foes – human prejudice. Only now did he fully appreciate the level of bitter local animosity towards Stielow and the ire that his investigation had aroused. One grand juror summed up Bond's predicament: 'We heard King tell his story which cleared Stielow, but … he can't be believed one way or another.'[24]

It later emerged that jury deliberations had been volatile, even hostile at times, and that seven members had voted for an indictment against King. Speaking outside the court one disgusted juror declared, 'I am convinced Stielow was not guilty.'[25] Another confirmed the widely held view that several jury members had been prejudiced against the investigation from the outset, driven by a belief that 'the state was attempting to put something over on Orleans County'.[26]

Yet another said, 'I am convinced King is guilty. His story was a straightforward one and tallied up with evidence others gave,' before adding, 'In my opinion the jury thought King was a liar from what they had heard of him before his hearing and doubted his story for that reason.'[27]

What this grand jury's verdict demonstrated more than anything else was the almost invincible power of the confession within the legal system. For most prosecutors it is the Holy Grail of evidence. They know just how reluctant most jurors are to embrace the notion that the police could beat or bully a person into admitting something that they had not done. Eradicating this entrenched stubbornness is well-nigh impossible. Setting aside the obvious argument in this case – that at no time did Stielow ever sign anything admitting guilt – it was enough that several law enforcement officers had claimed to have heard him do so. These were still the infant days of public naivety about jailhouse tactics and police truthfulness, and two juries had been sufficiently confident in the integrity of their law officials to believe that Charles Stielow had uttered the words ascribed to him. There was now nothing else that the legal system could offer this unfortunate man.

The first immediate effect of the grand jury's verdict was that the arrest warrant against Erwin King was automatically discharged. He still had the Little Valley perjury indictment hanging over his head, so there was no question of his being released, and that night, at the Powers Hotel in Rochester, in the presence of Charles Waite and various reporters, the itinerant junkman reiterated his confession. 'What I said was right and I ain't going to change a word.'

But the newsmen wanted more. 'Did you see the shooting of Charles Phelps and Margaret Wolcott?' asked one.

'Yes, I did.'

'Was Charles Stielow there – or Nelson Green?'

'No; they wasn't.'[sic] [28]

King went on to elaborate his actions following the crime. O'Connell, he said, had peeled about $80 (the sum had shrunk since he'd spoken to Bond) off the wad of bills stolen from the house and handed the money to him. After lurching drunkenly back to the Barge View Hotel, King had spent a fitful night. Next morning, nursing a sore head, he had made his way to the towpath of the Erie Canal, tied the cash to a stone, and pitched the bundle into the water.

To the listening reporters, King sounded genuine and no one could imagine any good reason to explain why someone would talk himself into the electric chair unless that story were true. At the conclusion of his statement, King pulled himself to his feet and was led away by a guard, in readiness for his return to Little Valley jail.

Waite watched him go, then turned to face the reporters. His face was a study in bewilderment. 'King went before the jury and confessed,' he said. 'He went into detail concerning his movements on the day of the slaying and it was established beyond reasonable doubt that he was in the vicinity of the slaying and that it was a physical possibility for him to have done the job. Besides that the state investigators produced sufficient evidence to convict King disregarding his confession. The action of the Grand Jury is unexplainable.'[29]

Unexplainable or not, it was an outcome that utterly delighted Orleans County. By the most conservative estimate, the legal bill had now soared beyond $25,000 – some put the figure much higher – a colossal sum for a county with such a low taxpayer base. Surely now, most locals prayed, a line could be drawn under a ruinous case that had pushed them to the brink of bankruptcy? Others weren't so sure. They worried that King would start mouthing off again. Knickerbocker soothed the doubters. He might have been banished by the voters, but he still knew the law. No matter how many times Bond – or any of those New York meddlers – tried to indict King, any grand jury proceedings would have to be held in Orleans County. And that requirement, smirked Knickerbocker, eliminated any possibility of a retrial, guaranteeing that Charlie Stielow would end his days behind bars.

Exasperated but not surprised, and certainly not defeated. That was the reaction of Bond and Waite after failing to secure the indictments against Erwin King that they felt the evidence warranted. Blinkered thinking by Knickerbocker and his cronies had contaminated the legal process ever since the day that Stielow was arrested, and it would have been foolish to expect it to cease now. Instead, the two government investigators returned to New York to begin work on a full report for Whitman. When completed it would run to more than 200 scrupulously researched pages on the Shelby shootings. They left no fact, no statement, no scrap of evidence unexamined. Throughout, they excoriated an Orleans County legal machine that first rigged evidence and then deliberately set out to thwart them at every turn. Bartlett and Newton were singled out for especially bitter criticism. When their joint ineptitude failed to uncover any viable suspect, and with the press baying for a solution to the most atrocious crime in local memory, they had been panicked into arresting two vulnerable saps who happened to live across the road. Whether by malevolent design or even a genuine belief in the rightness of their actions – at least at first – both investigators had given evidence that shifted like sand over the course of three hearings, shading their testimony to suit the latest developments, neither of them hampered by a desire for consistency. The report left no doubt that these two men had been at the heart of the conspiracy that arrested two innocent men. And it was Knickerbocker who sealed Stielow's fate, by insinuating a known shyster like Hamilton into the case. Hamilton's evidence at the trial was risible – photographing the 'wrong side' of the bullets, scratches mysteriously disappearing – yet Knickerbocker allowed him to drip-feed this poison into the jury's ear without a quibble. Bond despised Knickerbocker. Although he realised that, to some extent, the disgraced former district attorney was merely cleaning up the mess created by Newton and Bartlett, he felt that disbarment should have been the least of his punishments. As the county's highest legal officer, Knickerbocker had wheedled, connived and dissembled, as well as almost bankrupting the treasury in a wilful attempt to cover up a blatantly crooked investigation. But none of it had succeeded. Bond and Waite had seen through the subterfuge. At the conclusion of the report, Bond wrote:

> As a result of my investigation, and having regard to the new facts and evidence discovered, and of the confessions that have been made to me, I am fully convinced and give it as my deliberate opinion that Charles B. Phelps and Margaret Wolcott did not meet their deaths at the hands of Charles F. Stielow or of Nelson Irow Green, nor were Stielow and Green in any way accessories to the crimes, nor did they have any guilty knowledge of it.
>
> On the other hand, I am as strongly convinced and give it as my deliberate opinion that the three bullets that were fired into the body of Charles B. Phelps, causing his death, and the bullet that was fired through the heart into the body of Margaret Wolcott, causing her death, were fired by Clarence O'Connell ... and that Erwin King was with him at the time and aided him in the commission of the murder.[1]

The report landed on Whitman's desk in the early part of 1918. The governor sighed, at a loss to understand how a small-town murder had escalated into a national *cause célèbre*, elevating Charles Stielow into an American Dreyfus. It scarcely seemed credible. But this was an election year and the governor was desperate to extract every last inch of political mileage from what was an unprecedented situation.

As a veteran trial lawyer himself, Whitman knew that the courts offered Stielow no more options. Without an indictment against King and O'Connell, the big German was legally doomed to rot in prison until the day he died, while Nelson Green would be middle-aged before he once again breathed free air. Whitman grimaced: no gubernatorial candidate could afford to heft that kind of baggage to the polls.

Over the following days and weeks, Whitman dissected every word that Bond had written. He searched for flaws in Bond's logic and came up empty-handed every time. The breadth and depth of the dishonest machinations that had spawned this calamity were truly breathtaking, even to a battle-hardened cynic like Charles Whitman. An impartial study of the facts permitted only one conclusion: a gross miscarriage of justice had been inflicted upon two innocent men. Whitman twisted and turned. He'd been blasted by the press for perceived bias in the execution of Charles Becker; a rerun of that fiasco was unthinkable and would surely sound the death knell for his political career. Finally, after days of agonising, Whitman made up his mind. On 8 May he called a press conference to announce his decision:

After careful study of Mr. Bond's report, and after mature reflection, I have reached the conclusion that had the evidence which Mr. Bond has developed been presented to the trial court at the time Stielow was tried, such evidence would necessarily have resulted either in a direction of a verdict for the defendant or his acquittal by a jury. In other words, the character of the new evidence is such that at least a reasonable doubt of Stielow's guilt would necessarily have been created in the minds of the members of the jury.

Believing as I do, and there being no provision of law under which a new trial can now be had, I have reached the conclusion that it is my duty to commute Stielow's sentence and permit his discharge from custody.[2]

With just these few simple words, Whitman put an end to a three-year nightmare, overturning the worst miscarriage of justice in New York's history. At the same time, Whitman also pardoned Nelson Green.

That evening, an Auburn prison guard brought the news to Stielow in his cell, telling him: 'Better pack up: you're going out.' Charlie, phlegmatic as always, merely grunted: 'All right.'[3] By contrast, when Nelson was told of his impending freedom, the excitable youngster yelled out: 'I knew it! It was bound to be! God has been with us!'[4]

Someone equally overcome with emotion was Mischa Appelbaum. The highly strung founder of the Humanitarian Cult fired off a typically purple telegram to Stielow at Auburn. 'Heartiest congratulations on the pardon so humanely granted by our Governor. The Humanitarian Cult and its members are willing to support you so that you and your family may re-establish yourselves and have much happiness to offset the suffering you have endured.' Then came the *quid pro quo*: 'On Tuesday evening, May 14, at Carnegie Hall, we will celebrate your vindication and expect you and your family as our guests. The great Justice Guy who saved you will also be there.'[5]

But Whitman had already scotched any plans for a publicity coup. There would be no triumphal parades, 'no brass bands'[6] to mark Stielow's release; that was part of the deal. Everything had to be low-key. Whitman might have done the right thing in issuing the pardons, but he didn't want the state's legal system – or his own electoral chances – embarrassed any more than was necessary.

That evening saw a lot of activity. Laura and Mary Jane Green made the long trip to Auburn to welcome Charlie and Nelson back to the free world. Both women were secretly relieved with the governor-mandated privacy restrictions; in the past few years, they'd endured enough publicity to last them a lifetime. All they wanted was to take their men home. Laura's sister, Olive, was with them the next morning – 9 May 1918 – as they rapped on the main gate at Auburn Prison. But there was still more disappointment. Warden Harry R. Kidney announced that the pardon papers had not arrived and, without them, neither prisoner was going anywhere.

In the meantime, officials in Orleans County were giving their reactions to Whitman's decision. District Attorney Munson, pragmatic as always, saw little chance of any fresh development. 'I think it would be absolutely useless to present evidence to an Orleans County grand jury looking to the indictment of Erwin King,' he said. 'Unless some new evidence that I don't know anything about develops, I do not intend to make another presentation of the matter.'[7] He pointedly added that his own opinion remained unchanged: sufficient evidence *had* been presented to the special grand jury to warrant an indictment against King. However, from what he'd heard, a sinister 'controlling influence'[8] in the jury room had cajoled fellow jurors into ignoring everything except Stielow's reported confession and Green's subsequent admission of guilt.

Sheriff Swart also expressed pessimism: 'All I know about the governor's pardon of Stielow or his reasons for the same is what I have read in the newspapers. I don't intend to apprehend King until I have something more tangible.'[9]

Knickerbocker, uncharacteristically, was not available for comment. He left that to his associate, Thomas Kirby. 'I assume that all public officials do their duty as they see it,'[10] was all he had to say.

All day Laura waited outside the prison gates. She'd brought little Irene with her and the three-year-old was getting fretful. Afternoon came and went, and so did the sun. By 8:30pm, the shadows were beginning to lengthen along State Street and still there was no sign of the pardon decrees. Finally, at nine o'clock, with the daylight fast running out, a messenger arrived. He delivered the pardons to Clerk Allen D. Stout who checked that they were in order and then nodded at Warden Kidney. He handed Charlie and Nelson the few dollars that both men had earned during their time at Auburn, and made a point of accompanying them as they stepped through the main gate. Olive's eyes popped open when she saw Charlie in his cheap prison-issue grey suit. 'Why, he looks like a preacher!'[11] she blurted out. The comment acted as an icebreaker, making everyone laugh, including Warden Kidney. Beaming delightedly, he stepped forward and shook Charlie by the hand, wishing him well. He also put a fatherly arm around Nelson's shoulder and expressed his heartfelt hope that he would never see the young man again, at least not in a professional capacity. Little Irene, seeing everyone else shaking hands, decided to get in on the act, and extended a formal hand to the father she had only seen twice in her short life. Charlie responded by sweeping her up into his arms and hugging her for several minutes, standing off to one side. He never was that big on crowds.

The only non-family member in the welcoming party – Whitman had barred lawyers from attending – was Thomas O'Grady. The private detective saw this reunion as a good chance to publicise his own part in gaining the prisoners' release and he was ready to milk the opportunity for all it was worth. A couple of reporters, who'd caught wind of the low-key release, were on hand as O'Grady spoke to Charlie. He asked Charlie if he recalled the first time they'd met. Charlie looked puzzled, blue eyes squinting tight as he struggled with his faulty memory. Nope, he finally admitted. O'Grady reminded him of that morning three years beforehand, when the bloodhound had been working the foot-tracks outside the Phelps residence. Still, Charlie couldn't remember the chance encounter. O'Grady just laughed it off, leant forward, and whispered something in Charlie's ear. Moments later, O'Grady called the reporters closer. Charlie had an announcement, he said. Go on, Charlie, tell 'em! He spoke uncertainly: 'I am going with Mr. O'Grady, and he is going to get me work in Buffalo [in a meat-packing factory],' he said, before admitting to some doubts about city living. 'If I don't like it, I will go back to farming.'[12]

When one of the reporters asked Charlie how it felt to come so close to the electric chair, the big man smiled dubiously. His fleshy jaws worked rhythmically on the wad of gum that seemed to aid his recollection as he slowly drawled, 'Oh, I dunno. I didn't really think they were going to take my life. I was innocent and I knew that God wouldn't let me go.'[13] When O'Grady suggested a cold beer to celebrate, Charlie bashfully declined. He hadn't taken a drop of alcohol since this nightmare began and he wasn't about to start now. Besides, it was getting late: time to go.

As Nelson, who'd been understandably overshadowed in all the hubbub, began gathering up his meagre belongings, Mary Jane fixed her son with an accusing eye. 'You ain't forgot your Bible?'[14] she demanded. Nelson proffered the leather-bound volume and even Mary Jane's habitually stern demeanour softened just a little around the edges. Amid more laughing, everyone then headed for the Port Byron trolley car. Just before boarding, Charlie allowed himself one last look at the prison's menacing bulk. A quick self-conscious wave to the reporters, then he disappeared into the trolley car as it clanked off into the night.

With Buffalo well over 100 miles away, Charlie and Nelson spent their first night of freedom in downtown Rochester, at the Whitcomb House. Opened in 1872, the hotel had built its reputation as a favoured watering hole for visiting actors and travelling salesmen, and it was no stranger to riotous behaviour, but never before had it witnessed scenes quite like these. Word soon got around that Charlie Stielow was in town, and before long the glittering lobby, with its wide ceiling supported by exquisitely decorated cast-iron arches, was jammed with folks all fighting for a glimpse of the state's most celebrated ex-prisoner. Charlie had already gone to bed. But O'Grady, who'd assumed a highly proprietorial air towards his charge, wasn't about to pass up the chance to flaunt his triumph. At 1:30am, he hammered on Charlie's door, yelling for him to come and say a few words to the gathered throng. A few minutes later, still stuffing his nightshirt into his trousers, Charlie stumbled down the stairs. Not that he said much. When asked how it felt to be out of prison, he just smiled sleepily and mumbled something inaudible. Unlike Nelson Green. 'How do I feel?' the younger man exclaimed in answer to the same question. 'I feel just like a canary that has been caged for three years – separated from all those of its kind. And I am innocent. Both of us are innocent.'[15]

Charlie hovered for a while on the sidelines, then, at the first opportunity, he quietly slipped away to his room.

Next morning, Charlie and Nelson shook hands and said good-bye for the time being. The young man was going back to stay with Olive at her small farm in Royalton. Charlie, meanwhile, carried on to Buffalo. Once there, Charlie, Laura and the kids checked into the eight-floor Iroquois Hotel on the corner of Eagle and Main. For a farmhand who'd swapped a log cabin for a death row cell, the transition was astounding as he gazed upon the Iroquois' overwhelming opulence.* Charlie was similarly awestruck on the afternoon of 12 May, when a large man – almost as big as himself – suddenly rushed up and grasped him by the hand. 'Remember me?' the stranger asked. 'Think hard, Charlie. Think of them times in the cooler at Albion.'

Still Charlie looked blank. Then, slowly, the mists cleared. 'It's the wild man … Charley Reynolds.'

'Right,' said the other man, still pumping Charlie's hand.

'Didn't know you with the whiskers,' said Charlie. 'Nobody wouldn't know you in them good clothes, anyhow.'

---

* Curiously, Harold S. Blake, Knickerbocker's trial associate, died from a heart attack at the Iroquois Hotel on 8 June 1920.

'Wear 'em all the time now. I'm working steady on the Buffalo police force.'

Charlie's voice dwindled to an awed whisper. 'You – you – on the police? What of all them policemen you killed when you was a robber?'[16]

Charles Sparacino just grinned and sat Charlie down to explain. With each revelation, the big German's expression looked ever more incredulous. Sparacino explained how he'd been planted in the cell, in an attempt to get Charlie to confess, and how he'd never once admitted anything. 'You acted like an innocent man,' he said. 'I remember the day your people were outside the cell door, all crying, and your brother asked you why you did it. You were crying, too, and if there was ever a minute for a breakdown that was it. But you grabbed the bars and shouted, "I did not do it."'[17] Watching that heartfelt performance, Sparacino said, converted him to the view that Charlie was innocent. Unfortunately his doubts were not shared by his boss. Newton – one hand already on the reward money – wasn't about to let go any time soon, and he continued to belligerently insist that Stielow and Green were the guilty parties.

After another day spent schmoozing at the Iroquois, Charlie was ready to leave the luxury and splendour and to get on with his life in the canning factories of Buffalo.

When Charlie Stielow had entered prison, America was still a distant viewer of what some termed the 'European War.' By the time of his release, millions of young Americans were crossing the Atlantic to fight in the world's first global conflict. But the barbed wire and the bullets treated these doughboys no better than they had the old protagonists, and with US casualties spiralling horrifically, on 31 August 1918, President Wilson signed a bill amending the draft's upper age limit to 45. The government, after trying so hard to kill 39-year-old Charlie Stielow, was now desperate for him to kill others. His registration card, dated 12 September 1918, showed him still living in Buffalo and passed him fit for action. (Nelson had been drafted within a month of his release. Indeed, the military was so keen to get its hands on him that his registration card still showed his address as Auburn Prison.) By now, though, it was all academic. The tide of war had turned overwhelmingly in favour of the Allies and, two months later, hostilities ceased.

Just six days before the Armistice, Governor Whitman's career came crashing down. On election day, 5 November 1918, he was ousted from office by Al Smith (who would go on to become the Democratic presidential candidate in 1928). Whitman couldn't understand it; the omens had been so good. In the primaries, he'd carried every New York county except two: one a Democratic stronghold, the other Orleans County. Republican voters there never forgave the man who, they felt, had held up their judicial system to national ridicule. Come election day proper, Whitman still won Orleans County, but only with a drastically reduced majority, and that weakness radiated right across the state. Even so, it was a close-run thing; barely 14,000 votes separated him from Smith when the hotly contested count was finalised. How much the Stielow fiasco contributed to Whitman's downfall is unknowable, but with this defeat all his dreams of the White House evaporated. Never again would he hold public office. But he still had one last piece of unfinished official business. On 19 December 1918, Whitman fully restored Charles F. Stielow's American citizenship.

Ordinarily this process took at least a year from the date of pardon, but a special restoration request had been made by Grace Humiston. Since Charlie's release, Grace had uncharacteristically distanced herself from the Stielow ballyhoo. Normally a fixture in the front row at every press conference, she was suddenly hard to find. This new-found coyness dated back to the summer of 1917, when she'd won an injunction against the Universal Film Manufacturing Company to prevent them showing a movie called *Woman Lawyer Solves Ruth Cruger Mystery* that included images of her at the crime scene. Grace, keenly aware of her commercial value and eager to cash in on her new-found fame, had also filed suit for $100,000. And 'Mrs Sherlock Holmes',[18] as the press was now calling her, was always hungry for another headline-grabbing inquiry. It came in the autumn of 1917. Vague rumours reached Grace of a vast white slavery ring, with tentacles that reached into US Army bases across the northeast. Without checking any facts, she threw herself headlong into yet another high-profile investigation. This time her impetuosity proved calamitous. The charges were utterly spurious; there was no gang of military pimps, no drugged prostitutes, no soldiers lining up to take advantage of hapless victims, only a discredited investigator. Grace was utterly humiliated. She was forced to retreat to the sidelines to lick her wounds.

And there was worse to come. On appeal, her injunction against Universal was thrown out when the courts ruled that, as a public figure, she had no right to privacy. The decision caused plenty of guffaws in some circles, and nowhere was the jeering louder than at the New York Police Department. Grace had never enjoyed good relations with the police; she was always critical of their methods, sometimes recklessly so. As early as 1905, after solving a case that New York detectives had shelved, she'd made her contempt very public – saying 'the police are no good'[19] – and the NYPD had never forgiven her. And now she'd been routed. Revenge had never tasted so sweet.

She would go on to fight other battles and to gain the occasional minor victory, but the glory days and the headlines were behind her. Even the death row hard-cases shunned her. In June 1926, one inmate, George Bittle – just seven days from taking that final walk – couldn't even be bothered to talk to the woman who 'saved Charles

Stielow from the chair.'[20]* For Grace Humiston it was the final humiliation. All that was left to her now was the stewardship of her family's real estate empire. This trailblazing champion of justice and
human rights, who had once been the most famous female lawyer in
America, died, almost forgotten, in a New York hospital on 16 July
1948.

Her greatest victory also faded from the headlines. In Orleans
County there was no appetite – and even less money – for pursuing
King or O'Connell, so no charges were ever filed against them and
both men disappeared into the mists of time. As a result, the murders
of Charles Phelps and Margaret Wolcott remain officially unsolved.
Nor did any of the people involved in the investigation ever face
charges of perjury. Newton wriggled out of any type of legal censure,
but his reputation had taken a bad hit and he faded from view. Of
the other principals, Sheriff Bartlett and his deputy, Porter, both filed
libel suits against three New York papers that had accused them of
using third-degree tactics to induce a false confession from Stielow.
In 1919, realising the hopelessness of their claims, both men dis-
creetly withdrew their suits. While Porter continued in law enforcement, Bartlett opted for the gentler pastures of life as postmaster for
Albion, until ill health forced his premature retirement. He died on
11 August 1933.

Knickerbocker, similarly chagrined over press allegations of
prosecutorial chicanery, had also filed libel actions against several
newspapers, only to let them fall by the wayside. He continued his
lucrative private practice until succumbing to throat cancer on 18
May 1928.

When Charlie Stielow was released from prison, one paper wrote:
'The state owes this man something.'[21] It didn't happen. The man
who'd spent three years in prison and survived four dates with the

---

* Ironically, two days later, Bittle's sentence was commuted to life imprisonment.

electric chair for a crime he didn't commit never received a cent in compensation. Not that he ever asked for any.

———————

The Stielow case undoubtedly left a sour taste in the mouth. There were too many loose ends, too many unanswered questions, too many people walking around free who should have been behind bars. But there was one undeniably positive outcome. And it was all thanks to Bond's assistant, Charles Waite.

After he'd finished his work on the Bond report, Waite was seconded into government war intelligence work, where he ran a group investigating suspected alien activity in the United States. Waite was notoriously cagey and his obituary in the *New York Times* hints darkly that he was 'thought to be a secret agent of the British Government'.[22] Whatever the truth of this claim, one thing is certain; Charlie Stielow's ordeal – and the part played in it by Albert Hamilton – affected Waite profoundly. During his work on this case, a seed of an idea grew in his mind: he began pondering the possibility of raising firearms identification to the same level of courtroom credibility as that enjoyed by fingerprinting. During long discussions with Jones and Butts of the NYPD, Waite had listened to them argue that no two guns were identical. He now set out to test the truth of this theory. Following the Armistice, he began collecting guns, hundreds of them, and he test-fired every one. Then he examined the bullets under a magnifying glass. He saw that the markings on each were unique and repeatable. It didn't matter how many times a gun was fired, the markings didn't vary and he never found two weapons, even of the same manufacture and calibre, that produced similar striations. This repeatability intrigued him. Maybe the markings on a bullet really were as individual as a human fingerprint? In 1919, Waite opted for a career change with consequences that would reverberate around the globe to the present day – he abandoned the law and devoted the rest of his life to improving the science of fire-arms identification.

He began cataloguing every gun he could find. Most, he soon realised, were cheap 'Saturday Night Specials', made in Spain and dumped illegally in the US after the war, and available on the streets of New York and Chicago for a couple of bucks, or even less. Home-grown guns were much scarcer, and these were the main focus of Waite's attention. At the time there were fewer than a dozen manu-facturers of small arms in America and Waite contacted them, out-lining his remit and requesting their assistance.

All expressed a readiness to cooperate. He began his quest at Springfield, Massachusetts, where the Smith & Wesson company threw open its books to his inspection. The records, however, were disappointing, as most only covered current models. Since the com-pany was founded in 1856, it had made and discarded any number of models, and thousands of these obsolete weapons were presumably scattered around the country and might be used in the commission of a crime. Moreover, Waite learned that every manufacturer from time to time made minor changes in the rifling of the model. This was a persistent problem for Waite at every company he visited. No one – not the company bosses nor the ballistics engineers – had ever seen or heard of any data being kept about the obsolete types. Nor did the factory records show the dates when minor changes had been inaugurated in current models. Thanks to Waite, henceforth arms companies began keeping far more complete records of their prod-ucts, thus making the question of identification that much easier. This innovation, by itself, would help solve hundreds of crimes. But Waite wasn't finished, yet.

For years he laboured on alone, shouldering an almost impossible burden, travelling as far as Europe to broaden his knowledge. It was exhausting work. Gradually, overwhelmed by the enormity of the task he had set himself, came the realisation that, if he were to suc-ceed in his mission of cataloguing every handgun made in the US, he needed specialised assistance from the best available source. And that meant turning to Major Calvin H. Goddard. Although still only in his mid-thirties, Goddard probably knew more about firearms than anyone else in America. His background was unusual. In 1915 he had earned a medical degree, but that same year he took a commission in the army without having engaged in private practice. It was the military that provided the technical framework for his passion: firearms. He had an instinctive feel for handguns, one that Waite lacked, and he jumped at the chance to add his knowledge to Waite's quest. In 1925 Goddard wrote a paper entitled *Forensic Ballistics*, one of the first tracts to cover the systematic identification of guns and bullets. And in April of that same year, Goddard and Waite, along with a microphotographer named Philip O. Gravelle and John H. Fisher, a physicist, founded the Bureau of Forensic Ballistics (BFB), the world's first crime lab solely devoted to the study of firearms identification.

The title was more impressive than the premises – a spare room at the Hotel Latham on 28th Street in Lower Manhattan – but from this unlikely setting these four men revolutionised firearms analysis. Not only could they access Waite's unique database, but they were also able, for the first time, to authoritatively match bullets to guns. This came about because Gravelle had invented what remains the greatest advance ever in the field of firearms identification – the comparison microscope. In this device, two microscopes are connected by an optical bridge, which provides a split-view window, enabling two separate objects, such as bullets, to be viewed side by side. If the striations match, both bullets have been fired from the same gun. If they differ, it is overpowering evidence to the contrary. Gravelle always claimed that he first dreamt up the idea of the comparison microscope because he mistrusted his memory. Trying to remember the placement of the minute flaws and imperfections on the bullets was beyond him (or anyone else, for that matter). When it came to examining bullets, he wanted to see the crime scene bullets and the test bullets alongside each other. Only that way could he give a definitive answer to the question: 'Was this bullet fired from this particular gun?'

In 1926 Goddard published the BFB's latest findings in *Scientific Identification of Firearms and Bullets*, explaining how the Stielow case had been the catalyst for a ballistics revolution. Within the same pages, he lavished praise on Waite for his tireless work over almost a decade. Interestingly, the foreword to Goddard's article was provided by ex-governor Charles Whitman. He, too, eulogised the enigmatic former lawyer, saying: 'He [Waite] has earned the thanks of every prosecutor and every attorney for the defence who is sincerely desirous that the truth be told.'[23]

The first high-profile trial to feature BFB testimony was the sensational Hall-Mills murder case in 1926. What should have been Waite's finest hour turned to tragedy when his always delicate health finally gave way. He was scheduled to be a witness for the prosecution, but on 13 November 1926, on the eve of his testimony, he died suddenly at the Latham. Waite never did achieve his goal of cataloguing every American handgun ever made, but, because of his extraordinary single-mindedness, firearms analysis was elevated to the same legal status as that enjoyed by fingerprint identification. 'Waite's vision of a decade ago has become a reality,' wrote Goddard, adding that, thanks to 'the Waite method of bullet identification, the missile itself has been forced to give up its secrets.'[24] Goddard was in no doubt that Waite, unheralded and barely known, should rank alongside other great forensic innovators such as Edmond Locard, Hans Gross and Francis Galton.

Waite's place at the Hall-Mills trial was taken by Goddard. Although the defendants were acquitted, the validity of the comparison microscope was demonstrated beyond all doubt and before long Goddard was once again hitting the headlines, this time as a key witness in the long-running saga of Nicola Sacco and Bartolomeo Vanzetti, a pair of Italian anarchists who'd been convicted of shooting two guards during a 1920 payroll robbery in South Braintree, Massachusetts. The verdicts had sparked a storm of global protest, whipped up by left-wing agitators eager to convert Sacco and Vanzetti into martyrs to American capitalism, victims of a vicious 'Red Scare' campaign. Facts? Who needed them? This was all about politics, and Sacco and Vanzetti made marvellous victims. They languished on death row for years. Finally, in a 1927 review of the convictions, Goddard and his comparison microscope convinced even sceptical defence experts that Sacco's gun had undoubtedly been used in the murderous robbery. Shortly thereafter, to worldwide protest, Sacco and Vanzetti went to the electric chair at Charlestown State Prison.

In an ironic twist of fate, Albert Hamilton had also figured prominently in the Sacco/Vanzetti case. Like just about everyone else, he'd slithered unscathed through the Stielow debacle, and 1924 found him swearing before a committee that Sacco's gun was not the murder weapon. Hamilton was his usual slippery self. When handed Sacco's .32 Colt automatic to examine, he disassembled it slickly in front of Judge Webster Thayer, and compared it with two other Colt pistols that he'd brought into court with him and which he also disassembled. Then, just as smoothly, he reassembled all three guns. Demonstration over, he handed back the Sacco gun, pocketed the other two weapons and stood up to leave. Thayer stopped him short. He ordered that the other two pistols be impounded. Hamilton coolly handed them over. Later, one of the prosecution ballistics experts noticed that the barrel on the otherwise rusted Sacco automatic looked suspiciously new. Closer inspection revealed that it had actually come from one of Hamilton's other guns, and that the original barrel was attached to one of the weapons that Hamilton had attempted to remove from court. When confronted by this evidence, Hamilton admitted that a switch had taken place, but professed himself mystified as to how this could have happened. Had it not been for Judge Thayer's gimlet-eyed scrutiny, it is entirely possible that Hamilton's sleight of hand might have changed the course of criminal history, allowing Sacco and Vanzetti to go free. Despite grave suspicions against him, Hamilton again dodged any criminal charges, although he was thrown off the defence (but only after submitting a bill for $2,813.65). As setbacks go it was devastating, but not fatal. For another decade 'That Man from Auburn' continued to plunder the American legal system, auctioning his opinion to the highest bidder. By his own estimate, he testified in almost 300 homicide cases. Like many of his utterances, this should be taken with a hefty pinch of salt, but the fact that he testified at all is a terrifying indictment of a legal system that knew he was a charlatan and yet continued to hire him. Time finally ran out for Hamilton during the Manny Strewl kidnapping trial of 1934, when he was caught red-handed offering his testimony to both prosecution and defence, whoever would pay the most. Not even Albert Hamilton could smooth-talk his way out of this PR catastrophe. The miracle is that he avoided prison; maybe the courts took pity on a 75-year-old man. But the big-money paydays were over and never again did he figure in a prominent trial. The man who virtually invented the role of the crooked expert witness died at his Auburn home on 1 July 1938.

We don't know if news of Hamilton's death reached Charlie Stielow. By this time he was living back in Orleans County. He had never settled in the canning factories of Buffalo, his love of the soil was too great, and it didn't take him long to drift back to his former life as a tenant farmhand. Over the years his family added another daughter, Alice, and a son named Edward, and in December 1930 he and his family returned to Medina. When the Stielows settled in their small house on South Avenue, the press commented kindly on his return and there is no evidence that his arrival sparked any hostility. It had always been the same; people who met Charlie Stielow really liked him. Certainly no one could picture him as a double killer. One thing is certain: the ordinary citizens of Orleans County treated Charlie Stielow far, far better than did its elected representatives.

Like millions of other Americans, the Stielows suffered in the Great Depression. Money, always tight, dried up to a trickle. There was no compensation nest-egg to fall back on, nothing in the bank to cover the hard times. A rare – and entirely out of character – emergence from obscurity for the Stielows came in March 1936, when Laura, by now middle-aged, cropped up in a small newspaper advertisement, extolling the virtues of a vegetable tonic called 'Dr Pierce's Favourite Prescription'. It had, she said, 'Rid me of the headaches, and relieved me of the ache in the small of the back, I felt stronger and had more energy, too'.[25]

. But if Laura's health had taken a turn for the better, the same could not be said for her husband. Years of backbreaking toil, working the land in all weathers, finally took their toll. By the early 1940s his formerly ox-like constitution had withered to a shadow. Charlie Stielow's hard struggle with life came to an end on 9 August 1942, at his home on Church Street, Medina, after what the local paper called 'a lingering illness'.[26] He was 63 years old.

Laura, the rock who'd stood by him through the darkest days, was there to weep at his graveside two days later when he was laid to rest in Pioneer Cemetery in Akron, New York. She'd already said goodbye once to Charlie – in the death house at Sing Sing – now it was for good. She was made of tough stuff, though. Another three decades would pass before she joined her husband in the little cemetery on Hunt's Corner Road, dying on 17 February 1972 at the age of 86.[*]

Charlie Stielow's grotesque ordeal didn't clear the courts of pseudo-expert witnesses or eliminate phoney jailhouse confessions – sadly, they persist to the present day – but it did sound a warning bell about the dangers of junk science. The Stielow case marked a milestone

---

[*] Nelson Green outlived his sister by six years, dying on 2 September 1978.

in American jurisprudence; for the first time, scientific testimony helped to overturn a murder conviction. Those four gunshots fired on a snowy night in western New York State changed forever the face of forensic science and gave law enforcement agencies around the globe access to a system of accurate firearms analysis. That in itself is a fine achievement, but the greater and more lasting legacy of the Stielow case goes deeper than mere scientific accomplishment, right to the core of what it means to be human. Had it not been for a small band of dedicated supporters, an innocent man would have been put to death. What made his deliverance even more miraculous was that Stielow was a nobody. Americans were used to wealthy defendants literally getting away with murder, thumbing their noses at the legal system and walking free from the courthouse, or else serving their prison time under palatial conditions that wouldn't have disgraced the Waldorf-Astoria. 'You can't convict a million bucks,' the old saw used to run; and for the most part, the cynics were right. But Charlie Stielow broke the mould. By rights, he should have been electrocuted, buried and long-forgotten by now. Never before had someone on the very bottom rung of the social ladder, an illiterate immigrant without a dollar to his name and without any kind of influence, attracted such nationwide attention. In the end, the clamour was too great to ignore. His was the first great triumph in the war on miscarriages of justice. A hundred years on and we now have respected and highly influential organisations like the Innocence Project[*] and the Center on Wrongful Convictions[†] at Northwestern University, to carry the fight to the authorities. Given the appalling number of legal blunders that they have exposed and set right, we can only shudder as we wonder just how many friendless innocents have taken that final lonely walk to oblivion. When Charlie Stielow came within minutes of the electric chair, fighting the system was something new, and yet an improbable coalition of lawyers, prison

---

[*] http://www.innocenceproject.org/
[†] http://www.law.northwestern.edu/wrongfulconvictions/

officials and political activists somehow managed to pull off the greatest escape in New York penal history. For various reasons – from hubris, political ambition, a commission-driven conviction policy and sheer stupidity, to just plain stubbornness – a gang of misguided men did their damndest to kill Charlie Stielow. They didn't succeed because they overlooked one vital factor – the power of human outrage in the face of injustice.

Nelson Green's Confession: 20–21 April 1915

About two or three days after we moved over to the Phelps place Stielow and I were out by Stielow's barn and he told me that a fellow told him that Phelps has lots of money and he keeps it in his bureau drawer and he was going to have some of it, and I didn't say anything to him, and a few days after this, about Friday or Saturday before the murder, Stielow and I were near the chicken house over at Phelps' and Stielow said to me we will come over and steal Phelps' money Sunday night, and I told him No, that I didn't want to do it and Stielow said that we could get it and nobody would know it, and I again told him No, that I don't want to do it, and he told me that I could watch and nobody would know it, and I asked him how he was going to do it, and he said he would go in and steal the money, and try to get in the back door, and he would try and not kill them. He told me that he and John Lukeman stole money out of a clock at old man Barlow's, (this Stielow told me about one year ago.) Stielow told me that if I would help him he would give me fifty dollars, and I then told him Yes, that I would help him. This talk was in the evening, after we got through doing chores. We then went home. I am sure that this talk was on Friday or Saturday evening before the murder, and when we were crossing the road over to our house, Stielow asked me if I had a revolver, and I told him No, and he told me that he would take his revolver, if he had to use it. The revolver that Stielow spoke of was an American made revolver, a Young America revolver, with a hammer, double action hammer gun, seven shots, nickel plated, twenty-two calibre, long or short cartridges, and he kept it in a bureau top drawer upstairs in the South bedroom, and the cartridges of about half a box of twenty-two short, rim fire, with a letter U in the centre, in a red box also were kept in the same drawer. I know they were there, because I helped move the bureau upstairs and I saw the revolver and the cartridges in the top bureau drawer. Stielow got the twenty-two revolver from a fellow when Stielow was working for Fayette Day on his farm down near Grangeport, near Lockport, about eight years ago, he told me this about a little over a year ago. Last Fall Stielow traded an old breech loader gun with George Terrell for a thirty-two revolver but I don't know where this thirty-two revolver is now.

The Sunday evening of the murder, when we were doing our chores over at Phelps', Stielow told me that we would get the money about half past ten tonight, and after we did the chores we went home, and we finished the chores at our barn, then we went into our house and we stayed in our house until about twenty minutes after ten, then we went out to Stielow's barn, but before we went out to the barn, Stielow went upstairs and got his revolver, then we went out to Stielow's barn, then Stielow handed the revolver to me and told me to go into Phelps' and steal the money, as I could go in stiller, and it would be easier for me, and Stielow told me that the money was in the third drawer in the bureau in Phelps' bedroom, in the bottom drawer, in a long pocketbook, covered over with clothes, but I told him I wouldn't do it. Stielow said he would try the milk door first, and see if he could get in there, and he again told me that he would give me fifty dollars, and he coaxed me to go with him, and he told me I had better go along with him and watch, and I told him Yes, then he told me to go in and get the money as they would not hear me so quick. Stielow asked me if there was any use putting a handkerchief on his face, and I told him No. Stielow had a red handkerchief in his pocket, but I don't know whether he put it on his face or not. Then Stielow and I started for Phelps' house, and I left Stielow just as we went into the Phelps driveway, and Stielow told me to stand there and watch and if anybody came along I should whistle, this was about fifteen minutes to eleven at night. Then Stielow walked down the driveway into the Phelps yard, and he walked up and down from the kitchen door to the hen house several times, then he went around to the milk door, and he afterward told me that he tried this door, and found it locked, then he came back and went to the kitchen door and tried the door, and found it locked and then I heard him knock on the kitchen door, and in about two or three minutes Mr Phelps came out from his bedroom, carrying a lamp, and Mr Phelps opened the kitchen door, then Stielow shot Mr Phelps in the hand, and I could see the flash when the gun shot, and I heard the report of the gun, then Stielow went inside the kitchen and he shot twice, and Stielow told me that he shot Mr Phelps near the nipple and the third time he shot him in the head, then Stielow went into Mr Phelps bedroom, then in two or three minutes Miss Wolcott came running out of the kitchen door, and just as she was out the door Stielow shot her through the kitchen door. I heard her slam the door shut, then she ran across the road to Stielow's house and onto his front door step, and shortly after she left the kitchen door she screamed and said Help, Murder, and after she got onto Stielow's doorstep I was still standing near the tree and I saw her at Stielow's front door and I heard her moan and say that she was dying and to let her in, and I heard her pound on the front door, then I saw her fall in front of the door. A few minutes after Miss Wolcott came out of the kitchen door Stielow came out of the same door, and he ran down the driveway to where I was standing, and I saw him have the Phelps pocketbook in his hand, and he showed it to me and he told me he thought he had about two hundred dollars, then he ran down the side of the road towards Jenkins house for a short distance and went through the fence and cut across the field towards the Jenkins barn, and that was the last I saw of him for about one hour. I then walked down the driveway into Phelps and behind the house and through the orchard and over to the road and down the road and into our own driveway and when I was near our stoop I saw Miss Wolcott lying there dead, then I went into our house through the kitchen door, and when I got in my Mother asked me what the screams was, and I told her it was some woman screaming that went by, and my Mother said she heard the woman screaming out in front of the door and said she was dying and wanted to get in and she didn't dare let her in because it would make my Sister sick. My Mother said it must be the woman across the street by the sound. My mother was in bed when Stielow and I went away, but she was up when I came back, and she and I sat up until Stielow came back about one hour after I got into the house. I think it was about 11:15pm when I got back into our house and about one hour afterward Stielow came home, and my Mother asked him what that noise was, and he said it was some woman that went screaming by, Stielow was very nervous and his shoes were muddy. In a few minutes we went to bed, and Stielow came to bed five or ten minutes after I did. When we got bed [sic] Stielow told me to keep still and keep my mouth shut and they would get somebody else for the murder. After we got to bed Stielow told me he was going to keep the gun and the money in his breeches pocket, and he slept in behind and I slept in front and he hung his breeches on the bedpost by my head, and in the morning Stielow got up about five o'clock, and I got up a few minutes after he did, and he told me that he was going over to Jenkins' and tell him about the murder, and he told me to build a fire, and he was gone a little while, and when he came back he told me to get a canvass and cover Miss Wolcott up, and I did, then Stielow and I went up the road, South, and on the way up the road Stielow told me to keep still and not say anything, and he also told me that when he went out of our house this morning he went over to Phelps' and found Mr Phelps alive there yet and that he went out to the wood pile and got the mop and chopped the stick in two and went in and hit Phelps in the head so he wouldn't come to and tell anybody, then he saw Jenkins with a lantern at his barn and he didn't wait in Phelps' house because he was afraid Jenkins would hear him and come over. Stielow went to get Kohler up and I went and got Pogle up. When Stielow chops wood with one hand, I have seen him chop with his left hand and also with his right hand. The night of the murder Stielow was dressed in his overalls and a brown corduroy coat and a black cap with a front piece and his No. ten shoes, but I don't know whether he wore his rubbers or not, and I wore my felt boots, Size No. eight or nine, I wear a No. nine shoe, and I wore a blue flannel shirt and brown corduroy breeches and a short brown rain coat and a black, woolly cap, with a front piece.

I now remember that a few days after we moved over to Phelps Stielow told me a fellow told him that Phelps kept money in his bureau drawers, and I remember that Stielow said that it was William Pogle who told him about Phelps keeping money in his bureau drawers.

The Tuesday after the murder Stielow and I were out by our barn and he told me that he had buried the money and the revolver, this was when I asked him for the fifty dollars he promised to give me for helping him. Stielow told me that he buried the money and pocketbook and the revolver out by his barn, but I don't know just where.

Last Sunday I was down home at Royalton Center and my Mother also was down there, and she told me that Stielow told her to tell me that the Detectives had been there and that I should keep still and not say anything, and that one of them was awful smart and he didn't like him and if they asked me anything for me to keep still and not say anything, and my Mother asked me what Stielow meant, and I told her that he probably thought the Detectives might take Stielow if I said anything.

The next day after the murder Stielow told me that after he left the Phelps house after the murder he went through the lot over to Jenkins barn and down to the Transmission Line.

Stielow said that he buried the pocketbook in the manure pile by the corner of the barn on the tenant place, and that he dug the hole with a pitchfork, two or three feet deep, and the revolver also is in the same place.

The Monday after the murder and when the dogs were there Stielow told me that he thought the dog might get both of us, and he kept away from the dog, and when the dog went into the house I was out by the tree and I watched the dog.

Before I went away from Stielow's on the Wednesday after the murder and on the Monday morning after the murder Stielow told my Mother and me to say that we all were in the house when we heard the screaming of the woman and the pounding on the door, and that we all should stick together and say the same thing, and to say that none of us went out of the house and for us to say that we did not hear the revolver shots, and when we went to the Inquest at Medina and what I swore to about being in the house and on hearing the screaming and getting up with Stielow and looking out of the door and South window was not the truth, and Stielow and I were not in the house when the woman screamed.

No promise of pay or reward has been made to me, directly or indirectly, for the making of this statement. I am not making this statement on account of any feeling or grudge I have against Charles Stielow. All of the foregoing statement I solemnly declare to be true. I am willing to sign and swear to this statement.

NELSON IROW GREEN
Subscribed and sworn to before me
this 21st day of April, 1915.
F.W. Buell
Notary Public

Appendix 2

Stielow's First Statement: 21–22 April 1915

I was to start to work the Monday after Phelps was killed, for wages, although I did his chores before that time, and both Nelson and I worked together everyday doing Phelps' chores, and while doing these chores, Nelson Green and I did not have any talk about Phelps' money. The Friday night before the murder of Phelps, and after dark, Nelson Green and I talked together out by my own barn on my place. I think we was talking about going over that night to Wolcottville [*sic*] for potatoes, but we went the next day. Nelson and I did the chores together at Phelps' place both in the morning and evening the day of the murder, and after dark on that Sunday night Nelson and I were out by my barn talking, this was as late as eight o'clock in the evening, and everyone of us were in bed that night by nine o'clock, and Nelson and I did not go out of our house that night, after we had this talk about eight o'clock the night of the murder. At about eleven o'clock the night of the murder I heard screams, as if from a woman, and the voice came from about the middle of the road in front of my house, and I heard more screams and more screams until the screams got right up to my front door, and just before the screams I heard one report of a pistol, and Nelson and I got up and put our clothes on, and all the time the scream seemed to get closer to our house, until the scream got right up to our front door, then I heard a woman's voice say, 'Charlie, please let me in, I'm dying,' and she said this same thing several times, and in the meantime, Mrs Green said, 'It's the woman from across the road, she must be killed,' I heard a shot, and Mrs Green wanted me to lock the doors, as they all were unlocked, and I wanted to let this woman into the house, but Mrs Green would not let me do it, she said it might be some crazy folks and it would scare my wife, and I went around and locked all the doors, and I then looked out my front door at about half past eleven o'clock and I saw the woman laying there on the boards just in front of my front door, and she had something white on, but my folks would not let me go out, Mrs Green told me not to go out, and Nelson also looked out of the front door with me. Nelson was awake and up and with me all the time I was, and also Mrs Green, and my wife remained in bed all this time, but she was awake, and the children were upstairs asleep, and in the morning before I ever went out of the house I looked out of the window in the door and saw that the woman who laid there dead was Miss Wolcott, and I saw the blood on her night gown on her side, lots of blood near her armpit. This was at 5.20 in the morning, and I then told Mrs Green that that woman laid out there dead, and she said, 'Is that so?' and I said something must have been going on last night someway, and Nelson was just getting up and Mrs Green told Nelson about the woman laying there dead.

During the time that Green and I laid in bed that night, I laid on the back side of the bed and Nelson laid on the front side of the bed. I told Nelson to build the fire, and I went out of the house and on the stoop to the front of the house, a thing I never did before in my life, and I went up to the woman laying on the ground, and saw that she was dead, and I then went right across the road to Phelps' and found the kitchen door open, and a kerosene lamp burning on a stand near the door, and as I stood on the doorsill I saw Mr Phelps lying on the floor just inside the kitchen door, the door being open against his body. I bent over near Mr Phelps and could see and hear him breathe and could see that he was still alive. I did not see any blood on Mr Phelps, and I did not see any bullet wounds or any marks on his person. I did not try to assist him or arouse him or to do anything for him at all, as I was very excited. I stayed with Mr Phelps four minutes, then I saw across the lots a light in Jenkins's

barn, and I then left the Phelps kitchen and went through the little gate just opposite the kitchen door and across the lot and into
his sheep barn and asked him if he was Jenkins, and he said he was,
and I told him that the woman and Mr Phelps had been killed, the
woman laid in front of my front door and Phelps laid dead on his
kitchen floor, then I started, and Jenkins said he would be over just
as quick as he could reach the telephone and get the Doctor, and I
then said I would go on and notify the neighbours, and he told me
he would tell the Bensons and I then walked out his driveway and
onto the road and up to my house and told Nelson, who was out by
the pump, to get the canvas out of the buggy shed and put it over
Miss Wolcott, and he did this, and I started down the road toward
Howard Kohler's and Nelson right behind me, and I notified Kohler,
and Nelson told William Pogle. I told Kohler that something awful
happened, then Kohler said where, and I told him to Phelps [*sic*], and
I started back, and Kohler caught up with me, and also Nelson did
catch up with me, and when we got to Phelps there was several persons there, this was about 6:30am or 6:45am. Then at about 7 o'clock
we all went into Phelps' house at the time the doctor did, Nelson
was with us when we went into the house. We went and looked into
Phelps' bedroom and saw the bed and saw that the bureau drawers
had been pulled out on the floor, and Doctor Munson was looking
through the bureau drawers, then I went into the kitchen and into
the milk house and got the milk pails (Nelson was then outside.) and
I noticed that the door to the milk house was closed and locked on
the inside, Nelson was not with me, and he did not know that the
milk house was locked on the inside.

I fed the horses and Nelson was milking, and after I had the
horses fed, I helped Nelson milk the cows, then we took the milk to
the milk house, and we strained the milk, and he took the calf's milk
and I fed the hogs. I am positive that I did not that day tell Nelson
any place where Phelps had any bullet wounds, but when we was
eating breakfast at home at 9 o'clock I told Nelson that it looked as

though Phelps had a couple of marks on his face. Between nine and ten Nelson and I went back to Phelps', and we went back into the house and listened to what the people had to say, and we listened, but we did not say anything, then we went out doors and I helped cover up the footprints with a horse blanket, and I heard them say they was going to get a blood hound to track the murderer, and they said they was going to get these dogs from Oneida. About noon Nelson and I went over to my house for dinner, and came right back, and we stayed there until the dog came, and we watched him work. They put the dog onto the tracks on the side of the road that they covered up, and at first the dog worked good, but after he got over the fence he didn't work so good, then we went and done the chores, and by that time the dog was gone, then we went home and got our supper, and we stayed at home. The story that I framed up with my folks for us to tell at the Inquest was a lie, and we all swore to a lie. I tried to hide it that I saw Miss Wolcott dead when I looked out of my front door window that night. I also lied when I told the District Attorney and the Sheriff and the Detectives and others and the Coroner that I never had a revolver or a gun, and at the time I told these lies I did have a gun in my house, and the twenty-two revolver my wife might not have given to Raymond Green until after the Phelps murder, and when Mrs Green, my Mother-in-Law, went to Royalton Center last Sunday, I told her and all my folks to be careful of them Detectives, as they are clever, and they asked me lots of questions and they are foxy and they will catch the man that done it in time and the less they said the better it would be for all of us. About two weeks ago today or tomorrow I saw Raymond Green and about one week after the murder of Phelps I saw Raymond, he came to my house for his Mother to sign a note for him, and I think my woman let Raymond have the twenty-two calibre revolver at that time. I bought the twenty-two calibre cartridges at Hartland Corners from Frank Rind about ten years ago, it was from Mr Gill, instead of Rind. My idea of the fellow that killed Phelps is that Curt [*sic*] Tallman did it, because

Mr Phelps told me that Tallman lived in the same house I now live in and Tallman picked some apples for Phelps and sold the apples and never gave the money to Phelps, and Phelps told me he never got the money from Tallman. I also heard that Tallman moved to Rochester with his wife, who is a thin woman. We talked about getting a Lawyer to collect the salary due me from the Phelps Estate. I want to say on this statement that I have lied to you Detectives when you asked me about this murder. I wear a number ten leather shoe. Nelson Green left my house the Wednesday after the murder and went to his Sister's, Mrs Frank Smith, in Medina.

On the Sunday night of the murder, at about 8:00pm Nelson Green and I was out back of the hen coop at my house getting some rails for wood, I had on my black cap and overalls and jumper to match, the same as I have on now, and my felt boots and rubber overshoes that I now have on, and I had a red handkerchief in my pocket, like the one I have in my pocket now, and Nelson had on a black, woolly cap, the only one he has, and his short, light coloured rain coat, and brown corduroy pants, and felt boots, with rubbers, and the next morning after the murder when I got up I put on the same felt boots and other clothing that I had on the night before, and Nelson also put on the same clothes he had on the night of the murder.

You can go to my wife and her Mother, Mrs Green, and to Nelson Green and tell them that I sent you and they should tell the truth about the Phelps murder, and I know they will tell the truth and I will stand back of anything that any one of them tells you about this murder. I have told you all and everything that I know about the Phelps and Wolcott murder. I certainly don't know who committed the murder.

No promise of pay or reward has been made to me directly or indirectly by any person, and all of the foregoing statement I solemnly swear to be true, and I am willing to sign and swear to the same.

His

CHARLES FREDERICK STIELOW

mark

Subscribed and sworn to before me

this 22nd day of April, 1915.

F.W. Buell

Notary Public

Signature to the above statement

witnessed by George W. Newton

Robert A. Wilson

J. Scott Porter

Henry S. Schultz

Stielow's Second Statement (Unsigned): 23 April 1915

I, Charles Frederick Stielow, do make this further and additional statement, of my own free will and accord, without promise of immunity from prosecution, and without threat or fear, concerning the murder of Charles Phelps and Margaret Wolcott. The Wednesday before the murder, when Nelson Green and I were doing the chores at Phelps', in the evening, we talked about the money that Phelps had in the house, and talked about robbing Mr Phelps, Nelson and I were talking, and I told Nelson that Will Warner told me that Phelps always had lots of money in his house, and Nelson said, 'Let's go over and rob him,' and I said, 'Oh, shaw [sic], we don't want to do that,' then Nelson said, 'Yes, we will, we need the money, and we will go and rob him,' and I said, 'Alright, if you will do the work, I will go with you,' and he said, 'Alright.' That was all we said about it that night, then we went home. The next time we talked about the robbery was the Friday evening before the murder, when we again talked about the robbery out by my barn. Nelson said to me, 'Will we go and rob Phelps,' and I said, 'I don't know, I don't feel like doing it,' and he said, 'Oh, yes, you must do it,' I want to take this back what I just said about planning this robbery, the truth is that I planned the robbery, and on the Wednesday and on the Friday evening's [sic] above referred to, I told Nelson that Phelps had lots of money in his house, and I asked Nelson to go with and help me rob Phelps, and when we talked on this Friday night, I told Nelson that the best time to rob the house would be next Sunday night, and then on Sunday night of the murder, after we had done the chores at Phelps we came back to my house and done our chores, then we stood out by my barn and talked about what we was going to do, and I told Nelson that we better go to bed, and wait until about ten o'clock, then get up, and we will go over and stand by the side of Phelps' house and see if there is any rigs coming then I says if there hain't [sic] no rigs coming I will go down the transmission line, and see if there is anybody at Jenkins' and anybody stirring any other place, and then Nelson said to me, 'I will go down the road here a little ways and see if these neighbours are stirring around.'

Then we went into our house and went to bed about nine o'clock, and about ten o'clock Nelson and I got up, and we went out and stood back of our house and talked a few minutes, then Nelson said, 'I will go down towards Benson's and see whether they are up,' and I said, 'Alright, and I will go over to Jenkins' and see whether they are up.' Before we went to bed at nine o'clock, Nelson went upstairs and got the twenty-two calibre revolver out of my trunk.

After we had this talk, Nelson gave me the revolver, and said, 'Here is your Pop Mitchell,' (This is the nickname that we always have called this revolver.) I looked at the revolver and I saw that it was loaded, every chamber was full. Then we both walked out my driveway together, and we went to Phelps' and we saw Phelps and Miss Wolcott both sitting in chairs in the dining-room, and the hanging lamp over the table was lighted, they were sitting there talking, then we both came out the Phelps driveway together, and I turned and walked down the gullet [sic] beside the road for a short distance, then I went through the fence where there is a little opening. Those were the tracks I made, and the ones that I helped the Under Sheriff Porter cover up the Monday morning after the murder. We covered the tracks with horse blankets from Phelps' barn, to preserve them until they could get the bloodhounds there, those were my own footprints, made by my number ten leather shoes, and these shoes now are at my own home, in my bedroom. After I passed through the opening in the fence, I cut across the lot to Jenkins barn, and looked to see if anybody was up at Jenkins, but I did not see any light in Jenkins' house, or anybody around his place, then I walked down Jenkins' lane and cut through the orchard and over to the Transmission line, in a North-easterly direction, and when I came to the waterhole a little ways from the Transmission Line, I waded through this pond, or water standing on the land, and it was not very deep, and I got my feet wet, then I walked down the Transmission Line, West to the West Shelby Road, then I walked on the left, or Phelps side of the road down past Jenkins and Bensons, and did not see anybody up, then when I got to Phelps' I saw Nelson Green standing right by the maple tree at the corner of the Phelps driveway, and next to the corner of the fence. The reason I made this trip around by the Transmission line was to see if anybody was up and also to make it appear that the robbers had gone that way, by my footprints.

When I met Nelson at the maple tree I told him that I just made that trip around the Transmission Line so we could fool the Police, and make them think the robbers had gone in that direction, and Nelson told me that he had walked down the middle of the road down in front of Benson's, and he said that there was nobody up, then he came back and had been standing there waiting for me. I walked fast all the way on my trip. Then Nelson told me that Phelps and Miss Wolcott were up yet, then we walked in the Phelps drive-way, down to the chicken coop, and as we passed we saw that Phelps and Miss Wolcott were still sitting in the dining-room, the curtain in the dining room to the East of the outside door was down, but there was no curtain on the window in the outside door in the din-ing-room, and we could look through this window in the outside dining-room door, there was a stand in the dining-room in front of the outside door with plants on, and the window curtain to the West of the outside door also was down.

We stood there at the chicken coop, then we went back to the straw stack behind the barn, we went back there to hide and kill time.

Then we went back to the chicken coop, then we went to see if they was up yet, and we saw both of them leave the dining room, and Miss Wolcott went into her bedroom and Mr Phelps took the kerosene lamp out of the bracket in the kitchen and he put the dining room hanging lamp out, then he carried the bracket lamp and went into his bedroom, and Nelson and I stood right by the stone horseblock, almost in front of the dining room door, just West of it, and in a few minutes his light was out in his room. Then we went to the woodpile then I told Nelson to get the mop that was hanging on the dinner-bell pole just back of the house, or on the back of the house, I don't know which, I told Nelson to chop the mop part off, and I told Nelson that would make a good stick to hit the old man with if he shows fight, then I told Nelson now we will have to start it, and now we are going to do it, then I pulled out the revolver from my left outside pocket in my jumper. Just before we went over to Phelps that night I told Nelson that I heard that Phelps always kept his money in his bureau drawer.

When I pulled out the revolver from my jumper pocket I handed it to Nelson and told him that he could do the robbery better and much stiller than I could, and I told Nelson that he should kill the old Son-of-a-bitch and the woman, too, because if they saw either one of us they would tell the Police and it would be all off with us. I told Nelson to kill them with the mop stick if he could, but if he couldn't kill them with the mop stick, then to kill them with the gun, and I told him if he needed any help I would go in and help him, then Nelson said he thought he could do it alone. I told Nelson I would keep watch outside and see if anybody would come along, and if anybody did come, I would whistle to him, and if he heard me whistle he should come out of the house as quick as he could, and we could run behind the barns and the orchards and get away someway. I think this was about twenty minutes to eleven at night. Before we went into the house I went around the house and looked into Phelps' window of his bedroom, and I saw that it was dark in his room. This was after I had given the revolver to Nelson, and after I came back from Phelps' window, I went and tried to get into the milk room door, but it was locked on the inside. Then I told Nelson to go to the door and rap on the door, and to go ahead, and if he couldn't handle them alone, I would go in and help him, then Nelson said to me that he was pretty sure he could handle them alone, and I told Nelson I would stand right there by the kitchen door, and help him if he needed me, then Nelson rapped on the kitchen, after he tried the door and saw it was locked, then we saw Phelps light the lamp and come out of his bedroom and come to the kitchen door, and put the lamp on the stand by the window in the kitchen, then Nelson said, 'Open the door, I want to come in,' then Phelps opened the door, and Nelson went in and struck Phelps in the face with the mop stick. Before Nelson went in, I took a stick of wood from the woodpile, and I told Nelson that if he couldn't handle them, I would help him with the stick of wood, and I would lay them out. After Nelson struck Phelps in the face with the mop stick, then Phelps showed fight, and I stepped inside the house and pushed Phelps back away from Nelson, and I held Phelps' right arm and Nelson shot him in the left arm, then Nelson said he didn't hit him very good, and he better shoot him again, and then I told Nelson to go to it. All this time Phelps was hollering, but I can't remember what he said. Then Nelson shot Phelps two times in rapid succession, the second shot was in the body near the heart, then I let go of Phelps and he fell down, and he hit the pail with his head when he fell, then Nelson shot Phelps the third and last shot in the head after Phelps was laying on the floor. Phelps had his night clothes on all this time. Then I told Nelson, 'Now go after the money,' and he said, 'Alright, I will,' and I said I would go out doors and watch if there is anybody coming. Before I went into the house I said to myself, 'I don't need that stick of wood,' and I laid it down on the manure by the door, and when I came out of the house I picked up the stick of wood and kept it in my hand, then I went across the driveway, and stood there by the maple tree, and watched to see if anybody was coming, then I saw Miss Wolcott coming, running in the kitchen and to the kitchen door, and Nelson was right on her heels. When I went out of the house I closed the kitchen door behind me. Miss Wolcott opened the kitchen door and came out and closed the door behind her, and she put her arm up to her head and ran close to the house, and just after she closed the door Nelson was inside the kitchen and the door was closed and he shot her as she stood just outside the door, just as she started away from the kitchen door, and the shot went through the glass in the kitchen door. As soon as she left the house she started to holler, and she screamed all the way over till she got to my lot, and when she got up to my front door she pawed around on the front door, then she said, 'Charlie, please let me in, I'm dying,' and she said this several times, then I went down Phelps' driveway to the road and into my own driveway and when I passed her I saw her fall down on the boards in front of and close up to my front door, and I just stood there and I heard her say, 'I'm dying.' After Miss Wolcott came out of the house and ran to my house, Nelson came right out after her, and I threw the stick of wood over onto the woodpile and Nelson told me she was shot so she wouldn't last long. I did not tell the truth when I said that I went out of the house after Phelps was shot, the truth is that after Phelps was shot I took the lamp and Nelson and I went into Phelps' bedroom and I held the lamp and Nelson Green went through all the drawers in Mr Phelps bureau, he took the three drawers out and put them onto the floor, and I saw Nelson take the leather pocketbook out of one of the drawers. I think it was the lower drawer, the pocketbook was under some clothes. Nelson put the pocketbook into his own pocket. I was mistaken when I said that I was standing outside when Miss Wolcott came out of the house, and I also was mistaken when I said that Nelson and I went into Phelps' bedroom before Miss Wolcott was shot, the truth about it is that after Nelson shot Mr Phelps, while I was holding Phelps, I took the lamp and Nelson and I started to go into Phelps' bedroom to ransack, and just as we were going into Phelps' bedroom Miss Wolcott came out of her bedroom and ran into the kitchen and we followed her to the kitchen door, and she closed the door after she went out, then Nelson shot her through the window in the kitchen door, as I have described before, then Nelson and I went back into Phelps' bedroom and ransacked the bureau drawers as I have described just now, then we came out of the bedroom, and I put the lamp on the kitchen stand, and we took a look at Phelps, and I told Nelson, 'He's gone, alright,' then we both went out doors, and I picked up the stick of wood from beside the house and I threw it over onto the woodpile, then I ran down the Phelps driveway to the road, and into my own driveway, then I heard Miss Wolcott screaming at my front door, and saw her pawing around on my front door, and she kept saying several times, 'Charlie, please let me in, I'm dying.' Then I stepped in the driveway near the front of my house and took a look at her, then I went around my house and went into my house by the back woodshed door, and I walked slowly through Mrs Green's and my wife's room, where they both were in bed, but they did not say anything to me, although I know they both were awake at the time, and when I went through their room I heard Mrs Green talking to my wife and telling her keep quiet and not worry. I waited in my bedroom a few minutes. When Nelson and I came out of Phelps' house, I started toward my house, and Nelson went around behind Phelps' house, and he told me he was going around through the orchard to our house. That night I wore this same suit of blue overalls and jumper, and number ten leather shoes and my black cap, with a front-piece, and Nelson wore his brown corduroy pants and brown, short raincoat, and felt boots and rubbers over them, I don't know what size, and his black woolly cap, with a long front piece, and Nelson, before he went into the Phelps house, pulled the front piece down over his eyes, and the sides of the cap down over his ears, and his face was pretty well covered up. I waited in my bedroom a few minutes when Nelson came in, and a light, very low, was burning in the little sink bedroom and front room where Mrs Green and my wife were lying, this bed is in a little sink place just big enough for a bed, and is just off from the front room in our house, and the bed in which they were is not more than ten or twelve feet from the front door of the front room where Miss Wolcott was screaming and calling for help, there is one window and a glass in the front door in this room, and in the next room to the North there is one front window, and my and Nelson's bedroom is just off from this other room, to the West of the front of the house. When Nelson came into our bedroom, I was sitting on the edge of my bed, and when Nelson came through Mrs Green's and my wife's bedroom and the front room, which is all one room, and only a few feet from my bedroom, I heard my wife ask Nelson where he had been, and Nelson said he had been out doors, and when Nelson came into my bedroom I asked him if he heard that racket, and he said, 'Yes,' then Nelson and I went out into the room where Mrs Green and my wife were, then Mrs Green said, that she heard screams and a woman pounding on their front door, and she thought it was the woman from across the road, and that she must be killed, as she (Mrs Green) heard a shot, then I looked out of our front door window and saw Miss Wolcott laying there, then I told my folks that she was laying out there dead, and I told them I would open the front door, and Mrs Green would not let me do it, she said it might scare my woman, that she might take a kink and die, in the condition that she was. Then I went around and locked the doors, as we never used to lock our doors, then we all went to bed.

I think we all went to bed about some time after eleven o'clock. When I looked out of our South window I saw there was a light in Pogle's house, this was just before we went to bed. Mrs Green told us the next morning that soon after we went to bed a rig went by.

I slept on the back side of the bed and Nelson slept on the front side of our bed. At five o'clock in the morning after the murder I got up first, and got dressed, then I woke Nelson and told him to get up and build a fire, and that I was going to Phelps' to see whether Phelps was alive, and he said, 'Alright,' then Nelson and I went out doors and talked it over, we were standing back of our house, then I asked Nelson how much money he got in the pocketbook, and he told me he didn't get very much, then I called him a Son-of-a-bitch and told him to give me my share, as we had an agreement that we were to divide the money, and Green was to have a little more than half of the money we got, and I was to have a little less than half of the money, then I went over to Phelps' house, and I went into the house and I looked at him and I saw that he was still breathing, and I stayed there about four minutes, then I came out and went through the gate in the fence near the kitchen door, and through the lot and to Jenkins' cow shed or sheep shed, and I saw Jenkins there with a lantern, and I told Jenkins, and asked him if he was Mr Jenkins, and he said he was, then I told him that there had been some robbering [*sic*] going on at Phelps, and they must have been shot, then Jenkins said he would telephone to a Doctor and that he would notify Benson's, and I told him I was going to tell Kohler's, then I went out Jenkins's driveway and to the road and back to my house, and I saw Nelson outside behind our house, and I told Nelson to get the canvas and cover Miss Wolcott up, and he said he would, then I told Nelson to go and tell Pogle's and that I would go and tell Kohler's, which we did in the manner described in my former statement. A few days after the murder Raymond Green came to our house, and after he had gone my wife told me that she gave the Pop Mitchell (meaning the revolver) to Raymond, and she told him it was the gun that had killed the folks across the road. The statement I made in my former statement that I certainly did not know who committed the murder is not true, and I have now told you today all that I know about the Phelps and Wolcott murder. Nelson Green left my house I think it was the Tuesday after the murder, and he took with him the pocketbook we got from Phelps' bedroom, and he never gave me any of the money. All of the foregoing statement I solemnly swear to be true, and I am willing to sign and swear to the same.

UNSIGNED

The foregoing statement was voluntarily and freely made by the said Charles Frederick Stielow and written at the time by George W. Newton in our presence.

GEORGE W. NEWTON

CHESTER M. BARTLETT

J. SCOTT PORTER

ROBERT A. WILSON

Appendix 4

Timeline of Events

1915

March

13 Stielow and Green move into tenant house

21 Charles Phelps and Margaret Wolcott are murdered

22 Stielow finds the bodies

26 Inquest opens in Medina

27 Private detective George W. Newton assumes control of the case

29 Stielow gives firearms to Raymond Green to hide

April

7   Newton's first recorded visit to the Stielow house

12 Stielow family move to new home on Salt Works Road

20 Green arrested

21 Green confesses at 2:00am: four hours later Stielow is arrested

22 Stielow's daughter, Irene, is born

23 Stielow allegedly confesses: he and Green are charged with double murder

29 Second arraignment hearing at Albion

May

1   Albert H. Hamilton, ballistics expert, enters the case

6   Arraignment hearing resumes at Albion

7   RMS *Lusitania* sunk by German U-boat with the loss of 1,198
     lives, including 128 Americans

12   Arraignment hearing resumed and adjourned

June

21   Grand jury convenes to hear evidence in the Shelby killings

23   Grand jury returns indictments against Stielow and Green.
     Stielow will be tried first

July

12   Stielow's trial begins

23   Stielow convicted and sentenced to death in the week of 5
     September. Green plea-bargains a life sentence

26   Stielow arrives at Sing Sing

27   Stielow's death sentence is automatically stayed pending appeal

September

3   Five die in Sing Sing's electric chair in one night

October

31   Warden Thomas Mott Osborne takes medical leave from
     Sing Sing

November

28   Defence lawyer David White files further notice of appeal

1916
January

17   Warden Osborne charged with perjury

21   Stielow appeal is heard in Albany

February

22   New York Appeals court dismisses Stielow's appeal. Execution set for 14 April

March

15   Osborne's perjury charge dismissed

April

10   White petitions Governor Whitman for a new trial. Whitman stays death sentence until 19 April

17   Whitman issues 60-day stay of execution

June

7   Stielow given one-month stay of execution

16   Immorality charges against Osborne thrown out

22   Oresto Shilitano shoots Officer Daniel McCarthy and escapes from death row. Recaptured that same night

28   Grace Humiston agrees to investigate Stielow case

30   Shilitano executed

July

4   Stielow's scheduled execution date. Death warrant reveals a loophole and the date is rescheduled for ten days later

13   Motion for new trial made before Justice George W. Cole in Buffalo

14   Stielow's execution halted ten hours before scheduled time after Judge Cole issues a temporary reprieve

16   Warden Osborne returns to Sing Sing

26   Judge Cole dismisses Stielow's motion for a new trial. Stielow's death sentence confirmed for 72 hours later

29   Judge Guy stops Stielow's execution at 5:20am, just 40 minutes before he is scheduled to die. Issues a twelve-hour stay. Execution rescheduled for 11:00pm that same night. At 7:00pm

Judge Guy calls Sing Sing and extends the stay until at least 24 August

August

8   Erwin King arrested for another crime

10 King confesses his involvement in the Shelby murders to Grace Humiston

13 King repudiates confession

23 Appeal hearing before Justice Adolph J. Rodenback at Rochester. He adjourns the case until 27 September

September

20 District Attorney Knickerbocker and Sheriff Bartlett both voted out of office

27 Hearing continues before Justice Rodenback

30 King once again repudiates confession

October

11 Justice Rodenback dismisses the motion for a new trial

15 Osborne leaves Sing Sing, having resigned the post of warden

23 Defence lawyer, Inez Milholland Boissevain, is struck down by illness during a speech in Los Angeles

25 Stielow resentenced to death during the week of 11 December; the fourth time that he has faced the electric chair

November

25 Inez Milholland Boissevain dies

29 Governor Whitman chairs public hearing on the case

December

3   Governor Whitman commutes Stielow's death sentence

1917

January

30   Governor Whitman interviews Erwin King in secret

February

1   Governor Whitman appoints a Special Commission, headed by George Bond, to reinvestigate the Shelby murders

April

6   United States declares war on Germany

June

7   King confesses to Bond

December

12   Orleans County grand jury convenes to hear the Special Commission's findings

21   Grand jury advises the court that it has 'nothing to report'. The arrest warrant for Erwin King is discharged. Bond begins writing a report for Governor Whitman

1918

May

8   Governor Whitman pardons Stielow and Green

9   Stielow and Green freed from Auburn Prison

November

5   Governor Whitman voted out of office

1942

August

9   Charles Stielow dies aged 63 in Medina

Author's Acknowledgements

I am greatly indebted to several people and several organisations that have assisted in the preparation of this book. These are: the Library of Congress; the British Newspaper Library; Simon Flynn, Andrew Furlow, Najma Finlay and Sarah Higgins at Icon Books; David Andersen; Greg Manning; Angelyn Singer; Rebecca Hatcher; David Corbin; Nancy Metzer; Lou Fuller; Dawn Izydorczak; Tom Tryniski; Francis Sypher; Marge Goodrich Schultz; Janis Gillis; Jill Spiller; Marion Bach; Glorian Venturella; Professor Julio L. Hernandez-Delgado; Janet Bunde; Lauren Yannotta; Cheryl Mowatt; Nick Halliday for illustrations; Ed Knappman and everyone at NEPA; and Rachel Calder at Sayle Literary Agency. A very special vote of thanks goes to Anita Reeb and Mary Stack for their patience and persistence. Along with everyone else mentioned they gave their time graciously, but the usual caveat applies; any errors or omissions are entirely the responsibility of the author. As always, the final dedication is reserved for Norma.

Notes

1: Pity the Poor Immigrant

1. *The Times*, 29 June 1914
2. *New York Times*, 22 March 1915
3. Report by the Special Deputy Attorney (1917), p. 8a
4. *Medina Daily Journal*, 29 April 1915

2: Bodies in the Snow

1. Report by the Special Deputy Attorney (1917), p. 162
2. ibid., p. 196
3. *Rochester Democrat And Chronicle*, 20 July 1915
4. ibid., 16 July 1915
5. Report by the Special Deputy Attorney (1917), p. 53
6. ibid., p. 55

3: Out Of The Mouths …

1. *Buffalo Express*, 24 March 1915
2. *Rochester Democrat And Chronicle*, 24 March 1915
3. ibid.
4. ibid.
5. ibid., 26 March 1915
6. Report by the Special Deputy Attorney (1917), p. 55
7. ibid., p. 56
8. ibid.
9. ibid.
10. ibid., p. 161
11. ibid., p. 162

4: When First We Practise To Deceive

1. Report by the Special Deputy Attorney (1917), p. 59
2. ibid, p. 60
3. ibid,
4. ibid, p. 55
5. ibid, p. 61

6. April 1915
7. Report by the Special Deputy Attorney (1917), p. 175
8. ibid., p. 64
9. ibid., p. 66
10. ibid., p. 188
11. ibid., p. 71
12. ibid.
13. ibid., p. 143
14. ibid.
15. ibid., p. 144
16. ibid.
17. ibid., p. 191
18. ibid., p. 192
19. ibid., p. 193
20. ibid., p. 192
21. ibid., p. 194
22. ibid.
23. ibid., p. 195
24. *Medina Daily Journal*, 24 April 1915
25. Report by the Special Deputy Attorney (1917), p. 75

5: 'That Man From Auburn'

1. *Rochester Democrat And Chronicle*, 24 April 1915
2. ibid.
3. *New York Times*, 1 May 1915
4. ibid.
5. Report by the Special Deputy Attorney (1917), p. 75
6. ibid.
7. *New York Tribune*, 13 May 1918
8. *Rochester Democrat And Chronicle*, 1 May 1915
9. *Buffalo Express*, 21 July 1915
10. Report by the Special Deputy Attorney (1917), p. 76
11. *New York Times*, 17 March 1910
12. *Rochester Democrat And Chronicle*, 5 July 1938
13. ibid.
14. *Auburn Citizen*, 21 January 1910
15. Report by the Special Deputy Attorney (1917), p. 62
16. ibid.
17. *Buffalo Express*, 23 July 1915
18. Report by the Special Deputy Attorney (1917), p. 127
19. *Rochester Democrat And Chronicle*, 8 May 1915

20. ibid.

21. ibid.

22. *New York Times*, 8 May 1915

23. May 1915

24. Report by the Special Deputy Attorney (1917), p. 80

25. *Rochester Democrat And Chronicle*, 13 May 1915

26. *Washington Post*, 3 February 1935

27. Report by the Special Deputy Attorney (1917), p. 161

28. ibid., p. 62

6: The Trial

1. *Rochester Democrat And Chronicle*, 13 July 1915

2. ibid.

3. ibid., 15 July 1915

4. Report by the Special Deputy Attorney (1917), p. 204

5. ibid.

6. ibid.

7. *Buffalo Express*, 16 July 1915

8. Report by the Special Deputy Attorney (1917), p. 204

9. ibid.

10. ibid.

11. *Rochester Democrat And Chronicle*, 16 July 1915

12. ibid.

13. ibid.

14. ibid., 18 July 1915

15. Report by the Special Deputy Attorney (1917), p. 163

16. ibid.

17. ibid.

18. ibid.

19. ibid., p. 165

20. ibid., p. 166

21. ibid., p. 167

22. ibid., p. 167

23. *Rochester Democrat And Chronicle*, 18 July 1915

24. ibid.

25. Report by the Special Deputy Attorney (1917), p. 168

26. ibid., p. 163

27. ibid., p. 166

28. July 1915

7: Stielow Takes The Stand

1. *Rochester Democrat And Chronicle*, 20 July 1915

2. Report by the Special Deputy Attorney (1917), p. 168

3. ibid, p. 139

4. ibid, p. 144

5. *Rochester Democrat And Chronicle*, 20 July 1915

6. ibid.

7. ibid.

8. ibid.

9. ibid.

10. ibid.

11. ibid.

12. ibid.

13. Gerry Spence, *Of Murder and Madness* (New York: St Martin's, 1983)

14. *Buffalo Express*, 20 July 1915

15. Report by the Special Deputy Attorney (1917), p. 161

16. ibid., pp. 16 –62

17. *Rochester Democrat And Chronicle*, 21 July 1915

18. *Buffalo Express*, 21 July 1915

19. *Rochester Democrat And Chronicle*, 21 July 1915

20. ibid.

21. ibid.

22. ibid.

23. ibid.

24. Report by the Special Deputy Attorney (1917), p. 193

25. *Rochester Democrat And Chronicle*, 21 July1915

26. ibid.

27. *Buffalo Express*, 22 July 1915

28. *Rochester Democrat And Chronicle*, 21 July 1915

29. *ibid.*, 22 July 1915

30. *Buffalo Express*, 22 July 1915

31. ibid.

32. *Rochester Democrat And Chronicle*, 22 July 1915

33. ibid.

34. ibid.

35. ibid.

36. ibid.

37. ibid.

38. ibid.

39. *Buffalo Express*, 23 July 1915

40. ibid.

41. *Rochester Democrat And Chronicle*, 23 July 1915
42. ibid.
43. ibid.
44. ibid.
45. *Buffalo Express*, 23 July 1915
46. *Rochester Democrat And Chronicle*, 23 July 1915
47. ibid.
48. ibid.
49. ibid.
50. *Rochester Democrat And Chronicle*, 24 July 1915
51. ibid., 23 July 1915
52. *New York Times*, 24 July 1915
53. *Rochester Democrat And Chronicle*, 24 July 1915
54. *Buffalo Express*, 24 July 1915
55. Report by the Special Deputy Attorney, (1917), p. 205
56. ibid., p. 205
57. *Elmira Morning Telegram*, 20 August 1916
58. ibid.
59. Report by the Special Deputy Attorney (1917), p. 205
60. ibid., p. 39
61. ibid., p. 38
62. Edwin M. Borchard, *Convicting the Innocent* (New Haven: Yale University Press, 1932), p. 247

8: The Verdict

1. *Buffalo Express*, 24 July 1915
2. *Rochester Democrat And Chronicle*, 24 July 1915
3. *Buffalo Express*, 24 July 1915
4. *Rochester Democrat And Chronicle*, 24 July 1915
5. *Buffalo Express*, 24 July 1915
6. *ibid.*, 25 July 1915
7. *Syracuse Journal*, 26 July 1915

9: The Big House up the River

1. *New York Times*, 28 March 1927
2. ibid., 23 May 1914
3. *Washington Post*, 15 December 1912
4. *Mahoning Dispatch*, 30 July 1915

10: The Killing Machine

1. *New York Times*, 9 December 1914

2. Anthony Taylor, *The Prison System and its Effects* (Hauppauge: Nova Science, 2008)
3. *New York Times*, 31 July 1915
4. ibid.
5. ibid.
6. *Washington Post*, 4 September 1915
7. *New York Times*, 14 December 1915
8. ibid., 14 January 1916
9. ibid., 4 January 1916
10. ibid., 17 February 1916
11. ibid., 18 February 1916
12. ibid.
13. *People v. Stielow, 160 N.Y.S. 555 (1916)*

11: Mrs Humiston Lends A Hand
1. *New York Tribune*, 12 May 1918
2. ibid., 3 March 1916
3. *Washington Post*, 5 March 1916
4. *New York Times*, 16 March 1916
5. ibid.
6. *New York Times*, 3 October 1905
7. November 1906
8. *Crimes and Punishment* (BPC Publishing, 1974), vol. 16, p. 102:
9. *Washington Post*, 2 June 1916
10. *Poughkeepsie Eagle*, 12 August 1916
11. Report by the Special Deputy Attorney, (1917), p. 32
12. ibid.

12: Outwitting Detective Newton
1. *Auburn Citizen*, 15 August 1916
2. *The World*, 13 August 1916
3. ibid.
4. *New York Times*, 7 July 1916
5. ibid., 17 July 1916
6. *Buffalo Express*, 20 July 1916
7. ibid.
8. ibid., 21 July 1916
9. *New York Times*, 19 July 1916
10. *Rochester Democrat And Chronicle*, 27 July 1916
11. ibid.
12. *Buffalo Express*, 20 July 1916

13. ibid., 28 July 1916
14. ibid., 28 July 1916
15. *New York Evening Journal*, 28 July 1916
16. Kristen E. Jaconi, *Inez Milholland: The Suffragette Martyr* (Women's Legal History Project), p. 6
17. ibid., p. 17
18. Edward T. James, Janet Wilson James and Paul Boyer, *Notable American Women* (Boston: Belknap Press), p. 189
19. *Buffalo Express*, 28 July 1916
20. ibid., 12 August 1916

13: The Longest Night
1. *Buffalo Express*, 29 July 1916
2. *Schenectady Gazette*, 29 July 1916
3. *Washington Post*, 24 December 1916
4. *New York Times*, 30 July 1916
5. *The World*, 12 August 1916
6. *Clyde Herald*, 30 July 1916

14: A New Suspect
1. *Brooklyn Daily Eagle*, 30 July 1916
2. *Utica Herald-Dispatch*, 29 July 1916
3. Report by the Special Deputy Attorney (1917), p. 99
4. *Auburn Citizen*, 12 August 1916
5. ibid.
6. ibid.
7. ibid.
8. *People v. Bradford*, 218 N.Y. 729; 113 N.E. 1063; 1916, p. 198
9. *Auburn Citizen*, 12 August 1916
10. *Buffalo Express*, 13 August 1916
11. ibid., 12 August 1916
12. *Auburn Citizen*, 14 August 1916
13. *The World*, 12 August 1916
14. *New York Times*, 12 August 1916

15: Startling Confession
1. *Rochester Democrat And Chronicle*, 12 August 1916
2. *New York Times*, 12 August 1916
3. *Buffalo Express*, 11 August 1916
4. ibid., 12 August 1916
5. *New York Times*, 12 August 1916

6. *The World*, 12 August 1916
7. *Auburn Citizen*, 12 August 1916
8. *Buffalo Express*, 13 August 1916
9. ibid., 12 August 1916
10. ibid., 13 August 1916
11. ibid.
12. ibid.
13. ibid.
14. ibid.
15. *New York Times*, 13 August 1916

16: Knickerbocker Fights Back

1. *Buffalo Express*, 14 August 1916
2. ibid.
3. *Auburn Citizen*, 14 August 1916
4. ibid.
5. ibid.
6. ibid.
7. *Rochester Democrat And Chronicle*, 15 August 1916
8. *Buffalo Express*, 14 August 1916
9. ibid.
10. ibid.
11. *Oswego Daily Times*, 15 August 1916
12. ibid.
13. *Albany Evening Journal*, 16 August 1916
14. *Rochester Democrat And Chronicle*, 15 August 1916
15. ibid.
16. ibid.
17. *Utica Daily Press*, 16 August 1916
18. ibid.
19. ibid.
20. *Rochester Democrat And Chronicle*, 15 August 1916
21. *Auburn Citizen*, 16 August 1916
22. *Buffalo Express*, 17 August 1916
23. ibid., 16 August 1916
24. ibid., 17 August 1916
25. *New York Times*, 21 August 1916
26. *Buffalo Express*, 22 August 1916
27. *Syracuse Post Standard*, 24 August 1916
28. *State v. Trybus*, 219 N.Y. 18; 113 N.E. 538; 1916

17: Special Hearing in Rochester

1. *Buffalo Express*, 2 September 1916
2. ibid, 12 September 1916
3. ibid.
4. ibid.
5. ibid., 14 September 1916
6. ibid.
7. *New York Times*, 14 September 1916
8. September 1916
9. *Rochester Democrat And Chronicle*, 28 September 1916
10. ibid.
11. *New York Times*, 28 September 1916
12. ibid.
13. *Rochester Democrat And Chronicle*, 28 September 1916
14. ibid.
15. ibid, 29 September 1916
16. *Rochester Democrat And Chronicle*, 28 September 1916
17. *Waterton Daily Times*, 29 September 1916
18. *New York Times*, 29 September 1916
19. *Rochester Democrat And Chronicle*, 1 October 1916
20. *New York Times*, 1 October 1916
21. *Utica Daily Press*, 30 September 1916
22. ibid.
23. ibid.
24. ibid.
25. *Rochester Democrat And Chronicle*, 1 October 1916
26. ibid.
27. *New York Times*, 7 October 1916
28. ibid., 10 October 1916
29. ibid., 29 October 1916
30. ibid., 10 October 1916
31. ibid., 12 October 1916
32. ibid.
33. ibid.
34. Doris Stevens, *Jailed for Freedom* (New York: Knopf, 1967), p. 58
35. *New York Times*, 26 October 1916
36. *The World*, 26 October 1916

18: Reprieve!

1. *Poughkeepsie Daily Eagle*, 18 November 1916
2. *The World*, 12 October 1916

3. Report by the Special Deputy Attorney (1917), p. 34
4. All letters are taken from the Report by the Special Deputy Attorney (1917), pp. 35–36
5. *Philadelphia Evening-Ledger*, 21 June 1917
6. *Utica Herald-Dispatch*, 29 November 1916
7. ibid.
8. ibid.
9. ibid.
10. ibid.
11. *Poughkeepsie Daily Eagle*, 2 December 1916
12. *New York Times*, 4 December 1916
13. *Brooklyn Daily Eagle*, 4 December 1916
14. December 1916
15. December 1916
16. December 1916
17. *New York Times*, 7 December 1916

19: Governor Orders Investigation

1. Report by the Special Deputy Attorney (1917), p. 37
2. *Syracuse Post-Standard*, 3 February 1917
3. *Buffalo Express*, 10 March 1916
4. Report by the Special Deputy Attorney (1917), p. 156
5. ibid.
6. ibid., p. 194
7. ibid., p. 144
8. ibid., p. 79
9. ibid., p. 163

20: Hamilton Exposed as a Fraud

1. Report by the Special Deputy Attorney (1917), p. 87
2. ibid., p. 163
3. ibid.
4. ibid., p. 31
5. ibid., p. 95
6. ibid.
7. ibid., p. 97
8. ibid.
9. ibid.
10. ibid., p. 98
11. ibid., p. 100

21: Grand Jury Dashes Hopes

1. *Medina Daily Journal*, 12 December 1917
2. ibid.
3. *Rochester Democrat And Chronicle*, 14 December 1917
4. Report by the Special Deputy Attorney (1917), p. 6
5. ibid., p. 103
6. ibid., p. 111
7. ibid., p. 115
8. ibid., p. 116
9. ibid.
10. ibid., p. 115
11. ibid., p. 116
12. ibid., p. 119
13. ibid.
14. ibid.
15. ibid.
16. *Rochester Democrat And Chronicle*, 19 December 1917
17. Report by the Special Deputy Attorney (1917), p. 120
18. ibid., pp. 120–21
19. ibid., p. 122
20. *Rochester Democrat And Chronicle*, 21 December 1917
21. *Rochester Herald*, 20 December 1917
22. *Rochester Democrat And Chronicle*, 22 December 1917
23. *New York Tribune*, 12 May 1918
24. *Buffalo Express*, 12 December 1917
25. *Rochester Democrat And Chronicle*, 22 December 1917
26. ibid.
27. ibid.
28. *Buffalo Express*, 22 December 1917
29. *Rochester Democrat And Chronicle*, 22 December 1917

22: Freedom At Last

1. Report by the Special Deputy Attorney (1917), p. 162
2. *New York Times*, 9 May 1918
3. ibid., 11 May 1918
4. *New York Tribune*, 11 May 1918
5. *Brooklyn Eagle*, 9 May 1918
6. *Auburn Citizen*, 10 May 1918
7. *Rochester Democrat And Chronicle*, 10 May 1918
8. ibid.
9. ibid.

10. ibid.
11. *Auburn Citizen*, 10 May 1918
12. *New York Times*, 10 May 1918
13. *Auburn Citizen*, 10 May 1918
14. ibid.
15. *Rochester Democrat And Chronicle*, 10 May 1918
16. *New York Tribune*, 13 May 1918
17. ibid.
18. *New York Times*, 24 June 1917
19. ibid., 3 October 1905
20. ibid., 10 June 1926
21. *Albany Evening Journal*, 10 May 1918
22. *New York Times*, 15 November 1926
23. *Journal of the American Institute of Criminal Law and Criminology*, Vol. 17, No. 2, pp. 254–63
24. ibid.
25. *Schenectady Gazette*, 20 March 1936
26. *Medina Daily Journal*, 10 August 1942